D0184428

POPCORN

By the same author

This is Uncool: The 500 Greatest Singles Since Punk and Disco
Fear of Music: The 261 Greatest Albums Since Punk and Disco

POPCORN

FIFTY YEARS OF ROCK 'n' ROLL MOVIES

Garry Mulholland

Copyright © Garry Mulholland 2010

The right of Garry Mulholland to be identified as the author of this work
has been asserted by him in accordance with the Copyright, Designs and
Patents Act 1988.

This edition first published in Great Britain in 2010 by
Orion Books
an imprint of the Orion Publishing Group Ltd
Orion House, 5 Upper St Martin's Lane,
London WC2H 9EA
An Hachette Livre UK Company

10 9 8 7 6 5 4 3 2 1

All rights reserved. Apart from any use permitted under UK copyright
law, this publication may only be reproduced, stored or transmitted, in any
form, or by any means, with prior permission in writing of the publishers
or, in the case of reprographic production, in accordance with the terms of
licences issued by the Copyright Licensing Agency.

A CIP catalogue record for this book is available from the British Library.

ISBN: 978 0 752 88935 1 (hardback)

Typeset by Input Data Services Ltd, Bridgwater, Somerset

Printed in Great Britain by Clays Ltd, St Ives plc

The Orion Publishing Group's policy is to use papers that are natural,
renewable and recyclable and made from wood grown in sustainable forests.
The logging and manufacturing processes are expected to conform to the
environmental regulations of the country of origin.

Every effort has been made to fulfil requirements with regard to reproducing
copyright material. The author and publisher will be glad to rectify any
omissions at the earliest opportunity.

THE BOURNEMOUTH & POOLE
COLLEGE

LCH

WITHDRAWN

27/9/14

from C

SB

£16-99

791.436 MUL

250221134 K

www.orionbooks.co.uk

To Linsay, as always

Contents

Acknowledgements

The main source of information for *Popcorn* – as well as the original source book from which I made my list of movies to watch and write about – is *The Radio Times Guide to Films*, published by BBC Worldwide. Updated annually, it's the epitome of the comprehensive and informed movie reference book.

As constant fact-check sources, the online resources at Wikipedia (wikipedia.org), All Movie Guide (allmovie.com) and the Internet Movie Database (imdb.com) were invaluable.

Other books used for background on specific films, historical context or examples of how to interpret film were:

Seeing Is Believing – Peter Biskind (Bloomsbury)
1001 Movies You Must See Before You Die – Edited by Steven Jay Schneider
Stoned – Andrew Loog Oldham (Vintage)
Revolution in the Head: The Beatles' Records and the Sixties – Ian Macdonald (Pimlico)
Where the Girls Are – Susan J. Douglas (Times Books)
From Reverence to Rape: The Treatment of Women in the Movies – Molly Haskell (Penguin)
The Who: Maximum R&B – Richard Barnes (Plexus)
The New Biographical Dictionary of Film – David Thomson (Little, Brown)

Many thanks also to James Kendall and Ian Preece for lending me key films at key times. Ian has been the editor for all three of my books and deserves some kind of medal for patience and calm, as well as my heartfelt gratitude for keeping my writing on track and believing in me. Something similar could be said of Julie Burchill, with the addition of friendship way above and beyond the call of duty.

As always, the last but not least shout-out goes to my wife and best friend Linsay McCulloch. If you see an idea somewhere in these pages that you really like, it's probably one of hers. Cheers, Dollface, for everything.

If you have any comments or observations on, or corrections or criticisms of *Popcorn*, you can reach the author at garrymul@aol.com, or by visiting my website at www.garry mulholland.com

Introduction

I don't remember the first rock movie I ever saw. I have vivid recollections of going to the pictures with my mother to see *Jesus Christ Superstar* (1973 – Ted Neeley as a hippy Jesus with a screechy voice, and Judas the only character played by a black man); *Tommy* (1975 – Roger Daltrey as a deaf, dumb and blind hippy Jesus, with the person who peddles him drugs the only character played by a black woman); and *Elvis on Tour* (1972 – no Jesus nor hippies, nor black people; just a camera following the world's most famous man as he plays some shows, blissfully unaware that He will die for our sins within five years). My mum and nine-year-old me were such huge Elvis fans that we took our first cassette recorder to the pictures and taped the whole thing, in what I now realise was an innocent, sound-only precursor to the pirate DVD.

This early 1970s period represents the peak of rock movies – not necessarily in quality, but quantity. Feature films were made featuring the entirely uncinematic likes of Slade (*Slade in Flame*), T.Rex (*Born to Boogie*), Gary Glitter (*Remember Me This Way*) and even Mud (can't remember ... and can you blame me?). It was the equivalent of the millions of dollars now needed to produce, distribute and promote a feature film being spent on movies starring the Kaiser Chiefs, Amy Winehouse and Chris Brown. And who'd be dumb enough to do that?

I remember all these first cinema rock movie experiences fairly clearly, but I suspect that the first rock movie I ever saw was probably an Elvis or Cliff Richard film on our flickering black and white TV. But I don't know; not for sure. Yet I can almost give you the dates of when I first *heard* Elvis, and the Rolling Stones, and the Sex Pistols, so dramatic were their impact on my unprepared psyche. This, perhaps, is why there are a million books on rock and a million books on film – and pretty much none at all on rock films. It's not just that films about pop music don't appear to change

1

lives. It's that there's something about the respective qualities of the 20th century's two most popular art forms that seem to cancel each of them out. The complexities of the film-making process dilute the immediacy of rock 'n' roll.

Nevertheless, this much-maligned movie sub-genre contains some of the most vivid, famous and influential screen imagery of the last 50 years, even ... perhaps especially ... when that imagery pops up in an otherwise fatally flawed piece of film-making. Just as the promo video has gradually brought more of the film-maker's *modus operandi* to the making of pop music, pop injects its crass, vulgar, tasteless instincts for high-impact hooligan art into the normally more subtle practices involved in making a feature film. This book is an attempt to look at the whens, whys and wherefores of that strange 50-year love–hate relationship between the two modes of entertainment that dominate the Western world's mainstream popular culture.

The biggest help in this process is the fact that I come from a background in music journalism rather than film criticism. The most noticeable thing about the list that I'm looking at is how few of the films are part of the movie pantheon – that relatively small and wearingly predictable set of classics the endless adoration and analysis of which is a compulsory requirement for entry into the tiny world of film criticism – the most hermetically sealed boys' club this side of the Freemasons and the Magic Circle. The official pantheon might condescend to include *Easy Rider*. Possibly *Don't Look Back* and *Performance*. Maybe *A Hard Day's Night*. All 1960s guy films, naturally. Otherwise, forget it. The reason's pretty simple. The only reason anyone makes a pop film is exploitation. A pop star or pop trend has caught the commercial youth *Zeitgeist*, and a studio, its producers and the record companies promoting the star or the trend fall over themselves to cash in before the Kids decamp to Morris dancing or whatever weird noise someone's secretly concocting in a bedroom or garage near you. Film critics believe in art for art's sake and dismiss crass commercialism (and, by association, the suckers who fall for it). Therefore, all exploitation films are either ignored or revived as kitsch after a comfortable amount of time has passed. All can I say is: I love *Citizen Kane* as much as the next 'Ooh! Look at that tracking shot!', innovative-camera-angles-and-subtly-realised-Big-Themes junkie. But anyone who rejects the joy that the likes of *Grease* or *Footloose* or *The Rocky Horror Picture Show* have brought to millions of people without even attempting to engage with why such unapologetic trash works ... can't really be that interested in filmgoers at all. The most exciting thing about being a critic is finding an intellectual path through the eternal arm-wrestle between art and entertainment, and understanding why some things cross over between the two, and who they touch, and why. Reject films that touch the masses out of hand, and the entire point of the critical exercise is lost. *Film is a popular medium, not an academic one.*

Film criticism's elitism is something music journalists can't afford to indulge in. Pop's raison d'être is dragging the money from the pockets of people still young and energetic enough to do something other than listen to music. When pop journos fail to engage with what captures the young consumer's imagination, all our learned analyses of *Astral Weeks* and *Pet Sounds* will not save us from being branded dinosaurs and pensioned off to that great Mercury Prize judging panel in the sky. And quite right, too.

So ... that's the why. The meat of the matter is a list of what I believe to be the 100 most important rock movies in existence. The reason that the book is not subtitled 'The 100 Greatest Rock 'n' Roll Movies' is that there aren't 100 great movies about rock. At least half of the movies I'll be writing about are either mediocre or enjoyably trashy – or just plain awful. But they all star cultural icons, or say something important about rock's impact on the planet, as well as defining the genre.

I should also attempt to define, at this point, what I believe a rock movie is. For the purposes of this book: it's a film made after the birth of rock 'n' roll as a mainstream genre in 1955, which bases its central premise around pop music in the post-rock 'n' roll era. This includes movies about or inspired by soul, reggae, punk, disco, hip hop, dance music and forms of folk-roots music that cross over into the pop mainstream. It doesn't include films about jazz, pre-rock pop music, blues, classical or folk-roots music that doesn't cross over into the pop mainstream. It also doesn't include movies that have nothing to do with rock/pop music, but feature a rock/pop star in a lead role. I was toying with the idea of including these just so I could while away many happy hours ridiculing Sting – but my wife Linsay soon put paid to such foolish self-indulgence by the judicious application of one single question: 'So – you're really going to watch *Ned Kelly*?' Anyone who has seen Mick Jagger and Tony Richardson's turgid and baffling attempt to represent Australia's most famous outlaw as a plank of wood will understand why I was immediately brought to my senses.

I should mention here some movies that didn't make the cut, and a few reasons why. First, the movies that are not available on DVD, and that I couldn't track down on VHS, bootleg or the net. The most glaring omission is *Rock Around the Clock*, the 1956 Alan Freed/Bill Haley vehicle that marks the first attempt to make a rock movie and allegedly inspired an orgy of teenage seat-slashing at cinemas in the USA and Britain. A crucial slice of pop culture history. Not available in the UK. On any format. Bizarre.

Other movies with strong cult reputations that I finally ran out of time to track down were 1968 rock 'n' politics satire *Wild in the Streets*, Penelope Spheeris's highly rated *The Decline of Western Civilization* rockdoc trilogy, and 1980s punk comedy *Ladies and Gentlemen . . . The Fabulous Stains*. The absence of all four of the above galls, but there you go. Similarly, Madness vehicle *Take It or Leave It* and the Pet Shop Boys' *It Couldn't Happen Here* also remain missing in action.

The omission that most readers are likely to notice is that of *The Song Remains the Same*, Led Zeppelin's sole foray into feature film. If it was just a bad film it would have made the cut on the basis of being notable trash. But *The Song . . .* isn't just bad – it is unforgivably boring, even somehow contriving to make Led Zeppelin's live show look and sound dull. There seemed no point in kicking something more interesting to the kerb just to sneer or snore at it, so I didn't.

Others that fall into the too-bad-to-mention dumper included

The Wiz, Motown's misguided all-black remake of *The Wizard of Oz*, which even Michael Jackson and Diana Ross couldn't save, and similar is-nothing-sacred? remake nightmares featuring Neil Diamond (*The Jazz Singer*) and Barbra Streisand and Kris Kristofferson (*A Star is Born*). And no power on Earth could make me watch pop movie disasters *Absolute Beginners*, *Xanadu*, the Beatles-associated *Sgt Pepper's Lonely Hearts Club Band* and *Give My Regards to Broad Street*, or the 1987 Bob Dylan/Rupert Everett turkey *Hearts of Fire* again. Trust me. You're better off not knowing.

A few watchable movies were left out because better films had entirely covered their territory. So *The Buddy Holly Story*'s inclusion gave the chop to pleasant but bland rock biopics *La Bamba* (Ritchie Valens) and *Great Balls of Fire* (Jerry Lee Lewis). Disco movies *Thank God It's Friday* and Village People vehicle *Can't Stop the Music* suffered the same fate at the hands of *Saturday Night Fever*.

I adore Baz Luhrmann's senses-battering take on *Moulin Rouge* – but, in the final analysis, it's a modernized period musical which chooses to use contemporary pop songs rather than an original score, and I just couldn't justify it as a rock movie. Similarly, Robert Altman's brilliant 1975 satire *Nashville* is a must-see for any movie fan – but its use of the country music scene to take America's post-Watergate temperature is, in the end, nothing to do with rock or pop. And the same can be said of Spike Lee's masterpiece *Do the Right Thing*, even though rap is crucial to its treatise on racial conflict.

Hip hop is, without a doubt, the most ill-served musical genre in film, in stark contrast to its influence on popular culture. 50 Cent vehicle *Get Rich or Die Tryin'*, OutKast's *Idlewild*, the recent Biggie Smalls biopic and rap 'comedies' *CB4* and *Fear of a Black Hat* are just plain lousy, and not in a fun way. And, on a personal note . . . having spent most of my formative years working in record shops I really wanted to include a film about the strange world of music retail. But *Empire Records* and *High Fidelity* stink. So I couldn't.

So let's get back to what does merit inclusion. All of the rock-and pop-orientated movies here fall into seven basic categories, which, despite enormous changes in the languages of pop, film direction, dialogue, fashion and acting styles, remain virtually unchanged. They go a little something like this.

1. *The Pop Star Vehicle*

Some bright spark decides that the best way to drag maximum moolah from their spanking new musical sensation is to make a cinematic homage to their boundless talent, charisma and sex appeal. Sometimes, the bright spark is the musical sensation themselves, who has really always wanted to be a movie star because movie stars have a credibility and 'A'-list master of the universe quality that pop stars don't. The pop star vehicle is, therefore, the most extreme, expensive and ego-frenzied example of status anxiety known to humankind. And, as a general rule, they are disasters and give us mere mortals a chance to laugh at our supposed betters.

2. *The Pop Star Biopic*

A biography of a musician, usually a dead one. This enables record companies to sell back catalogue, and film-makers to dish an entertaining amount of dirt on said icon without fear of legal action, while simultaneously playing up to the 'they died for our sins – but will always live on through their music' death cult sentimentality that has hung around rock like a bad smell ever since Buddy Holly's plane crashed. These films generally walk the well-meaning but uneventful line between the genuinely authentic and intelligent (*I Walk the Line*) and the laughably inane (*The Doors*).

3. *Digging the Scene*

Undoubtedly the most creatively productive of our seven categories, these films largely ignore pop stars and focus on the teen scenes and youth cults that use a fashion style and a particular pop genre as their major inspiration. Apart from the nostalgic possibilities of the whole 'this was the soundtrack to our lives' shebang, most of these rites-of-passage movies are driven by troubled hip kids who, by movie's end, will learn valuable lessons about the pain of growing up.

4. *The Rock Musical*

Like the musical, only with bad versions of rock music replacing bad versions of operetta. There is obviously a large crossover here with Category One, as the plot often only exists to allow sensational new pop star to burst into song at every available opportunity, and can barely hold itself back from reminding you that the soundtrack is on sale now at your local Tescos after every dodgy tune.

5. *About the Biz*

Movies about making it in the modern music industry, usually presented as moral fables about the evils of men in suits and the perils of fame. Easily the most satirical of our seven categories, offering soul-less corporate bastards the chance to be self-aware about being soul-less corporate bastards, while taking ample opportunity to lecture the peasants about how fulfilling your dreams inevitably means ingesting heroin through a squirrel's rectum and either dying or learning a valuable lesson and becoming humble and, Lord Help Us, down to earth. Often produces the most hysterical rock movies, therefore getting closest to the frantic idiocy of great pop music.

6. *The Rockumentary*

The advent of ever cheaper ways of shooting real life, and the increasing proliferation of DVDs packaged free with new albums, means that there are now far too many documentaries about rock music, most of which just follow some incredibly dull musicians around while they tour. Here, I limit myself to the most fully realised and discussed docs that got a full cinema release. At its best, the rockumentary not only captures a moment in pop cultural history more vividly than a conventional feature, but reveals that major pop artists and the hubbub that surrounds them are more surreal and unlikely than any work of fiction can imagine. This category also includes films of live music events where, again, I limit myself to the culturally significant likes of *Woodstock* and *Gimme Shelter*.

7. *Rock Comedy*
Comedies about rock.

As we'll see, many rock movies contain more than one of the above elements. For example, the 1957 Elvis Presley film *Loving You* is mainly a pop star vehicle, but is also a rock musical, a satirical comedy and a cynical look at the rise of the fledgling rock 'n' roll scene *and* rising to fame in the music business, which is also liberally sprinkled with fictionalised elements of Presley's early career. Almost the full set.

But, 50 years on, the rock flick song essentially remains the same ... the Kids go wild, chaos ensues, valuable lessons are learned. What does change between eras is how the films choose to end ... always the biggest clues as to what film-makers are trying to leave their audience believing, thinking and feeling; always a key cultural barometer, in terms of the message The Man thinks we *want* to hear. In the 1950s and early 1960s, rock films were aimed squarely at supposedly innocent teens, and endings were happy and com-forting – as much to let parents know that this still relatively new and scary youth phenom wasn't going to turn their kids queer or lead them to consort with black men. At the end of the 1960s and through the 1970s, this is turned on its head. Endings become tragic and shocking, a way of both tapping into Western youth's more sophisticated and rebellious attitude, while still warning The Kids that sex, drugs, non-conformity and individual artistic achievement could only lead to destruction.

In the 1980s, it was all about individual achievement, and endings were triumphant, the cinematic equivalent of money from the sky and high fives all round. As the 1990s have progressed into the 21st century, endings have remained largely optimistic, but muted. The final triumph has often come from deprived beginnings, and at a cost, and it doesn't make *everything* all right. The rock film has become therapy.

Yet something has happened since the year 2000, with the likes of *Ray*, *I Walk the Line*, *8 Mile* and *Last Days* reviving the idea of serious, heavyweight rock and pop movies, while the exceptional likes of *The Filth and the Fury*, *DiG* and *Anvil: The Story of Anvil* have forced the rock-doc to come of age and present their subjects as fully rounded human beings. Moreover, the accepted movie pantheon is getting old and weary through repetition, and, just as my books about great singles and great albums, *This Is Uncool* and *Fear of Music*, sought to find an alternative pantheon, where accepted greats nestle alongside inspired trash and obscure hidden treasures, *Popcorn* is an attempt to look at a different kind of classic film, from a different, less elitist perspective, and to acknowledge these films' relationships with unashamed exploitation vehicles, grimly fascinating cinematic horrors and, most importantly, us . . . the kind of people who grew up obsessed with pop and movies.

Yet it was only after writing about the 100 movies that editor Ian Preece and I finally decided to arrange the book chronologically, as we had with my books on singles and albums. I'd thought that the rock movie was too erratic and chaotic a medium to lend itself to a historical narrative – I was wrong. There is a clear journey through various levels of cynicism and optimism that fits our perceptions of the late 20th century very neatly indeed. By the time I'd travelled from the shallow dismissals of youth culture of 1956's *The Girl Can't Help It* to the profoundly disturbing and quintessentially adult tragedy of 2009's *Telstar: The Joe Meek Story*, I realized that the rock movie had followed a parallel path to its musical soundtrack – a journey from misunderstood adolescence to uneasy middle-age. And, along the way, I learned some valuable lessons. I hope you do, too.

Garry Mulholland
September 2009

The 20 Best Rock Movies Ever Made ...

The big lesson that I learned from my two previous list books is that, no matter how often you insist that your book is arranged in chronological order, the first question everyone asks is: 'What's number one?' So I figured that, this time around, I'd get off the fence right from the get-go and provide a simple list of what I believe to be the best rock and pop movies of all time. A whopping six of the Top Ten are from my favourite sub-genre of rock-orientated film – a run of savage, sepia-tinted British rock/pop movies, from 1959's *Expresso Bongo* to 1979's *Quadrophenia* that evince a bitter, cynical, blackly humorous and bravely surreal take on the perennially grey British landscape and its ongoing battle with the vivid colours of rock 'n' roll. An English perspective – right down to *Spinal Tap*'s piss-take of dumbass Brit metal bands – dominates my 20 faves, so I may as well own up to my bias and wave the flag for British pessimism.

1) *Privilege*
2) *Expresso Bongo*
3) *Easy Rider*
4) *Performance*
5) *Stardust*
6) *Slade in Flame*
7) *This Is Spinal Tap*
8) *Quadrophenia*
9) *The Filth and the Fury*
10) *Gimme Shelter*
11) *Hairspray*
12) *Beyond the Valley of the Dolls*
13) *The School of Rock*
14) *Superstar: The Karen Carpenter Story*
15) *Saturday Night Fever*
16) *24 Hour Party People*
17) *DiG!*
18) *Catch Us If You Can*
19) *Beat Girl*
20) *Bulworth*

1950s

• •

The Girl Can't Help It

1956

Starring: Tom Ewell, Jayne Mansfield, Edmund O'Brien, Little Richard, Eddie Cochran, Fats Domino, Gene Vincent and the Blue Caps
Dir.: Frank Tashlin

★ ★

Plot: Legs and jugs and rock 'n' roll.
Key line: 'She ain't Rome! What we're talking about is already built!'

If *The Girl Can't Help It* had been made in any other year but 1956, it wouldn't be here. Despite some critics' attempts to give this glossy sex(less) comedy revisionist props (John Waters bigs it up on the DVD featurette; Truffaut allegedly called it 'a masterpiece') it's actually a tiresome, boring film from a creaking Hollywood studio system which was rapidly losing its flair for screwball funnies. But it remains a crucial rock movie because it has beautifully filmed performances from four of rock's major pioneers, which casually subvert the 1950s mainstream, and therefore helped change the world for the better. Little Richard, Gene Vincent, Fats Domino and Eddie Cochran – not to mention the Treniers, the Platters and jazz singer Abbey Lincoln – allow this film to stand when similarly unfunny comedies of the period have long slipped into obscurity. If your curiosity about early rock onscreen compels you to see it, just be warned that *The Girl Can't Help It* surely ain't no *Some Like It Hot*.

The plot, such as it is, involves washed-up gangster Marty 'Fats' Murdoch (O'Brien) employing drunk agent Tom Miller (Ewell) to make his reluctant girlfriend Jerri Jordan (Mansfield) a pop recording star in six weeks. Jerri can't sing but Miller finds a way to make her famous anyway, Tom and Jerri (chortle, guffaw) fall in love, and then it turns out that Jerri can sing, and Fats becomes a pop star instead, and everyone gets what they want, which is marriage and kids, in Tom and Jerri's case. The musical sequences are woven into the plot by virtue of the leads turning up in nightclubs and studios, and the musical turns perform straight to a static camera, which somehow works perfectly.

Aside from the fact that the acting stinks and the dialogue sucks, the film largely fails because it can't make up its mind whether to bury rock 'n' roll or praise it. On the burial hand, the story attempts to satirise teen stupidity . . . you can sell any din to them as long as it has a gimmick. But this premise is undercut right from the beginning, as Ewell archly introduces the film pre-credits and has his old-school showbiz speech interrupted and blown gleefully off soundtrack and screen by Little Richard's title track and the sight of a seven-inch single spinning on a deliciously iconic art deco jukebox. Director Tashlin seems to take pleasure from the scandal and noise of this rock stuff, and perhaps the film's problem is that he's caught between the demands of exploitation cynicism and his own foresight about the burgeoning power of rock 'n' roll.

What's more, the rock performances are made timelessly thrilling by the loving way they are shot. The Colour Deluxe film stock makes our rockin' heroes look incandescent, and Tashlin understands that there is so much natural action in the faces and movement of Vincent (and his heroic, gum-chewing, proto-punk guitarist Paul Peek), Cochran (framed with visionary prescience by a television screen) and the hugely underrated black vocal group the Treniers (Little Richard is dashingly handsome but oddly stiff and ill at ease) that he just points a camera at them and stays stock still. 20th Century Fox's chief arranger Lionel Newman chooses cutting-edge, 'real' rock at a time when the US music biz was reinforcing the racism of middle America by sending Pat Boone off to cover R&B hits so that radio could stay happily segregated and parents could stay in denial about the screaming black jungle music that their little treasures were actually listening to on bedroom Dansettes and black radio. And Tashlin gave his black acts equal prominence to the white ones, subtly establishing that this new teen phenomenon was absolutely about racial miscegenation without having to hammer the point home. 'This is the new showbiz – deal with it, America!', *The Girl Can't Help It* seems to say, in a good-natured, don't-scare-the-horses way. It may not be a good film. But it is one of the most influential and subversive films in this book.

As for the non-rock bits, there are two justly famous scenes which transcend the rest of the film's fudge and lack of decent jokes. First . . . trussed up in the tightest suit imaginable, Jerri/Mansfield walks down a street to Miller's house. If you've never heard of Mansfield, she had a brief flush of fame in the late 1950s as the low-budget Marilyn Monroe – a parody of a parody of the Blonde Bombshell. She couldn't act a lick but she had an hour-glass figure, platinum-blonde hair, perfect teeth and unfeasibly large breasts which were transformed into heat-seeking missiles by the torture devices they called underwear at the time. She got the death such a public life demanded, too, when, at the age of 34, her car ploughed into a tractor-trailer, and a photo was released which appeared to prove that her head had been severed by the impact. Dispellers of this urban myth insist that the 'head' was nothing more than a blonde wig, but what kind of ghoul wants to believe something as mundane as that?

Anyway, she walks down the street and the torrid and terrifying licence to leer that is Little Richard's 'The Girl Can't Help It' soundtracks her ludicrous sashay. A man is delivering ice. He turns to gawp. The mountain of ice melts in a pussy juice gush. She walks up the stairs past a geeky milkman. He gawps. And he metaphorically cums, as his milk bottles pop their caps and blow their load. Another set of stairs inside Miller's building, and an old bloke is picking up his milk from his doorstep. He gawps. His glasses crack and he appears paralysed with shock and awe. The scene ends when she gatecrashes an embarrassed Miller's bedroom and has a conversation with two full bottles of milk held up in front of her torpedo bazooms. The sexual connection between so many bodily fluids and functions has never been so memorably conveyed.

And Tashlin also finds time to invent the conceptual pop video. Miller comes home to his empty flat after a long night of drowning his sorrows. The major source of his angst is Julie London, the real-life sophisto-jazz chanteuse that the story insists Miller discovered. She was the love of his life but has long since departed, leaving him a washed-up lush. He puts on London's big hit 'Cry Me a River' ... and a ghostly apparition of London appears, taunting him. He runs drunkenly from room to room and out of his flat, but no matter where he turns, Julie's there, vaporous and vengeful. It's genuinely haunting, and the song is a torch classic ('Told me love was too plebeian', goes the most extraordinary line. Too *plebeian*?! And it gets rhymed with, 'Told me you were through with me, and'! Man, they really don't write love songs like that any more!), and it all seems like it's been bussed in from a better, sadder film.

And actually ... I'll add another scene, in the interests of fairness. Eddie Cochran's weird, brilliant, Elvis-in-a-straitjacket performance of 'Twenty Flight Rock' is blasting out of a TV, and a black maid starts dancing for joy. By twisting reality on its head – it was black rockers who were making white folks break racial taboos and dance like negroes, of course – Tashlin wrings just a little more pleasure out of the inevitable end of artistic apartheid. The guy had moments. Just not enough of them to carry an entire film.

• •

Loving You

1957

Starring: Elvis Presley, Lizabeth Scott, Wendall Corey
Dir.: Hal Kanter

★ ★ ★

Plot: Troubled but well-mannered orphan hick manipulated to musical stardom by ambitious female PR. Anti-rock grown-ups, press outrage and bizarre emotional baggage intervenes. Problems solved by hick singing simpering ballad on telly.
Key line: 'Who's fighting sex? It's a healthy American commodity.'

The second Elvis movie is a key text in the career of the 20th-century's leading musical icon. It neatly establishes the public arm-wrestle between the Elvis that could have been – a dirty, rebellious ball of licentious sexual energy – and the Elvis that was – the simpering all-round entertainer, standing for all things Mom and all-American. Indeed, screenwriters Hal Kanter and Herbert Baker show quite extraordinary prescience by reflecting the cynicism of Elvis's legendary manager Colonel Tom Parker (credited as the film's 'technical adviser') through the sarcastic, contemptuous dialogue of several of the main characters. It's almost like they know where Elvis is going, and they don't much like it, but find the charade pretty damn amusing. Add the genuinely creepy neuroses that provide the plot twists, and you have a movie that represents the death throes of the repressed 1950s and the desperate need for liberation that characterised the 1960s . . . a decade that Elvis largely spent starring in gut-wrenchingly bad versions of *Loving You* while the rebels he inspired invented the modern world. *Loving You*, in its clunky, compromised way, seems to predict all the follies of Presley's future.

Kanter's attitude to the small-town Southern states where Elvis was born and raised add another prophecy ... there's a Jewish intellectual contempt for 'Hicktown' in this movie's opening scenes that meshes neatly with Presley's posthumous biographer Albert Goldman's loathing of the redneck. Although Kanter's lack of directorial talent (the sitcom and gag writer scuttled back to TV soon after *Loving You*, going on to produce the hugely successful American *Till Death Us Do Part* equivalent *All in the Family*) becomes more obvious as the film progresses, the opening pre-Elvis scenes are rather extraordinary: a country band in cowboy threads playing on a small-town bandstand, there to help elect a fat and obviously corrupt governor, who cuts short a political speech to sell health tonic, surely a barbed comment on the carny hustler background of Col. Parker. Within minutes we learn that the country bandleader is a fake and that his partner in insincerity is a woman. Glenda Markell, played by Lizabeth Scott, stands out like a sophisticated sore thumb among the dumbass country suckers, her glamour, poise and verbal elegance a symbol of the Big City, which is held up throughout *Loving You* as a beacon of progress and thrill. When bandleader Tex Warner sneers at the hillbilly music that pays his rent, Glenda smirks, 'Don't knock country music. It's the voice of our nation,' with enough jaunty irony to raze Nashville to the ground.

When Elvis finally arrives onscreen, a humble delivery boy, he is beautiful: all in be-jeaned blue, immaculate jet-black quiff, hooded eyes and curled lip, his whippet-thin bod a slow-rolling metaphor for all things laconic and horny. Glenda eyes him like meat. Deke Rivers is persuaded to sing, performs 'Got a Lot o' Livin' to Do'. The women pant like dogs. The men recoil in bemused horror. The one black boy in town – in the entire film! – grins delightedly and dances. Admittedly, this isn't a subtle reminder of where Elvis's beats and gyrations hail from, but it makes its point. When Elvis hands back his borrowed acoustic to the goofy country guitarist, a string is broken. The goofy guitarist looking resignedly at a broken string becomes a recurring motif, a snappy little symbol of rock's destruction of the Old Ways. By the time these scenes have finished, Kanter, Presley and Scott have introduced us to all the cultural, racial and sexual impulses that made THE SIXTIES!!! inevitable.

Sadly, the compromises inherent in producing a 1950s pop star vehicle with an all-ages rating prevents *Loving You* from being the rock 'n' roll *Sweet Smell of Success* it could've been. Songs intervene, gloss pervades, plot gets silly. Nevertheless, Kanter does his best to smuggle in smart dialogue and dark plot developments. Elvis/Deke falls for older woman Glenda, who doesn't reciprocate, and the film implies (before backing off, clunkily) that she fucks him to keep him working for her. Just as 'Tex' turns out to be a fake called Walter, Deke Rivers turns out to be a fake called Jimmy Tompkins, who stole the Rivers name from a tombstone after running away from a children's home. Glenda, meanwhile, is busy providing blueprints for Malcolm McLaren, paying middle-aged ladies to express their disgust at Elvis's pelvic gyrations so smitten female fans get into fist fights for photographers. The entire film displays a knowing amusement at female lust, and, taken in tandem with Elvis/Deke/Jimmy's ingenuous sexual manipulation by an older woman, his status as all-dancing sex object turns gender roles around and feminises Elvis. The most famous scene, where Elvis performs the tough, sexist blues of Ray Charles's 'I Got a Woman' before beating up a jealous greaser, is utterly undercut by the groupie scene, where the greaser's girlfriend breaks into Elvis's dressing-room and challenges his entire sexuality: 'You are afraid! You don't *sing* scared . . . You're a phoney!' Elvis doesn't argue. By the time the two are discovered kissing, it's too late. Elvis is revealed as an impotent sex tease, and a rock 'n' roll fake. For a guy who spent much of his career penning gags for Bob Hope, this Kanter guy had a shrewd take on Elvis's lack of balls.

Loving You also provides a checklist of future rock and rock movie clichés: nerdy, screaming girls as objects of both horror and comedy; stage door chaos, band overshadowed and dumped by dominating singer, gaudy car as ultimate symbol of freedom and upward mobility, greedy PR cynicism. But, after all the crafty subversion, *Loving You* ultimately seeks to comfort its intended audience. After Scott's Glenda spends the entire film either manipulating or castrating every man she meets, she is forced, in typical 1950s Hollywood manner, to reject all personal ambition in order to prove herself worthy of her man's love. After all, even Elvis's sexless good girl love interest Susie (Dolores Hart) knows the score, observing the sexual hysteria our nice boy provokes and sneering, 'He's male. Every female wants one.' At the film's climax, Elvis welcomes Glenda, Susie and Tex into a happy-ever-after group hug, a tableau of the perfect nuclear family our orphan wants so much more than fame, money or sex. By that time, Kanter and Baker have struck so many false notes with all four, the happy ending becomes a dark joke.

Loving You isn't a great movie: it's just too badly made to be that. But it's a genuine curiosity and a must-see for anyone interested in Elvis Presley. The man was shoved from pillar to post by Parker, the music and movie businesses, and the public's desires until he died young having no real idea of who he was or why his unmatched success had brought him so low. That process begins right here.

• •

Jailhouse Rock

1957
Starring: Elvis Presley, Judy Tyler, Mickey Shaughnessey
Dir.: Richard Thorpe

★ ★ ★ ★

Plot: Elvis kills a man with his bare hands. Learns to sing in the Big House. Becomes star. Fucks it up.
Key line: 'That ain't tactics, honey. That's just the beast in me.'

Elvis Presley is so great in this movie. Everything's in place for a career as a top leading man in top films. Smouldering good looks. Method-style subtlety. Vulnerability. Pent-up anger. Sexual threat. He flirts with other characters, not with the camera. He's utterly natural, barely strikes a false note anywhere here, refrains from indulging his love of self-parody. His onscreen bad father–errant son relationship with the excellent Mickey Shaughnessey as fellow con Hunk Houghton shows that he has a natural talent for the give-and-take of ensemble playing. He's especially great at throwing a wild, realistic punch. He obviously enjoys every second of playing a selfish, greedy, petulant redneck wanker, desperate for flash cars and fancy cufflinks. The bling-obsessed rapper? A new idea? Nope. Elvis is pure hip hop in *Jailhouse Rock*. The camera adores the animal grace with which he walks, talks, slouches and sneers. He's a Brando, Dean or Clift in the making. Oh Elvis . . . where did it all go wrong?

Thorpe's gritty monochrome and feel for the harshness of prison life gives a sense of authenticity to what is, plotwise, a potentially very silly potboiler. Fork-lift truck driver Vince Everett, as played by Elvis, gets in a pointless fight in a bar. He kills his opponent, goes down for manslaughter. His cellmate Hunk is an old country singer who guides Vince through prison and teaches him how to play guitar. When Vince gets out, he bumps into a pretty record plugger called Peggy Van Alden (Tyler) who guides him to stardom. Hunk gets out of chokey, wants a piece of Vince's action. After proving himself too old-school for singing success, he settles for being Vince's lackey. But Vince has become a monster, and his sadistic humiliation of the hapless Hunk leads to a deserved punch in the throat. Will Vince ever sing again?

Jailhouse Rock isn't perfect. The sudden introduction halfway through of Vince's lawyer Stokes as narrator is smartarse and superfluous. The Hollywood bit is a facile preview of the beach bum banality of Elvis's future film career, and features the least convincing kiss in screen history. Presley himself obviously feels the falseness of the scenes . . . his acting suddenly falls apart.

Another slight drawback is the soundtrack. Dominated by Leiber and Stoller songs, this is not their best work, and the performances – the delicious 'Treat Me Nice' and the 'Jailhouse Rock' dance routine aside – aren't as incendiary as those in *King Creole* (see p.25) and *Loving You* (see p.17). But then, Thorpe is more interested in making a believable drama rather than a pop musical. The dialogue is tough and Elvis spits his lines with trailer-trash fervour. Apart from the ending, there are few Hollywood clichés in the tale . . . when Vince first gets to sing in front of a crowd, they ignore him. Rather than win them over with his pure Elvisness, he gives in, loses his temper, smashes his guitar in a fit of pique. When he makes his first record, an established star steals the song and arrangement and has the hit. When Vince gets his first radio play, it's as a soundbed for a dog food ad. Early rock films were all cynical about the biz, but *Jailhouse Rock* takes its pops at money men, not pop itself.

Elvis is not presented here as natural star or even a good man . . . he has to work the system, like anyone else who can sing a bit. The movie's emphasis is almost entirely on Vince, Peggy and Hunk as characters, rather than Elvis as a star. It's a good 1950s social-realism melodrama – not quite *Rebel Without a Cause* or *On the Waterfront*, but not that far away.

The early prison scenes are especially fine. We get a sneak preview of Elvis's future army haircut. He still looks great. And at one point topless Elvis takes a whipping from a prison guard and looks as if he's cumming rather than suffering. Did 1950s Elvis have a gay following? 'Jailhouse Rock' was always a queer lyric, in both senses. 'Number 47 said to number 3/You're the cutest jailbird I ever did see/I sure would be delighted with your company/Come on and do the jailhouse rock with me.' I mean, you're really not needing a diagram about what a rock in an all-male jailhouse would look like, are ya?

It's a full 25 minutes of all-male prison drama before we finally get introduced to the love interest. Judy Tyler as record plugger Peggy is one of Elvis's curiously unattractive leading ladies – he got a fair few of 'em – but their first scene together in a bar is fabulous. Vince is a rude, sneering, sexually threatening bully . . . irresistible, in other words. And perhaps, as it is a Presley vehicle, it's poor Tyler's job to be blown offscreen and rendered asexual by the sheer animal magnetism of Presley's presence, which she duly is.

You can't help wondering if notorious Elvis manager Colonel Tom Parker's ears were burning when he clocked the Hunk

Houghton character. An ageing country singer jailbird who happens upon Vince by chance, not seeing the talent, but quickly seeing the potential for money. Parker never sang and probably never did time – although his life remains so clouded in mystery, you never know – but he came from the country music world and sold his protégé like a carnival huckster. Houghton cons Vince into signing a dodgy contract while they're still sharing a cell – the kind of move that surely would've drawn approving nods from Parker.

The most famous scene is the celebrated 'Jailhouse Rock' dance routine, but there's a recording studio scene which is arguably more significant. It's essentially a distillation of Elvis's breakthrough moment at Sam Phillips' Sun Studios in Memphis, when a snap decision to play his blues and country covers harder, faster, blacker and sexier invented Elvis, rock 'n' roll, the modern world. Here, Vince runs through a limp version of blues tune 'Don't Leave Me Now' (with Scotty Moore and Bill Black, the guitarist and bass-player who backed him at Sun, right there onscreen with him), recoils in horror when he hears how ordinary he is, and then records it again with a deeper beat and a dirtier voice. It's a wonderfully subtle reconstruction of Elvis's eureka moment.

But it's not the most important scene in Elvis's movie career. That would be the bit where Peggy takes Vince to a posh party thrown by her rich and educated parents, where the gathered sophisticates are into modern jazz. Vince tries to shock them by telling them he's just out of jail, fails miserably. Instead, mom implores her husband to put on the new record by 'Stubby Right-mire', and the party guests say things like, 'I think Stubby has gone overboard with those altered chords, don't you?' and 'I say atonality is just a passing phase in jazz music.' Elvis, of course, gets his great class-warrior moment: his eyes hood, his lip curls, and he simply says to mom, 'Lady ... I don't know what the hell you're talking about', and storms out, managing to convey, just by the way he shoves his hand in his pocket and swings those pussycat hips, that modern jazz and the upper middle classes are both utterly fucked. Rock 'n' roll and everything it means is in this three minutes of screen soothsaying. It's as crucial to the whole shebang as Little Richard's first shriek on 'Tutti Frutti'.

This is all build up for the 'beast in me' line, Elvis's most infamous movie moment, as he forces his tongue down Peggy's throat and defines hooligan potency for a generation of girls who were deciding that hiding their sexual desires was a busted flush. You can almost feel the swooning in the cinema from 50 years ago, even now.

Fascinatingly, much of the story hinges on Vince and Peggy starting their own record label. Yep . . . *Jailhouse Rock* presents Elvis Presley as a pioneer of Indie Rock. Bizarre. Brilliant.

Of course, it all goes horribly wrong when Hunk gets out of prison and comes to claim his 50 per cent. The implication is less that all jailbirds are bad news, and more that, by driving away Peggy and replacing her with 'the most expensive flunky in the world', Vince is rejecting the civilising influence of a strong, intelligent woman, thereby ensuring his inevitable demise. Must have appealed to Elvis, a man who was never the same once his sainted mother died. But considering how many expensive male flunkies he surrounded himself with throughout his life, Elvis never did learn the lesson.

Jailhouse Rock is, in the final analysis, a morality tale about hubris. Vince provokes Hunk into the punch that almost ends his career through sheer sadism. He gets what he deserves, even if the ending shits out and gives him Hollywood redemption. And Elvis is at his best playing this cruelty . . . this hubris was in him from the beginning. All the words written about the most famous man of the 20th century . . . but you'll find most of what you need to know about Elvis Presley from this, his best movie by far.

• •

King Creole

1958

Starring: Elvis Presley, Carolyn Jones, Dolores Hart, Dean Jagger, Walter Matthau, Vic Morrow
Dir.: Michael Curtiz

★ ★ ★ ★

Plot: The last sighting of Rebel Elvis.
Key line: 'You're a pretty fancy performer, ain'tcha Kid?'

It's no surprise at all that Elvis Presley routinely cited *King Creole* as his best movie. The final Elvis vehicle before he joined the army and the last to be filmed in black and white, *King Creole* was based upon a proper novel (*A Stone for Danny Fisher* by Harold Robbins). It had *Casablanca* director Michael Curtiz pulling off an unlikely blend of fun musical and ghetto crime story, included heavyweights Dean Jagger, Walter Matthau, Carolyn Jones and classic 1950s juvenile delinquent Vic Morrow in the supporting cast, and was originally offered to James Dean before his death. The score boasted classics in 'Crawfish', 'Hard Headed Woman', 'Trouble' and the title track, hard and bitter dialogue from Herbert Baker and Michael Vincente Gazzo, and the tough, *noir*-ish plot and authentic New Orleans setting gave the whole enterprise a gravitas that Presley's film career never approached again. But hey … what did Elvis know about picking film roles compared to his manager Colonel Tom Parker? *King Creole* isn't even in the Top Ten grossers of Elvis's filmography. Number one? The appalling *Viva Las Vegas* (see p. 45). The public gets what the public wants.

Danny Fisher is a young singer, living with sister (Jan Shepherd) and Dad (Jagger) in among the whores and seedy clubs of Bourbon Street. Mom's been dead three years and the family ain't over it. Dad's a coward and a loser, shoved around by his pharmacist boss, living for the day Danny graduates from high school and becomes more like him. But Danny's graduation is constantly held up by his violent streak and the hours he puts in as the dogsbody in dodgy nightclub the Blue Shade, which is full of greasy criminal types who drink until sun-up and treat women like the jaded Ronnie (the wonderful, smoldering Carolyn Jones, who spits out poet-slut lines like 'I was supposed to be home by midnight. I forget whose', with Dietrich-esque knowingness) like shit. Somehow, Danny has to make money, get the nice girl Dolores Hart (the dull virgin always has to triumph over the fascinating mature slapper), beat bad guy Maxie Fields (Matthau) *and* make Dad proud. Trouble is, for a superhero, Danny is a bit of a tosser. His idea of a romantic first date is booking a room in a seedy motel. He's a little too easily seduced by the idea of easy, dodgy money. He's a little too obsessed with Bad Dad. And he really likes hitting people.

The early 'Crawfish' scene, where Danny swaps vocals with a hot fishwife from his window, isn't just a glimpse of Elvis's movie potential. Its sensual, jazz and gospel-influenced blend of rock toughness and loungey soul would have been a perfect direction for Presley's music too, if anyone around him had been interested in art or quality in the early and mid 1960s. Hearing him duet with soul wailer Kitty White exemplifies both his instinctive grasp of black music *and* how much he found his own distinctive, white style within it. It's a short scene, but the most purely pleasurable one in the Elvis movie canon.

But, mostly, *King Creole* gives you a full look at the serious, sexy and threatening actor Presley could have been. He has great, believable moments throughout *King Creole* – rescuing Ronnie from two thugs with two broken bottles in hand, scared, but brave enough to sneer, 'And now you know what I do for an encore.' The blistering performance of 'Trouble'. The dirty flirting with Ronnie in her gleaming convertible. And a scene where he has to cry over his father in hospital where you believe every tear.

There are very silly scenes, too ... hints of future Elvis fiascos, like when Morrow's gang persuade Elvis to sing the rubbish 'Lover Doll' in a store to create a distraction for their crime spree. But the assault on Danny's father in a rain-soaked street at night is a classic *noir* set-piece. And for the film's final scenes the rock musical is forgotten and *King Creole* becomes a beautifully shot, dark, pacey thriller with wise insights about the nature of courage and the beauty and sadness of Ronnie's character, and visual dimensions way beyond the standard pop star vehicle. Even the ending refuses to tie everything up in a neat, happy bundle.

King Creole is a great, great movie. Funny thing is, it would still have been a great movie without Elvis's songs. But it's hard to imagine without Elvis's acting. That's how good he is here.

● ●

Expresso Bongo

1959

Starring: Laurence Harvey, Sylvia Syms, Yolande Donlan, Cliff Richard
Dir.: Val Guest

★ ★ ★ ★ ★

Plot: Early Cliff Richard film leads writer to question validity of modern life and his own existence.
Key line: 'You've got a chip on your shoulder and an H-Bomb in your pants!'

Even the credits are a masterpiece – a montage of tracking shots of 1950s Soho in all its gaudy, sleazy, black and white glory, with the cast's names appearing on billboards, shop fronts and jukeboxes. Big band jazz blares and everything about the magic fantasy of pre-1960s Soho – the slumming rich, sex and gambling, hookers and handjobs, Italian deco and trashy cheesecake, fags and fast food, coffee bars and dance clubs, dodgy deals and dodgier dealers, a London speeding towards its swinging peak – comes tumbling off the screen and mainlines its way into your heart.

The world of *Expresso Bongo*, the first truly great rock 'n' roll movie, based on the first great rock 'n' roll stage musical, is a world so cosmospolitan that the first person onscreen is a terrifyingly young and hard-looking Burt Kwouk, in plaid shirt with turned-up collar, barking 'Get with it, chick! Why come if you don't go for the beat?' The future *Pink Panther* and *Harry Hill* favourite is not presented as an exotic or a symbol of alien otherness . . . just another teen in the thrilling neon melting-pot of London on the cusp of modernity.

In seconds we get our first look at our star Laurence Harvey, fresh from his breakthrough role in Jack Clayton's proto-yuppie classic *Room at the Top*. He's reading the *New Musical Express* in the sharp grey suit, bow-tie and pork-pie he'll be wearing for the rest of the movie as fast-talking, comically Jewish hustler Johnny Jackson. Johnny was a drummer but has decided to cash in on the craze for teenagers playing music in Soho espresso bars. He's the kind of man who lies so much he can't detect his own bullshit. One minute he's on about his first million, the next he's dreaming of making an impact 'from Willesden to Croydon'. He's beautiful and brilliant and has loser written all over him.

His girlfriend is Maisie (Sims), a gauche stripper attempting to better herself by becoming a singer ('I don't want a man. I want a manager'). She drags the reluctant Johnny to a basement club, where teens who all look like designer hillbillies dance brilliantly to in-house band the Shadows. After stopping off to whiplash a chick through a contemptuous pastiche of jiving, Johnny settles down to sneer at the forthcoming young rock act which we immediately see is Sir Richard of Cliff. 'Here he comes,' Johnny leers. 'If we're lucky we'll be witness to an affray.'

He's still snippily unimpressed when the pudgy young quiff-meister starts playing the bongos, surrounded by hyperactive teens. But then Cliff starts to sing . . . and it's quite a thing. The song is a speedy, twangy little sub-Elvis rocker and Cliff is just fabulous, with his melodramatic lip-curling and St Vitus dancing. It's a real 'Where did it all go wrong?' moment.

'That child's got more sex than age', Maisie quips. Johnny sees the light. 'I've got the perfect setting for all this teenage violence.' He's soon hustling a bewildered Cliff aka Bert Rudge, who keeps insisting that all he wants to do is play drums 'for kicks'. Being no match for Johnny's speed-jive, the slum kid is soon Bongo Herbert, resident teen sensation at the equally bewildered Leon's espresso bar, which Johnny has transformed into the Tom Tom Club. A few sharp cons at the expense of record labels, the BBC (a great self-mocking turn from real-life documentary maker Gilbert Harding: 'We have the most eminent people coming to discuss this Bongo and his symptoms ... I mean, art.') and a lovely Bongo performance of 'A Voice in the Wilderness', and Johnny is suddenly in 'be careful what you wish for' territory. How well can his master-plan go, when his in-house songwriter is a 'bint'-obsessed jour-neyman called Beast who pens classics like 'I Beat My Chick With A Solid Rock'.

Old-school showbiz arrives in the shape of past-it American chanteuse Dixie Collins (the excellent Donlan), who interrupts her jaded diva-isms long enough to take Bongo under her ... ahem ... wing ('I've always done everything I can to help young talent', she leers) in what becomes a reverse-gender *A Star is Born* scenario.

Harvey's own ears must have been burning when he read the *Expresso Bongo* script. As well as spending his life hiding his Jewish-ness, which perhaps explains a performance that parodies Jewish-ness to the point of self-loathing, the Lithuanian-born heartthrob was also a closet queen. In order to conceal this throughout his short life (he died of stomach cancer at 45) he took up with a string of older women, the first of whom was Hermione Baddeley, a distinguished Oscar-nominated English character actress who was twice his age and mentored him through his early years in the British theatre. For added weirdness, she has a supporting role here as a comically ancient Soho hooker. No surprise, then, that Johnny's downfall isn't one of the ageing Jewish businessmen who make money from music and kids they loathe, but an unholy alliance of Bongo's selfish and bitter white-trash mother and Dixie, the worldly wise mother substitute. And no surprise either that Bongo's pass-port to superstardom isn't teenage sex and violence, but faked Christianity and an unapologetically oedipal ballad.

You watch this song, and the way that Richard nails this parody of shameful showbiz schmaltz, and you really can't help

THE BOURNEMOUTH & POOLE COLLEGE LRC WITHDRAWN

marvelling at how closely his subsequent career follows this exact blueprint (As Richard, as Bongo Herbert, asks in the film: 'Why is everybody always on with this *girlfriend* routine?'). But if it's all been a 50-year scam based on a satirical skit from a musical, then the man truly deserves that knighthood on the grounds of sheer evil genius.

This was Richard's second role, coming straight after his debut in the same year's excellent juvenile delinquent drama *Serious Charge*, a film I would've included for its insightful presentation of British pre-1960s terrors if Cliff had got to burst into song a few more times. Richard is the redeemable troubled teen in this provocative little movie about a small-town vicar falsely accused of homosexual molestation and, even though Richard can't really *act*, as such ... there's just something *right* about him. And he's exactly the same in *Expresso Bongo*; when you first watch it you feel he's just the hapless teen gimmick steamrollered by Harvey's overwhelming chutzpah. But the more you see *Expresso Bongo*, the more perfect for the role he is. His stilted emptiness is entirely evocative of the kind of dumb but ambitious innocent who is both easy to manipulate and ripe to become quickly corrupted by success. Any stronger in the part, and he'd make Bongo too sympathetic. And sympathy is something *Expresso Bongo* doesn't have for anyone involved in the London entertainment industry.

For a 1950s mainstream hit of stage and screen, *Expresso Bongo* is a bilious sick-fest, a parade of barely repressed perversions and none-too-subtle hints at the real Sodom-and-Gomorrah abuses and neuroses that have always fuelled British show business. Twenty years before punk, and the gleeful celebration of decadence, greed and nihilism on show here makes *The Great Rock'n'Roll Swindle* (see p. 206) look like *Little House on the Prairie*. But, because of the censorship rules of the time, what can't be shown has to be suggested by allusive dialogue and cunning implication. If you've read John Niven's savage 2008 Britpop-meets-*American Psycho* comic novel *Kill Your Friends* and not known whether to giggle or retch, then understand that the music biz scenario it describes is pretty much accurate, and that it's just *Expresso Bongo* with added cussing, blood and semen.

Wolf Manciewicz's waspish, crackling dialogue, Harvey's characterisation (based on Manciewicz himself) and Guest's *mise en scène* vie for top billing in pop's greatest movie (*Privilege*, my choice as this book's best, is pure *rock* movie by virtue of its apocalyptic pessimism). Guest makes the tale's theatrical origins into pure cinema by making London the star, presenting the penthouse and pavement extremes of the wild West End with such sleazy glamour you wish you could just jump into a time machine and drown in its irresistible corruptions and chaotic, pre-corporate franchise dens of iniquity. A mixture of my mum's reminiscences, Colin Macinnes's *Absolute Beginners* novel and *Expresso Bongo* have conspired to convince me that my curse was being born in the right place at the wrong time, 20 years too late for a London being conquered by greedy and reckless youth, where tribal allegiances to music and fashion mattered enough to change the world, and even corruption and cynicism were innocent enough to be revolutionary.

Watching *Expresso Bongo* makes me deliriously happy and furious simultaneously. Because Britain doesn't make films like this any more. Writers who can write, directors with vision and actors who can create shaggable monsters like Harvey's Johnny are actively discouraged until they move to America or just give up. *Expresso Bongo* creates a world so vivid and full of life and spit and desirable danger that like, say, the alternative worlds of *Buffy the Vampire Slayer*'s Sunnydale or *The Wire*'s Baltimore, you visit and don't want to come home to whingeing, prurient, smoke- and fun-free England. We drown in vats of mimsy middle-class mediocrity.

Once upon a time we were so good at making movies that we could tell stories so wicked and strong that Cliff Richard couldn't ruin them. Now we make *The Boat that Rocked*. *Expresso Bongo* is about a London that was poised to be the centre of the world. Now we've lost so much interest in ourselves that our films are about Indian call centres, funded by the game shows they're promoting.

A nation is only as healthy as its culture. Twenty-first-century Britain is slumped in a grey hospital bed, attached to drips.

1960s

Beat Girl

1960

Starring: Adam Faith, David Farrar, Gillian Hills, Noelle Adam, Christopher Lee, Shirley Anne Field, Peter McEnery, Oliver Reed
Dir.: Edmond T. Gréville

★ ★ ★ ★

Plot: Crazy beat music and Bad Dad lead pouting nymphet down seedy path to sin and degradation.
Key line: 'Do everything. Feel everything. Strictly for kicks!'

Beat Girl opens with one of the best scenes in the dubious history of the rock movie.

A twangy guitar – courtesy of the John Barry Seven – rings out over a stark monochrome shot of a scruffy staircase. Sharp dressed young pre-mods descend the staircase. One girl stops, holds centre-screen. Blonde, luscious of lip and wearing hip-hugging sweater and slacks, she pouts, her expression an intimidating mix of disdain and lust, of fuck-you and wanna-fuck-you.

The camera slams in closer, and the legend 'Beat Girl' frames her impossibly cruel face.

She finally moves forward and we move with her, into a small basement room with a band in the corner and a dance floor full of boys and girls in various states of downbeat sartorial splendour. They bop and frug with the kind of spectacular comic abandon that only happened when people danced on camera in the 1960s. Our Beat Girl begins to dance – pure sex, almost as if drugged – and we see that her plaid-shirted partner is ... Oliver Reed. Who could have believed that Britain's leading booze-bully thespian had ever been young!

As the credits continue to roll the camera looks down at the kids' feet – pedal pushers, pumps and rumpled jeans, all made gorgeous by the stark, French New Wave-influenced black and grey. As the

camera arcs and the scene ends, Beat Girl stares us down, a taunting, defiant, hungry predator. It's less than two minutes that
completely defines the eroticism and danger of both rock and rave's
eternal promise of dirty, stylish kicks. If the film had stopped right
there . . .

But *Beat Girl* doesn't stop. It gets right on with the job of
being a B-movie masterpiece. In its eagerness to exploit adolescent
sexuality, rock, beatniks, middle-class slumming, prostitutes, strippers and sly intimations of lesbianism and incest – not to mention
teen rock idol Adam Faith – it gleefully presents London's Soho as
an island of thrilling perversity in an England so repressed that a
married couple can't even snog on a train without some proto-
Mary Whitehouse skewering them with murderous disapproval. It
had to be directed by a Frenchman.

Beat Girl's seriously weird plot goes like this: Paul Linden, a
stuffy upper-class architect, goes to Paris for a few months to get
over his divorce and comes back with a French dolly-bird wife
who's only eight years older than his daughter. Said daughter
Jennifer, who is already being turned into a Bad Lot by art school
and hanging round Soho coffee bars listening to cool jazz and
hot rock with other rich brats and token authentic working-class
existentialist Adam Faith, gets really hostile. Meanwhile, a chance
meeting with Soho stripper Greta reveals that stepmum has a sordid
past. Jennifer is handed a chance to both expose the hypocrisy of
Bad Dad while watching strippers in a sleazy club with just a little
too much interest. Club owner Kenny (a marvellously cadaverous
Christopher Lee) sees *his* chance to lure the disco dolly to a life of
vice. It all ends in blood and chaos.

Around this sleazoid framework director Edmond T. Gréville
hangs a set of provocative digressions and brilliant set-pieces. A
rock 'n' roll rave in Chislehurst Caves, which isn't just a startling
revelation that acid house didn't invent the illegal rave in the
country, but also moves into a conversation between The Kids that
contends that it's World War, rather than their parents, that causes
them to huddle in this dark, underground place, scared and alienated. Then there's Adam Faith's superb Eddie Cochran pastiches,

dropped suddenly into the action, with backing from jukeboxes and a vocal echo chamber beamed in from nowhere, plus Shirley Anne Field singing a disturbing slice of Popera called 'It's Legal'.

Thrill, also, to a very British version of the infamous 'Chicky Run' from *Rebel Without a Cause* (Gréville is definitely in thrall to the Nicholas Ray/James Dean classic that remains the Daddy of all teen angst movies) where The Kids have to rest their necks on the rails of a country train track while a train hurtles towards them. Last one to get up is the winner, and Beat Girl Jennifer symbolically castrates Faith's Dave by proving herself the least scared to die.

And strangest of all, a gratuitous pop at 1960s town-planning when Bad Dad reveals his obsessive plan for a 'City 2000', blocking out his wife and daughter as he stares at his tiny cardboard city comprising rows and rows of identical high-rise blocks, and breaks into a blood-curdling lecture: 'Psychologists think that most human neuroses come from too much contact with other humans. Now in my city, a man can be as alone as if he was 10,000 miles from anywhere.' Remarkably prescient, *n'est ce pas?* Dad may be a 'square' socially, but in his work he is an arch-modernist. And in *Beat Girl*'s world, this makes him the equivalent of all those mad scientists from 1950s disaster flicks ... and mad scientists always have to be taught a valuable lesson about the follies of playing God.

No wonder, then, that Jennifer's gone beat crazy, hovering on the precipice of polymorphous perversity, before her father and his kind succeed in banning human interaction completely. She hangs around a group of people who certainly have a way with words. 'Say, Babe, are you feeling terpsichorical? Let's go downstairs and fly!' 'Great, Dad, great! Straight from the fridge!' 'He sends me! Over and out!' And a fledgling stripper's sneering rejection of Faith's advances: 'Fall down, Juvenile!' Screenwriter Dail Ambler has top fun at the expense of middle-class Brits trying to talk beatnik jive, reminding us that the wigger is no new invention. A bewildered Dad asks his errant Beat Girl what the heck all this teenage argot actually means, and gets a response which hits the enduring teen cult rebellion nail squarely on the dome, Daddio: 'It's all we've got. Next week ... Voom! Up goes the world in smoke! And what's the score? Zero! So now, while it's now, we live it up. Do everything. Feel everything. Strictly for kicks!'

Now, I hope I'm getting you real juiced up about seeing this movie. But a word of warning: the supporting cast are all great, especially Faith, Lee and Peter McEnery. But the three leads are *atrociously*, stunningly, jaw-droppingly bad. Farrar, once a charismatic and accomplished star of Powell and Pressburger classics *Black Narcissus* and *The Small Back Room*, is obviously dismayed and embarrassed that his career has come to this. Ms Hills would have been a superstar in the silent era, blessed as she is with one of those faces where every feature is too big and prominent and just screams 'SEX!' at you from every angle. But when the girl talks . . . *ouch*. And Noelle Adam as strumpet stepmum is patently not too comfortable with English and reacts to everything with the same scared and vacant expression.

But, somehow, this all works in the film's favour. While the characters that populate the rave and sex club scenes are alive and vivid and (super)natural, the scenes in Dad's ultra-modern glamour flat are as uncomfortable as the surroundings. There is a tension between the skill behind the camera and the bumbling haplessness in front of it which just makes *Beat Girl* feel even more perverse and transgressive.

Beat Girl was an X-rated movie . . . but did you know that, in 1960, X movies were for those aged 16-and-over? That the powers that be actually put the age *up* to 18 in 1970? I mention this because *Beat Girl* often has the feel of a film aimed at dirty old men. Especially in a striptease scene starring a black woman called Pascaline which wouldn't be out of place in a rap video . . . except that the context – a sudden switch from Pascaline's big behind fucking the stage to the supposedly 16-year-old Beat Girl watching with quizzical excitement – makes it seem far filthier than anything on MTV Base. It isn't long before Beat Girl herself is stripping for the entertainment of her friends, and Faith watches her, face contorted into an ugly grimace, his hand spanking the phallic guitar he carries everywhere. What could they be trying to say?

At the film's violent end, Faith has had his guitar smashed by Teds – those *truly* bad *working-class* thugs – who are only partly impressed by his oft-repeated pronouncement that 'fighting's for squares'. The reunited family walk away from the scene of Beat Girl's shame, and you could read that as a family-oriented happy ending. But the scene they walk into is pure *noir*, and the three, huddled together, are dwarfed by the garish neon flash and the looming dark alleys of the Soho night. The family is going to get royally fucked by modern times, it seems to say, and whether you take that seriously or with a pinch of kitschified salt, *Beat Girl* stands as both a stunning rock movie and a stunning British B-movie of the kind they just don't make any more.

• •

The Young Ones

1961
Starring: Cliff Richard, Robert Morley, Carole Gray, The Shadows, Melvin Hayes, Richard O'Sullivan
Dir.: Sidney J. Furie

★ ★

Plot: Let's do the show right here.
Key line: 'Cheer up! It may never happen!'

Writing about Sir Cliff Richard is the most redundant task in music journalism. Partly because he's really litigious. But mainly because saying that Cliff Richard is rubbish is like saying that toast makes a great snack – everyone agrees but nobody cares. But you can't write about rock movies from a British perspective without acknow-ledging the popularity of Sir Cliff's 1961–73 run of six family-orientated musicals. As they're all more or less identical, though ... one is enough (*Serious Charge* and *Expresso Bongo* [see p. 27] don't count as Cliff Richard musicals. He just happened to get in the way). So, *The Young Ones* gets in ahead of *Summer Holiday* and

Wonderful Life because it's the first, marginally the best, and because it named and ironically inspired an iconoclastic British TV sitcom. And the theme tune's cute, too. Go on. Admit it.

The opening is immediately somewhat curious. The first six minutes or so consist of various characters knocking off work in what one assumes is London (it's really sunny, clean and friendly, so maybe it's some inter-dimensional West London you reach by climbing into a wardrobe) and getting dressed for a Friday night out. The action is carefully choreographed in a traditional MGM musical sort of way, and the long musical suite accompanying the rush of happy, wacky images is more Gene Kelly than Elvis ... although much worse, naturally. It possesses the same jaunty, theatrical take on Englishness as *Oliver!* and *Chitty Chitty Bang Bang*.

But then ... a sudden jump cut to a podgy-faced and bequiffed Cliff, Presleying his way through a neat little Shadows-backed rocker called 'I've Got a Funny Feeling' in a dancehall decorated by murals of black people playing jazz, to a frugging collection of well-dressed 'kids' who, in time-honoured tradition, actually look around 30. *The Young Ones* is unusual in wanting to have it both ways with its target audience, going all out to splice the rock-sploitation movie and the heavily orchestrated 'quality' family musical. Later Cliff movies like 1964's *Wonderful Life* dispense with rock 'n' roll and the frisson of tribal youth altogether. But *The Young Ones* is caught somewhere in the middle, unsure, pre-Beatles, whether to stick with this rock 'n' roll fad or twist the clean-cut star and his frothy sidekicks firmly into the middle of the road.

Back to the youth club. When the Cliffster shudders to a really-not-that-unsexy halt, we learn that a property magnate called Hamilton Black (the reliably ludicrous Morley) has bought said 'youth club' and wants to close it down. While club members with suspiciously working-class accents suggest violent protest, Cliff's Nicky is the very epitome of good olde English middle-class resignation. 'We'll just go to another club, toodle-pip, what-what' sort of thing.

Before we can get embroiled further in the complexities of the perennial class struggle, Furie breaks for one of many old-school song-and-dance routines involving Nicky giving leading lady Toni (Gray) some peppy platitudes while walking her home through a deserted Stepfordised London. This would be dull, except that: (1) it's genuinely amazing how much Richard has come on as a screen actor in the two years since *Expresso Bongo* (see p. 27), where he can only dream of being as good as a plank of wood. He's no Astaire or Sinatra, but he carries off the routine pretty well. (2) It's neatly surreal when he suddenly swings slowly around the top of a lamp-post in honour of Russian cosmonaut Yuri Gagarin. And (3) The routine ends when, after walking the bint home, he says a breezy and sexless goodnight *without even kissing her*, thereby establishing his entire future public persona before literally vanishing into thin air. Give Furie his due … he did his best to give this schlock at least a little bit of 1960s weirdness.

But here comes the twist – the big bad property chap is Cliff's dad! The ideas that fuelled 1960s British pop films reveal themselves as suspiciously few and far between once you watch them one after the other. They all have Bad Dads. They're all obsessed with innocent young singers/actresses/models being bullied by all-powerful father figures. And, as *Beat Girl* (see p. 35) gained some success by having Bad Dad being a modernising architect, *The Young Ones* just goes right ahead with precisely the same premise. What was this English creatives' horror about fathers and builders and progress all about?

Basically, it all comes down to putting on a show to save the club. The 1960s is put on hold as Cliff runs in terror from the sexualised showgirl woman and falls with relief – of a kind – into the arms of the sexless girl, and Daddy's hard, thrusting edifice fails to penetrate the London skyline. But on the other hand, it mentions the Finsbury Park Empire, which always gives me a nostalgic glow, and it bigs up the subversive qualities of pirate radio, so, you know, Fight the Power, Boyeeee.

The film music is *awful* while Richard's own stuff is fine (Hank Marvin of the Shads is a guitar God, lest anyone forget). The dance routines get progressively worse but the colours are very pretty. I wanted to argue that its onscreen innocence is more appealing than the cynicism of a modern manufactured pop movie like *Spiceworld* (see p. 323), but I can't fake the lie. The relentless banality just reveals a different kind of cynicism and reminds us that we got all jaded and postmodern because it was less boring than family-orientated showbiz, which is the dullest entertainment on Earth.

Everything has some use, though. *The Young Ones* and the other Richard musicals do have the unplanned effect of making you realise that all those Elvis vehicles weren't really *that* bad after all.

● ●

Play It Cool

1962

Starring: Billy Fury, Michael Anderson Jr, Dennis Price, Anna Falk, Maurice Kaufmann, Richard Wattis
Dir.: Michael Winner

★ ★ ★

Plot: When rock stars were nice guys and rich girls were grateful.
Key line: 'Daddy! When we get back from Brussels we must give a big dance at Claridges! And Billy and the boys *must* play!'

Play It Cool feels like a last lovable blast of Britpop innocence before the Beatles popped our collective cherry. A light, pop musical vehicle for the first great British rock star Billy Fury, it charms through that terribly chirpy stage-school cockney over-acting famil- iar to anyone who has watched the cinematic works of Cliff Richard and Tommy Steele, and the wonderful, heavily orchestrated, Buddy Holly-influenced pop-rock songs of Norrie Paramour, who dominated British pop production in the pre-Beatles era. Fury is stunningly beautiful, with a sweeping blonde quiff (a haircut copied and acknowledged by ABC's Martin Fry), a sheepskin-collared coat, and a constant shy smile. Not to mention perfect pop star cheekbones, coathanger shoulders and the best *faux*-Elvis voice of his time. The boy talks throughout in the weirdest accent, though; you can barely make out a word he says. But it just makes him seem more enigmatic and odd. Unlike Richard, Steele, Marty Wilde, Adam Faith and the other members of the Larry Parnes stable of archly monikered British pop stars of the pre-Beatles era, Fury had genuine animal magnetism and an aura of mystery.

There's an undertow of tragedy and quintessentially English underachievement to the Fury story, which is probably why Morrissey is such a fan. Born Ronald William Wycherley in 1940, the Liverpudlian initially approached Marty Wilde at a local show to sell him his songs. One look at him, and Larry Parnes had changed his name to Billy Fury and put him on the bill of his travelling show. A few hits later, and local boys the Silver Beetles were auditioning to be his backing band. Parnes offered them £20 a week if they sacked then-bassist Stuart Sutcliffe. John Lennon refused. Two years later, and Fury was the Beatles' major UK chart rival during their early Beatlemania years.

But not for too long. Like all the early Britpop idols, Fury and his manufactured, matinee idol post-Presleyness was made redundant by the beat groups. In 1967 he went into hospital for the first of many heart operations. His condition finally claimed his life in 1983 at the age of 43, after a less-than-successful attempt at a comeback. Aside from his ill-health, Fury's main problem was that he couldn't go completely MOR like Richard and Steele. He was an authentic rocker and songwriter, and fell uncomfortably between the two stools.

But *Play It Cool* preserves the legend at his peak. Fury's band, Billy Universe and the Satellites, are off to play at a twist championships. Of course they are. The Satellites' fellow passenger is heiress Ann Bryant (Falk), who has been sent away to

Belgium by her overbearing posh Dad (Price) after being involved in a scandal with rock star Larry Granger (Kaufmann). When the plane gets marooned in London, Billy persuades the lovelorn heiress to hang out with the band and search for Granger. They go to bohemian dance clubs in London's perennially beautiful and dangerous Soho (see *Beat Girl*, p. 35 and *Expresso Bongo*, p. 27) and a twist club where the turn is Shane Fenton, who'd be better known in the 1970s as Alvin Stardust. This is, naturally, the cue for the greatest of all cinematic marvels, the 1960s disco dance scene. Fury himself has one of the campest and sexiest dance styles in pop, and all is good. Although he's soon left behind in the camp stakes when the one and only Lionel Blair gets to do a sub-*Guys and Dolls* routine in an equally gorgeous cellar club.

This is one extra-special Soho night, in fact. In the Chinese-themed Lotus Club, husky-voiced Helen Shapiro is the headline chanteuse. Things go a bit Pete Tong when we have to endure a song by American Buddy Holly copyist Bobby Vee, but he was a big star at the time and his presence probably got the film distributed in the States, and the song is blissfully short. It's at the Lotus Room that the gang find Granger, who of course turns out to be a no-good cheating cad and bounder. The gang foil his despicable plans, outwit a nosey press photographer and Bad Dad, and Billy plays it cool.

The surprise is how great the film looks, shot in super-stylish monochrome and deliciously evocative of its times. It makes it hard to believe that Michael Winner went on to become such a notoriously tasteless director. The film, in terms of story and *mise en scène*, is a template for *Catch Us If You Can* (see p. 57), except that the world changed so much in those three years that the Dave Clark Five vehicle twists the 'two potential lovers on the run from authority' storyline into an existential critique of teenage culture. Here, it's still innocent fun and glimpses of the unsquare world ahead. Of course, when I say innocent, I'm referring to our young heroes and heroine. Once again, early rock films are full of cynics and conmen. But they're all on the business and media side, while the talent is largely naive and well-meaning. Young is good. Middle-aged, is old, is bad.

The film is so careful not to offend anyone with its visions of youthful sex that Billy Universe doesn't get the girl. This is one of the reasons why *Play It Cool* is a *fin de siècle* film ... the last time rock 'n' roll as virginal teenage fun ever played to anyone as cool.

• •

Viva Las Vegas

1963
Starring: Elvis Presley, Ann-Margret, Cesare Denova, William Demerest
Dir: George Sidney

★

Plot: Don't be silly.
Key line: 'That's what I call a real sporty model.'

It's no coincidence that America's two most popular 20th-century male entertainers are so closely associated with Las Vegas. But Frank Sinatra never let Las Vegas eat him.

This film is essentially an 80-minute ad for the gaudy delights of the planet's least authentic city, yet it still stands as the best of Elvis Presley's notoriously appalling post-army movies. This says nothing substantial at all, of course. These films are so bad no amount of applied trash aesthetic can save them. It's not the shallowness or sexism or awful music that makes them so bad. It's the fact that they're all very, very boring.

Sinatra might have been as corrupted by Vegas as Elvis, but the guy had a real film career that brought the best out of him, and even managed to make great music while he did so. The movies Presley made between 1960 and 1969 took a decade of art out of his life, and fuelled the depression which caused the addictions that finally killed him young. They also did more to destroy rock 'n' roll's innocence and self-confidence than any one other factor, at the very same time as the Beatles and Dylan were symbolising its depth and power. The Elvis movies and their relative commercial success are the reason why rock is split into mainstream and alternative, why Louis Walsh and Simon Cowell make more money out of pop than your favourite artist. In short, you can't write a book about rock movies without discussing at least one of the wretched things, and as *Viva Las Vegas* has a Ray Charles cover, the best theme song and the sexiest leading lady, it might as well be the one.

So Elvis is a racing driver called Lucky and he falls for hot tamale Rusty, played by Ann-Margret. His rival in love and racing is a rich European Count (Danova), but Elvis's all-American charm wins, well, everything. Songs are sung, dances are danced, jokes aren't funny, the camera trains itself on Ann-Margret's pert arse like a perv at a peep show and another nail is hammered into Elvis's supersized coffin at the grand old age of 28.

As you can probably tell, it was a low point in the writing of this book just trying to find something useful to see in, and say about, this movie. Every line of dialogue is like an extract from an after-dinner speech at a footballers' dinner. Every scene is set like provincial am-dram filmed by a monkey. Every Elvis performance is like Ricky Martin with severe back spasms. Every song is like some kind of evil parody of actual music. It had been a long time since I'd seen an Elvis movie (I should point out here that the phrase 'Elvis movie' doesn't apply to the pre-army Elvis films or the 1970s documentaries discussed elsewhere. 'Elvis movie' means the 1960–69 dross, the worst of which, if you're that kind of ghoul, is a 1969 disaster called *Change of Habit*, where the love interest is Mary Tyler Moore as a singing nun) and I was shocked that time and a few years of being given a proper education in screen musicals by the missus had made me realise that they're even worse than the Cliff Richard musicals, probably because the waste of talent is far more dramatic.

But using *Viva Las Vegas* as a launch-pad for one of those

critical Elvis ponderings on the theme of 'What if?' would be an irrelevance, really. The truth is that Elvis Presley's days as an innovator were over on the day he signed for RCA, because he'd only come up with the magic formula for fusing black and white music and performance out of hunger and ambition – once there, he was happy, as a non-songwriter and instinctive performer, to do whatever manager Colonel Tom Parker assured him would make money. The Elvis movies are a key part of the Great American Tragedy that was Presley's life, and without them the story wouldn't have the ominous middle bit that gives the story its meaning.

The most notable thing about *Viva Las Vegas* is the oddly named Ann-Margret, a beautiful and talented American actress doomed to be abused by leering directors (see *Tommy*, p. 164). Ann and Elvis had a well-publicised affair on the set of *Viva Las Vegas*, despite Presley already being betrothed to future wife Priscilla, and much has been made down the years of the pair's onscreen chemistry. In truth, this seems like a great job done by the studio's publicity machine because Elvis is too stiff and stilted throughout the film to steam a kettle. But Ann-Margret's dance scenes, where she frugs with gay abandon in tight sweater and hip-huggers, are a key moment in bringing beatnik girl style to the mainstream. She's more iconic than the 20th-century's greatest icon here – although, admittedly, a sock-puppet would have given the somnambulant star a run for his Vegas dollars too.

Viva Las Vegas does point out something key about Presley, though. When watching this film . . . I literally felt loathing for the guy and everything he stood for. I watch the 1968 'Comeback' TV special, or listen to any of his 1950s Sun sides or late 1960s Memphis sessions, and I adore Elvis with a devotion bordering on the obsessive. Has there ever been another entertainer capable of inspiring such extremes of love and hate in us?

If you're answering, for example, Michael Jackson at this point, you've got to realise that it's simply not the same thing: any revulsion Jacko inspires in us is caused by what we think we know about his sexual proclivities . . . plus what he's done to his face, the colour of his skin, to children that he's dangled off balconies. In short, any loathing of Jackson is entirely dependent on his offstage character. Little was known about Presley's private weirdness until his death, and, even then, the worst that can be said about him, once you read all the posthumous biographies and exposés, is that he never grew up. It's his music, his performance, his sheer presence in the universe that inspires intense positive and negative emotions, and it's that that makes Elvis Presley unique.

Las Vegas was always the perfect backdrop for the demise of the most charismatic American of his age, the Empire of Neon Tackiness and rampant greed that any poor kid from Tennessee would see as the symbol of being Top of the World, Ma. It's fitting that the theme song from *Viva Las Vegas* has been covered by myriad smartarse alternative bands and has become as much of a totemic Elvis song as 'Heartbreak Hotel' or 'In the Ghetto'. It *is* the American Dream that the planet won't accept is really a nightmare.

But would I, one day, go to Las Vegas? Hey ... buy me a ticket and I'm on that plane to Hell. And I'd probably shell out for the kitsch Elvis wedding too, if I hadn't already settled for a nice council employee in Hackney. Because I, like you, have been programmed to be beguiled by American shite. But not efficiently enough to love Elvis Presley's 1960s movies.

• •

A Hard Day's Night

1964

Starring: The Beatles, Norman Rossington, Wilfred Brambell,
John Junkin, Victor Spinetti
Dir.: Richard Lester

★ ★ ★

Plot: A day in the life of Beatlemania.
**Key line: Journalist: 'What would you call that hairstyle
you're wearing?'**
George: 'Arthur.'

I watched this film for the first time in many years for this book,
and came out of the experience confused. It's obviously an accomplished and influential movie, but I was strangely bored by it.
I couldn't get to the bottom of why. Finally, my wife Linsay came
to my rescue with a bit of spot-on lateral thinking. *A Hard Day's
Night*, she said, reminded her of the opening credits of the long-
running TV cartoon series, *The Flintstones*. Specifically, the bit
where Fred Flintstone goes to a takeaway and buys dinosaur ribs.
The simple visual joke is that Fred puts this enormous slab of meat
and bone on the side of his little stone-age car, and the car collapses
sideways with a splat. 'This film', Linsay reckoned, 'collapses under
the weight of everything you know about it. It can't carry the
dinosaur ribs.'

What we know about the dinosaur ribs is this. Conceived to do
nothing more than exploit the imagined fad of Beatlemania in the
wake of the Beatles' extraordinary first visit to America, *A Hard
Day's Night* was shot in 16 weeks on a budget of £200,000. Richard
Lester, a British-based US director, who had cut his teeth working
with John Lennon's favourite comedy team the Goons and later
directed a couple of Christopher Reeve Superman movies, used
the limitations in a visionary way. Whereas Elvis and Cliff movies
were all pretty location and bursting happily into song, Lester shot

in dour, newsreel black and white in claustrophobic train carriages and hotel rooms, pinching his *mise en scène* from Italian neo-realism and the French New Wave, and giving rock its first shot of self-conscious, modernist art. That, the Beatles' naturalistic performances, and the film's surreal 'a day in the life' non-plot seduced anti-rock movie critics who had expected to hate the film. Their universal praise made a film for kids into a film for everyone and *A Hard Day's Night* grossed over £2 million in six weeks, even gaining Oscar nominations for scriptwriter Alun Owen and Beatles producer George Martin.

It's fun to wonder what would've happened to the Beatles without this shot of credibility and the confidence that intellectual approval brings to any young artist. But the effect the film had on rock, popular culture and post-war Britain's self-esteem is incalculable. The first classic Beatles album, *Rubber Soul,* was still almost 18 months away when *A Hard Day's Night* was released, yet the film granted the Beatles highbrow critical acceptance at a time when they were still penning clever but slight teen love songs. The Beatles fit for all ages and classes presented in *A Hard Day's Night* were sexless, but relentlessly cool: whiplash smart prickers of pretension who were impossible to control, lived every second on impulse, yet still turned up on time to play a perfect pop show for girls who screamed so hard that one of the real camera operators had to go to an emergency dentist straight after shooting because the hormonal din had loosened all his fillings. Owen may have written the witty script; Lester may have shaped the look and the sense of surreal chaos; but it was made to feel like the Beatles were making it all up on the spot. The scenes where John, Paul, George and Ringo make monkeys of various upper middle-class journalists, fashionistas and theatre luvvies are crucial, because they paint the Beatles as fearless purveyors of working-class intellect, the kind that plays dumb for effect but can then suddenly accuse an elder and better, as Ringo does to the camp TV director played by Victor Spinetti, of 'hiding behind a smokescreen of bourgeois clichés', knowing full well that the phrase itself is a parody of self-proclaimed intellect. The movie is even clever enough to subvert its own youth rebel premise by making the most anarchistic character an old man. Paul's grandfather, played brilliantly by Wilfred Brambell aka Old Man Steptoe, spouts Irish nationalist cant at policemen, springs up through a trapdoor while the band entertain the multitudes and is a constant, seditious loose cannon. His malicious mischief inspires the movie's best and most poignant segment when he convinces Ringo that the rest of the band look down upon him. A convinced Ringo goes AWOL and embarks upon a mini-quest for his working-class roots, strolling through an already dying world of urchin boys and pubs where workers play shove ha'penny. Ringo ends up getting thrown out of the pub, not because he's recognised as a Beatle but simply for not fitting in, and you feel the Beatles' inevitable loss of anything like a normal life.

A Hard Day's Night plays these bittersweet class-warrior games incessantly, because Owen spent time with the Beatles before and during the writing and tapped perfectly into the four's blend of macho Liverpool banter and bohemian references picked up at art school and among the nocturnal beatniks of Hamburg in their pre-record-deal days. There's even a very odd little nudge-nudge-wink-wink scene, particularly in the light of the later rampant rumours that Lennon was bisexual and had some kind of affair with Beatles manager Brian Epstein.

The Beatles and entourage are backstage at the theatre. John points out that Ringo is reading a magazine called *Queen*. 'That's an in-joke, you know,' he quips, more to us than anyone else. Brambell's granddad declares them all a bunch of sissies. Then Norman Rossington, playing the band's long-suffering (and very un-Epstein) manager, threatens to 'tell 'em all the truth' about Lennon, unless he stops leading the boys astray (the film very much elects Lennon the undisputed leader of the band). 'You wouldn't', mumbles John . . . who is now wearing a false *beard*! At another point Lennon sniffs something off the top of a can OF COKE!!!, and we see that *A Hard Day's Night* is also the beginning of the sinister rumours that surrounded the Beatles throughout their time together, most of which they happily started themselves.

I'm not saying that every kid who watched *A Hard Day's Night* in 1964 caught the references or took them as permission to take Class As and get bi-curious. But enough did, consciously or not, and the sense of freedom and benign rebellion the Beatles conveyed in *A Hard Day's Night* has as strong a claim to inventing the experimental, liberal and anti-establishment 1960s as Elvis, JFK, Vietnam or the Cold War. If you were young and ordinary in 1964, these four men must have looked like everything you dreamed of becoming ... particularly as none of them had the unattainable glamour and weirdness of Elvis, Dylan or Jagger.

But these more provocative and substantial scenes don't dominate; they're the best bits among 89 minutes of larking about and singing a bunch of bland, samey pop songs. For a movie to be a timeless classic, as critical consensus insists this is, you have to see these enormous achievements when you watch the film, not because someone keeps telling you that the first jazzy chord of the movie's theme song was a symbolic clarion call to youth revolution ... blahblahblatherblah. And *A Hard Day's Night*, after 40-odd years of geeky blokes with guitars, their defensive in-jokes, their manufactured gang mentality, their miming to their songs in parks or on train carriages; 40-odd years of arty black and white, and the young cocking a snook at the old, and we're free to be (to buy) whatever we want any old time, of revolt into style; 40-odd years of women being dismissed as screeching hysterical pre-pubes, sexed-up bimbos or sexless hags, as *A Hard Day's Night* casually does; 40-odd years of bands pushing the 'I'm working class and down to earth' card while aiming to get the exotic bird and the mansion in the country at the earliest possible opportunity; 40-odd years of the forced jollity and stiff poses of the pop promo; 40-odd years of the world the Beatles helped create ... *A Hard Day's Night* is a small, empty vehicle which collapses under all the good and bad things the 1960s have come to mean.

Among the extras on the current DVD version is an interesting 'making of' documentary called *Things We Said Today*. It gives director Dick Lester the opportunity to relate a telling little story. It turns out that he was sent 'a parchment scroll' quite recently, thanking him for being 'the father of MTV'. Lester relates that he wrote back to the music TV channel demanding a blood test. Nice joke, but MTV, in the end, is the real meat of what *A Hard Day's Night* invented. The rest of the baggage is … well, actually, it's 'hiding behind a smokescreen of bourgeois clichés', when it comes right down to it. The dinosaur ribs look like a feast on the plate. But it's hot air and bare bones once you bite into it.

• •

Help!

1965

Starring: The Beatles, Leo McKern, Eleanor Bron, Victor Spinetti, Roy Kinnear
Dir.: Richard Lester

★ ★ ★

Plot: Bizarre eastern cult can't leave Ringo's ring alone.
Key line: 'We're risking our lives to preserve a useless member.'

I'm probably the only Beatles fan and film fan in existence who likes *Help!* better than *A Hard Day's Night* (see p. 49). Don't get me wrong; they're both boring. But *Help!* has more great ideas, and is definitely more lovable, in a Saturday morning pictures sort of way.

The first 30 minutes, in fact, is just plain, um, fab. I love the device of switching to black and white for the first performance of 'Help!', in a bit of self-reference to *A Hard Day's Night*. The Beatles look so stupidly cool with pudding-bowl hair and existential black rollnecks. This first performance of 'Help!', as the credits roll and the mysterious bad guys throw darts at them while watching them on a screen, definitely ranks high among any compilation of best pop song renditions in a movie. The way director Lester picks out tight angles on their faces and profiles, the joy the four bring to the simple act of miming a pop song. If you're one of the few mystified by the appeal of the Beatles at their peak, then this three minutes of simple pleasure will explain everything.

Then there's the whole parade of old-school Brit character actors doing their usual farcical turns ... McKern, Kinnear, Bron, John Bluthal, Warren Mitchell, Patricia Hayes, Alfie Bass, Patrick Cargill, Dandy Nichols, Gretschen Franklin (Ethel off *Eastenders*) ... a host of post-Ealing Comedy faces that lit up TV during the 1970s and 1980s, and remind one of a kinder, funnier England that treasured eccentricity, and saw a happy beauty in the grumpy and frumpy.

Lester might be accomplished in monochrome, but the colours of *Help!* are rich and vivid and somewhat surreal, especially in the bravura scene where the suited and booted four walk into separate, neighbouring doors on a terraced street ('Lovely lads ... and so natural. I mean, adoration hasn't gone to their heads', froths Ms Franklin's old biddy, waving excitedly, and neatly summing up what we Brits want from our stars, even as we worship them like gods). Of course, the four doors lead into one giant space-age bachelor pad that only the unnaturally wealthy could want or afford. The pad itself is a parade of weird visual puns and jokes at the expense of modern art, and it is the house that I want to live in when you all buy this book and make me a billion pounds. I never really dwelt much on wanting to be a Beatle, but the first minutes of *Help!* are the exception. God, I wanna be in this gang, playing a Wurlitzer organ in a room with a lawn, wearing Savile Row pinstripes with a hangdog fall guy called Ringo. If they'd just stayed in this house and kept away from girls they would never have split up.

If *Help!*'s comedy doesn't make you laugh, blame the Goons, the 1950s radio stars led by Peter Sellers, Spike Milligan and Harry Secombe who revolutioned British comedy overnight by bringing a collegiate absurdity to the art of silly voices and stoopid gags. Lennon was a huge Goons fan, Lester had cut his teeth co-directing a Goons short with Peter Sellers, and *Help!* is basically a Goons film with added pop gems, a touch of Tex Avery cartoons, and a Swinging London modernist aesthetic. *A Hard Day's Night* is self-conscious and self-regarding. *Help!* is the invention of everything most seductive about the concept of band as gang. And the Beatles turn out to be funnier when they're the butt of the joke, rather than the source of it.

The visual invention and flair for the absurd with which Lester pastiches Bond throughout *Help!* would have made this a pretty decent genre parody without the Beatles. But one of the major reasons why *Help!* wallops *A Hard Day's Night* is because the music is better. The Beatles were months away from *Rubber Soul*, the album that transformed them from jolly purveyors of kiddie love songs into poets and artists who defined their times, and the title track, 'The Night Before', and 'You've Got to Hide Your Love Away' and 'Ticket to Ride' are the great works that opened Lennon and McCartney's eyes to how far they could take this talent for melody, arrangement and lyrical succinctness. Lester, given more time and money than he had for the hastily conceived *A Hard Day's Night*, responds with stunning templates for how all pop performances should be filmed, tripping on his love of interesting faces, shooting them on lush and fascinatingly detailed sets, finding new angles, making room for sly jokes, and leaving the performances in the previous film looking stilted and repetitive, which is exactly what they are.

Watching *Help!* again makes Monkees film *Head* (see p. 71) an even more embarrassing experience. *Head* is a note-for-note rip-off of *Help!* (as was the TV show, in a less offensively cynical way) but manages to make everything great about *Help!* into visual sewage. The moment in *Help!* when the movie abruptly comments upon itself by interrupting plot to introduce the Beatles' own intermission – the four pratting around in some woods for five seconds – is cheeky, funny and cute here. *Head* – and a whole bunch of postmodernists with even less to recommend them – take similar ideas and render them smug and immature. Is this because the Beatles are so adorable? Or because Lester is one of the most underrated geniuses in modern film? Bit of both. Not that Lester was entirely original. Once again, Jean-Luc Godard and the French *nouvelle vague* prove the biggest influence on rock and pop film-making, with Lester chucking Godardian captions at us, and ending the movie on a beach.

One odd similarity to *A Hard Day's Night* is the amount of quality screen-time awarded to each Beatle. Watching both films leads you to the unavoidable conclusion that the most naturally talented actor among the Beatles was probably McCartney. Yet, in an echo of the earlier film, Lester gives Macca a bit of quality time at the beginning of the movie . . . and then concentrates almost exclusively on John Lennon and Ringo Starr. At one point, he contrives to shrink Macca to the length of a cigarette and makes him hide in an ashtray. You can't help wondering whether Lester just didn't like Paul very much. See *Let It Be* (see p. 109) and work out for yourself why *that* might be.

But *Help!* isn't, in the end, a great film. It's a great 45-minute short stretched out into 90 occasionally wearing minutes by way of much somewhat tedious larking about. If it had stopped at the comedy intermission . . . actually, it's amazing how many times this exact same caveat is coming up in this book, isn't it? Something about pop being a medium best sampled in thrilling three-minute bursts, and how even the most talented film-makers struggle to find an hour-and-a-half of substance in something that depends on brevity and immediacy. *Help!* gets on your nerves after a while, especially when it makes the mistake of moving out of the dream pad on the terraced EveryStreet and gets all travelogue in its eagerness to be comedy Bond. And, even though the Indian stuff that provides the daft plot doesn't strike one as explicitly racist, there's enough blacking – well, browning – up and *It Ain't Half Hot, Mum* accents to become tiresome and borderline offensive.

But if *Help!* had stopped at the intermission, you wouldn't have got the bit where the Beatles have to tame a tiger by singing 'Ode to Joy' in a Richmond pub that suddenly becomes 60,000 people at a Burnley vs Spurs match . . . and then where would we be? What you want, in the end, is for the lame skits to sod off and John, Paul, George and Ringo to get on with the next song. We're always being told by fledgling film stars that the reality of filming is boring – endless waiting around to do endless takes of the same thing from a hundred different angles. But the Beatles make everything they do look spontaneous and first-take, and as if they are having the time of their lives. I mean, I'm a Stones man. Always have been. But significant parts of *Help!* make me wish I'd been a Beatle. I can't put it fairer and squarer than that.

• •

Catch Us If You Can

1965
Starring: Dave Clark, Barbara Ferris, David De Keyser, Robin Bailey, Yootha Joyce
Dir.: John Boorman

★ ★ ★ ★

Plot: Two crazy kids run away from the lousy, hollow sham that is Swinging London.
Key line: 'But that's why you chose her, isn't it? That's her image. Rootless, classless, product of affluence . . . typical of modern youth.'

There are more superficially bizarre movies in this book. *Sympathy for the Devil* is more abstract. *Beyond the Valley of the Dolls* is more hysterical. *Beat Girl* is more perverse. *Performance* is more surreal. But context is all, and none of those films are a cheapo vehicle for a dull, second-rate Merseybeat-via-Tottenham pop group. This, for my money, is the strangest rock movie of all time.

The Dave Clark Five were among the more unlikely beneficiaries of the Beatles and Stones-inspired 'British Invasion' of America, scoring a healthy bunch of US chart hits between 1965 and 1967. But this was a band so ordinary that their leader was the drummer. Whoever decided that their one-and-only cinematic vehicle should be a bleak, black and white, Jean-Luc Godard-influenced road movie about the emptiness of the society of spectacle, the fleeting nature of human connection, and the inevitable failure of youth rebellion, directed by a documentarist and future highbrow director, was obviously high on their own prodigious supply. But it's moments of madness on the part of some anonymous suit who releases the money that allows follies like *Catch Us If You Can* to be made. So bless you, whoever you are. And I hope your time spent at the business end of popular culture didn't all turn out to be as depressing as this movie suggests.

As for John Boorman, who would go on to a pretty glorious directing career which included three bona fide masterpieces in *Point Blank*, *Deliverance* and *The Emerald Forest*, his mission, for his film-making debut, appears to consist of drowning the whole idea of youth culture – and making a film to promote a dumb pop group – in so much grim irony that he very nearly succeeds in killing the rock movie infant while it sleeps. That he doesn't quite pull that off is, naturally, down to the Dave Clark Five. The Beatles or Elvis (or Adam Faith, for that matter) would have got the joke and run with it. The DC5, you suspect, have no idea why they are there at all, and just do as they're told, with the complete absence of presence that only an entirely absent mind can create. Clark is the leading man, and he's awful, and he's just one irony too far to make this a five-star film. The rest of the band are reduced to extras in their own movie, with one, Lenny Davidson, never getting to speak at all (at one point he turns up at a fancy dress party as Harpo Marx – geddit?), and another, Denis Payton, misspelled on the credits as Paynton.

So you'll be delighted to learn that the Dave Clark Five actually *play* extras. Really. They are a group of extras-forward-slash-stunt-men who, for reasons that are never discussed, all live together in a disused church called Action Enterprises Ltd which is a shrine to the detritus of Pop Art. As the credits roll, and the theme song kicks in, and you see and hear the ticking of a giant clock, the boys woken by a blaring pipe-organ, the madness of the customised church, a poster of a happy-go-lucky model captioned 'Lot Of Body', the building of a log fire on a giant hotplate that hangs from the ceiling, the boys working out by blowing up a rubber dinghy and trampolining, and then jogging in a military line around the park – you're all set for an imaginative, pop-art take on the jolly pop group japes of *A Hard Day's Night*, which the look of *Catch Us If You Can* is obviously indebted to. But instead, the film casually paddles downriver toward its own, very British, Heart of Darkness, when Steve (Clark) and Dinah (Ferris), the model star of the meat commercial he's working on, decide to nick the on-set E-type Jag and run away. Dinah isn't enjoying being the national face of meat, and dreams of a buying an island off the coast of Devon and living completely alone. Steve also hates the cold, grey, broken London that cinematographer Manny Wynn captures so evocatively and fancies Spain. So the pair make a bolt for it, with the giants of the meat marketing trade snapping at their heels.

Except . . . that isn't the case. Dinah's mentor Leon Zissell (played with admirably sleazy jadedness by David De Keyser) obviously taught Alastair Campbell everything he knows about spin and exploits the runaways for maximum publicity by saying Dinah was kidnapped. Now the whole of southern England knows all about 'The Butcher Girl'. The more the pair run away from celebrity, the more infamous they become.

I'm tempted, at this point, just to run through the entire plot, with all the key scenes described and the best of Peter Nichols' extraordinarily incisive dialogue included, because it does hit you pretty early that the ending isn't going to be a happy one. But, on first viewing, I was constantly surprised by scene after scene, as the pair encounter junkie beatniks, the army, a vampiric upper-class couple (show-stealing turns from Bailey and future *George and Mildred* star Yootha Joyce) and Steve's old youth-club leader, and Zissell gradually reveals a relationship between himself and Dinah that it's disturbing even to contemplate, and everything ends, in true situationist fashion, on a beach, as the pair reach the inevitable limits of their rebellion at what Steve calls 'the last resort'. So I'm not going to give things away. It's an amazing film and you must see it. And most particularly because it was made in 1965 – the high point of Swinging London and the year when the Beatles' 'Rubber Soul', Dylan's 'Like a Rolling Stone' and the Stones' 'Satisfaction' changed the teenage dance craze that was rock 'n'

roll into the adult art form that is rock. Yet *Catch Us If You Can*
refutes all the rebellions that those characters and records would
bring to fruition in 1967 and 1968, and predicts, with foresight
and finality, that the counter-culture will inevitably fail, because,
no matter how hard it tries to pretend otherwise, all it's really
interested in is getting a job that means being rich and famous, or
worshipping other people who got a job being rich and famous.
And if *Catch Us If You Can had* to have a pop group in it – to get it
made, if not to lend it meaning – then it was fitting that it should
be the mid-1960s equivalent of ... I dunno ... Scouting for Girls;
an empty vessel that won't undermine the central premise by just
being too sexy and interesting to mock, as the Beatles or the Stones
surely would have been. So, instead of a typical example of what
Robin Bailey's Guy, while showing the guileless Dinah his collection
of pop-art artefacts, calls 'the desperate measures that people have
taken to immortalise the moment' (and yes, almost all the dialogue
is *that* good), Boorman made a film that, in various prophetic
images and themes, predicts Andy Warhol's banana sleeve for the
first Velvet Underground album, *Slade in Flame* (see p. 147), the
final shots of Godard's *Sympathy for the Devil* (see p. 74), insane
cult TV sci-fi series *The Prisoner*, Lindsay Anderson's public school
revolution classic *If . . .*, Fellini's *Satyricon*, Michael Powell's *Peeping
Tom* and the Monkees. And *The Truman Show.* Oh ... and every
failed revolution of the last 40 years. Not bad, for a Dave Clark
Five movie.

• •

Don't Look Back

1967

Starring: Bob Dylan, Joan Baez, Donovan, Alan Price, Albert Grossman
Dir.: DA Pennebaker

★ ★

Plot: The court of King Dylan, England, 1965.
Key line: 'Would you ask the Beatles that?'

Between 2004 and 2007, the manager of the football team I support, Tottenham Hotspur, was a Dutch feller called Martin Jol. The most interesting thing about him is the way he deals with questions from the gentlemen of the press. The first word in every answer is 'No.' Great result, Martin. You must be very proud of your boys today. 'No . . . I thought we did well first half.' Robbie Keane's second goal was a beauty, wasn't it? 'No . . . he does it every day in training.' Would you at least agree that this win has got you three points? 'No . . . it got us three points.' And so on. I wondered if his habit of issuing a disclaimer before even the most mundane public utterance was learned in some Dutch PR school for budding sporting personalities. But . . . no. It was obviously learned from careful study of D.A. Pennebaker's celebrated documentary about Bob Dylan's 1965 solo tour of England. Never has one man's paranoia about being quoted, pigeonholed or defined in any way, shape or form been so repetitively exposed. 'No, I'm not angry.' 'No, I don't have any message.' 'No, I'm not Bob Dylan . . .' – and yes I did make that last one up, but hey ho on it goes. If that sounds like a frustrating or even dull thing to be watching . . . it is. Yet *Don't Look Back* is one of the most praised and influential rock movies of them all.

Well, here's my opinion, with no disclaimer. I'm a big fan of Bob Dylan, and I think this film is a life-draining experience. But then, I don't get a kick out of watching surprisingly inarticulate brats surround themselves with flunkies and intimidate anyone unfortunate enough to want to speak to them. I've had to watch it, in real life, and no amount of talent possessed by said brat lends the spectacle any dignity or entertainment value.

The thing that can't be denied about *Don't Look Back* is that it is beautifully shot and ahead of its time. Much like Lester for *A Hard Day's Night* (see p. 49), its director Pennebaker was a genuine innovator and used an evocative monochrome and a restless moving camera to fix an iconic artist with an iconic look, therefore establishing a way that rock stars would be shot until this day. Pennebaker's invention of a portable 16mm camera and sound system set-up made him one of the pioneers of *cinéma vérité*, and *Don't Look Back* is the first major film to use techniques we now barely notice through their ubiquity. But it's shocking to note that this yawn-inducing 95-minute parade of Dylan and hangers-on in hotels desperately trying to be hip and groovy comprises the *highlights* from *over 20 hours* of film. Jesus ... how fucking dull was the other stuff?

What isn't dull is the one piece of staged action. The film's opening is, arguably, the single most influential visual image set to music. *Don't Look Back* finds it hard to live up to the justly celebrated 'Subterranean Homesick Blues' sequence, where Pennebaker illustrates Dylan's first 'electric' rock single by having Dylan stand in an alley, stage right, haphazardly parading the song's lyrics on cue cards, while beat poet Allen Ginsberg and A.N. Other stand chatting, stage left.

The day before finishing this entry, my friend Jo sent me an email. The subject header reads: 'Bob Dylan has a message for you, from Jo.' I click on a couple of links, and the familiar 'Subterranean ... ' clip clicks into gear. Except, instead of 'Basement', Dylan's first cue card reads, 'Howdy Garry'. The message from my friend continues, replacing Dylan's allusive cut-up poetry, and my jaw drops so hard to the floor in front of my desk that it dislocates my entire body.

Amazing what they can do with computers, especially when Bob Dylan's 115th *Greatest Hits* compilation needs a good, hard marketing. And being a child of spectacle, pop promo, advertising and onscreen special effects, I'm impressed. But it sets off a chain of thought about all the millions of people over the last 40 years who've watched that piece of film, and felt that something enormous and essential was being communicated directly to them, and put the pictures of words into their personal filter, and enjoyed the joy of deciphering the Dy-Vinci Code. Now, he really is giving you a personal message – whatever you want it to be, if you fancy sending yourself Bob Dylan telling you that your penis is huge or that you are the fairest in the land – while its foundation message is finally revealed in all its glory. Buy Bob Dylan records. Buy them again. Isn't he cool?

So, watch *Don't Look Back* and marvel at the young revolutionary as he becomes paranoid and patronising over the moderate success of Donovan and quietly humiliates Joan Baez while his manager Albert Grossman harangues hotel staff and haggles with a TV impresario over chump change. It's not that Pennebaker didn't show the – or, at least, a – truth. It's just that the truth of Bob Dylan in 1965 was obviously nowhere near as exciting as we (still) fantasise. It should've killed the Dylan myth in its tracks, yet didn't, which remains mystifying in itself.

In his 2004 book *Chronicles, Volume One*, Dylan writes brilliantly about his post-1966, post-motorcycle accident retreat from Conscience of a Generation status. 'I don't know what everybody else was fantasizing about,' he writes, looking back at riot- and protest-torn America in 1968, 'but what I was fantasizing about was a nine-to-five existence, a house on a tree-lined block with a white picket fence, pink roses in the backyard.' *Don't Look Back* proves he's not lying. Great singer, songwriter and writer. But not much fun to hang around with, and no interest in changing the world. It's not like he was hiding it.

● ●

Privilege

1967

Starring: Paul Jones, Jean Shrimpton, Mark London, Max Bacon
Dir.: Peter Watkins

★ ★ ★ ★ ★

**Plot: He's not the Messiah. He's the pawn of a future fascist
British government. And a very naughty boy, obviously.**
**Key line: 'Steve's song, which has been specially written for
this occasion, may have certain auto-suggestive qualities to
it from which the sick may derive some internal benefit.
Therefore the less fortunate than us will be brought before
Steve in invalid chairs which we shall be providing, if I may
say, free of charge.'**

Inspired by John Lennon's infamous mid-1960s crack about the
Beatles being 'more popular than Jesus', *Privilege* is the Rock
Messiah trip taken to its illogical conclusion. With a story supplied
by Johnny Speight, who would go on to create hugely popular TV
racist Alf Garnett in BBC sitcom *Till Death Us Do Part*, English
director Peter Watkins employs his extraordinary skill at making
fiction look, sound and feel like newsreel to attack just about
everything that Britain holds dear. Watkins' previous film was *The
War Game*, a notorious fake documentary about the aftermath of
nuclear war that the BBC bottled out of broadcasting and which
ironically won the Oscar for best documentary. *Privilege* uses the
same mock-doc techniques and anti-establishment pessimism to
create a stunningly intense film experience – part rock movie, part
science-fiction chiller, part satirical polemic.

The tale is set in a near-future Britain and concerns Steven
Shorter, a rock star played by former Manfred Mann blues crooner
Paul Jones. We open on Shorter being given a ticker-tape welcome
on his return from an American tour. We're soon looking at a
concert stage with a cage at its centre. A narrator is explaining the

whys and wherefores of Shorter's unprecedented popularity, in the matter-of-fact manner of a BBC documentary ... a *Panorama* or *Arena*.

The film switches to still photographs, shots of Shorter being handcuffed by prison guards. It turns out that Shorter served time and that this stage act is based on his experiences. By now, you are suitably freaked out by what the hell this stage act consists of. It's that terribly English, objective, academic narration that's doing it, the kind of voice that implies that we are all just animals, being observed by our betters for our own good.

Shorter is led to the stage with a blanket over his head, and then literally thrown down onto the stage. He's led into the cage, as the vaguely psychedelic rock begins to play. He begins to theatrically smash himself against the bars of the cage in a futile attempt to escape, while two guards grin maniacally and smash the bars with batons in return. The ramping up of the violence causes the girls in the audience to scream orgasmically. We see two of the girls. Even though the narration has informed us that this is all taking place 'in the near future', they are pure 1960s chicks: beehive hairdos, pastel-coloured clothes, false nails and lashes. The actresses have clearly been chosen for their homeliness, and their mania and their make-up renders them hideous.

Jones/Shorter begins to sing, a great, doomy operatic rock tune imploring the audience to set him free. The guards oblige, and Shorter rips his clothes into shreds as if trying to free himself from his own skin. A frumpy girl is lowered onto the side of the stage. She appears to be part of the act, as the guards don't react to her as she reaches Shorter and starts to lead him offstage ... at least, not at first. Then suddenly, as the music hits a crescendo, one of the guards slaps her hard to the floor. The still-handcuffed Jones hits the guard, and all hell breaks loose. Shorter gets in some good shots in the free-for-all, but, inevitably, the guards overwhelm him and give him a good kicking.

By now, you're being strongly reminded of *Tommy* (see p. 164), Pink Floyd's *The Wall* (see p. 248) and *A Clockwork Orange* ... films that hadn't been made yet, lest we forget. Never seen this mentioned as an influence by any of the writers or directors of those films, though. Funny that.

The other thing that has struck you is that, despite the narrator explaining that this show is for the benefit of 'the public', the audience is entirely composed of girls. Actually, women too, including the middle-aged and the elderly, all of whom are in a state of weeping, wailing, agonised ecstasy. Seems like Watkins, Speight and fellow screenwriter Norman Bogner have been to some pop shows, and, like many a man before them, been completely intimidated and threatened by the manic release of female sexual tension. So far, the major problem of British society being identified in *Privilege* is the repressed sado-masochistic sexual urges of ugly birds. Well . . . it is the 1960s.

One song and the performance is over. So no surprise when said congregation of ugly birds storm the stage and start a riot. As mayhem ensues, the narration returns and calmly begins, 'There is now a coalition government in Britain . . . ' We're not in an Elvis movie any more, Toto.

We're soon being introduced to the supporting cast. Swinging London model icon Jean Shrimpton is Vanessa Ritchie, an artist who has been commissioned by the Ministry of Culture to paint Shorter. She has enormous eyes, the cut-glass accent of a minor royal and the acting talent of Kate Moss. Then we meet press officer, manager, publisher, etc., in some kind of club that looks more like an East End pub. All of them are scum. Everyone is grotesque. In a very pre-*Spinal Tap* (see p. 264)/*The Office* style, everything is presented as if it's a fly-on-the-wall documentary, and the characters are always painfully aware of the camera. Steven himself is largely silent, glancing at the camera incessantly, always on the verge of tears, his eyes still imploring the audience – us – to set him free. Whatever this movie is going on to say, the unavoidable fact is that it is, stylistically, several light years ahead of its time, even making the thoroughly New Wave *Catch Us If You Can* (see p. 57) look traditional in comparison.

There's even the odd decent gag. The fake documentary maker interviews Shorter's 'administrator'. He asks him what his job entails, and the thuggish-looking chap – who is pumping weights – explains that he got his client out of a paternity suit. 'I procured an abortion and arranged for the young lady to be paid £500.' 'I see,' responds the interviewer, dubiously. 'And how did you account for this expenditure?' 'I put it down to petty cash.'

Enter the aristocratic merchant banker who owns Steven Shorter Enterprises. As I'm beginning to realise, the British rock movie pre-*Quadrophenia* always insists that the youthful pop celebrity is actually nothing but the hapless puppet of an Old Etonian. But this particular shadowy upper-class Kingpin is actually concerned that his superstar protégé is being worked too hard, and might be heading for physical and mental breakdown.

The central thrust of *Privilege* is that this near-future Britain is in such political, economic and spiritual chaos that the establishment need the country's most popular star to paper over the cracks. His influence is such that, when the country finds it has grown too many apples, Shorter has to immediately film a commercial ordering everyone to eat apples. If the increasingly fraught boy takes a holiday, the country will slide into anarchy and revolution. Shorter is, officially, the opium of the masses.

So the powers-that-be's plan for Steven is a simple one. Having become the most influential person on the planet by appealing to everyone's need for pantomime sex and violence, Shorter must now publicly repent and urge his supine flock to conform and unite against the agents of communism and anarchy. Cue a spectacular scene where a beat band record a rock version of 'Onward Christian Soldiers' in front of a mean-looking bevy of bishops. 'At one time, the church used the methods of the Inquisition to gain converts,' the Archbishop tells the press in due course. 'We find Mr Shorter a little less painful.'

When you've become the most worshipped human icon in the world – and reached 'commercial saturation' to boot – there's only one career move left. They make him Jesus. The big Christian coming-out gig is a quasi-fascist rally, complete with burning crosses and stiff-arm salutes from the black-shirted band. William Blake's 'Jerusalem' is turned into Nazi Merseybeat. It's totally over the top. But I really, really *love* totally over the top.

Of course, it may not necessarily be a great idea, convincing a boy on the verge of a complete nervous breakdown that he is, in fact, the Second Coming. Less than hilarious consequences ensue.

The Big Theme is fabulous, but there are great, smaller scenes dotted throughout the movie. Like Steven posing for his painting, stalking the room, unable to relax. He has a radio built into his watch. He switches it on. It's him. Vanessa asks him to change stations. He does. It's him. She asks him again. The same song again, in exactly the same place.

Or the scene where Steven's press officer patiently explains to camera: 'He doesn't belong to himself. He belongs to the world. And therefore, he no longer has any right to himself,' and you're thinking of every tabloid editor and journalist who you've ever heard argue, without a hint of either irony or compassion, that anyone they deem to be a public figure has no right to a private life. Or the bit where Shorter accepts an award and begins to make the desperate, tearful speech that destroys him, and the narrator simply talks over the top of him, as uninterested as everyone else in the reality of the man. The passage of narration pointing out that the British coalition government is working because of the complete lack of difference in ideology between Labour and Conservative, in the midst of the Christian rally, is just plain chilling in its foresight, 30 years before Blairism.

Jones and Shrimpton really are appallingly bad actors. But this is deliberate. They both look like everything fashionable and iconic about the swinging sixties, but they're empty vessels. Watkins, one suspects, sees pop culture as an empty vessel, which is why he believes it be dangerous. It's just too stupid, narcissistic and greedy to understand that it's being used. Just as Watkins surrounds the hapless Jones with great character actors who make everything happen, the character of Steve Shorter is also surrounded by movers and shakers, who, unlike Shorter, know what is going on, and make everything happen. All Jones and Shrimpton need be is pretty eyes, cheekbones and legs to hang clothes and manipulation of the masses upon. An exaggerated version of the truth, sure . . . but pretty much the truth about pop stars, nonetheless. See the way they're still wheeled out for charity, to distract us from the reality that whatever disaster they're asking us to solve has been caused by their sponsors! See how blankly they stare and how emptily they smile, and see how we line up to believe that they actually care, even when we *know* that charity PR is worth its weight in adopted Third World children and cosmetic surgery! The more banal a celebrity is – Diana, the Beckhams, Kylie, all the screeching divas – the more we can project our own fantasies of transcendence upon them. Considering that this was made when the Beatles, Dylan and Morrison were *appearing* to change the nature and substance of celebrity, Watkins' understanding that the new rock icons had just found a way of marketing a veneer of substance was remarkably prescient and bravely unfashionable.

No wonder *Privilege* has sunk into obscurity. *Privilege* has an incandescent loathing, not just of government, corporate capitalism, organised religion, consumerism and the privileged classes, but of rock's success at inviting large groups of potential young revolutionaries into a draughty hall, encouraging them to act out an energetic and cathartic fantasy of transgressive sex and violent revolution ... and then sending them home sated, drained and ready to get up in the morning and continue to be good little wage-slaves. Watkins thinks we're *all* dumbass dupes and sell-outs. The guy's a Sex Pistol ten years before the fact. If only he'd directed *The Great Rock 'n' Roll Swindle* (see p. 206).

Privilege also presents an unusual and innovative form of sci-fi dystopia. Because this England looks the same – old buildings, green fields, red buses. The dystopia is entirely psychological and political, emanating from the minds and mouths of a British population that, from prime minister to prole, has lost all sense of direction, morality and soul. Whether rock is a cause or a symptom of this casual descent into the abyss is never made entirely clear. But I think we can safely conclude that it hasn't helped.

One thing I learned too late from doing press for *This Is Uncool* and *Fear of Music* is that, no matter how you order your list in a list book, the first question everyone asks you is, 'What's number one?' So, in the unlikely event that anyone asks this time around, I've come prepared. *Privilege* is the Number One. Yup ... even better than *Quadrophenia* or *Performance* or *Gimme Shelter* or *Hairspray*. It is a work of insane genius, and, although there are a fair few of those covered in this book, there isn't another one that's turned out to be so utterly and ferociously right about everything. It's hard to believe that its withering critique of the supposedly revolutionary nature of rock and its inevitable co-option was made in the same year that *Sgt Pepper*, San Francisco psychedelia, Hendrix and The Doors sent perceptions of rock's world-changing potential into a frenzy of deluded optimism. And it's equally hard to believe that nobody's heard of the damn thing.

Privilege was completely unavailable when I was writing this book. I managed to get hold of it on a dodgy bootleg, and I definitely had no plans to apologise about it because it was a disgrace that it hadn't been rediscovered and re-released. At a time when the British film industry is a global embarrassment, we need what's left of it to worship films like this as a reminder that Britain used to routinely make cutting-edge masterpieces on tuppence-ha'penny, and make us grateful that the likes of Lynne Ramsey and Shane Meadows still keep that flame burning, despite their lack of interest in hiring Hugh Grant or making Mr fucking Bean.

But happily the BFI have re-released this movie. And now everyone can see it for themselves and tell me that I'm talking out of my arse when I say that it is, officially, The Greatest Rock 'n' Roll Movie Ever Made.

• •

Head

1968
Starring: The Monkees
Dir.: Bob Rafelson

★

Plot: Boy band force-fed drugs and abused by hippy fuckwits.
Key line: 'The tragedy of your times, my young friends, is
that you may get exactly what you want.'

Head is one of a selection of movies I'd never seen before writing
this book, and it was probably the one I'd been most looking
forward to watching. I love Monkees records and the TV show.
Head was made in the most exciting year in post-war counter-
cultural history. And it was the first break into movies for Bob
Rafelson and Bert Schneider, who had created the Monkees' show
and went on to produce *Easy Rider* (see p. 80), *The Last Picture
Show* and *Five Easy Pieces*, which in turn kick-started the whole
New Hollywood, 'movie brats' era that ended up giving us *The
Godfather*, *The Exorcist* and *Taxi Driver*. Plus the goddamn film was
co-written by Rafelson and *Jack bloody Nicholson*! I mean, how
could this be anything less than thrilling?

And then *Head* hits you with its best shot straight away, as,
after some bemusing stuff about a mayor opening a bridge, Micky
Dolenz jumps into a river and hangs suspended in the water as the
lush psychedelia of 'The Porpoise Song' serenades him. The water
goes through a blissfully lysergic spectrum of lurid colours, mer-
maids appear, Davy Jones is singing that 'The porpoise is
laughing/Goodbye, Goodbye', and you realise that an ersatz version
of 'I Am the Walrus' can be just as good as the real thing . . . better
maybe, unencumbered as it is by any pretence of deep meaning.

If you want to explain the pop end of the 1960s to that proverbial
alien visitor, this scene is the one to choose.

But sadly . . . it's a red herring. Or maybe a purple porpoise.

Because, from that moment on ... *Head* is the worst rock movie ever made.

After the water frolics, we cut straight to a blonde girl snogging all four out-of-it-looking Monkees in turn. It's eight minutes in and we've had references to The Man, Vietnam, LSD and free love. The screen splits into 20 separate TV screens – most showing Vietnam footage, naturally – and the Monkees are singing an ironic cartoon ditty which goes: 'Hey, hey we're the Monkees/You know we love to please/A manufactured image/With no philosophies.' Finally all the screens switch to a man being executed by a soldier. Apart from one, at the far bottom, which pictures a girl screaming hysterically. Of course, she's not screaming at the violence, but at the Monkees. See what they did there?

And so it goes on. The film has no plot, so Dolenz blows up a Coca-Cola machine with a tank. Women only appear as sexual fantasies. American film conventions – Westerns, horror flicks, war movies – are spoofed with no point and no laughs. Dolenz gets to tear down the fourth wall, or somesuch, and tell Bob to stuff his fake movie and walk right through the backdrop, which Mel Brooks must have watched before doing it properly in *Blazing Saddles*. Peter Tork gets to whistle a bit of 'Strawberry Fields Forever'. Victor Mature and Frank Zappa do in-jokey cameos. Toni Basil dances with Davy. TV, adverts, cops and war are *very bad things*.

Former world heavyweight boxing champ Sonny Liston, having been humiliated in the ring twice by Muhammad Ali, has insult added to injury by Davy Jones and Dolenz. Nicholson, Rafelson and Dennis Hopper make brief appearances as themselves. The film endlessly comments upon itself, but doesn't have anything useful to say. *Head* is everything bad about the 1960s – as the world entered the very real turmoil of 1968, a bunch of white middle-class smartarses got busy using all that horror and anger and oppression and violence as foundations for glittering careers, re-branding revolution as lifestyle cool for weekend rebels.

I'm sure the justification was subversion ... you know, the teeny Monkees fans go into a cinema to scream at their idols, but come out with an education on the military-industrial complex from their elders and betters. But what *Head* amounts to, 40 years of Hollywood hypocrisy later, is nothing less than more American imperialism … a bunch of college boys on their way to wealth and stardom, using Vietnamese war victims to bolster their own self-image as rebels, utterly disinterested in the Vietnamese as people, but fascinated with them as found footage to lend credibility to their godawful sixth-form revue 'satire'. The Monkees themselves are still puppets … but now they're pretty props for Rafelson, Nicholson and Schneider to hang their modish counter-culture pretensions upon. What's worse, the film keeps chucking that in your face, ensuring that everyone gets their cake and eats it. Except for the Monkees themselves. They just look like utter tools.

There *is* a good druggy disco scene. But it's a known fact that it's impossible to shoot a bad 1960s druggy disco scene, so it doesn't count. All four Monkees get to revel in the river to 'Porpoise Song' at the end, an acknowledgement, one suspects, that this was the only good idea Nicholson and Rafelson had managed to come up with. The song goes, 'Goodbye, Goodbye', and we're saying goodbye to the Monkees, their careers ruthlessly murdered by the dicks that made them.

Head is such a joyless, self-serving enterprise it's almost enough to put you off *Easy Rider, Five Easy Pieces* and the best of Jack Nicholson's career. Hell, it's so cynical that it gave me a new-found respect for the pure schlock of Westlife. The whole movie tries desperately hard to be ironic, but only one piece of irony hits home. The only thing that stands up in *Head* is the music, and the wonderful 'Porpoise Song' is written by those old-school hit-factory hacks Jerry Goffin and Carole King. Manufactured Pop 1; Counter-culture 0.

• •

Sympathy for the Devil

1968
Starring: The Rolling Stones
Dir.: Jean-Luc Godard

★ ★ ★

Plot: The Rolling Stones rehearsing 'Sympathy for the Devil' juxtaposed with surreal scenes from The Revolution That Never Happened.
Key line: 'I'd jump over ten nigger bitches just to get to one white woman.'

Before you freak out completely, I should point out that the line of dialogue above is not said by a member of the Rolling Stones. It is read out of a book of Black Panther Eldridge Cleaver's writings by a man playing a black militant in one of a number of scenes shot in a car scrapyard by the Thames where a fantasy cell of black male radicals stockpile guns, shoot white women and make speeches about the inevitable triumph of Black Power. This film was savaged by the critics and seen by virtually no-one. If only Mick and Keef could have written a 'Yellow Submarine' . . .

But this is what makes the Stones *the Stones*. Their Scouse rivals get an American to pay wacky monochrome homage to French New Wave director/icon/iconoclast Jean-Luc Godard in *A Hard Day's Night* (see p. 49) and become loved by everyone and her mum. The Stones get the man himself who, by 1968, has renounced all his earlier work, become a revolutionary, started shooting every-thing in colour, rejected linear narrative wacky or otherwise, can hardly get round to making a film for joining the revolutionary hijinks of the May 1968 Paris insurrection, and is about to physically attack one of his stars, Ian Quarrier, at the 1968 London Film Festival, for tacking the Stones' finished recording of 'Sympathy for the Devil' on the end of his film (which Godard also wanted to title *One Plus One*). The Beatles, no matter how fucked up or unhappy they were, attracted light and mainstream approval. The Stones, no matter how ordinary or businesslike they really were, attracted darkness, chaos ... and troubled French mavericks who saw them as the Five Horsemen of the coming counter-cultural apocalypse. Whatever the Stones really made of a film like this, I'm glad it exists. Because, if you want to know why the swinging, love-will-conquer-all mid-1960s quickly hardened – for some – into violence and terrorism, and why this failed (and why, perhaps, we're all lucky it did), then this incredibly strange film will give you much of the info you need.

Sympathy for the Devil consists of beautifully shot film of the Rolling Stones writing, rehearsing and recording their most dance-able evocation of evil, interspersed with Godard's surreal skits on the subject of the 1960s counter-cultural revolution and Sean Lynch's ironically old-school voice reading out stuff about porn and guerrilla warfare. It is neither a documentary nor a linear work of fiction, but an ambiguous, annoying and hypnotic discourse on the New Left politics of the time. The Stones, in that sense, are merely props; they are not interviewed and have no lines except boring band-at-work stuff like 'Can you turn it up in Keef's cans?'

Yet they are stunning (and revolutionary) to look at; Mick so thin and beautiful; Keith so cool and elegant; Charlie so deadpan and monkey-faced; Bill so ... well, Godard doesn't bother much with him, anyway. And the late Brian Jones? Godard either knows or senses that Jones is on his way out – of the Rolling Stones, of existence – and almost always shoots his non-presence from the back. When we get to see his tired, pudgy face, it's in the first run-through of the familiar, Afro-funk version of 'Sympathy for the Devil', in which you can hear every separate instrument ringing loud and clear ... except Jones's guitar. It's a haunting portrait of a man being gently pushed out of his own life.

All the scenes with the black militants are disturbing, acute and ambiguous enough to be considered both racist and misogynist. Godard's enthusiasm for his Panthers' clothes, mannerisms and weapons is the ultimate example of the hard-on so many white middle-class 1960s radicals had for angry, sexy black men with guns who didn't like women. All echoed, 40 years later, in middle-class white boys' fascination with black rappers with guns who don't like women. Why don't you all just get a room?

Nevertheless, there are jokes here at the expense of all this testosterone. There is a scene where Jagger is recording a vocal for 'Sympathy for the Devil', and, as he gets into it, he starts giving it the full-on, hip-thrusting, sub-James Brown, jive-ass dandy wiggerisms that made his name. 'Yes y'all! Git down!', he grunts. This cuts straight to a title card for the next skit: 'Inside Black Syntax'. All of the dramatic scenes are easy to laugh at, in fact, and Godard seems to be satirising the language and poses of the 1960s left as much as celebrating them, while relishing the racist and misogynist nastiness of the burgeoning consumer culture, as much as slamming it. That's what makes this a great movie. It's all down to the viewer, and what you decide Godard's message is here will say more about you than it will about him, or the 1960s. I'd always figured that Godard was an *auteur* who didn't respect his audience's intelligence. *Sympathy* . . . suggests the opposite.

What else do I love about this movie? I love finding out that the original of 'Sympathy for the Devil's most famous line sees Jagger declare that the Kennedys were killed by 'only me', meaning 'the Devil', before it was changed to 'you and me', making us all culpable. And the feel of chaotic, horrifying events in 1968 changing art in a heartbeat, as the assassination of Robert Kennedy during filming changes the line from 'Kennedy' to 'the Kennedys'.

I love the clothes. Everyone in this film looks so heartbreakingly cool.

I love the little Situationist pun towards the end, as the most famous slogan of the May 1968 uprising in Paris – 'Under the paving stones, the beach' – becomes, as a title caption for the final scene, 'Under the Stones, the beach'.

Most of all, I love the way Godard's camera prowls slowly, around the Stones, around his actors and locations. It lingers on something interesting, gets bored, moves on, and takes in every detail of its surroundings on its way to the next thing worth lingering upon.

Godard's camera is as great an art thing as the Rolling Stones were in 1968, and that is a very good thing indeed.

Jean-Luc Godard – so famous and feared in his 1950s/1960s heyday, so obscure and marginalized now – famously stated that, to make a film, 'All you need is a girl and a gun.' He gives us those, at the end of *Sympathy for the Devil*, as he films a film crew filming a girl running and shooting, and being shot, on a beach, of course. She is hoisted into the blue sky upon a camera crane, because she is only *playing* dead, as so many characters are in Godard movies. The Stones' song plays and the image of the girl freezes and, for better or for worse, I wish that it was 1968, and I was 19, and someone had handed me a girl, a gun, a guitar ... and a camera.

• •
Yellow Submarine

1968
Starring: John Clive, Geoffrey Hughes, Peter Batten, Paul Angelis, Dick Emery, Lance Percival (voices)
Dir.: George Dunning

★ ★ ★ ★

Plot: The Beatles vs the Blue Meanies in the animated high-point of mainstream psychedelia.
Key line: 'Nothing is Beatle-proof.'

The best Beatles film famously doesn't feature them at all until the final scene. Still smarting from the failure of their *Magical Mystery Tour* television special, the Fab Four jumped at the opportunity to fulfil their three-movie United Artists contract without having to do anything when Canadian director Dunning suggested a cartoon feature based upon their most celebrated children's song. With a short story provided by Lee Minott, a script team that included *Love Story* author Erich Segal, a 200-strong team of artists to reproduce the Beatles' likenesses and actors impersonating their voices, all the band had to do was provide the soundtrack, most of which was plucked from *Revolver* and *Sgt Pepper's Lonely Hearts Club Band* anyway. An American Beatles TV cartoon series which Dunning also worked on, and which the band disliked, made them reluctant to participate further until they were shown *Yellow Submarine* and, suitably impressed, agreed to appear in the final, singalong live action sequence. The result was one of the most lovable rock movies and animated features ever, and a great commercial success. Yet, at time of writing, *Yellow Submarine* remains unavailable on DVD or video; an almost forgotten 1960s period piece. This is just mental.

The plot is simple but ingenious: the Beatles must travel in a Yellow Submarine to free Pepperland, an undersea paradise which has been enslaved by the sadistic Blue Meanies, who have turned all the vibrant psychedelic colours to grey and banned music and the word 'Yes'. They travel through seven mildly hazardous seas which give them the excuse to wisecrack and play Beatles songs. And they win the day, of course.

But the film is all about the overall *mise en scène*, not the plot. Art Director Heinz Edelmann crafted a spectacular, surreal form of limited animation influenced by Magritte, Escher and Edelmann's pop art contemporary Peter Max, which combines cartoon and photograph, movement and tableau, collage and visual pun, in a style further defined by Terry Gilliam in the animated sequences for the Monty Python movies and TV shows. Iconic 20th-century images and pop culture references dot the landscape, with everything from superheroes and Monroe to hamburgers, King Kong and Rolling Stones banners exploding from doorways or cluttering the screen as furniture. The cartoon Beatles and various fantastical supporting characters career through this magical landscape, spitting out droll one-liners and whimsical wordplays, interrupted only by witty and wonderful visualisations of many of the Beatles' best late-period songs.

Despite being entirely suitable for children, *Yellow Submarine* is not all sweetness and light, with the comic darkness of crazed warmongers the Blue Meanies matched by sequences such as the interpretation of 'Eleanor Rigby', where a grey and dirty Liverpool is depicted as a place full of 'all the lonely people', endlessly repeating mundane tasks in ugly, ominous streets.

Brilliantly trippy, particularly in the 'Sea of Science' sequence backed by George Harrison's sonically outrageous 'Only a Northern Song', *Yellow Submarine* obviously taps into the era's obsession with LSD, endlessly winking knowingly at the hipsters among us. But this is never allowed to overwhelm the good nature and charm of the movie. The ideas that stand – like an attack of whales fended off by the submarine breaking into a toothy grin, or the creature that sucks up everything in its path through its Hoover-like snout until it devours the entire movie and finally itself, or the childlike sadness invoked by the workaholic Jeremy, the gratuitously rhyming 'Nowhere Man' who lives in a literal white void – do not require experience in hallucinogenics ... just imagination and a sense of visual humour. The film's freewheeling feel of crusading adventure without real threat feels less like an acid trip and more like an especially good dream.

All this charm and pleasure and innocent fun? In a rock movie? Of course, *someone* has to spoil it. In the commentary that accompanied the most recent DVD release, Production Supervisor John Coates reportedly suggests that making the Meanies blue amounted to a play on the word 'Jew'. This disturbing revelation seems to gain some credence when you re-watch the Pepperland chase sequence toward the end of *Yellow Submarine*; a Blue Meanie approaches a poorly disguised Beatles and asks, 'Are you bluish? You don't look bluish.' When the Beatles escape their inquisitor by dropping an apple on his head, the angry Meanie rubs his hand over his face causing his flattened nose to spring up – a gesture that draws attention to his abnormally large nose.

There has always been a tendency to attach significance to Beatles lyrics and peripheral events that was simply never there. As someone who has loved this movie since his childhood, and who always thought that the Meanies were obviously blue because that's the colour of conservatism, the idea that there's a surreptitious anti-Semitic agenda buried within something so apparently all-embracing fills me with dismay. I just hope this Coates feller is way off target, or that he's been crudely misquoted.

Because *Yellow Submarine* defines, with its deluge of innovative ideas and beautiful images, everything we love about the Beatles, pop music and the naivety of the hippie ideal ... whereby the good-and-plenties really can change the world just by being brighter, funnier and nicer than the bad people. When actual actors or musicians act this fantasy out, it just amounts to a self-aggrandising argument for apathy. In the lush cartoon form of *Yellow Submarine*, it convinces you that 'it's all in the mind' anyway, this peace, love and freedom stuff. Do all that, and make it a seminal work of art, and you've hit the pop nail on the rock 'n' roll head.

● ●

Easy Rider

1969

Starring: Peter Fonda, Dennis Hopper, Jack Nicholson
Dir.: Dennis Hopper

★ ★ ★ ★ ★

Plot: The road trip that killed Hollywood.
Key line: 'We blew it.'

Where to start with such an iconic movie – a film so surrounded in legend that the DVD's accompanying *The Making of ...* documentary is better than 80 per cent of the movies in this book?

First, *Easy Rider* is one of three movies in *Popcorn* that one could argue aren't rock movies at all. Like *The Loveless* (see p. 242) and *Bulworth* (see p. 330), *Easy Rider* is not about the rock business, doesn't feature pop stars and isn't a musical. But the 1960s rock featured in *Easy Rider* is a crucial character in the movie, providing the cultural context for its tale of broken counter-culture dreams while enabling scenes of two men riding customised Harley-Davidson motorbikes to take on mythic status and comment upon the passing landscape, the situation the pair have just left, the inevitably darker one that they're travelling to. No more joyful and adrenaline-pumping moment exists in movies than when Steppenwolf's 'Born to be Wild' explodes over the credits and the beginning of Peter Fonda and Dennis Hopper's journey into a Conrad-esque heart of American darkness. To think that Hopper's record collection was just a stopgap until Crosby, Stills and Nash wrote a 'proper score'. Thankfully, the trio admitted that they couldn't better it and *Easy Rider* became the first movie with a soundtrack sourced from rock 'n' roll radio.

And, speaking of music and darkness, it's weird to see a boyish Phil Spector playing a drug dealer in the film's pre-credits airport scenes. Spector, a good friend of Dennis Hopper's, already had wife-beating and gun-toting form in 1968. Forty years later and his recent fate encapsulates the American horror at the heart of *Easy Rider*. His face, in 2009, is the nightmarish visage of someone who has looked into a fathomless abyss and seen horrors too perverse to bear.

Spector is the 'Connection' as Captain America aka Wyatt (Fonda) and Billy (Hopper) do a big cocaine deal via Mexico and Los Angeles. Having deposited the cash in the tank of Wyatt's Stars and Stripes-festooned chopper, they ride across America, theoretically to retire in Florida and live it large on the proceeds. But we know there's no rest for the wicked. As acutely relevant songs from Jimi Hendrix, the Byrds, the Band and Dylan serenade their progress, these hippy outlaws meet rather too much of Real America, in the shape of hippy communes, an alcoholic lawyer (Nicholson), hippy-hating cops, hippy-hating rednecks, New Orleans' Mardi Gras, cinema's least slutty hookers and one hell of a bad acid trip. The real bad trip ends in the middle of the beautiful but hostile American nowhere.

The campfire scenes lie at the heart of *Easy Rider*, giving shape and focus to what could have been an aimless journey. On-set conflict, half-formed script ideas, endless improvisation and copious amounts of dope give these scenes a spontaneity and intimacy rarely found in film. The rambling, informal scenes also mean that, when one of the protagonists finally makes a clear statement, it seems to take on endless levels of meaning. The first of these scenes, a three-hander between Fonda, Hopper and Luke Askew's enigmatic hitchhiker Jack, is even more fun when you learn that the antipathy between Hopper and Askew and the senseless statements followed by stoned giggles were not being 'acted'. Tons of rambling garbage were probably left on the cutting-room floor, but the editing is incredible, especially as almost everyone involved in the movie had their cutting-room say as Donn Canbern did the hard work of getting Hopper's three-hour version down to something manageable.

The commune scenes are leisurely and include a long, circling shot of the hippies that is both a tribute to the character of faces and an elegant capture of the sadness and defeat of the hippy dream. The commune represents Wyatt's chance to find what he's looking for, as his cool façade cracks and he relaxes with the alternative vision of family life the commune represents. But Billy is agitated, bored, desperate to leave. Billy may look like a cowboy-styled hippy, but he's punk through and through, and all this rural idyll and impromptu performance art leaves him cold. Even though the 'things to do' that he rants about are obscure, he wins. 'Your time's running out,' the hitchhiker tells Wyatt, matter of factly. But Wyatt has already thrown away his watch, symbolically ending time. From that moment, you know that happy endings are out of the question. But the futility of the commune – the cowardice and confinement of escape from the real world – makes Billy right, too. It's a no-win situation.

Before they leave, they get to do naked skinny-dipping with a couple of the women. The actresses were uncomfortable with nudity and agreed only if the set was closed. When an onlooker peeked down on the scenes of splashy frolic, an actress complained and an extra fired a gun to scare him off, missing the onlooker by inches. The peeping tom was Bert Schneider, the executive producer whose money the entire film depended upon.

Westerns are also an obvious inspiration for the outlaw poses of *Easy Rider*. Wyatt and Billy are named after Wyatt Earp and Billy the Kid, and the pair travel through Monument Valley, the stunning desert landscape where John Ford shot his most acclaimed films. The Westerns of Ford, Howard Hawks and Anthony Mann haunt this update on their elegiac visions of the battles between old and new America.

Nicholson's George Hanson is an American Civil Liberties Union lawyer who, due to his addiction to booze and try-anything-once enthusiasm, comes along for the ride. There's nothing wrong with the performances of the laconic, cat-like Fonda and the hyper Hopper, but Nicholson blows them off-screen and almost all the way back to Mexico. George is lovable, hilarious, fragile, indefatigable, sexy and entirely composed of the dead-eyed ticks and shit-eating grins which the world would fall hopelessly in love with over the next 40 years and counting. While Wyatt and Billy are, by necessity, ciphers, George brings the viewer onboard; like us, he's too smart to miss the fun, but too blind to see the consequences. He is the fearlessness and optimism of liberal-minded youth, willing to see the best in everyone and everything, an angel waiting to be de-winged.

The Fonda–Hopper–Nicholson campfire scene is a legend and justly so. Forty years of lame cinematic stoner scenes have neither matched it nor dimmed its majesty, as the genuinely stoned Nicholson slips in the script's best wink-to-the-hipster in-joke – an initial, unconvincing refusal to take the joint punctuated by 'It leads to harder stuff' – and then heads into alien conspiracy theories and the kind of authentic stoner wisdom/gibberish that kills precious time to this day. But it's a sober George that defines the political terms of the Western World ('It's real hard to be free when you're bought and sold in the market-place'), and has to be punished accordingly.

The end of *Easy Rider* is, essentially, 25 minutes long. I only saw the film for the first time a few years ago, and was lucky enough to be shocked by the ending, which meant that an awful lot of film critics had been kind enough not to spoil it for me over the previous 20 years of acclaim and analysis. So there's no way I'm going to spill. But it includes a screen acid trip that no-one will ever match for both accuracy and visual splendour; the result of Fonda being bullied by Hopper into using the real-life suicide of his mother as emotional spice for his heady recipe; and prophecies of counter-cultural failure so prescient that it's hard to believe that the film was shot before Richard Nixon's presidential election win, Altamont and the Manson Family murders, and while the effects of the Martin Luther King and Robert Kennedy assassinations, the Soviet crushing of Prague and the failure of the Paris 1968 insurrections were still being processed.

It was Fonda's idea to boil a semi-written handful of summing-up dialogue to one, quiet, sullen phrase: 'We blew it.' It was a masterstroke. 'We' and 'it' means something different to every viewer, and has ended up being hotly debated ever since. For this viewer, 'we' and 'it' feel immense enough to swallow history.

The similarities between *Easy Rider* and the equally seminal *Performance* (see p. 89) are unavoidable. Both were made in 1968 and saw their releases delayed for re-editing at the behest of bemused producers. Both were made by indie producers working with distribution and money from major studios. Both feature jump cuts, experimental camerawork, subliminal shots, lots of drugs and nudity, lots of rock 'n' roll, and lots of amateur actors. Both are black comedies fuelled by pessimism, where 'freedom' isn't defeated by state power, but by working-class violence and traditional values. Both were seat-of-the-pants projects where an inspired but mercurial director was saved by innovative and brilliant cinematographers in *Easy Rider*'s Lasklo Kovacs and *Performance*'s Nicolas Roeg, who were able to make the most spontaneous and chaotic ideas look gorgeous. And both are doomy prophecies of the end of the 1960s.

But *Easy Rider* was an instant huge hit while *Performance* initially failed commercially and had to settle for enduring cult status. This was probably down to the striking contrast between big American landscape and small British interiors, and the fact that *Easy Rider* at least flirts with freedom before outside forces introduce the oppressive reality. While *Easy Rider*'s characters run, the protagonists of *Performance hide*, in a twisted take on the old 'Every

Englishman's home is his castle' cliché. They *know* that there's nowhere to go. So, even though *Performance* is more deliberately comic than *Easy Rider*, there's no-one who possesses the potential for freedom and pleasure that Jack Nicholson represents in *Easy Rider*. There's no 'Born to be Wild' moment.

The very last shots of *Easy Rider* are haunting and heartbreaking and leave you with a feeling that you've caught a glimpse of oblivion that you can't quite get out of your mind. The reason why it's such an astonishing film – a film popular and unique enough to put the final nail in the coffin of the old Hollywood studio system and create an entirely new market for commercial films that contained harsh truths – was that it wasn't, in the end, about hippies or rock music or the 1960s. *Easy Rider* is about one violent, universal and timeless human truth: everybody wants freedom. But nobody wants to allow it.

1970s

Performance

1970

Starring: James Fox, Mick Jagger, Anita Pallenberg, Michele Breton, Johnny Shannon
Dir.: Nicolas Roeg and Donald Cammell

★ ★ ★ ★ ★

Plot: Gangsters and hippies go mad in Notting Hill.
Key line: 'You've got the wrong house, mister.'

Way back in the 1980s, I was in a band. Just as it felt as if we were starting to get somewhere, the bassist and guitarist moved into a West London squat. It was an enormous abandoned hotel in Bayswater; a warren of tiny rooms, twisting corridors and dank basements which now housed an ever-growing number of itinerant bohemians and punkish outsiders.

The house seemed, at first, like the perfect place for the band. One of the larger basement rooms offered free rehearsal facilities any time of the night or day. There was a ready-made collection of potential fans, roadies, groupies and creative fellow travellers . . . a scene. And, best of all, it was a house free of rules and restraints. Every time you walked in there seemed to be a party of some kind on the go or on the boil . . . an unending private bacchanal with hot and cold free-flowing sex, drugs and endless possibilities.

But no matter how many lights you switched on in this house of rock 'n' roll fantasy, it was always, *always* dark. So much so that day and night blended into one. People moved in and, after a few weeks, stopped going out. As I said, sex always seemed possible there. But the only time I actually got laid I got my only dose of the clap. I took my first acid trip there too, and spent what seemed like hours watching the yellowing walls crawl like armies of bugs, and crawled home to my girlfriend a blubbering wreck (I still have no idea how I got from Bayswater to Brixton, or why the girlfriend in question didn't dump my cheating ass). The house sucked you in like a black hole, and infected you with its darkness.

Within three months of moving in the guitarist was a junkie and the bassist was dealing heroin. The band dissolved. The bassist, who was one of my best friends at the time, realised what the house was doing to him when his beautiful girlfriend kicked him to the kerb. He moved in with me to escape, and then disappeared to California. The last time I saw the guitarist he was begging outside Tufnell Park tube station. I still believe that if I hadn't effectively split the band by refusing to enter that house anymore it would have got inside me and fucked me up too. That house in Bayswater was a killer.

I always think back to this when I see my favourite shot in *Performance*. It's not a particularly celebrated scene in one of the all-time great cult films. But it gets me, in the gut. It simply involves James Fox, as gangster-in-hiding Chas, standing in the narrow entrance hall of a house in Notting Hill, a (rolling) stone's throw from Bayswater. We look down on him from above, as he is dwarfed by a wooden stag's head and the rude drone of Jack Nitzsche's Moog synthesizer. He is wearing a blue trenchcoat and shades – he still looks pretty much like a gangster – but in this dark, Gothic tunnel, he is a puny human observed by quizzical gods and monsters. Small, trapped and doomed. It's exactly how I felt every time I walked into that damned hotel.

Performance is a legend as well as a great movie. Made in 1967–68, it marked the various cinematic debuts of Mick Jagger, writer-director Donald Cammell and director-cameraman Nicolas Roeg. Its legend is suffused with the narcotic, violent and devilish elements that it toys with; Cammell made just four more failed films (two of them released posthumously) before committing suicide; James Fox got into a drug called DMT, quit acting and became an evangelical Christian; Rolling Stone Brian Jones drowned, months after Anita Pallenberg dumped him for bandmate Keith Richards, and Jagger and Pallenberg cavorted naked for Roeg's camera. In fact, Roeg, Jagger, Fox and Pallenberg have all gone on to live happy and fruitful lives but, hey, why let facts get in the way of a good rock story? The black comedy of *Performance* lends itself to the sensation and apocrypha of rock legend.

One element of the myth can't be dismissed. The version that Cammell first delivered to Warner Brothers executives so bewildered and disgusted them that the film wasn't released until two years and many frantic edits later. And you can sympathise. They splash out in the hope of getting a *Hard Day's Night*-style cash-in on the popularity of the lead Rolling Stone – and what they get is a surrealist gangster movie based on the works of Argentinian writer Jorge Luis Borges, where Jagger doesn't appear until almost halfway through, the 'love interest' (Breton's Lucy) looks like a boy, and with an ending that no-one involved in the film has ever professed to understand. One piece of possible apocrypha relates that the wife of one of the Warners executives was so shocked by the sex, drugs and violence that she starting vomiting in the screening room.

But a word of warning here: in a world where the *Saw* movies exist, anyone coming to *Performance* expecting some kind of hippy snuff movie is going to be sorely disappointed. The gangsta violence is mild and played for weird laughs. The sex is tasteful and soft-focus. And the main drugs on display are magic mushrooms. The times they have a-changed.

The plot is unlikely, to say the least. Chas (Fox) is head pretty-boy thug for the Cockney firm run by Harry Flowers (Shannon). Having gone rogue by killing betting shop owner Joey Maddocks (Antony Valentine), Chas goes on the run. An overheard conversation at a railway station persuades him that the best course of action is to dye his hair blood-red, pose as a musician, and move into the Notting Hill home of retired rock star Turner (Jagger) and his two nubile concubines Pherber and Lucy, played by Pallenberg and Breton. They feed Chas drugs and fuck with him mentally and physically. But eventually, the gang tracks Chas down and the inevitable violent climax ensues.

Which takes us neatly to the ending. I'm not going to reveal the brilliant monkey puzzle that is the movie's last shot. Not because I don't want to spoil it for a first-time viewer but because I don't know what it means. No-one does. No-one can. But what one of the best endings of any movie does succeed in doing is both illuminating and destroying everything leading up to it, while also leaving you haunted for, in my case at least, years afterwards.

Perhaps the best way to look at the film is as a male-orientated and much funnier remake of Ingmar Bergman's 1966 arthouse classic *Persona*, in which two very different women, one of them famous, are thrown together in claustrophobic circumstances, enter into a psychological power battle, and metaphorically and visually merge into each other. *Performance* appears to suggest that the personas of rock star Turner and thug enforcer Chas are merely flipsides of one and the same thing; both are performers who need the male ritual of violence in order to please their chosen crowds. 'The only performance that makes it, that really makes it, that makes it all the way, is the one that achieves madness,' Turner announces, all done up like a leather cosh-boy, playing out the rock iconography update on Antoine Artaud's Theatre of Cruelty.

The rest of the movie is in the detail. Roeg's astonishing camera-work and Frank Mazzola's invention of the random crash-edit. Fox's Chas taking a sado-homoerotic beating, getting hold of a gun, and sneering 'I am a bullet', before murdering Joey Maddocks. Shannon's Harry Flowers turning to camera and announcing, 'My bath's running'. A small urchin girl dressed like a boy (or is it the other way around?) called Lorraine (played by Laraine Wickens) hanging around to take the piss out of Chas and then disappear, but not before delivering history's verdict on Mick Jagger. 'I fancied him. Old rubber lips. He had three number ones and two number twos and a number four.' Pallenberg tormenting Chas with mirror tricks that dissolve his masculinity. The brilliance of Jagger's performance of 'Memo from Turner' – his first solo recording – with slicked-back hair and gangster suit. The many and varied lines from our Dadaist gangsters – 'It's Mad Cyril!', 'I like a bit of a cavort', 'I like that! Turn it up!' – that turn up on future songs by Happy Mondays and Big Audio Dynamite, and effectively invent the post-modern, word-mangling gangsters of Guy Ritchie and Jonathan Glazer's *Sexy Beast*.

The best of those lines comes from Chas, and is directed at

Turner, but is really all about Mick Jagger: 'Comical little geezer. You'll look funny when you're 50.' He was right about old Lippy Mick, of course. But I prefer to think of it as poor, doomed Donald Cammell accurately predicting the future of rock 'n' roll.

• •

Beyond the Valley of the Dolls

1970

Starring: Dolly Read, Cynthia Myers, John La Zar, David Gurian
Dir.: Russ Meyer

★ ★ ★ ★ ★

Plot: Fresh-faced girl group are chucked into a drug-crazed whirlpool of sex and violence by the immoral perversities of Los Angeles.
Key line: 'The oft-times nightmare world of show business!'

One of the all-time great cinematic trash-fests, *Beyond the Valley of the Dolls* tramples gleefully on all received notions of good taste in its hysterical enthusiasm for spoofing everything. Directed by former US army cameraman and King of the Nudies Russell Albion Meyer and co-written by film critic Roger Ebert, *BVD* gives a cheerful kicking to hippies, rock music, LA, straights, gays, Phil Spector, the Manson Family, marriage, soap opera, Douglas Sirk melodramas, and, most significantly, Hays Code-era Hollywood movies, where studios had their cake and ate it by using sanctimonious voiceovers and morally correct happy endings in order to justify whatever perverse and violent images they'd been happy to assault the viewer with over the previous 90 or so minutes. And all this is before you get to the most direct object of ridicule, Mark Robson's 1967 film of Jacqueline Susann's bonkbuster bestseller *Valley of the Dolls*. *Valley of the Dolls* was a huge hit and Susann had submitted two screenplays for a sequel to 20th Century Fox, both rejected. So Fox approached Meyer and Ebert. The result was such a scabrous take on the original's tale of showbiz-turned-sour that *BVD* had to open with a disclaimer to any connection with *Valley of the Dolls*. Fox had also demanded that Meyer tone down his enthusiasm for soft-focus shagging and enormous knockers in order to ensure an 'R' rating for cinemas. One look at this insane sick-fest and the censors slapped it with the inevitable 'X'. Meyer responded by asking to shoot more scenes of gratuitous nudity. The studio declined and rushed the movie out. Made with a $1 million budget, *BVD* has thus far grossed $40 million and counting. In 1970, the mainstream film industry still hadn't cottoned on to the cross-generational appeal of anything deemed too nasty to watch. *BVD* played a minor but crucial role in the upsurge of sex and violence in 1970s film.

And what has all this got to do with rock? Glad you asked. The basic plot revolves around a three-piece girl group called the Kelly Affair, led by happy hippy Kelly McNamara (played by Dolly Read) and managed by pretty-boy hipster Harris Allsworth (David Gurian). Their frothy, over-the-top Jefferson Airplane-ish sound has so far got them as far as playing high school proms. This has its perks, of course, as after the show we see the band's black drummer Pet Danforth urge good girl bass-player Casey to 'split' because 'the Principal's gonna hit me with a coupla caps of acid!' But woman cannot live by LSD alone and it turns out that Kelly's dead mother was rich and left it all to Aunt Susan in Los Angeles. This cues a magnificent scene where the pros and cons of going to LA are debated, in voiceover, by Kelly and Harris in debased Kerouacian rhyme.

So the band decamp to LA, where Susan offers Kelly a third of the million-dollar inheritance against the wishes of her leering, hippy-hating attorney-boyfriend. The band go to a party thrown by a producer called Ronnie 'Z-Man' Barzell who speaks entirely in Shakespearian cadence and signs them on the spot, changing their names to the Carrie Nations. They make it big, guzzle too many drugs, Harris is pushed out of the picture by the apparently gay Z-Man and a gigolo called Lance. Cult 1960s psych band the Strawberry Alarm Clock perform their fabulous 'Incense and

Peppermints'. Z-Man has a sordid party every night. Everyone has weird sex with someone they shouldn't. Harris is emotionally castrated by a dominatrix porn star ('You're a groovy boy. I'd like to strap you on sometime'), is beaten up by Lance, makes Casey pregnant in a drug-fuelled rape and attempts to commit suicide by diving from a lighting gantry onto the stage where the Carrie Nations are doing a live TV broadcast. The doctor at the hospital informs the shocked band and entourage that Harris has 'massive nerve dysfunction' but will 'have a rewarding life as a paraplegic'. Casey is seduced by a sneaky lesbian who persuades her to have an abortion. Randy Black, the Heavyweight Champion of the World, turns up in his boxing gear, seduces Pet with cracker-barrel philosophy, and then beats up her nice boy trainee lawyer boyfriend a couple of times. 'Everyone's guilty', reasons Pet, and you can see what she means.

All this is a set-up for the last act. Revealing the plot for this bizarre and brilliant endgame is so tempting. But ... I'm going to assume that most readers of this book will not have seen this film, and I don't want to spoil it, because it is shocks galore. And not just because there are bizarre gender twists, violent deaths and miracle cures that no-one could see coming because the makers didn't see it coming ('The movie's story was made up as we went along, which makes subsequent analysis a little tricky,' Roger Ebert has confessed since). But because the entire tone of the movie changes so dramatically, from comedy soap with added sex and drugs and rock 'n' roll, to crazed slasher movie, to slapstick satire. Suffice to say ... it feels like a cartoon version of the notorious Charles Manson's August 1969 Hollywood killing spree (*Valley of the Dolls* star Sharon Tate was the most famous victim). A true nightmare about the world of show business. Watch out, also, for the darkly comic use of 20th Century Fox's own signature fanfare, and prepare to be stunned by just how scary and jolting a pair of tits can be if revealed by way of out-of-the-blue surprise and spectacular low-angle camerawork and *noir* lighting.

Because Meyer, who died in Hollywood of pneumonia in 2004 aged 82, was a great cinematic stylist. *BVD* is shot in stunning colour, is edited with a jolting surrealism that subverts movie and TV conventions, and is able to switch between the light-hearted and the nasty with a visual logic that few could match. For example, the opening of the film prints the 'oft-times nightmare world of show business' line as part of the disclaimer, and then shows a woman and a Nazi being chased through the gardens of a mansion by a man who looks like King Arthur. The Nazi gets stabbed and King Arthur forces a sleeping woman to fellate a gun. By the time you've worked out what this has to do with anything, you've also worked out that it's a brilliant framing device which makes the last act all the more horrific and uncomfortably funny.

Meyer chose to pursue a (very profitable) career of making exploitation movies rather than 'serious' films. And because of that, his merits as a true *auteur* – Meyer wrote, directed, shot and edited all of his films – will always, inevitably, be underrated. But *BVD*, along with his extraordinary massive-tits-'n'-feminist-violence cult masterpieces *Faster, Pussycat! Kill! Kill!* and *Supervixens*, are vivid winners because they march to the beat of their maker's unique, grotesque, ironic and oddly innocent worldview. If I was to analyse the ending of *BVD*, it would be easy to come to obvious assumptions about the film's moral 'message', and damn Meyer as essentially right-wing. But I'd be wrong, because the film scrambles any easy assumptions, mocks American screen piety with savage gusto and leaves you feeling that, among the deliberate dumbness and dubious use of porn imagery, something strange and true has just been conveyed to you.

Roger Ebert, on his *www.rogerebert.com* website, ends his essay on the film he co-wrote with an odd story that goes some way to explaining what I mean. 'The strange thing about the movie is that it continues to play successfully to completely different audiences for different reasons. When Meyer and I were hired a few years later to work on an ill-fated Sex Pistols movie called *Who Killed Bambi?* we were both a little nonplussed, I think, to hear Johnny Rotten explain that he liked *Beyond the Valley of the Dolls* because it was so true to life.' The collaboration failed and the fall-out was salvaged by Julien Temple and renamed *The Great Rock 'n' Roll*

Swindle (see p. 206). But you can entirely see what Rotten might have meant, and why McLaren wanted Meyer to make that film.

BVD isn't about rock ... but, on some almost subliminal level, it is about the decadent imagery that rock plays with to sell itself to the common man. I mean, Manson did hang out with the Beach Boys and co-opt Beatles songs into his warped psychopathy, lest we forget. So it's about all that, and Meyer's fervent belief that small breasts are a crime against humanity. Watch this movie, and its stunning last act, and you'll see what I'm getting at.

● ●

Woodstock

1970
Starring: Hippies. Lots of them.
Dir.: Michael Wadleigh

★ ★ ★ ★

Plot: Three Days that Shook a Field.
Key line: 'The brown acid that is circulating around us is not, specifically, too good. It's suggested that you stay away from that.'

The most famous rock festival of all time almost never happened. Originally planned for a place in New York state called Middletown, the Orange County residents successfully lobbied to refuse permission for an August 1969 music and arts festival designed to entertain 50,000 people. When dairy farmer Max Yasgur offered to lease the organizers 600 acres of his land in nearby White Lake, Bethel (43 miles southwest of Woodstock, New York), the Bethel town council again refused to issue the agreed permits, but backed down through fear of being invaded by thousands of sex and drug-addled ravers anyway. Once the festival had got under way, the 186,000 ticket-holders were joined by an estimated 300,000 chancers who simply smashed through the perimeter fencing. Already stuck with a resulting shortage of food, sanitation and first aid, the organizers then had to reckon with the inevitable rainstorm which caused so much illness and hardship that the government had no choice but to declare the festival a disaster area and fly in a fleet of US army doctors to tend to the sick and wounded. One person died of a heroin overdose, another when they were run over by a tractor as they lay in their sleeping-bag.

Despite the chaos, Woodstock has been seen for 40 years as the high point of 1960s youth optimism, even as said optimism was being instantly crushed by the gruesome details of the murders committed that August by Charles Manson's hippy 'family', and the coming December's Altamont festival nightmare, captured for posterity by the *Gimme Shelter* documentary (see p. 104). Woodstock, the movie, is both the reason why the festival holds its place in history, and proof that what the organizers and the huge hippy tribe achieved in those three days in August really was one of the most extraordinary and inspiring public events in history.

Director Michael Wadleigh also almost failed to persuade Warner Brothers that the film was a good idea. Ironically, it was Wood-stock's enormous global success that saved the ailing company's bacon, making the film a key element in American cinema's shift from traditional studio system escapism to the post-rock experiment and controversy of the Movie Brat era. The film's excellence and commercial success depended heavily on the expert cutting of thousands of hours of footage, and the pair responsible were editors Thelma Schoonmaker and Martin Scorsese. It was genius Brit director Michael Powell's wife Schoonmaker who was nominated for the editing Oscar and who went on to collaborate with Scorsese on all of his best movies. Woodstock also won 1970's best documentary and best sound Academy Awards.

Indeed, Woodstock is so successful that it keeps, literally, growing. Originally released in cinemas at an already pretty challenging 177 minutes, the DVD version I've reviewed here is a 225-minute 'director's cut'. In June 2009, a couple of months too late for the writing of this book, a 40th anniversary version is being released that bumps the movie's running time up to a full four hours, with another two hours of previously unseen footage included on the DVD. There's at least another six hours that Warners have kept in reserve. By the time of the 60th anniversary, a three-day running time plus the technology to reproduce virtual mud, blood and naked dancing hippies will make you feel like you were really there.

And here begins the scoffing, yes? Well, yes ... but I'll try and keep it to a minimum. Hippy culture has never quite recovered its cool cachet from the scorching it got from punk – although the rave era gave it a jolly good go – and as an ex-punk I know how easy it is to laugh at the naivety, sneer at the hypocrisies and gag at the personal hygiene of the 1960s counter-culture. But no other generation or youth tribe managed to get over half a million people to party without police and create a utopian city for a weekend in the face of potential outright loathing from what was, at the time, a virulently anti-youth, anti-counter-culture, militaristic state. The Woodstock festival was both a triumph of organization on the part of its makers, and a triumph of communal living and good behaviour from its patrons. And the Woodstock movie's achievement lies in its refusal to be fooled into seeing this as anything so mundane as a music festival. It is, in many ways, a glimpse of humanity, as we could be: at our best, if left to our own devices. Which is very, *very* inspiring.

So ... why is Woodstock great, even for hippy haters?

Wadleigh and his crew shoot it beautifully. Early doors there is a shot of a group of long-hairs standing around a half-erected teepee. The camera makes it iconic by pulling away slowly and gracefully, framing the tableaux with a fish-eye lens. But Wadleigh isn't content to let anything stand without using something else, for contrast or comment or juxtaposition. So the scene plays out while the voice of an unseen member of blues-rockers Canned Heat complains that he can't find anywhere to take a piss, immediately contrasting the magical optimism of getting it together in the country with the practical problems of the entire weekend.

No movie has ever used split-screen as well, as the film constantly juggles its reams of information using the volume of the soundtrack to push your attention from one image to another.

The makers get strong interviews to provide context. The exchange early on between a fresh-faced middle-aged couple vacationing in the area and one of the guys the husband calls freaks is short, sharp and full of insight. Is 'freak' a good or bad thing? What does 'behaving yourself' entail? And how does it feel to watch hundreds and thousands of unkempt youths roll past your holiday home, 'like an invading army'? A beaming female shop-owner calls the festival-goers 'beautiful people' with no irony intended, and you find yourself shocked, for the first of many times, that 'old', straight, short-haired America is capable of such kindness and good grace.

The best interview is with a beautiful, unspoiled young hippy couple, talking about their open relationship, drugs, their commune, the schism that the hippy lifestyle they've chosen has caused with their parents. They're frighteningly articulate and wise about what we now can see as the end of the hippy era, as the boy describes the drug-driven counter-culture as 'contrived . . . I don't wanna have a mass change because a mass change only brings around mass insanity.'

When asked why so many are pouring into Woodstock, he replies: 'People that are nowhere are coming here because there's people that they think are somewhere. Everybody is really looking for some kind of answer, you know, where there isn't one . . . Is music *really* all that important? *I* don't really think so. But people don't know how to live, and they don't know what to do, and they think they can come here and find out what *it* is . . . People are very lost, I think.' It's this boy, so modestly accurate at such a tender age, who shares top Woodstock billing with Jimi Hendrix.

More reasons why Woodstock is great? For a fly-on-the-wall documentary, it tells a great story. When the rain comes on the second day we get suspenseful layers of portent. Announcers plead with kids to move back from the huge, teetering lighting towers. Roadies scuttle to cover the potentially deadly banks of electrical equipment. There are darkening skies and apocalyptic winds. Everyone takes up a chant of 'No! Rain! No! Rain!', and, of course, it's at that very moment that The Heavens open, because The Man even controls the weather, right? You think I'm joking . . . two guys accost the cameras to angrily posit their theory that the planes flying overhead are *making it rain*. The conspiracy theory – the biggest self-defeating element of a doomed counter-culture – is already talking its toll by 1969.

The cameras capture the storm so wonderfully well, and it feels like Woodstock can only become a nightmare. But it doesn't. What it does do is define the dominant image we all have of rock festivals – crazy young people, playing in mud. The Kids create impromptu mud slides and start pretty impressive tribal chants backed by found percussion. And one of the things that strikes home around about now is how glamorous this bunch of hippies are: almost all are slim, muscled, tanned and wholesomely pretty. Maybe it's an editorial decision on the part of the documentary makers, but you do find yourself wondering where they hid all the bony, pale, fat and ugly people.

You increasingly understand that the music is almost certainly not what any of the gathered throng took from Woodstock. A community really is formed here. A lost, confused and occasionally paranoid community, maybe. But one largely lacking in negativity, selfishness, or the consumerist craving for canned entertainment or convenient luxury. Where did we all go wrong?

And then there's the music. You thought I'd forgotten, about the music, at this famous music festival, didn't you? Well . . . I almost did. It's just not anywhere near the most interesting or significant thing about this movie, or, I suspect, the event itself. But then, I would say that, because I hate most of it.

Here's the thing . . . it's all a matter of personal taste. If you love self-consciously rustic *faux*-folk ditties, cosmic witterings and endless pub-rock white blues jams, then the music of Woodstock will give you gooey, sticky feelings. If you possess an ounce of pop aesthetic, it won't. So, for me, the live performances in Woodstock are what the fast-forward button on a remote control was invented for. So big up the four performances that deserve their place in musical history, even for a glam-disco-punk head like me.

Joan Baez – The *grande dame* of the US folk revival heads to the stage while her husband languishes in jail for Vietnam draft-dodging. But even without that kind of direct context for an appearance at a festival that crystallises the less militant side of the anti-war movement, her a cappella version of 'Swing Low Sweet Chariot' would be something special. Baez's perfect vocal diction and doe-eyed performance style is incongruous amongst all the grunting wiggers, and she performs the spiritual framed by utter darkness, giving an eerie dread to the dignity and virtuosity of her voice and bearing.

The Who – How did the working-class thug-mod Roger Daltrey become the tassled, leonine hippy rock God, inventing Robert Plant along the way? And how great Pete Townshend looked in his anti-hippy white boiler suit, and how violent and unholy his guitar sounds on a version of Eddie Cochran's 'Summertime Blues' which connects Woodstock to the tough, teen rock 'n' roll that first gave a voice to the schism between the post-war generations.

Country Joe McDonald – Country Joe's satirical anti-Vietnam singalong 'Feel-Like-I'm-Fixin'-to-Die Rag' feels like the only song that really focuses what the festival might be about. It's huge, as the song becomes more insistent and more and more of this enormous crowd stand and sing, and you really see, right there, that these are the boys who might/could/will be faced with a choice of fighting the Vietcong for reasons unknown or fighting their own government. This cleverly heads into a segment where locals debate whether the festival is disaster or triumph, disgrace or example, and it is fantastic to see ordinary, older Americans argue about whether these kids are degenerates or Golden Children. The generosity of some of these folks as they pool all their resources to feed whoever needs food is perhaps the most moving part of the story.

Jimi Hendrix – Well, obviously. If you've never seen or heard his solo guitar assault on 'The Star-Spangled Banner' ... it might just be the most powerful live music statement ever made, as he uses feedback and effects to paint a picture of bombs dropping, guns raging, children screaming, people dying. It is that 'shock and awe' that George W. Bush actually spoke of as something for America to be proud of. I've never been able to listen to it without crying tears of fear and shame, and just seeing Hendrix perform it feels like an honour.

'The Star-Spangled Banner' is intense enough to comment upon and subvert previous scenes from the movie. The film's 'Interfuckingmission'. On-site telephones and fresh-faced kids calling their parents to assure them that they're OK and that this isn't 'another Chicago' – a reference to the riots at the 1968 Democratic convention in which Mayor Richard Daley's police declared open and brutal welfare on protesters, as the cameras caught it all. The altogether unlikely and jaw-dropping moment when the US Army flies in doctors and medical supplies to the festival by helicopter. How closely the *après*-storm Woodstock resembles a war zone. The Swastika pendant worn by a member of Jefferson Airplane.

And, at one crucial point, the organisers pointing out that at least 300,000 people have had a party with no police and no trouble, and explaining how rock festivals are a way to establish a self-governing counter-cultural world without the laws and repressions of the old order. The man saying this is Michael Lang. A couple of months later he agreed to organise Altamont.

● ●

Gimme Shelter

1970

Starring: The Rolling Stones, Jefferson Airplane, the Flying Burrito Brothers
Dir.: Albert Maysles, David Maysles, Charlotte Zwerin

★ ★ ★ ★ ★

Plot: The Stones, and Altamont, and the killing that killed the sixties.
Key line: 'It's creating a sort of microcosmic society, y'know, which sets the example to the rest of America as to how one can behave in large gatherings.'

The lines above are spoken by Mick Jagger, in a press conference held just days before the Rolling Stones headlined the December 1969 free concert at Altamont Speedway near San Francisco. By the time the concert was over, four people were dead. Four babies were also born, in that place, on that day, if you're a person who believes that God really does have a plan. Altamont taught us all a great deal about how one *can* behave in large gatherings. One can, for example, turn up mob-handed on motorbikes with knives and sawn-off pool cues, take over a crowd of 300,000 people with a couple of dozen men primed for violence and intimidation, fill yourself with free beer, hand out a summary beating to anyone who annoys you, and, inevitably, stab and kick someone to death just yards from where the Greatest Rock 'n' Roll Band in the World are singing a song called 'Under My Thumb'. You can do all that, and be caught on camera doing it, and find yourself in history books, and never serve time, and even find that you and your gang, the Hell's Angels, get a place ahead of Richard Nixon, the Beatles and Charles Manson as the official Killers of Sixties Optimism. And best of all, you'll find your deeds immortalised in a proper film in cinemas around the world, and you'll be a movie star!

Gimme Shelter is the story of that notorious day and it's a shock to the system. I'm a big, big Rolling Stones fan, but I'd never seen the film before seeing it for this book. I don't have a reason for that, except that it rarely surfaces anywhere. I even had to borrow a copy on bootleg DVD because it's not available in Britain at the moment. So I watched it, and I cried, and I watched it all over again with the commentary from co-director Albert Maysles, editor Charlotte Zwerin and production manager Stanley Goldstein, and I cried again. It wasn't sadness or sentiment that brought the tears. It was shock. I began watching a music documentary and an hour later was watching a man called Meredith Hunter being murdered. Believe me, I have clocked up some serious hours watching screen violence in my 45 years. And I knew what happened at Altamont before I watched the movie. But none of that prepared me for the reality of guns and knives and fear and blood and a life snuffed out in front of a concert stage. And what's more, the makers of *Gimme Shelter* plot this film like a tragic thriller – one of those *noirs* which start with the hero bleeding to death on the floor and then tell you the story in flashback. It's a masterpiece of *vérité* storytelling and the best fly-on-wall documentary I've ever seen. Why is it so much less famous than *Woodstock* (see p. 97) or *Don't Look Back* (see p. 61)?

I guess the obvious answer to that is that *Gimme Shelter* is depressing and hard to stomach, and that's not what punters or critics want from rock movies. One of the many things that it's about is the clash between the wildness and darkness and evil imagery that is the major part of rock's appeal, and how frail and specious and spoiled all that seems when confronted with *real* wildness, darkness and evil. The Hell's Angels, are, after all, a rock 'n' roll gang. The Angels were at Altamont because a tradition had developed at late-1960s rock festivals whereby the Angels were given a space near the stage and a crate of free beer in exchange for guarding the equipment. This was an arrangement that had worked fine at previous American festivals, and the Stones had done a free show in London's Hyde Park a few months earlier where British Angels – a less violent breed, by all accounts – had provided an 'honour guard' for the Stones as they'd taken to the stage. The Hyde Park show was even more peaceful and incident-free than Woodstock.

Another strong subtext that permeates *Gimme Shelter* is that Altamont was partly a product of middle-class England trying to lord it over Anglophile America – and being firmly put in its place. At the concert at New York's Madison Square Garden that begins *Gimme Shelter*, the Stones look huge. Jagger is wearing a Stars 'n' Stripes hat that affectionately mocks American patriotism. They command the stage and it's a stage that looms above the gathered throng of young fans. They are Rock Gods. At Altamont, the hastily built stage is just four feet above the ground. The film shows how road manager Sam Cutler had gradually lost control of the entire stage area throughout the day, and the band are beset from all sides by fans, hangers-on and Hell's Angels. At one point, an Alsatian casually strolls across the stage in front of where Jagger is performing. The contrast with the New York show, where over-enthusiastic but harmless stage invaders are quickly bundled off the Stones' stage, is striking. At Altamont the Stones, too, had lost control of their domain.

The sound system is inadequate for this huge space and crowd, and, although the Stones' playing is extraordinary under the circumstances, the noise is tinny and insipid. Jagger and Keith Richards try to stop what is going on in front of them, but they have no authority over the Hell's Angels. Although they are spared being knocked unconscious as Jefferson Airplane's Marty Balin had been earlier in the day, one story that emerged later is that Richards was ready to walk offstage until Sonny Barger, the Angels' leader, shoved a gun into his ribs and ordered him to finish. The film doesn't capture this – it doesn't capture *everything* – but no-one who watches *Gimme Shelter* would be surprised if it was true. The Rolling Stones are reduced to nothing at Altamont ... except the providers of a mocking soundtrack of songs about violence and cruelty and death and Satanic poses ... 'Sympathy for the Devil', 'Gimme Shelter', 'Street Fighting Man', 'Brown Sugar', '*Under My Thumb*', for God's sake, and the events that unfold just feet away from them do not, as many journalists like to suggest, lend those songs even deeper, scarier meaning. They make them sound shallow and irresponsible and . . . silly.

Gimme Shelter also succeeds in doing something to me that I'd never imagined possible: it makes me feel sorry for Mick Jagger. Really, *really* fucking sorry for the guy. 'Cos we can all have a dark laugh at that 'microcosmic society' stuff he says at the press conference – but how was he to know that a bunch of homicidal thugs would make him look like such a cunt? Who amongst us hasn't had a moment of unbelievable hubris, and how lucky we're not so famous and adored and idolised that those moments lead to people dying? It's no wonder that Jagger veered abruptly away from 'spokesman of a generation' ambitions after Altamont, and has spent the last 40 years concentrating on making money out of the most efficient touring machine in musical history. I mean, what did he get for allowing himself to get carried away with all this flower children jive? In *Gimme Shelter* he gets a good kicking, frankly, and it's some testament to him that he signed the necessary papers to allow the film's release.

Why poor Mick? Here's why. The film's dastardly cleverness lies in the way it chooses to frame its chronology of events. The makers invite the Stones to watch the footage as it's edited. It seems that only Jagger and drummer Charlie Watts accept the invitation. We begin with this and end with this. We're watching Altamont with the Stones themselves, in other words. Near the beginning, Jagger and Watts are played a San Francisco radio phone-in that has become a post-mortem of the event. And big, bad Sonny Barger himself wants everyone to know that it wasn't his fault. 'This Mick Jagger put it all on the Angels, man', he rages. 'We were the biggest suckers for that idiot that I can ever see!' The camera is on Jagger and he tries to keep his cool. But he can't help reacting to this like he's taken a punch. Barger explains that one of these 'peace creeps' had kicked his bike. 'So they got got.'

In the film's key scene – the murder of Meredith Hunter – we are suddenly taken away from the nightmare that is night time at Altamont, and reminded that we're watching this with Mick Jagger. He is with David Maysles, watching the moment, and he asks for the film to be rolled back. Maysles points out the lanky black man who, as well as the victim, is also the most remarkable image onscreen. He is a fancy-dress pimp in a lime-green flared suit and black frilly shirt, standing out like a big neon sign in a crowd of white hippies. Maysles freezes the film and points out to Jagger – to us – what had happened too quickly in real time to take in. Hunter reaching into his pocket and producing what is clearly a gun. Him raising and pointing it at something – it could be one of the Hell's Angels who are attacking him, it could be the stage, it could be Jagger himself. A burly white man coming from behind his left shoulder and, with great deftness, simultaneously pulling the gun down with his left hand, leaping into the air, and bringing an enormous knife down into Hunter's back. Jagger watches, silently.

Now here's where things get entirely down to an individual's perception of Jagger's reaction. Many who have seen the film feel that Jagger's inability to burst into tears or agonised screams at this point means that he doesn't have any feelings about what he has seen. This, I feel, would be the sort of person who, in the wake of any tragedy, demands that some public figure come on television and express our emotions for us. For me, Jagger's lack of a flamboyant 'reaction' on camera is the sign of someone actually understanding that a tragedy is something more than an opportunity for good PR. If I was him, I'd be numb. Numb is what Jagger seems to be.

At the end of the movie, we see Jagger watch the end of what we've watched ... and sigh, quietly, wearily, helplessly. He says goodbye to Maysles and co., and gets up to leave. Still no BIG emotions. But as he's getting out of the room, he looks at the camera, for a split second. You could easily miss it. But editing genius Charlotte Zwerin didn't miss it ... and captures one of the most extraordinary freeze-frames in celluloid history. For Jagger's real feelings have been caught against his will. And those feelings are, quite clearly ... guilt and shame. A shame so deeply felt that Jagger's face has regressed to childhood. Gone is the rock star. And the failed politician and his 'microcosmic society'. And the stoic Englishman watching his personal disaster with as much adult dignity as he can muster. All that's left is a bereft child, paralysed with shame.

I suspect that anyone watching the wealth of brilliantly edited detail of the events leading up to the murder of Meredith Hunter will come to their own conclusions about whose fault it was, and whether Altamont really was 'the death of the sixties' or just a bad trip that happened to happen at the end of 1969. But I hope that not everyone sees it as another sexy part of the Stones' 'Satanic Majesties' legend. *Gimme Shelter* is about something much more important than that, something about life and death and order and chaos and how quickly paradise can become Hell. 'Rape . . . murder . . . it's just a shot away', is how the song 'Gimme Shelter' puts it. It's on an album called *Let It Bleed*.

• •

Let It Be

1970

Starring: George Harrison, John Lennon, Paul McCartney, Ringo Starr, Yoko Ono
Dir.: Michael Lindsay-Hogg

★ ★ ★

Plot: The most famous band break-up in history, in all its depressing glory.
Key line: 'I'll play whatever you want me to play. Or I won't play at all if you don't want me to play. Whatever it is that will *please* you, I'll do it.'

In January 1969, the warring Beatles, who hadn't played a live show since 1966, gathered together at Twickenham Film Studios in London to rehearse for a one-off eight-song live show to be filmed at the Roundhouse in Camden, north London. It was McCartney's idea. The sessions were such a disaster that the show was never played, and was replaced by an impromptu show on a roof. The sessions were filmed by Michael Lindsay-Hogg, who got, instead of a standard making-of doc, the mutual loathing and weary boredom of four former best friends exhausted by the pressures of being the Symbols of the Sixties. To the Beatles' everlasting credit, they allowed United Artists to release it, just so that every Beatles fan could see that the dream – whatever 'the dream' had been, exactly – was painfully and terminally over. The resulting film is the perfect mirror to *Gimme Shelter* (see p. 104), that other, more obviously horrifying filmed document of the end of the 1960s, starring the band that had been the Beatles' shadow throughout the decade. It's a matter of debate as to which of the two films is more sad and pessimistic about the failure of youth culture's attempt to replace the status quo with dancing and fucking in the streets.

At the beginning of the film, of the sessions, things appear ... OK. Lennon and McCartney lark about with each other while they sing, the four play great versions of 'I've Got a Feeling' and rockabilly stomper 'One After 909', and the Beatles seem sort of like the Beatles, albeit with questionable facial hair. But the studio feels dark and oppressive, the ever-present Yoko Ono obviously intends to never let Lennon out of her sight, and McCartney has elected himself boss. This had happened years ago, in fact, around the time of 1967's *Sgt Pepper*. But his insistence that every tune be led by him, and that every note be played the way he wants it to be played is irritating to the viewer, let alone his bandmates. According to the late Ian Macdonald, writing in his towering *Revolution in the Head: The Beatles' Records and the Sixties*, McCartney was operating as musical director and forcing the Beatles to work because he was lying awake at night worrying about the band's split. He believed, in essence, that the family that plays together, stays together. And fair enough ... but the three wealthy, successful grown adults that he was working with didn't want to be told what to do, by their bass player or anyone else. In fact, Starr wanted to act, Harrison wanted to make country-rock in California, and Lennon wanted to make avant-garde art happenings with his beloved Yoko. *Let It Be*'s major triumph, the hit single 'Get Back', was McCartney literally telling the band and the world that the Beatles should get back to basics, playing rock 'n' roll, playing live, keeping it real. Sadly, the rest of the Beatles had no intention of going back to where they 'once belonged'. They wanted to head their separate ways, and get out from under Macca's dictatorial tendencies and the expectations of their pop audience.

So, as you watch, you begin to realise that three of the Beatles are barely present at their own rehearsals. It's *all* about McCartney, holding court, talking in that phoney mid-Atlantic twang he acquired somewhere around *Sgt Pepper*, bullying Harrison. We're less than 17 minutes into the film when George hits back at Macca with that infamous, heavily sarcastic, 'Whatever you want' line, subtly emphasising the words 'please you' in an impersonation of a small, obedient child. You, like poor Ringo, put your head in your hands and shift uncomfortably on your seat in embarrassment.

When the whole divorce from Heather Mills affair was going on in the press, I wondered why I wasn't going along with the national notion that Mills was the gold-digging Devil Woman-incarnate, and Sir Paul was the poor old rich goober being victimised by the mad bitch. Was it gut-reaction feminism, or was I just being con- trary for the sake of it? I realise now, as I watch this movie for the first time in 35 years, that it was buried memories of McCartney in *Let It Be*.

Anyway ... each song starts to sound a little more like an awful pub-rock band. The atmosphere of sheer boredom seems to pervade everything. The only glimpse of pleasure is when John and Yoko waltz to George's 'I Me Mine', in love, and temporarily oblivious to the band politics.

After 23 minutes, the 'action' switches to the Apple building. According to Macdonald, Harrison had finally tired of Macca's nagging at the Twickenham rehearsals and stormed out, effectively ending the planned gig. But Macca wouldn't let it lie. He persuaded his fellow Beatles to convene at Apple a week later, record songs for a new 'no overdubs' album, and rehearse enough to play the legendary rooftop set on 30 January, an event that would stop traffic, make headlines, almost get them arrested and inspire

Lennon's much quoted 'I hope we passed the audition' wisecrack.

So things get a bit better. A version of Harrison's 'For You Blue' with some great slide guitar from Lennon. And Paul explaining to the rest of the band that he'd just got hold of a film of their Maharishi Yogi misadventure, and how they'd allowed all their personalities to be submerged by the controversial guru. It isn't exactly the least strained conversation you've ever seen. But much of the darkness has been left in Twickenham. Except that Macca ends on a joke, and Lennon dutifully laughs, but turns away with the beginnings of a piss-taking sneer for the benefit of someone off-camera. Lindsay-Hogg cuts away quickly, almost as if his embarrassment has outgunned his desire for great shots.

There is much forced larking about. But nobody's laughing. It dawns on you, right about now, that you're watching something that only a handful of people got to witness first-hand ... the world's greatest pop group playing together! I mean, it's the fucking Beatles, right? But ... that's the point. All those ornate pop masterpieces since *Rubber Soul*, where producer George Martin was the fifth Beatle and the Abbey Road studio was the sixth, and arguably most vital, member of all. This was, by 1969, a band who *didn't* play together. You're not watching the Beatles. You're watching four solo artists who don't like each other much trying half-heartedly to find some musical – and personal – common ground. I mean, this isn't visual fireworks. But it's strangely compelling, and oddly shocking. A car crash in *painfully* slow slow-motion. When black American organist Billy Preston and McCartney's daughter Stella appear in the studio, and the band run through a version of Smokey Robinson's 'You Really Got a Hold on Me', it should be a joyful communal reminder of one of their biggest musical influences. But it's miserable, as is a perfunctory rock 'n' roll medley. They're just not those pop-loving kids any more. And they can't even fake it convincingly.

All the songs that they succeed in recording properly and perform to camera as a series of promos are sombre McCartney ballads. The most significant among them is 'The Long and Winding Road', which Beatles students will know as 'The Song that Split the

Beatles'. When the band compiled these 'Get Back' sessions into 1970's *Let It Be* album, Lennon, who had been impressed by legendary wall-of-sound producer Phil Spector's work on Lennon's debut Plastic Ono Band solo album, hired Spector to drown McCartney's heartbreaking ballad of regret in sugary strings. McCartney freaked, tried to stop the track's release, failed . . . and announced that the Beatles had split. 'The Long and Winding Road' went to Number One in America, a final joke at McCartney's expense. It was a tawdry end to an enterprise that had symbolised youth, enthusiasm and the idea that best friends could stick to their guns and change the world.

The lovely, stately performance of McCartney's 'Two of Us', staged and played to camera as a proper pop promo, carries the weight of the rift between Lennon and McCartney. 'You and me chasing paper/getting nowhere' is widely interpreted as a reference to the lawsuits that would begin to engulf the Beatles in the coming weeks. 'You and I have memories/Longer than the road that stretches out ahead,' is self-explanatory. And McCartney's face as he ends the song – 'We're going home . . . Goodbye' – is a picture of sullen resignation. There may be lawyers and betrayals and money wars ahead. But you feel that the Beatles break up, irrevocably, as 'Two of Us' grinds to an inappropriately jaunty halt. 'Let It Be' – the song – is a pretty PS saying, you know what? Just leave this alone. It ain't getting no better. Time to move on.

But before 'Let It Be' can do that, there's a rooftop concert to perform. It's genuinely moving, watching passers-by and office workers in neighbouring buildings stopping, puzzling and, when the penny drops, scurrying to various vantage points to see what they can't possibly know – that they are witnessing the last ever performance by the Beatles. How could they know, when the band sound tough and tight and Lennon and McCartney seem as close as they ever were? Maybe McCartney was right. Maybe if they'd just got over their differences and nerves and laziness, and just toured . . .

Well – we'll never know. What I do know is that I still boo when the posh boss killjoys of Baker Street force the police to stop the show. And that two days after the rooftop triumph, Lennon, Harrison and Starr asked Stones manager Allen Klein to sort out their labyrinthine money problems, and McCartney, who wanted his girlfriend Linda's family management company to do it, sued the rest of his band. And that somehow, in the midst of all this, the Beatles got through the making of one more album, *Abbey Road*, which they began recording just three weeks later.

The muted discomfort of *Let It Be* is a very different 'end of the sixties' than the one the Rolling Stones would endure 11 months later at Altamont, captured by the Maysles Brothers in the extraordinary *Gimme Shelter*. But it is, in its way, as ominous and final as the long, dead piano note at the end of 'A Day in the Life'.

• •

Elvis: That's The Way It Is

1970
Starring: Elvis Presley
Dir.: Denis Sanders

★ ★ ★

Plot: Elvis Presley just before the fall.
Key line: 'So those of you who's never seen me before will realise tonight that I'm totally insane, and I have been for a number of years.'

The first Elvis Presley documentary established the world's dominant view of Elvis the performer. The King ... a dark-haired, sweaty medallion man doing karate moves and stylised poses in a white jump-suit over big-band, MOR-tinged pop-rock on a stage in Las Vegas. It was directed by Denis Sanders, who had won two Oscars, for a 1955 short fictional war film called *A Time Out of War* and a 1970 documentary called *Czechoslovakia 1968*. The movie is based around shows at the International Hotel in Las Vegas in August 1970, and makes good use of the era's Hollywood film gimmicks like split-screen and Panavision. Some idea of the hoops Sanders had to jump through to make his hit documentary is given by the presence, among the credits, of Presley's omniscient manager Col. Tom Parker as 'technical adviser' and the nine names that make up Presley's legendary Memphis Mafia entourage as 'technical assistants'.

We're quickly introduced to 1970s model Elvis, rehearsing with his crack band for the shows. This is the last beautiful Elvis the world got to see; rakishly slim although slightly chubby of cheek, jet black hair and big sideburns, deep tan, purple aviator shades, flowery silk shirt and tight black loons. His voice is already showing signs of wear and tear, the neglect of a man who has convinced himself, correctly perhaps, that he didn't have to work at remaining a great singer. But the music is tough as well as solidly professional, and Elvis, at this point, is a soul-tinged country rocker, rather than the schlock-purveyor he would become after two years of boredom with the endless run of similar shows with the same musicians.

But Sanders does have a critical agenda, and we see its first fruits around six minutes in as we suddenly cut to two bespectacled, nerdy girls sitting on a bed. They are Elvis fans; the kind of darkly funny obsessives that use their idol to replace the excitement and hope that is missing from their own lives. They are comically serious as they talk about their fandom.

'She's only about eight months old, but she's a good fan,' the stone-faced one called Sue explains.

'Certainly. She loves to listen to Elvis,' her earnest friend adds. ' . . . She likes his Vegas album, 'cos it's gotta lotta action in it.'

'She' is Tinker Bell, their cat.

Sanders was definitely a smart cookie, and not just for employing Sam Peckinpah's director of photography Lucien Ballard to shoot the gorgeous Panavision live footage. Anyone making any kind of Elvis movie, let alone his first documentary, had to deal with the power of Col. Tom Parker. Parker was a control freak and made sure that his client was presented positively, to Parker's satisfaction, in every circumstance. Indeed, Parker smelled a rat when presented with the first cut of . . . *That's The Way It Is*, demanding – and getting – more live footage and less of the fan interviews and slyly critical scenes of Las Vegas tackiness. Nevertheless, the version that hit the cinemas still makes its point. By cutting from rich, beautiful Elvis and his arse-licking entourage goofing about with forced hilarity, to desperately serious and frankly very unattractive fans talking to camera about his Godlike qualities, Sanders subtly presents a picture of an uncaring, narcissistic King and his white trash subjects, who reinforce their loser status by their worship of a somewhat ridiculous false idol. It's a surreptitiously cruel film at the expense of Elvis fans, and a clever criticism of stars who don't live on the same planet as those who pay their wages. And it heavily implies that no-one who worships Presley possesses either a brain or a life.

The sub-plot is provided by interviews with money men in bad suits about the organisation around Elvis and how much revenue he generates. Again, it's a subtle way of taking the magic out of both Elvis and the business of show as we see that an Elvis gig in Vegas means block-bookings for corporate parties – a stop between the golf course and the strip club, presumably. The split-screen gimmicks juxtapose Elvis with the preparations of food; Elvis gets smaller and smaller as the meat his ever-thrusting groin is being used to flog gradually dwarfs him.

Col. Parker doesn't appear in the film, but his orders and demands are everywhere. It's the TCB ('Taking Care of Business') idea that Elvis and his entourage of lickspittle leeches loved so much. And it's the sort of impressive but mundane organisation and number-crunching that a reactionary viewer might admire, and anyone with a counter-cultural bent would find immediately off-putting.

If you're waiting for me to say that Sanders' point is destroyed by Elvis's music and charisma . . . it isn't. . . . *That's The Way It Is* captures Presley on close to top form and in rude physical health; but he still comes out of this film as a dislikeable man who doesn't deserve the levels of misguided devotion he inspires. A man who is being carried by his excellent band, who are also being paid to laugh at his relentless class-clown schtick. And who, by 1970, is loved only by hotel owners, Christian rednecks, the terminally unhip and homely women who have the air of potential stalkers.

Nevertheless, Sanders' objective eye ensures that this is all down to perception. An uncritical Elvis fan would just see an uncritical fan film, and fair enough. Especially as Sanders' other trick is unlikely suspense. The goofing at Elvis' rehearsals becomes increasingly irritating or nasty, and, on opening night, Presley's pre-show jokes take on a fretful quality, Tom Jones sends a 'funny' telegram, Cary Grant and Sammy Davis Jr take their seats, and Elvis finally dons the white jump-suit that is destined to become the ultimate symbol of his tacky majesty. As all this pre-show detail builds you want to know what happens when the man finally hits the stage. Is Elvis a god? Or the 20th century's most successful mass illusion?

And? Oh, neither, naturally. But when Elvis eventually swaggers onstage, there is an immediate change. He takes a humble bow and sweetly acknowledges his nerves with a blow of the cheeks and a shake of the head. And then he kicks off, surprisingly, with a version of his first ever single, 'That's Alright Mama', which is, of course, underwhelming, because its skipping blues eroticism is submerged beneath a breakneck tempo and too many damn instruments and singers, all crashing and bashing and chirping away to no great effect. But you can see why sitting in a room seeing *Elvis Presley himself* standing legs akimbo and actually *playing an acoustic guitar* would make anyone's heart skip a beat. You're charmed by how often Elvis makes eye contact with a specific member of the audience, revealing his insecurity or mocking himself with a look, making it personal. He's also very lithe and very sexy, and it's bizarre to think that this extraordinary presence will be a bloated corpse within seven short years.

Sanders continues to intersperse the show with subtly hilarious and tragic interview footage ('When he walks onstage there's no normal woman that can't get excited'; 'Mother likes a lot of action, and, I must admit, I do too'), including great stuff from a fan convention in Luxembourg ('So, lo and behold, Elvis appeared, and he presented me with this magnificent tandem'), acknowledging the truth that 45 minutes of live footage, even of beautifully shot Elvis live footage, is boring unless you're lucky enough to be in the room, immersed in the sound, charged by the communal electricity a star generates. Or maybe not; because, in the early part of the show, shots of the crowd reveal a passive, polite but almost entirely *un*excited audience.

But then, just before a really scary male fan in comedy binocular specs threatens the film-makers ('If I don't like this film, if I think it's done wrong ... I'm gonna call you up and tell you all about it or something. I'm just gonna write you a dirty little letter'), things very abruptly change. A self-mocking Elvis ramble about his early career is interrupted by malfunctioning microphones, and although his attempt to ad lib his way through his barely repressed fury at the technical ineptitude is uncomfortable, it seems to break the ice between performer and audience. 'Love Me Tender' becomes a mixture of contempt for the song and Elvis' desire to snog every woman in the front row, before, out of nowhere, the stage is invaded by a leggy platinum blonde Amazon who attempts to suck all the oxygen out of his face while clinging on to him for dear life. Interestingly, the onstage security takes his sweet time rescuing his boss. An unfazed Elvis keeps right on snogging, though, and straight-looking husbands are forced to be public cuckolds as their wives clamber over tables and Tammy Wynette haircuts to get some lewd public tongue action with the King. It's all brilliantly weird, and nothing like the priapic stud-god superiority of the supposedly cooler rockers of the era. The band look frightened and confused, and struggle to know where they are in the song, as the music is overwhelmed by the excited chatter of the crowd, and women start running from the back of the auditorium to try and get their fair share of regal saliva.

From then on, the show becomes sporadically fascinating, as Presley's unpredictability becomes the show's point, his voice and performance veering wildly between intense commitment and dis-tracted self-mockery, often within one line of a song. For example, Elvis had been worrying, pre-show, about whether he could remem-ber the words of a ballad called 'I Just Can't Help Believin'. He kicks off its introduction with a deadpan joke at the expense of its writer ('BJ Thomas has a new record out . . . I don't particularly like it') which elicits embarrassed titters from the audience, before demanding a piece of paper with the lyrics. Yup . . . Elvis Presley, at a live show in front of 4,000 people that is being filmed for a major cinematic release, *reads the words of one of the songs*. And then . . . pulls off a performance so restrained, sincere and lovely that the result became the soundtrack's big hit single (and the first single my mum ever bought me, which is why I especially love it).

One of the most curious things about the Vegas-era Elvis shows was his preference for performing covers of others' greatest hits over the songs that he had made his own. A mediocre 'You've Lost that Lovin' Feeling', a self-indulgent take on Tony Joe White's 'Polk Salad Annie', a good 'Bridge Over Troubled Water' and an awful version of Neil Diamond's 'Sweet Caroline' come and go, given a far more whole-hearted performance than the perfunctory, truncated run-throughs of the likes of 'One Night', 'Blue Suede Shoes' and 'Heartbreak Hotel'.

But you suspect that this is a musician who has fallen out of love with music. At one point Elvis orders the band to play anything they like while he clambers offstage and goes walkabout amongst his thrilled flock, utterly untroubled by the physical contact that sends rebel-rockers into paroxysms of terror. This was a man who received a serious death threat a few months after this show and barely let it change his touchy-feely attitude to public performance. Why should he fear stabbing or shooting when the guy was going to be so efficient at slowly killing himself?

If the NBC 1968 TV Special is the last word on the talent and charisma of Elvis Presley, then *Elvis: That's The Way It Is* is the best film about the Elvis phenomenon, and the connection between the white trash eccentricity of the icon and the white trash eccentricity of those who loved him after all those godawful movies. If Elvis in 1970 had nothing to do with rock 'n' roll's dominant counter-cultural aesthetic anymore, he also had nothing in common with the smooth, classy entertainers that were his competitors in Rat Pack Vegas. The guy had the face and voice of an angel, and the mind of a truck-driver who didn't believe that this superstardom thing could possibly last for someone like him. Sanders catches him before the fear and boredom and insecurity and self-loathing and responsibility involved in being the King finally overwhelmed him, and drove him mad, and led him to stop caring about whether he lived or died.

But you can see it all coming, in his childish desperation for attention, in the terror that often flickers onto his face, in the careless dismissal of his musical talents, in his inability to take himself seriously. The film forms a useful end-of-sixties-rock-optimism documentary triptych with *Let It Be* (see p. 109) and *Gimme Shelter* (see p. 104), and makes a sneaky argument that Elvis, and therefore rock 'n' roll, is already a busted flush.

• •

Cocksucker Blues

1972
Starring: The Rolling Stones
Dir.: Robert Frank

★ ★

Plot: The most infamous unseen rock movie of all time.
Key line: 'This is the most uninteresting drive in the world.'

The notorious *Cocksucker Blues* is a documentary about a Rolling Stones tour. The 1972 American shows to promote the magnificent *Exile on Main Street* album were the first in the US since the Altamont debacle (see *Gimme Shelter*, p. 104). The significance was understood by Robert Frank, a Swiss photographer and beatnik film-maker who had worked in the 1950s with Jack Kerouac and Allen Ginsberg. He brought a friend, Daniel Seymour, and a collection of cameras which anyone could pick up and use. The Rolling Stones looked at the end results and baulked, suing Frank to stop it being released. The judge came up with an odd compromise, ruling that the film could only be shown when the director was present in the cinema itself. This effectively killed the movie and established a legend ... that this was a film so wild, pornographic and evil that even the Satanic Stones didn't want anyone to see it. As always, legends are more fun than truths.

I managed to get hold of a copy on a dodgy bootleg DVD. It's occasionally difficult to discern whether the bad sound, chaotic editing and out-of-focus camerawork is down to the film or the format you're watching it on. But one thing was beyond reasonable doubt. It's 90 minutes that feels like 90 days.

Frank's film is pure *vérité*, meaning no captions, voiceovers or contextual interviews to explain what you're watching. It's more or less a montage of images with no obvious thematic link. Offscreen sounds, of music, of dialogue, constantly interrupt or obscure the conversation or onscreen music, leading to an eerie, drugged feeling of dislocation. Images come and go, so quickly sometimes it almost feels like they just didn't edit the film properly. The vast majority of the 'action' takes place in hotel rooms and dressing-rooms at gig venues, and there is more footage of anonymous members of the Stones' entourage than there is of the band. Everybody is constantly half-naked, on drugs and talking about drugs. I know this sounds thrilling in theory, but the truth is that people on drugs are only interesting if you happen to be on the same drugs. Otherwise, drug addicts are dull and embarrassing.

Early on, we see a mysterious Mick Jagger strop at a piano; a clothed male masturbation scene (Is it Jagger? We see a shot of him pointing a camera at us straight afterwards that implies it is, but I don't entirely believe it) and a press interview where both Jagger and Keith Richards are politely bored as they field silly questions about whether they should write a hit for Chuck Berry.

It's not long before we're on The Plane, a private Stones jet on which the stuff happens that has sustained the *Cocksucker Blues* legend for almost 40 years. It goes like this.

As we hear various portentous tributes to the Stones clipped from radio shows, suddenly, a big pair of tits appear before us. A minute or so later, the back, in shadow, of a naked couple fucking on an airplane sofa. You can't see their faces. Then a crowd of men watch as one beefy bloke – we assume a roadie – helps a giggling girl take off her top. We realise that the Stones are leading a crowd of men who are encouraging the girl to go further by verbal cajoling and the beating of drums. Another girl is roughly manhandled into toplessness by the meathead ... she's laughing, but it still feels uncomfortable. He succeeds in pulling off her jeans despite her feeble attempts to fight him off. Finally, he succeeds in lifting the first girl, now completely naked, onto his shoulders, horizontally. Look – no hands! Jagger and Richards look on with grinning but still somewhat half-hearted approval. A very large penis being held by another girl appears so briefly it's almost subliminal. One of the girls, who appears to have shaving cream on her back, gets dressed, looking annoyed.

This whole scene makes a lot more sense when you know that Frank admitted that it was staged. 'It would be nice to have something happen', he explained. The biggest shock in seeing something that has been whispered about for so many years is how tame and tawdry and empty the entire charade is.

Perhaps it's the scenes of backstage coke-snorting and hotel-room heroin use that led the Stones to stop the film's release. Not because anyone would be shocked that this band took drugs by 1972, but because this was bang in the middle of the Stones' high-profile drug bust years, and it would just seem like an invitation to be arrested again. But in essence, nothing about the way the Stones or their entourage behave is as unpleasant as the live performance here of 'Midnight Rambler', with Jagger going all out to pay tribute to the Boston Strangler, cheered on throatily by an audience dominated by men.

The best moments are the essence of *Cocksucker Blues*. They're when Frank manages to get himself in a room with a Stone, point the camera, turn off the sound ... and capture some desolately beautiful shots that speak volumes about the boredom and alienation of life on the road. But the missed opportunities become maddening. At one point, Keef is nodding out, apparently smacked off his mullet, while Mick is doing what he's always doing; talking business with a suit. But for all Frank's access, we never learn a single thing about what either felt about that, and how that relationship has worked for so long. Frank seems uninterested in anything that matters, to the point where anything Jagger or Richards say is partly obscured by another sound.

Andy Warhol, Bianca Jagger and Tina Turner pop up ... for seconds before disappearing. There's a chaotic live performance of 'Uptight' and 'Satisfaction' with Stevie Wonder which is interestingly shambolic. But it's eventually left to girls (you'd need a degree in advanced Stones trivia to know who the girls are and whether they are significant) to provide shock entertainment in hotel rooms. One shoots up, another is naked and half-heartedly plays with herself. The film becomes more and more depressing; no conversation seems to mean anything, no act goes anywhere, no-one who isn't in the band seems to have any point to their existence.

Things hit bottom when Keef and a sax player throw a TV out of a hotel room window. 'Tell us when', Richards says to the cameraman, which does say a great deal about rock rebellion. The film snaps briefly into focus towards its end when a fan outside a San Francisco gig is interviewed. She complains about how terrible her life is, especially as the state took her baby into care. 'I mean, what's wrong with having a baby on acid? He was born on acid,' she says, proudly. If Frank's point was that the Stones existed in a vortex of nihilistic amorality so seductive that even their fans were unapologetic scum, and that that is much duller than you might imagine, then job done, I guess.

You can't decide whether Frank's study of the tedium of being a Rolling Stone on tour, and the endless frustration of not being able to hear or focus on anything that looks potentially interesting, like Jagger's visit to a black pool hall, is a deliberate artistic statement or just a result of Frank's ineptitude. He seems so enamoured with being a part of the Stones' entourage that he just might have been too ... um ... distracted with other stuff to concentrate fully on his job.

Nevertheless, it's some achievement to be handed full access to the greatest rock 'n' roll band in the world at their peak, naked babes who will do anything they're told, tons of smack and coke, the landscape of America ... and still end up making something boring. The truth about *Cocksucker Blues*? Robert Frank made a bad film. That's why the Rolling Stones didn't want it released.

● ●

Born to Boogie

1972

Starring: Marc Bolan, Ringo Starr, Mickey Finn, Geoffrey Bayldon, Elton John
Dir.: Ringo Starr

★ ★ ★

Plot: Pop star plays gig and arses about with a Beatle.
Key line: 'Nah, he wasn't rich. He had a lot of money, y'know? He sometimes used the sun as a tambourine.'

T.Rex were huge in 1971. Million-selling, tabloid-bothering, bigger-than-the-Beatles huge. And this, in itself, remains weird because Marc Bolan was so much more art-house than chart-tart, on paper. Having established Tyrannosaurus Rex as a free festival cult in the late 1960s by singing about wizards, elves and girls called Deborah, who were just like a zebra, over acoustic guitar and bongo drums, his sudden change to electric warrior and scream idol was akin to Devandra Banhart suddenly exchanging excessive facial hair and campfire folkisms for six-pack and gold chain and making a fortune out of Usher-like R&B. Bolan actually got girls screaming at minimalist, postmodern, pre-Ramones art-rock, while footy hoolies faked a flamboyant gayness to emulate him. Bolan's raunchy, re-tooled 1950s rock, and pouting, preening and deliciously pointless sex pixieness, was just what Britain needed after the Beatles split and rock's flood of deeply concerned and monstrously dull *faux*-rustic singer-songwriters, and his success was so vertiginous that the Beatles financed this cinematic vanity project.

Said vanity project consists of highlights from two superbly filmed concerts at the Empire Pool, Wembley (now Wembley Arena) interspersed with a studio jam where T.Rex are joined by director Ringo Starr and Elton John, and surreal and whimsical skits inspired, it says on the DVD's 'Making Of' documentary, by Fellini. Suffice to say that, as art-house directors go, Ringo turns out to be a really good drummer. But this is part of what makes *Born to Boogie* a great watch; it's an exercise in hubris and laziness masquerading as creative spontaneity that tells you everything you need to know about the self-regard and innocent uselessness of rock after the lofty intellectual peaks of the 1960s golden age. Plus the fans are so beautiful and make me so nostalgic for the 1970s … tank tops and too-tight sweaters, make-up all wrong and a completely non-aggressive, joyful abandon. The shows are like a geek and nerd convention, and you fondly imagine that they all became artists and writers and sexually ambiguous punk pioneers. But they probably became estate agents and shop assistants, just like the rest of us.

Born to Boogie looks like a straight concert movie until 'Baby Strange' ends and we're suddenly at the end of what seems to be an airport runway watching a red car drive towards us. Even when it's still some distance away, you know that the figure standing in the dinky sports car is Marc – a man so special, Ringo seems to be telling us, that you can spot that it's him from 100 yards away. He's wearing a brown wizard's hat and he's swatting the driver with a fly-swatter. The driver is a man in a mouse suit. A phone rings and Bolan answers as his furry friend joins him in the back seat. He has an obtuse conversation about a man in New York. Bolan then beckons to someone off-camera and a figure appears – poof! Magic! – out of nowhere. It is a midget in a superhero costume. Marc swats him. The Supermidget eats Marc's wing-mirror.

Another sudden shift and we're watching Bolan, Ringo and Elton John playing a terrible pub-rock version of 'Tutti Frutti'. Then Elton accompanies Marc on a version of 'Children of the Revolution' which he sings as a disembodied head inside Elton's piano.

And I think you must be getting the idea by now. But it is somewhat extraordinary to see Elton and a Beatle being Marc Bolan's sidemen. This is how huge and cool Marc Bolan was in 1971.

The bit where Bolan and Starr keep corpsing as they attempt to perform some kind of skit to camera based on the lyrics of Elvis Presley's 'Party' is uncomfortable viewing, because Bolan is quite obviously forcing the laughter, and Ringo is trying and failing to hide his impatience with his silly, self-indulgent star. It feels like the point of the film; Bolan's contrived personality, so thrilling as soon as he's playing his guitar and singing, is an empty vessel once the music stops and we're left with poor Ringo's inability to find any substance within it. Bolan may still look thin and beautiful and be at his peak of popularity here. But you can see his future decline in every frame. All of his creative intelligence had been used up in his invention of glam-rock, and it's fascinating to watch a film where you can see that the star's failure is inevitable while the star himself believes his every idea and utterance is solid gold and easy action. Chilling more than fascinating, actually. If his death in 1977 had been a suicide or a drug overdose or a murder this all becomes suffused with portent, but a car crash as he was becoming punk's fairy godfather undercuts the death angle completely.

After the striving for revolutionary meaning of late 1960s rock, the 1970s backlash was rock 'n' roll as an end in itself. 'Cosmic Dancer', performed wonderfully here, contains the nub of the crux: 'I danced myself right out the womb/Is it strange to dance so soon?' The answer would be no, naturally, because in the rock aesthetic that Bolan invented, that's all there is. Children (of all ages) dancing to rock 'n' roll, forever dreaming, forever innocent. A magical fairyland of pointless pleasure. Sounds fine to me. But the 1970s was far too cynical a place to sustain that for long.

The DVD includes a 'Making Of' documentary fronted by Marc's son Rolan. It's a hagiography, of course, but it does have lots of useful trivia and some lovely monochrome footage of young, hippy-era Bolan and his early cheerleader John Peel. What it ain't going to mention is that Bolan ruthlessly kicked Peel to the kerb as soon as he got big enough to hang out with ex-Beatles, nor that

Peel went on to become the universally admired legend that Bolan didn't.

So, fact fans: tickets for the Empire Pool shows were 75p. The gardens in which the Lewis Carrollesque tea party is filmed are in John Lennon's house, and the hamburgers consumed were from Fortnum & Mason. The waiter at the tea party is played by Geoffrey Bayldon, who got the gig by playing the title role in a really quite brilliant 1970s kids TV show called *Catweazle*, about a medieval wizard who finds himself transported through time to the 1970s and has to get to grips with the perceived magic of 'eleck-trickery' and 'the telling bone'. One mulleted T.Rex fan insists that he wants to blackmail the British government. Bolan once kicked Tony Visconti in the bollocks. And, of course, Marc had a premonition that he'd die in a car crash.

Visconti, who produced both Bolan and David Bowie's greatest records, remarks to Rolan: 'Your Dad was arrogant enough to believe he could go onstage with no props.' He was right to be arrogant. In *Born to Boogie*, you see that T.Rex work on a tiny stage, no frills, no light show, none of Bowie's theatrical trappings. But he's still better live than Bowie, and it explains why Bolan was so adored by punks, with their stripped-down aesthetic. Punk was not modest. It was sure that the charisma of its stars and the intensity of the music was more of a spectacle than flying pigs and lasers. In that sense, Bolan was punk's greatest inspiration.

Born to Boogie is a key rock film because it's a perfect example of rock's constant failure to live up to its revolutionary hype, and of the inevitable folly of a grown man pretending he's better than us because he plays an electric guitar. But also because it's one of the very few films in this book where a live performance makes your hair stand on end, your arse wiggle and your lips pout in white man's overbite homage to the genius that was Marc Bolan. If it is, at times, embarrassingly bad, then it only serves to remind that rock 'n' roll was better when it revealed its lies and weaknesses, and shrugged and grinned, and wiggled its crotch in your face anyway.

• •

The Harder They Come

1972

Starring: Jimmy Cliff, Janet Bartley, Carl Bradshaw, Basil Keane, Bobby Charlton
Dir.: Perry Henzell

★ ★ ★

Plot: Country bumpkin becomes Ultimate Rude Boy killer. Makes reggae record on the way.
Key line: 'You want me to go and beg work for $10 a week for the rest of my life. I tried that. I'd rather die.'

Based on the true story of Rhyging, a cop killer from the late 1940s who became a Jamaican folk hero to the point where thousands attended his funeral, *The Harder They Come* established the concept of the 'rude boy' – the young black rebel-hooligan – in the mainstream, prepared the way for the coming of reggae's first superstar Bob Marley, and was such an enduring cult item in America that it played at San Francisco's Orson Welles cinema every week for eight years. Not bad for a low-budget film made by amateurs and locals in a country with no real film industry, and where the dialogue is dominated by inpenetrable Jamaican patois.

Director Perry Henzell transported the legend of Rhyging to the music business of early 1970s Kingston, casting singer Jimmy Cliff as Ivanhoe Martin, a country boy who moves from the mango farm to Kingston when his grandmother dies, and, after quickly recognising that conventional unskilled employment in the city brings nothing but exploitation and humiliation, turns to music and drug-dealing to fuel his naive dreams of getting rich quick. If that all sounds familiar, then, yep, it really is the entire *raison d'être* of gangsta rap 15 years or so before the fact. The tale of the poor and angry but talented and charismatic black boy who would rather kill or die than stay broke is one that just about every male on the planet is fascinated by, and *The Harder They Come* is one of the key benchmarks of the gangsta myth.

The first half of the movie justifies its success and reputation. Henzell's *mise en scène* completely evinces the heat, buzz and chaos of Kingston, a city of hustlers. Grainy documentary film stock, fast editing and naturalistic acting adds to the feeling of reality. Having one of the all-time great movie soundtracks as a constant presence, commenting on the action, doesn't hurt either. Scotty's 'Hold Your Brakes'. The Slickers' 'Johnny Too Bad'. Desmond Dekker's '007'. Toots and the Maytals' 'Pressure Drop'. Jimmy Cliff's stunning title track. Golden Age reggae classics that balance sweetness with roughness, just as Henzell's pacy patchwork of shanty housing, abandoned cars, dust and dirt, balances the scary with the joyful, the ugly with the beautiful, which is what all the most exciting and deadly cities invariably do.

But, for all its authenticity and influence, *The Harder They Come* drags. It's far too long at 103 minutes, and while the non-acting might add to the reality, the lack of charisma and technique of the players makes the characters impossible to engage with. Cliff, in particular, is an empty shell. His wooden style leaves you unable to judge whether Ivan is a decent man corrupted by poverty, or a prize prick who deserves what he gets. Morality tales and thrillers need their central characters to be either hero or anti-hero. Ivan is neither ... he just shrugs and does what the movie's plot tells him to do. One assumes that Henzell never got asked the 'What's my motivation?' question by Cliff. And he simply doesn't have the looks or presence to hold the viewer's attention, nor suggest a back story or even a basic personality.

The only time Cliff really comes alive is when he performs 'The Harder They Come' in a recording studio. Making the sloppy spliff/T-shirt/jeans ensemble look as glamorous as Bolan in full glitter, dancing and sweating and singing one of the all-time great fuck-you songs in pop history. There's still no glory here, though. Evil record label chief Hilton (played by Bobby Charlton – sadly, not *that* Bobby Charlton) offers Ivan £20 for his masterpiece. He refuses to sign and finds that the cigar-chewing, light-skinned mogul has Kingston music sewn up like the Mafia. No Hilton, no radio play or promotion, no chance. Turns out a police detective controls the drug trade, too.

The Harder They Come depicts Jamaica as a naturally beautiful country corrupted by imperialism, where the rich idle within gated communities while the huddled masses bully, con and kill each other over chump change. Aggression and humiliation is default for everyone in a poor society with no work. This is a place where men cut each other to bloody pulps over bicycles. Wonder what the Jamaican Tourist Board made of it.

There are some justly celebrated scenes. The point of us seeing a rowdy group of Kingston citizens watching spaghetti western *Django* in a chaotic cinema only becomes clear in the movie's shockingly abrupt ending, as a grown man believes himself the Western hero for real, fuelling his delusions of invincibility by imagining the cinema audience watching him, unable to separate fact and fantasy.

The gospel music scene in a Baptist church makes convincing connections between Jamaican and Afro-American life. But Christianity doesn't come out of this movie too well. The Preacher who gives Ivan a job is a tyrannical zealot with inappropriate feelings towards his adopted daughter, Elsa. But Elsa defies Preacher to move in with Ivan, who is soon dressing himself to kill and poncing her last $2 off her for a night out, as she tells him he's a dreamer. 'Who's a bigger dreamer than you?', Ivan responds. 'Always talking about milk and honey in the sky. There's no milk and honey in the sky.' And, if you want a weepy bit, then dopeheads the world over must have cried buckets at the scene where the army burns enormous bushes of ganja.

The film's second half is obviously strongly influenced by early American blaxploitation movies – fearless, trigger-happy black men, the murder of women presented as soft porn, gratuitously daft plotting. The twist that Ivan is so desperate for fame that he's willing to take on every cop, soldier and gang member in Kingston for notoriety's sake could have been great *grand guignol*, as well as a neat satire on showbiz. But there's been no clue beforehand that

Ivan's that mad, and there's no humour in the movie at all. The dialogue becomes increasingly functional, and the film gives up on being a critique of Jamaican society and settles for being male wish-fulfilment fantasy. Women here are nags or victims, irrelevant bystanders as the men make everything happen.

The punks' adoption of the reggae sound was a great thing musically. But their adoption of Jamaicans as icons of cool based largely around Rastafarianism and this film – check out the lyrical references to Ivan in the Clash's 'Guns of Brixton' – was always deeply suspect. When Whitey's feeling a bit geeky and lost for new ideas, he always steals from the black in an unconscious echo of slavery and colonialism. The punks' worship of the black male outlaw always smacked of a somewhat racist perception that all black men are more virile and instinctively rebellious than white men, which in turn gives them the right to be misogynist and homophobic. All that white middle-class bollocks about the noble savage and what a great sense of rhythm the black man has, in other words. I've never heard a woman express a love of this movie, but then, women don't generally live in constant fear of sexual inadequacy.

Nevertheless, the novelty of seeing black men in an authentic environment – plus the majesty of the music – made *The Harder They Come* a surprise commercial success and an influential cult film. Selling a story about the music biz and dope as a mixture of gangster flick and Western was the stroke of genius that made wannabe bad boys fall in love with the idea of being an Ivan. The clothes are cool, too.

Sadly, Henzell's lack of interest in actors and character betrays his lack of interest in people, which rather undercuts whatever message he thinks he's giving us. *The Harder They Come* simply helped make black music more popular by lending it criminal cool. Whether, in the wake of queer-bashing dance-hall records and a commercial rap culture that celebrates black-on-black violence, that counts as an achievement, is a whole other bag.

• •
American Graffiti

1973

Starring: Richard Dreyfuss, Ron Howard, Paul Le Mat, Charles
Martin Smith, Cindy Williams, Candy Clark, Mackenzie Phillips,
Wolfman Jack, Harrison Ford
Dir.: George Lucas

★ ★ ★ ★

**Plot: Four Californian boys drive around a small town to a
1950s/1960s soundtrack. Valuable lessons learned.
Key line: 'Rock 'n' roll's bin goin' downhill ever since Buddy
Holly died.'**

American Graffiti begins with a shot of a classic 1950s American
diner set against a blood-red sunset, soundtracked by Bill Haley's
'Rock Around the Clock'. It's a mercilessly cool opening, but it's
worth recalling that, in the early 1970s 'movie brat' milieu where
director George Lucas was working, this was just about as uncool
as it got. So much so that the big gripe amongst Lucas's fine
ensemble cast was over being forced to wear 1950s clothes and
have 1950s hair. They were children of the casual, unkempt, hairy
1960s, you see ... but then, that was the entire point of *American
Graffiti*. It was an anti-1960s film disguised as a modern rites-of-
passage movie. And once it had hit home, at just the moment where
Vietnam and Watergate had left America in a state of communal
self-loathing, it pointed to a place, before the Tet Offensive and the
Kennedy assassination and the Beatles and the Stones throwing
American music back in America's face and race riots and Nixon,
a place which had better clothes, better hair, better music, better
dreams and better times. A world where the only revolutionary
movements that mattered were the spin of customised wheels on a
gleaming automobile and where ugly geeks got the Homecoming
Queen. A happy land ruined by the 1960s. The *real* America.

If you're detecting some sniffiness here about the subtext of

American Graffiti, then you're right. The film's fondness for simpler times and its massive success paved the way for George Lucas's *Star Wars* in 1977, and that film's reduction of the complexity of conflict into black and white paved the way for Reaganism. But none of this makes *American Graffiti* into a bad movie, or even a movie with sinister implications. Its nostalgia is sincere and it remains a model for how to make a great, commercial picture on a tiny budget. It is also a reminder that financial limitations can force directors to subvert conventions by making the best of what they can afford.

A perfect example is the constantly playing soundtrack of early rock nuggets, which cost so much to licence that Lucas could not afford to commission a score. The result works in the movie's favour as dramatic scenes are played out to the background noise of streets and woods, lending a reality which a traditional score would have hampered. This lends greater authority to the Lucas masterstroke of using the voice of legendary DJ Wolfman Jack as the major soundtrack element. His ribald croak pierces the night and the action, delighting with its pre-rap jive talk and speed of thought, making Lucas's argument – that things were just *hipper* in 1962 – for him. Many years before the notion of the superstar DJ, Lucas goes one better and makes the Wolfman a Superhero DJ, complete with secret identity.

So what happens is that four high school boys – played by the very 20-something Richard Dreyfuss, Ron Howard, Paul Le Mat and Charles Martin Smith – embark on one night of hometown fun in Modesto, California before Curt (Dreyfuss) and Steve (Howard) leave for college the next morning. The four end up separated and have adventures that define the term 'mild peril' (even a high-speed car crash barely breaks a fingernail!), each of which teaches them things about themselves and illuminates their destinies. We know what those destinies are because, in a much-parodied final scene, the futures of the four boys are written onscreen as a plane carrying one of the characters flies east. I'm being coy about the ending because, if you haven't seen *American Graffiti*, I don't want to spoil it. Not because the fates of the characters are that much of a surprise, but because the tragic futures of (most of) these fictional characters are most of the point of the movie, and lend a poignancy that the rest of the film lacks. It's a devilishly clever Lucas invention in a career defined by words rolling portentously across a big screen ... itself a throwback to the 'innocence' of the silent movie era.

Of course, this is the 1970s – the era of post-hippy Hollywood misogyny – so the female characters' futures are not revealed because they don't matter. This is all about the fate of the American male. Nevertheless, the best performance in the film isn't from future *Jaws*/*Close Encounters* star and method midget Dreyfuss, nor from a very wooden and hilariously gay-looking Harrison Ford as a cowboy-hatted drag racer. It's from 12-year-old (at the time) Mackenzie Phillips, who plays 14-year-old Carol in the best of the film's vignettes. Laconic tough John Milner (named after Lucas's macho moviemaker mate John Milius and played by the authentically greasy Paul Le Mat) gets accidentally lumbered with Carol as he cruises for car/girl action, and has to fend off her romantic advances while finding a way to get her home safely. What could have been a slimy scenario is handled with such good faith and honest confrontation with the reality of adolescent sexuality that it turns out to be the most modestly touching of the film's simple tales, and Phillips perfectly conveys the film's smart balance between innocence and knowingness. These characters are not squeaky clean virgins – rape, orgies and incest all get a mention in the film's fruity dialogue – but neither are they cruel, jaded or damaged. They're ordinary, with an ordinary amount of carnal knowledge for their age. And it's this that hit home with teen audiences of the 1970s, who weren't about to accept a Disneyfication of rock 'n' roll and teenage kicks at this late stage.

And as far as that rock 'n' roll goes ... Lucas begins his film with Bill Haley and ends it with the Beach Boys. Offscreen, in 1962, the Beatles are preparing for the release of their first single. Within a year, Beatlemania, the British Invasion and Dylan will have made the jive and rockabilly and matinee idol pop and doo wop of *American Graffiti* redundant overnight. *American Graffiti* doesn't explicitly reject 1960s rock. But it does make a compelling argument for the youthful hedonism and romantic drama of early rock, and the possibility that it meant more than 'serious' rock because it rang more true. The revolutions that various rock trends have sold us since in the end turned out to be exactly that ... rebellions for sale. *American Graffiti* makes you feel the sadness of that, without ever hitting you about the face over it. But most of all, it's just genuinely in love with the everlasting link between teenage wildlife and radio pop. Or, as Wolfman Jack roars it, in that crackling croak ... 'I can't believe it! Feelin' so good, 'cos you're 16!!!'

● ●

That'll Be the Day

1973

Starring: David Essex, Ringo Starr, Rosemary Leach, Robert Lindsay, James Booth, Rosalind Ayres, Billy Fury, Keith Moon
Dir.: Claude Whatham

★ ★ ★ ★

Plot: The rock 'n' roll *Alfie*.
Key line: 'I suppose it's because I'm a bit of a prick.'

This key example of 1970s Britrock movie realism begins with the drabness and poverty of the post-war years. But setting the context for Britain's need for sexy rock thrills isn't the major reason for these early scenes. James Booth plays yet another Britrock movie Bad Dad ... albeit a more lovable and human version than earlier models. Unable to settle down with being a domesticated shop-keeper after his wartime adventures, Mr MacLaine abandons the family home, therefore supplying the Freudian reason why future Rock God Jim MacLaine will be a total bastard to women, mates and small furry animals over the course of two films. *That'll Be the Day* and *Stardust* (see p. 141) may not be the best rock films ever made (although *Stardust* is a contender) but MacLaine's story is by some way the most convincing fictional rock character in the shady history of the rock and pop movie.

Screenwriter Ray Connolly's tale of what rock stars are made of has a psychological and social plausibility that rock movies generally can't be arsed with. And the two movies together are plotted like good character study novels, full of back story and a sense of tragic inevitability. The pair borrow liberally from the 'Angry Young Man' novels of Sillitoe, Storey and Barstow and the dark side of 1960s sexual liberation presented by Tony Richardson and Rita Tushingham's groundbreaking *A Taste of Honey* and Lewis Gilbert and Michael Caine's *Alfie*. Uniquely, Connolly and director Whatham weren't content simply to present us with the all-singing pretty boy and hope we just accepted that he was unpleasant, damned and willing to be both the giver and recipient of abuse. They want us to know why Jim McClaine is a fully rounded cunt; a representative of the crucial mix of charisma, talent, sex appeal, narcissism, selfishness, low cunning and greedy ambition that makes a star so compelling and in need of our love. As a generation more obsessed with celebrity than any before us, we should have made these films far more famous, acclaimed and influential than they are. They're amongst the best and most important British films ever made, and simply not enough people have seen them to know.

And a word about our star. David Essex may not be in the Angela Bassett/Laurence Fishburne class as an actor (see *Tina: What's Love Got to Do with It*, p.309). But he is a magnificent Jim MacLaine . . . a blank, beautiful canvas on which to project our fantasies about rock stars, with a slow cockney voice that sounds like someone who believes that everyone, except for himself, is beneath his contempt. His arrogance and disdain oozes from the screen but remains seductive in itself, as it has to. Every time the guy catches sight of his next sexual conquest, even when he's playing a virgin boy, flirting shyly in his school uniform, his doe eyes become alternately soft and vulnerable and hungry and hateful, like a vampire sniffing blood. You know no woman would resist, even as she immediately knew that it would be the death of her.

Critics reckoned that he was outshone by Starr in this film and

Adam Faith in the sequel, but their characters *were* characters. Essex is playing a cipher who, because of the detail of the story, has to display more humanity than Jagger in *Performance* (see p. 89) or Jones in *Privilege* (see p. 64) or Daltrey in *Tommy* (see p. 164), while keeping that 1970s rock movie sense of being an alien. He pulls this off brilliantly in his first film roles, and deserved a better subsequent screen career than the likes of *Silver Dream Racer* and that awful 1980s TV rom-com about the Gypsy gave him. Both the MacLaine movies and his early records suggest that Essex was a major talent wasted because the music and screen businesses just thought he was pretty and nothing else. Sometimes good looks can be a curse for an artist ... as Elvis and Marilyn could have told you.

But unlike *Stardust*, *That'll Be the Day* also has to convincingly re-create a period ... the British 1950s, where our parents gave birth to the modern world in coffee bars, while drinking Coke, listening to jazz and early rock on the jukebox, and trying to get all the sex that they were convinced that their parents never got. The film has that sepia tone that makes the mundane look like art and history, and the clothes and hair and interior design is immaculately conceived. In the chirpy cockney accents that the young cast – which includes the likes of Robert Lindsay, Karl Howman and rock film mascot Johnny Shannon – adopt, there's a nod to the early 1960s pop musicals of Cliff Richard, Adam Faith and Billy Fury, a knowledge that these light works are what we think we know of the period, and a desire to subvert them completely. It's an extraordinary moment, then, when Fury appears essentially playing himself as a holiday camp singer called Stormy Tempest, still looking as dashing and strange as he did in the early 1960s. Even better that he's actually a knowingly dodgy self-parody, and that when we look behind the drumkit there's a greased-back Keith Moon rolling his eyes. *That'll Be the Day* is in love with the history of British rock, but from a mocking perspective, portraying it as rooted in the small-town, seedy and delusional. As in *Slade in Flame* (see p. 147) there's no rose-tinted nostalgia or A-list glamour here. (There *is* an annoying false note, though, when Fury and band perform the defiantly 1970s Who song 'Long Live Rock' at, of all things, a jive competition. No wonder the dancing's shite . . . 'Long Live Rock' is about as jive-friendly as, well, The Who.)

The major subject of the first film isn't rock 'n' roll, though . . . it's the bravado and lies of insecure young men. Jim and Ringo Starr's Mike are fakes, constantly lying about their sexual prowess, success and experience. Their first agenda, always, is how they appear to other young men, which makes them both typical boys and perfect to reflect the secret truth of rock 'n' roll's all-conquering success. Unreconstructed rock stars may love to dwell on female groupies and wink broadly at us. But the vast majority of their worshippers are always young men. They're bragging to impress other boys. This latent homosexual subtext fuelled rock's rise, and is expertly written and portrayed in the relationship between Jim and Mike, who compete for women in order to seduce and impress each other. Nope . . . they're not gay, they don't shag. But the shared obsession with each other's sex lives – and each other's cocks and bums – is one step from jerking each other off. The homely Mike is doomed to lose the battle of course, and there's a masochistic edge to his character that suggests he's more in love with Jim than any woman in the movie. This is key 1970s buddy-buddy movie stuff . . . where the anti-feminist backlash inspired a host of Butch and Sundance clones, gazing longingly into each other's eyes and dreaming of a world where women would just fuck, cook and leave the guys to their pre-*Brokeback* bonding rituals without trying to castrate them with all those civilised responsibilities and babies and cries for equality.

The pair end up shacked up together at a holiday camp because Jim ran away from his exams. 'Please sir . . . can I leave the womb?', he sneers, memorably. Like Dad, Jim sees his mother as nothing more than the smothering symbol of boredom, conformity, routine and entrapment. Once he's settled at the seaside, his next humiliation at the hands of womankind is taking two birds to the fair and being forced to pay for everything while they pretty much ignore him. When he runs out of cash, they shrug and scoot. We get the message loud and clear . . . every bit of rough treatment Jim's going to hand out to women ... well, they asked for it. Rosemary Leach, incidentally, is wonderful as Mum, taking her rejection by men she loves with that guilt-inducing blend of stiff and quivering upper lip, suffering in near-silence, forcing you to see that this is the very reason why feminism was on its way.

The most vile sexism mainly comes from the perpetually perving gob of Ringo's Mike. Casting the ex-Beatle as the itinerant Scouse Ted was a masterstroke, as Starr's relish at being able to relive his Ted roots is palpable. He does a selfless job of travelling from leering big brother figure – even a game of Crazy Golf is nothing more than an excuse to bang on about putting things into holes and gripping the end with both hands – to humiliated fraud, and, again, it's strange that it wasn't the beginning of a serious career for Starr as a likeable comic actor.

One of the key factors in the success of *That'll Be the Day* was its revelation of the unlikely pleasures of working the dodgems at a funfair. As Jim doesn't actually join a rock 'n' roll band until *Stardust*, escaping home and higher education to work at a fair serves as the symbol of freedom, independence and rebellion. Basically ... you roam from town to town, you wear cool clothes, you do cooler balancing things on the rides, you rip off both punters and boss, you get laid. All this prefaces what was, when I first saw the movie as a ten-year-old, the most shocking moment, when MacLaine seduces the boss's middle-aged wife. It wasn't just the age difference. It was that she's no Kim Basinger version of a MILF. She's an ordinary, frumpy middle-aged woman who looked like one of your mum's friends. Really, Whatham and Connolly left no secret adolescent male fantasy unexplored.

This probably says a great deal about the onscreen sexual politics of the time. Because, by the time Jim has had his mature oats (while his bestest friend Ringo is being hospitalised by a gang of Teds!), he's already date-raped a schoolgirl. There are few instances where two full-length films have been devoted to telling the story of such a despicable human being as Jim MacLaine, and gained a popular audience. We were bleak and grim in the 1970s, and all the better for it.

But this wouldn't be a British kitchen-sink movie without its share of class war. And, in time-honoured Brit tradition, it is status anxiety that provides its most memorable scene. Jim's old school friend Terry (Lindsay) comes to visit him at the fair. Terry is now a proper, early 1960s student – duffle coat, Lenin beard, CND badge and a Master's in well-read beatnikisms. He fixes Jim up with a double-date at the college dance – a draughty hall full of young poshoes 'stomping' to trad jazz. After the requisite ironic comment on the future of music – 'Oh come on, admit it – rock was just a craze!' – the night goes from bad to worse, as Jim's attempts to impress the college girls with truths about the fair and lies about writing a novel are met with silent embarrassment and downright loathing. A humiliated Jim makes a bolt for it, to the obvious pleasure of Terry, who has finally trumped his smarter, prettier, more confident schoolmate in the sex and class stakes.

Admittedly, in the real world, although middle-class girls might not see pretty rough boys as marriage material, they don't generally have a problem with the sexual attraction bit. But the scene is deliciously uncomfortable and is pivotal to the point of the two movies. Jim is too lazy and restless for academia and a white-collar career, but too bright and ambitious to settle for casual labour and being sneered at by the petit bourgeois – not to mention being rejected by girls who represent sophistication and upward mobility. After raping the schoolgirl at the fair, Ringo's Mike remarks that Jim should 'pick on someone yer own size'. When Jim does he gets his dick chopped off.

So what else can a po' boy do, except sing in a rock and roll band?

The scenes where a chastened Jim returns home, rebonds with mum, exchanges his motorbike for a van to help with the shop, and shyly romances childhood friend Jeanette all appear to be recommending family, conformity and sexual abstinence as the answer. But this is, literally, only half the story. The ending is only a beginning, but is still far too good to give away here, as it reaffirms MacLaine's credentials as working-class stud-avenger and prize bastard, and wittily explains why 1950s rock 'n' roll became redundant in the face of beat modernism, before leading to one of the most romantic and exciting final shots in British film history. Suffice to say, in the eternal struggle between a girl and a guitar, there can only be one winner. And Bad Dad gets the blame and the credit.

That'll Be the Day is the best movie made about why young men want to be rock stars. If it says nothing useful for or about women, then that's only right and accurate. Rock said nothing useful for or about women until punk forced it to.

• •

Stardust

1974

Starring: David Essex, Adam Faith, Larry Hagman, Ines Des Longchamps, Paul Nicholas
Dir.: Michael Apted

★ ★ ★ ★ ★

Plot: The rise and inevitable fall of the ultimate working-class zero.
Key line: 'You and I deserve each other.'

To recap: In 1973's *That'll Be the Day* (see p. 135), we saw pretty, poisonous late-1950s Londoner Jim MacLaine (Essex) run away to work at the fair, before running back to the bosom of family and marriage. All this was played out against the backdrop of the rise of rock 'n' roll amongst working-class youth, and its slow change towards the R&B-based beat group. *Stardust* begins with Jim right back at the fair, having inherited his father's wanderlust and hatred of domesticity. For the next 106 minutes, we're going to be treated to the most melodramatic rise and fall of a rock star in movie history, one that has as much in common with Caligula and Faust as it does with *Jailhouse Rock* (see p. 20). Ever wondered just how extreme the vertiginous highs and morbid lows of superstardom might be? Ever wondered whether you'd laugh, cry or die if you experienced them? Then *Stardust* is the film of your wildest dreams and nightmares.

Stardust is shot in the same gritty *vérité* style as its predecessor, showcasing a scruffy, grey, dank England at its most ugly-beautiful. We see footage of the Kennedy assassination so know this is 1963, the most momentous year of modern times ... JFK murdered. The Beatles at Number One. The first Rolling Stones album. A notoriously harsh and deadly British winter. *And* I was born. Our hero meets with Mike Medari (Faith) at the fair. They don't exactly appear to be friends. Jim asks Mike to be his band's road manager. A love story from Hell is born.

Johnny (Paul Nicholas) is lead singer/guitarist of the Stray Cats, while Jim plays bass and sings a bit. They wear leather jackets and are playing a tough version of a Buddy Holly song in a club that looks like a cavern, so it's all very early Beatles.

At these early shows, we're shown how, in early 1960s England, the previously separate tribes have started to merge, in preparation for the Golden pop-rock Era that would unify most of our youth culture. Beatniks, Teds and folky bohos are all in the same club, lines between hairstyles and threads have blurred; there's even a black girl. Apted is great at this stuff, showing the revolt into style of 1960s youth without telling, revelling in the details of hair-length and trouser-width.

The band is interesting too. As well as Essex and Nicholas, the Stray Cats comprise Karl Howman, pub-rocker Dave Edmunds (his real-life musical partner and future Elvis Costello producer Nick Lowe has a cameo playing bass for a girl-group), and the legend that was Keith Moon. There's a great little moment when the band interrupt their covers set to play a self-penned song, provoking bored shrugs and a bolt from the dancefloor from the punters. A reminder that, until the Beatles changed everything, British bands made their living covering hip American songs. British rock was considered uncool. The Kids worshipped America.

From there, *Stardust* is a film in three acts. Part One is the rise of the band in kitchen-sink style – Mike's devious and ruthless machinations, dumped band members, investment from launderette magnates, posh music biz vampires, an enthusiastic recreation of the 1960s *NME* pollwinners' concerts at Wembley, boys playing silly buggers and buggering about with silly birds.

Humour is provided by a neat running joke . . . every time Mike puts his arm round a shoulder and asks, 'Fancy a drink?', the owner of said shoulder disappears, from the band, the film, the world. Jim acquires a chic French girlfriend called Danielle (Des Longchamps), the kind of sophisticated and educated arm-candy that humiliated him in the first film. She's a surrogate Yoko Ono and the only woman in Jim's story who has his number: 'For a working-class hero, you can be very bourgeois', she sneers when he tries to bully her.

Part Two is Power Corrupts, as MacLaine becomes huge, breaks America, unleashes his already elephantine ego, gets dumped by the Stray Cats, is alienated from his roots and becomes an insane solo rock messiah on drugs. Two years before punk hit, the film satirises rock with classical pretensions as both a ludicrous sonic and visual disaster and a betrayal of the relevance and working-class energy of three-minute, three-chord rock 'n' roll. Prophetic stuff. The irony in this relentlessly well-written script is that the quasi-classical suite which tips Jim over the edge, mentally and artistically, is an operatic 'deification of woman' inspired by his arty girlfriend and dead mother. It's deliberately and magnificently awful, the one lie that this serial liar and loather of women can't pull off. Except that the sucker fans fall for it completely. Ouch and double ouch.

And part three . . . well, we'll come back to that. It's mental.

But *Stardust* is really all about the psycho-sexual love/hate relationship between Jim and Mike. Faith's Mike is a more rounded (and better acted) Cockney version of Ringo Starr's Mike from the first movie . . . the sidekick who becomes wife and mother to the monster that is MacLaine. As Jim is a misogynist doomed to reject commitment to women, but who is also far too weak and needy to be independent, he needs a man both to look after him and be the willing victim of his penchant for humiliating those close to him. The gay subtext is made explicit by Danielle, who eventually comes right out and accuses Mike of being in love with Jim, becoming the inevitable loser in the bizarre love triangle when Mike does for Jim the one thing she can't … procures him women. Danielle's heartbroken departure essentially ends any chance of redemption for MacLaine or Mike.

The rules of this twisted queer relationship are set early in the movie when Mike sets up a booty call with two members of a girl-group, only to find that Jim has seduced both of them and locked the hotel-room door. Mike can't resist peeking through the keyhole to see his stud friend in action. Jim meets his gaze – and ours – and leers triumphantly. He's performing for the benefit of Mike and we male viewers, and our approval is far more important than that of the brainless, giggling girls. Apted makes the film's view of sex as shots in an unending gender war explicit by contrasting Jim's threesome (conducted under a fur blanket with a wolf's head!) with the boxing commentary Mike ends up listening to alone in his room: 'A left and then a right … they're coming from every angle!' As Jim cums and the insatiable sluts carry on without him, Mike leers with approval … for the knockout in the fight, apparently. But the film leaves you in no doubt about what winning means to men.

Mike doesn't just accept his place as hand-maiden to the Master Cocksman … he's happy to masochistically bathe in his studly aura. When Danielle later catches Jim in a similar act, we see Mike, sitting fully clothed on the sofa, treated, this time, to a ringside seat for Jim's knockout performance. He's got rid of his love rival (without even having to buy her a drink) and he would rather watch the love of his life fuck than do it himself. Jim and Mike are one of the most dysfunctional couples you'll ever see in a superficially mainstream film.

Nevertheless, the presence of Danielle and the fact that her departure signals Jim's descent into the abyss turns everything we've seen previously in both films on its head; homosexuality – latent or otherwise – suddenly becomes the unnatural choice that corrupts the healthy male. Screenwriter Ray Connolly's attitude to sexual politics seems to be … love men only, but fuck women only.

That'll Be the Day and *Stardust* are prime examples of misogynist 1970s film-making in the wake of the success of male-bonding movies like *Easy Rider* (see p. 80), *Butch Cassidy and the Sundance Kid* and *The Godfather*. In a conscious backlash against the increasing power of feminism, movies sidelined women completely, using them only as victims, whores or mothers. The love interest in these films was between the leading men, whose intense bonding and fully rounded characters suggested that men would be happier if they dispensed with women completely except as breeders and carers. Women were the evil tamers of the natural wild spirit of we male hunters and gatherers, seeking only to castrate us with responsibilities and the hellish boredom of domestic civilisation. For the best account of this period in film-making, check out Molly Haskell's extraordinary 1974 book *From Reverence to Rape* (Penguin). If you think the title's over-doing it a bit, peruse the evidence and have your mind changed.

But as you've no doubt noted, *Easy Rider*, *Butch Cassidy* . . . and *The Godfather* were great movies. Sometimes great art is fuelled by bad faith. And so it goes with the Jim MacLaine films. To a large extent, that was what the excellent British 2005–7 *Life On Mars* TV show was getting at . . . that our politically correct culture has thrown the baby out with the bathwater and opted for a bland, anodyne culture rather than say anything that might potentially offend anyone at all, ever. *That'll Be the Day* and *Stardust* will tell future generations about the kind of fear and loathing women and gays were up against in the 1970s. *Mamma Mia!* will tell future generations that noughties women have a bizarre fetish for Colin Firth and holiday karaoke. A culture that hides what it feels about crucial issues is an unhealthy one. Repression eventually makes evil fantasies into realities.

Anyhoo . . . back to this little pop film that I like. There are bit parts for Faith's early 1960s pop rival Marty Wilde, future *Rock Follies* star Charlotte Cornwell, *Blue Peter* presenter Peter Duncan, US 1950s teen idol Ed Burns who also pops up later in *Grease* (see p. 178), and Larry Hagman of *Dallas* fame, getting in some serious training for being J.R. Ewing by playing Jim's cold-eyed corporate manager and all-round greedy bastard.

The weakest thing about the film is the music, which, with the more than notable exception of the spooked, dubwise psychedelic soul of Essex's self-penned closing theme, is vapid and unconvincing throughout. In truth, Jim MacLaine wouldn't have got anywhere making this shite. The film also appears to shift the Apollo moon landings back to 1966, which is just plain weird.

But not as weird as the third act. At one point, Mike tells Danielle that his successful plan to jettison the Stray Cats was 'not about the money', and he ain't bullshitting. It was about buying everyone that loved Jim a drink until he finally got what he really wanted – Jim MacLaine, all to himself. Having performed his cod-operatic travesty to a global TV audience of 300 million people via satellite, the exhausted Jim quits. He and Mike buy a crumbling castle in rural Spain. Jim replaces the hangers-on of the biz with a village full of peasants, dependent on him for their economic survival. This potential rural idyll is corrupted into a prison by the corruption of Mike and Jim's souls, until it becomes a Hell worthy of pulp thriller king Jim Thompson's El Rey from his novel *The Getaway*. While Mike at least attempts to integrate, playing football in the courtyard with the natives and buying a dog, Jim becomes a ghost, taking baths in his white clothes and tormenting himself with films of the old days with the Stray Cats.

The odd couple box, viciously, for the amusement of the locals. Jim responds to defeat by poisoning Mike's dog with acid so that she miscarries her puppies. Years pass. Hagman's Porter Lee Austin convinces the broken MacLaine to do a TV interview, a stunning set-piece which Essex and Apted should have won awards for. And . . . I can't give away the ending. Except to say that its final few lines of dialogue amount to the most brutal and cynical undercutting of a tragedy that I've ever seen in a movie.

Stardust is one of a fair few classic British movies in this book which have been almost written out of the pantheon. Too tasteless and hysterical, perhaps, and lacking the various anointed luvvies that the British film industry dotes upon. It's undoubtedly a film of its time, evidence of the misery and anger that had descended upon Britain in the 1970s. But *Stardust* is a masterpiece nonetheless and one that exemplifies just how much tougher – scratch that: better – Britpop films were than American rock movies.

Bully for us. How much sexier would that statement be if it wasn't quite so past tense?

• •

Slade in Flame

1974
Starring: Slade, Alan Lake, Tom Conti, Johnny Shannon
Dir.: Richard Loncraine

★ ★ ★ ★ ★

Plot: The dark underbelly of the traditional rock 'n' roll rags-to-riches fairy-tale.
Key line: 'You make a few records – that's all right. The rest is just bleedin' gangsters in dinner jackets.'

I went to see this movie the week it came out. I was 11, and Slade were my favourite group. The first group I ever saw live, in fact, at the Rainbow in Finsbury Park, London, in 1972 (Thin Lizzy and Suzi Quatro supporting, can you believe? Gawd bless you, Mum!). I wasn't alone – Slade had an unlikely bigger-than-the-Beatles moment between 1971 and 1974, at least, they did in Britain. Nowadays, almost every Number One single in the UK goes straight in at the top and quickly tumbles. Back in the early 1970s, when the singles market was huge and records weren't played on radio months before their release, even the biggest groups had to be content with entering low and hopefully climbing. Slade, however, had three successive singles go straight in at Number One, a feat that no-one came close to emulating until The Jam, The Police and Duran Duran managed it a few times between them in the 1980s.

So ... I do have distant, sketchy memories of going to see *Slade in Flame* with my mum. But it isn't the excitement or anticipation of seeing my favourite band onscreen that I recall. All I remember is sitting, wide-eyed and open-mouthed, at the film's abrupt, depressing ending. I just remember feeling ... *upset*. Again, I suspect I wasn't alone. Slade's fans were mainly little boys, mainly my age. And chart positions don't lie. Slade never got close to a Number One in singles or albums after this film's release. By March 1977 they were releasing an album called *Whatever Happened to Slade?* It bombed, too. *Slade in Flame* killed Slade's career.

On the DVD's illuminating making-of featurette, Slade's sand-paper-tonsilled screecher Noddy Holder remarks that *Flame* 'killed the myth ... of the jolly, jolly band' that Slade were seen as. But this deliberately gritty, grubby tale of a 1967 Midlands rock band's rise to fame and swan-dive into disillusion did more than that. To a young pop fan who watched it, it killed the myth of rock stardom. It contended that the movers and shakers of the music business were either thugs or posh conmen; that fame was specious and the rock 'n' roll lifestyle a bore; that the members of bands loathed each other; that they were so thick and guileless that they had no control over their own lives; that every great thing about rock 'n' roll – cars, girls, even playing your songs to adoring fans – was meaningless. What's more, it didn't even bother to suggest what else a poor boy could do that would have any more meaning. There is some crude and silly humour in *Slade in Flame*, but the odd guffaw still doesn't shed any light upon the world it presents. This rock world is dour, smelly, violent, cold ... a dead end. Guitarist Dave Hill, speaking in the featurette, still believes that they should have made a happy-go-lucky, *A Hard Day's Night*-style larking-about-with-songs movie. From the perspective of a sensible career move, the facts speak for themselves. But from the art-for-art's-sake perspective, I'm glad he was out-voted. Because *Slade in Flame* is a big contender for Best Rock Movie Of All Time, as well as being a prime example of British *cinéma vérité*, pitched somewhere between the Angry Young Man melodramas of *This Sporting Life* and *Saturday Night, Sunday Morning* and the docudrama modernism of Alan Clarke, Mike Leigh and Ken Loach. Really. *Slade in Flame* is almost as good as *Kes*.

Like all great British realist films, *Slade in Flame* is primarily about class war. After forming Flame from the ashes of two amusingly dire club bands, Stoker (Holder), Paul (Jim Lea), Barry (Hill) and Charlie (Don Powell) get spotted by an advertising agency run by upper-class money-grubber Seymour (Tom Conti, in only his second film). They take Flame to fame by selling them like supermarket product. But each publicity stunt and marketing wheeze sucks a little more soul out of the four already cynical lads. Meanwhile, their first agent, a small-time gangster called Harding (Johnny Shannon), and loser pub singer Jack Daniels (the superb Alan Lake), crawl out of the woodwork of Flame's past, wanting more than their 10 per cent. Mayhem ensues, and Flame's career staggers to an inevitable, anti-climactic finish.

The story was built out of real-life rock stories told to director Loncraine and screenwriter Andrew Birkin by Slade and their manager Chas Chandler as the pair accompanied the band on a few weeks of an American tour. Some of those stories are about Slade and some aren't. You suspect gangster music agent Harding has some loose basis in notorious manager/bully boys Peter Grant (Led Zeppelin) and Don Arden (Sharon Osbourne's dad), whose biggest successes came from Midlands-based bands. But those guys achieved A-list money and reputation. Harding appears to have won his war with upper-class money by smashing feet with iron bars and terrifying Seymour's family. But the geezers don't beat the toffs in movies like this, no matter how hard they are. By the time Harding gets control, Seymour's company have sucked Flame dry. His triumph lasts for about ten seconds of screen-time before he's left staring, gobsmacked and facing a life of fiddling fruit machines and creaming off the local bingo. His stunned expression neatly reflects that of the viewer, as the film veers away from the expected *grand guignol* finale of drug overdoses, spectacular violence or, at the very least, a big old fist-fight about the fact that Stoker has nicked Barry's bird, and just shrugs, smiles a bitter smile and steps into The Void.

Loncraine, who went on to make *The Missionary*, *Brimstone and Treacle* and *Wimbledon*, admits that he didn't really know what he was doing in what was his first feature. But his mistakes end up doing *Flame* a favour. We know the film is initially set in 1967 because 'New York Mining Disaster 1941' by the Bee Gees comes on a transistor radio. But other than that, the events depicted could take place over five weeks or five years ... there are no clues as to time-frame anywhere. We also assume that Flame are from Wolverhampton for no other reason than Slade themselves are from Wolverhampton. But that doesn't explain why the man from Seymour's terribly London ad agency finds himself watching Slade play in their local working men's club, or why the local music agent is a toy town Reggie Kray with requisite Cockney goons, or why everyone seems to walk directly from dank Midlands slum to shiny West End money. This bizarre dislocation of time and place undercuts some of *Flame*'s ultra-realism and makes it feel like someone's bad dream. It's this surreal undertone that haunts and adds strangeness to Loncraine's superb realisation of the drabness of 1960s Britain. In this film, Swinging London, Haight-Ashbury and the white heat of youth counter-culture are non-existent – which they weren't in the 1960s I grew up in. This is why rock became so huge, so loved, *so needed*. It was the only splash of colour, sex, rebellion and exotica in a land of belching chimneys and greasy hair, police cells and broken toes, dark satanic foundries and seedy dance halls, all depicted perfectly here as Loncraine captures an England that reminds us that things really weren't better in the good old days.

The realities of the cast shadow the movie too. Loncraine's smartest move was making everyone underplay every scene, so that Slade weren't relentlessly embarrassed by their lack of acting chops. To this end, he hired a cast who only had to play themselves. Conti is posh and aloof, and sickly in his boyish inscrutability, and on his way up, to Oscar nominations and stardom. Johnny Shannon is a Cockney geezer who fell into acting after *Performance* (see p. 89) and managed to convince most of Slade's cast that he really had been an East End gangster.

Beating pop to a pulp – appropriately lurid publicity poster for *Beat Girl* (p.35)

Images © The Kobal Collection. Picture captions by Linsay McCulloch and Garry Mulholland

KING CREOLE

Elvis Presley

Elvis as jazz modernist – rare publicity poster for *King Creole* (p.25)

← Desperate for black music to cross over, the young Elvis takes dat Al Jolson shit to tha next level in *Jailhouse Rock* (p.20)

↑ The greatest trousers in rock 'n' roll – sweet Gene Vincent makes sure *The Girl Can't Help It* (p.13)

← Attached to a drip – Laurence Harvey takes issue with Cliff's shorts in *Expresso Bongo* (p.27)

'I know. Great poet. But his stone-cladding leaves a lot to be desired.' Bob warns The Kids not to hire Allen Ginsberg as a builder in *Don't Look Back* (p.61)

When in Southern California visit Universal City Studios

THE RAW, SHOCKING MOVIE OF A POP SINGER WHO MAKES IT BIG!

UNIVERSAL PRESENTS the JOHN HEYMAN / PETER WATKINS PRODUCTION

PRIVILEGE
TECHNICOLOR®

Co-starring
PAUL JONES · JEAN SHRIMPTON
with
WILLIAM JOB · MARK LONDON · JEREMY CHILD · MAX BACON
Screenplay by NORMAN BOGNER · From an original story by JOHNNY SPEIGHT · Directed by PETER WATKINS · Associate Producer TIMOTHY BURRILL
Produced by JOHN HEYMAN · A WORLDFILM SERVICES LTD. / MEMORIAL ENTERPRISES LTD. PRODUCTION · A UNIVERSAL RELEASE

How many people saw this film, Paul?
Publicity poster for the neglected *Privilege* (p.64)

⬇ The cancer stage of capitalism – Keith Richards remains unmoved by the revolution of the black proletariat in Godard's *Sympathy for the Devil* (p.74)

⬇⬇ Hippy dream becomes biker nightmare – Hell's Angels introduce Stones fans to reality in *Gimme Shelter* (p.104)

↓ Phil Spector fluffs his lines in *Easy Rider* (p.80)

↓↓ A true revolution? The hippy dream of 'good' violence in *Woodstock* (p.97)

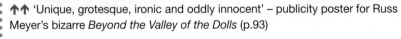

↑↑ 'Unique, grotesque, ironic and oddly innocent' – publicity poster for Russ Meyer's bizarre *Beyond the Valley of the Dolls* (p.93)

↑ 'Delicious, pointless sex pixieness' – Marc Bolan clowns around with Ringo an Elton in *Born to Boogie* (p.124)

The extraordinary Lake – whose life-story would make a damn fine movie – was a jailbird drunk and failed singer who snatched disaster from the jaws of triumph by marrying Britain's greatest sex symbol Diana Dors, getting slung in jail after a pub brawl and finally committing suicide in 1984. It's Lake's Daniels that gets his feet broken by Flame's thugs, allowing Loncraine to refrain from showing the actual blow with an utterly realistic depiction of (literally) naked fear and agony that still makes my feet jerk involuntarily, even after absorbing 35 years of graphic movie gore and spectacular onscreen blood-letting.

By forcing his experienced actors just to be themselves, Loncraine allows Slade to do the same and ensures their performances come out fine. Powell – who had only recently recovered from a car accident which had affected his short-term memory and made learning his lines almost impossible – is funny and lovable; Lea and Holder play their memorable two-hander scenes in a lift and a pigeon coop with modest aplomb; and Hill . . . well, they don't give him much to do anyway.

I really could go on and on about *Slade in Flame*, but I'm going to finish by contradicting myself a little. I used the word 'depressing' above and that's never a good way to urge people to sample something you love. *Slade in Flame* isn't depressing because it's exhilarating to see someone put the truth about the music biz onscreen and hope the viewer has the wherewithal to take it straight. As a singer and music journalist I can honestly say that I've never been exposed to any gangster violence. But I have been in bands who only hired the drummer because he had his own kit, and only let someone be manager because they had a van, and who split up because we were all too macho to talk about our feelings and just got bored with the mundanity of it all. And I've been at many a music biz soirée where everyone there is a wannabe or a hanger-on or a corporate hack who can barely be arsed to mask their loathing of their new hit band, because, when it comes down to it, they are so in control of these desperate puppets that they don't even have to fake enthusiasm. *Slade in Flame* is funny because it's true, and a great film because the story could be about any bunch of working-class blokes in any get-rich-quick profession, and comes from a time way before British film-makers became beguiled by the lie of 'the classless society' and banned the working class from public scrutiny, lest we rise up in our hoodies with our chav glottal stops and junk-food breath and insist we still exist, and bring down the fucking banal tone of what now passes for a British film industry.

And while I'm in self-contradiction mode, I'm not sure *Slade in Flame* did kill Slade's career. That might have been Slade, actually. Because Slade's 1974 tunes sound fine while you're watching the movie, but are pretty lousy when you just listen to the CD. I loved 'Cum on Feel the Noize' and 'Merry Xmas Everybody' but I still reckon that *Slade in Flame* is their best shot. Hill may not get it, but Holder and Lea, who've long moved on from Slade, do understand that they left something dangerous and brave and really quite wonderful to posterity. Not bad for, as drummer Powell refers to Slade on the DVD featurette, 'four scumbags from Wolverhampton'.

●●●●●●●●●●●●●●●●●●●●●●●●●●●●●●●●

Phantom of The Paradise

1974
Starring: William Finley, Paul Williams, Jessica Harper
Dir.: Brian De Palma

★ ★ ★

Plot: The *Rocky Horror* version of *The Phantom of the Opera*.
Key line: 'Nobody cares what anything's about.'

In a parallel universe that could have only existed in the 1970s, a boy-man called Swan (Paul Williams) runs the entire music industry, having single-handedly 'brought the blues to Britain . . . Liverpool to America . . . folk and rock together.' His big band is now a lame high-concept 1950s revival act called the Juicy Fruits, but his big project is the building of a Xanadu-like 'rock palace' called The Paradise. When nerdy-but-angry singer-songwriter Winslow Leach (Finley) crashes a Juicy Fruits show, Swan decides that Leach's music would be perfect to open The Paradise. Trouble is, he wants the song not the singer. Swan's henchman Philbin nicks Leach's song-suite about Faust and frames the gangly sap for slinging smack. Leach breaks out of prison to get his just desserts, but only ends up with his face disfigured by a record-pressing machine. He is now a hideous monster, destined to haunt The Paradise, seeking revenge. This all happens in the first 23 minutes.

Another prime example of violent 1960s/1970s *grand guignol* rock movie madness to join *Privilege* (see p. 64), *Stardust* (see p. 141), *Beyond the Valley of the Dolls* (see p. 93), *Tommy* (see p. 164) and *Jubilee* (see p. 199), this early musical by Alfred Hitchcock *pasticheur* Brian De Palma begins at a deafening hysterical pitch and then turns it up all the way to 11. Shot in lurid colours and over-acted with Olympian gusto, it uses its comic opera scenario to give the rock industry – and rock music itself – a solid kicking. This is a place where female singers audition by being gang-banged and where the Big Boss looks like a cross between a midget, a toad and Elton John. Paul Williams was a big songwriter in the 1970s – he even guested on a *Muppet Show*! – and was presumably chosen for his unfortunate hideousness, seeing as he's a terrible actor. The music is resolutely appalling, whether pastiching glam, singer-songwriter or 1950s rock – but it's definitely meant to be. And there is a wonderful prediction of our auto-tuned pop future, as Swan manages to transform the guttural rasp of the Phantom (sounds a bit like The Residents, actually) into a great voice using nothing but production tricks.

Obviously, as the Faust legend is involved, it's all about the downsides of various characters selling their souls to various devils. But it's also about Winslow/the Phantom's top superhero costume, complete with bird-like metal mask and black leather jumpsuit. The movie never takes itself remotely seriously, and

De Palma, as he would continue to do throughout the next 30-odd years, devotes too much of his energies to making things look striking to really care about any form of emotion ... even laughter. Although there is a very funny pastiche of the shower scene from *Psycho* involving an idiot glam-rock star called Beef and a toilet plunger.

But make no mistake – *Phantom of The Paradise* is as much a film about post-1960s disillusion as *Slade in Flame* (see p. 147) or *Quadrophenia* (see p. 220). There's an anger at and contempt for rock, pop, showbiz and art that gives what could be an awful movie a kind of furious zeal. It's a world where nothing matters except money, where artists will suffer any indignity for fame, and where The Kids lap up anything they're given: there's something actually quite *X Factor* about it all. Except that Simon Cowell is much scarier than Swan.

The film ends up being a madly over-the-top metaphor for the artist's battle for creative control of his art, and for the horror of how low even the sweetest wannabe star will go for the validation of the masses. But it's also charmingly silly, and would have been even better if De Palma hadn't cast a bunch of drab and talentless actors as the leads. As it is, *Phantom of The Paradise* is still a strong choice for that mondo gonzo bad taste rock movie party you've always wanted to throw.

• •

The Rocky Horror Picture Show

1975

Starring: Tim Curry, Susan Sarandon, Barry Bostwick, Richard O'Brien, Charles Gray, Jonathan Adams, Patricia Quinn
Dir.: Jim Sharman

★ ★ ★

Plot: The world's favourite cross-dressing sci-fi monster rock movie.
Key line: 'I wanna be dirty!' (from 'Touch-a Touch-a Touch-a Touch Me')

The Rocky Horror Picture Show is the film version of Richard O'Brien's stage musical *The Rocky Horror Show,* which opened in London in June 1973. Despite lukewarm reviews and commercial failure on release, it has gone on to be the film world's biggest cult phenomenon, grossing $140 million from an original budget of $1.2 million. It became the longest-running theatrical release in film history after the Waverly Theater in New York began showing it as a weekly midnight movie in 1976. Fans would turn up dressed as characters from the film and join in with dialogue, songs and dance routines. This interactive relationship with *Rocky Horror* was repeated in cities all over the world, and, despite many releases on video and DVD, the film is still on theatrical release 36 years after it opened.

The story is related by Charles Gray's criminologist/narrator, reminding us of the perennial joys of hearing dumb rock 'n' roll lyrics recited in plummy English tones. It concerns a white-bread engaged couple Brad and Janet finding themselves in a spooky castle where a sexually predatory mad scientist transsexual alien called Dr Frank N. Furter is leading a group of his fellow Transylvanians (*Trans*ylvanians. *Trans*sexuals. See?) in a round-the-clock sex orgy while also making a blonde muscle-boy monster called Rocky to be his personal sex monkey. People occasionally burst into song, and the soundtrack has become massively popular in its own right, even spawning a proper hit in dappy dance number 'The Timewarp'. But the film largely hinges on the overwhelming performance of English actor Tim Curry as Frank. It's all in the mouth; the ridiculous feminine lips, the unstoppable smirk, and the brilliant accent, charged with a delicious exaggeration of posh, husky sexual perversion.

So, I'll take a stab at analysing the extraordinary cult appeal of *TRHPS*. If you're actually a Frank N. Furter, you're far too busy actually having disgusting sex to act out a fantasy of it in public. But if, in the end, you are Brad or Janet, you are one of the vast majority of us who long to explore your every decadent fantasy, but don't, because that would involve a genuine removal from the mainstream of society, which is too frightening to contemplate. So you go see this movie, which gives you permission to dress up and misbehave, amongst other Brad and Janets who are on your side. For 95 minutes you sing and dance in the aisles and you are Frank or Magenta, laughing at Brad and Janet and therefore people who are too straight to even know what *The Rocky Horror Picture Show* is, never mind cross-dress in public. Because of the mob mentality of the cult, you have safety in numbers, sort of like an alternative stag or hen party. You go home rejuvenated by a risk-free fantasy of polymorphous perversity, pay the baby-sitter, have slightly better straight sex in the missionary position than usual, and plan tomorrow's trip to IKEA with a lighter heart.

Probably sounds like I'm sneering, but I'm not really. It's hard being what you really want to be and few of us have the guts for it. There's something in Tim Curry's performance that encapsulates the truth of deep sexual fantasy ... the idea that someone so sure of themselves and what they – and you – want will coerce you into doing terrible, degrading things with your mind and body that make you feel free of life's mundane compromises – but with no physical pain or psychological consequences. What this androgynous, undiscerning and perennially amused sexpert looks like or has between their thighs is irrelevant, really. They're there to release the willing victim in you, and someone too pretty or straight is incapable of that. And the reason why *Rocky Horror* has tapped into that shared frustration for so many people for so long is because it's far too silly to force you to dwell on the darker implications of either your sexuality or the lack of freedom you've settled for. It congratulates you for getting as far as wearing suspenders, but doesn't require you to actually rebel. Perfect.

So ... why is a film that has achieved such a unique form of audience escapism and been so enduringly loved not a five-star masterpiece? Well ... it's me, really. This is not something I tell a lot of people about, but ... I have a bit missing. It's embarrassing ... shameful, actually. But I've learned to live with it and my therapist says that sharing it openly will lighten the load and make me understand that I'm not alone. So here goes.

I don't have the kitsch gene.

It's true. While the rest of the human race blithely takes their kitsch gene for granted, bonding and sniggering conspiratorially over the pleasures of things that are so-bad-they're-good, I sit alone and unloved, cast out of my species by my sad insistence that bad things are actually bad, and good things are actually good. Therefore, every time this musical actually gets musical, I just see and hear terrible tunes with lousy lyrics played by awful musicians, performed by lunkheads like Meat Loaf and Christopher Biggins who can't sing or dance. There's a whole bit in the lab after Frank has brought his blond hunk monster Rocky to life in old-school Frankenstein style that just involves song after song for what seems like days, and I get bored, and want to see Tim Curry shag something. I realise that an irony eunuch like myself can't hope to understand the ways of normal people, but ... shouldn't music, singing and dancing be, you know, musical, in some way? Don't judge me. I'm still a person, too. I'm just ... special.

Having got that off my ample chest, special mention must be made of the performances of Sarandon and Bostwick as the hapless innocents, bringing 100 per cent enthusiasm and commitment to being the equivalent of Benny Hill stooges, running around in their underwear and being guilelessly available to anything that Tim Curry's overpowering charisma requires. It's genuinely surprising when Frank comically seduces Brad, and Sarandon is the very essence of someone who couldn't possibly grow up to be a heavyweight serious actress, liberal activist and star of a movie where two Amazons in a car define a generation of women's rebellion against a violent patriarchy. Hopefully this promising young comedienne had a full and rewarding career doing commercials for sanitary towels or something.

TRHPS is often referred to as a horror or sci-fi spoof, but it's a send-up of pretty much everything. Especially (1) repressed sexuality and straight couples; (2) stage musicals; (3) bawdy sex farce; and (4) pretentious rock musicals like *Tommy* (see p. 164). The year of its release is interesting, too. The originators of London punk are always quick to name their influences as intellectual underground stuff like the Velvet Underground, Guy Debord and Situationism, *Cabaret*, anti-Nazi artist John Heartfield, the New York Dolls and hardcore gay porn. Yet, in the very year punk kicked off down the Kings Road, here was a subversive comedy with a cult following where everybody dressed in fetish-wear, wore Alice Cooper fright-mask make-up and sang songs based on up-tempo versions of glam or 1950s rock? Uh-huh. Watch this after *The Great Rock 'n' Roll Swindle* (see p. 206) and *Jubilee* (see p. 199) and those key London punk films look increasingly like more pretentious versions of *Rocky Horror*, with their goth-faced dominatrix chic and chaotic perversity. Adam Ant, Jordan and Toyah were virtual clones of *Rocky Horror* characters. Richard O'Brien was actually in *Jubilee*. Could it be that it was O'Brien, rather than Malcolm McLaren or Johnny Rotten, who invented punk? For shame!

Defining a little sub-section of *grand guignol* rock musicals among rock movies – along with *Beyond the Valley of the Dolls* (see p. 93), *Tommy* (see p. 164), *Phantom of The Paradise* (see p. 152) and the recent, hugely *Rocky Horror*-influenced *Hedwig and the Angry Inch* (see p. 362) – *The Rocky Horror Picture Show* is one of those films that will always bat well above its weight. For all its musical flaws and occasional losses of focus, it neatly depoliticises the glammy end of rock's preoccupation with busting free of sexual constraints and being happily naughty, in a conservative-baiting but ultimately harmless way. By the time this book is published, a remake produced by MTV and Rupert Murdoch's Sky should have been released and I think I can predict fairly confidently that no man will ever queue outside cinemas at 11.30 p.m. in stockings and a basque to see it. This film is rooted in its time, a 1970s where the big British battles about censorship were still being fought, lending a comedy musical about a sadistic but irresistible bisexual alien murderer at least an edge of counter-cultural frisson. It's difficult to imagine what gleefully depicted taboos could titillate our jaded palettes now. Unless they've cast Dick Cheney as Frank.

● ●

Confessions of a Pop Performer

1975

Starring: Robin Askwith, Anthony Booth, Doris Hare, Bill Maynard, Jill Gascoine, Bob Todd, Peter Jones
Dir.: Norman Cohen

★ ★ ★

Plot: Carry On up the Hit Parade.
Key line: 'I know who you are! You're Mick Jagger! You're making a comeback, aren't you?'

In the entry for *The Rocky Horror Picture Show* (see p. 155), I idly wonder whether the musical's creator, Richard O'Brien, was really the secret inventor of punk rock. But maybe Malcolm McLaren nicked the idea of working-class London sex-rock outrage from an even less likely source: a soft-porn comedy knock-off made in the very year that McLaren formed the Sex Pistols.

Get this: a London rock band come to instant infamy. Their music is a faster and more minimalist version of glam-rock, with brash lyrics about beating people up sung in a thuggish Cockney accent. Their rapid ascent gains press notoriety, causes riotous chaos, and eventually ends by directly insulting Her Majesty the

Queen. I mean, McLaren was into porn, wasn't he? Could he have nicked all his best ideas from a dirty book hack called Christopher Wood?

But that piece of essentially pointless conjecture is not why one of the despised *Confessions* ... movies is in here. This second in a series of four nudie excursions into the sexual adventures of Timothy Lea is weird, funny and strangely disturbing, as if some one had taken all the bleak and dysfunctional fantasies and ugly-beautiful settings of the classic early 1970s British rock movies and rearranged them for an audience of urchin children and dirty old men. It's the first *Confessions* ... movie I've seen (honest), and undoubtedly the last ... but ... *Pop Performer* turns out to be far more memorable, imaginative and oddly right about rock than many more serious and tasteful rock movies made by respected directors.

The *Confessions* ... movies consisted of four *Carry On* ... / Benny Hill-style sex comedies which achieved some commercial success and notoriety in the 1970s. They all starred various veteran character actors whose careers were largely on the slide, and a pug-ugly bloke called Robin Askwith, whose slightly Mick Jagger-esque bearing was meant to convince the viewer that every woman he met wanted to have sex with him. This was all played completely for typical British seaside postcard laughs, though; partly because every woman in the *Confessions* ... world wanted to have sex with absolutely anyone all of the time, and partly because Askwith's Timothy Lea was an accident-prone, squeaky-voiced oaf of Frank Spencerian proportions. When going through the big *Radio Times Guide to Films* to make my list for this book, I noticed that one of the series was about Lea's adventures in the rock biz and figured that I should give it a watch, just in case it had interesting things to say about how the strictly anti-art end of 1970s culture saw the world of rock 'n' roll. And it does.

The plot goes like this: Bonk-brother-in-law-band-shag-gig-rumpy-pumpy-TV talent show-hump-Royal Variety Show-tits-chaos-end. But it's the little things (wa-hey!) that stick in your mind: strikingly elaborate slapstick set-ups, the fastest rise to pop fame in history, the sheer, Dada-esque weirdness of the sex, and how director Cohen and writer Wood manage to fit 1970s rock and pop into the narrow confines of trash comedy and sexploitation.

But before I go any further, I have to mention one Jill Gascoine. Ms Gascoine is a coolly beautiful British actress from Lambeth, south London, who rose to fame in 1980s Britain playing authoritative women in control, particularly police woman Maggie Forbes in TV thrillers *The Gentle Touch* and *C.A.T.S Eyes*. She married heavyweight thesp Alfred Molina and went on to be a successful novelist. In short, she was the kind of mature, sophisticated, classy English upper-crust beauty who was so out of any ordinary bloke's league that it seemed too depressing to even fantasise about. But ... who's that? ... blimey, it's Jill Gascoine! ... and what's she doing ... no ... surely not ... she's fake-shagging a repulsively ugly British character actor called Bob Todd! ... and ... Bloody Nora! ... I've seen Jill Gascoine's tits! And bush! And *everything*!

This is, to a man of my age, akin to finding out that Dame Judi Dench began her career as a fluffer on the set of *Emmanuelle Does Dallas*. Within minutes, *Confessions of a Pop Performer* has made a mockery of the world I believed in. There are some things a man should just never see ...

Robin Askwith's tiny arse is undoubtedly another one. But you see it a great deal in this movie, more than you see anything naked and female. If these movies were aimed at dirty old men – and the amount of dirty old men who get seduced by young totty in them suggests that they were – then market research must have uncovered their unhealthy fascination with pert and pale young male tail. In Y-fronts and those old-fashioned pants that always make you think of skid marks. Weird.

More casting fun ensues with the prominent role played in all the *Confessions* ... movies by one Anthony Booth, who would go on to be the prime minister's father-in-law. This is where he made the money to give Cherie Booth the best legal education money can buy. She must have introduced Tony to Dad with such pride.

Booth, as Timmy's brother-in-law Sid, plays a major role in a good, old-fashioned British orgy of nonsensical rudeness. Jill

Gascoine shags Sid. Fathers wander into the family home in gorilla suits. Jill Gascoine shags Timmy. Timmy eats fag butts. A woman powders her nose with a marshmallow. The hideous Bob Todd is sexually irresistible to every single woman in south London. Iain Lavender out of *Dad's Army* gets some. Rula Lenska and 'Diddy' David Hamilton don't. Bill Maynard and Doris Hare don't either, but they are fabulous, especially when Maynard makes a stirring political speech about the importance of working-class family unity and the baby pisses on him. And nothing I've just written will make an ounce of sense to anyone under 40.

In amongst this, Sid signs a pub band on Monday, gets them an afternoon gig populated entirely by old ladies on Tuesday, gets a rave review and a recording deal on Wednesday, gets them on a TV talent contest on Thursday, hypes their record to Number One on Friday, gets them a charity gig at 'the London Palaceum' in front of Her Madge on Sunday. It's like the rise of the Arctic Monkeys.

What happened Saturday? Shagging. Falling over. Every band needs a day off.

Oddly, one of Kipper – that's the band – looks *exactly* like Liam Gallagher. Identical. Could be brothers.

This is punctuated by weird sex – obviously – and the kind of slapstick scenes that, if they turned up in Buster Keaton or Jacques Tati movies, would be hailed as masterpieces. Askwith's gallant lighting of a lady's fag sets off a sequence of events which results in the apocalyptic destruction of an entire office. The stage of an imaginary London Palladium is laid to waste by two women's desperation for autographed Y-fronts and with such scattershot logic that amazement almost overwhelms amusement.

But best of all is a scene where Timmy gets his end away with the dolly bird shop assistant at a record store. As they make the entire building bounce with their Olympian thrustings, they are literally buried by an avalanche of pop. Buttons are hit on stereos until we're hearing a Burroughs-style cut-up of pop styles, including, bizarrely, a pastiche of 'The Ying Tong Song' by the Goons. Records fly from shelves and fall on to their naked bodies. A seven-inch single balances on Askwith's arse as the pair wrap themselves in audio tape. Surely the director is saying that the youth of today are being deluged by the tacky sexual imagery derived from pop's information overload, being kept from their natural sexual selves by a mediated saturation of packaged sensuality? Indeed, Kipper can be seen as a manifestation of symbiotic counter-culture. At least, that's what one of the characters tells the drummer.

One of the surprises about ... *Pop Performer* is its benign view of the comedy of sex. I'd been fully expecting a slew of racist, homophobic and particularly misogynist gags ... but they never come. OK ... *one* homophobic gag, but this is not the usual barely concealed seething misanthropy of the British 1970s. No woman is judged as a whore for wanting sex. It's as if the makers wanted to give the kind of frustrated working-class man who would actually pay money to see a *Confessions* ... movie a glimpse of the possibilities that the swinging sixties presented, with all of the routine self-loathing and repression stripped away. It's an oddly innocent take on porn ... wife-swapping with no stigma, sex with no angst, women more sexually confident and in command than men, and absolutely no-one judged for their sexual behaviour. A somewhat different idea of porn to the explicit and brutal one that rendered soft-porn movies redundant in the post-internet world. A strangely counter-cultural one, in truth.

But, when all is said and shagged, what does *Confessions of a Pop Performer* tell us about pop music? That the frantic movement of pop's here-today-gone-tomorrow momentum mirrors the urgency of the final thrusts and rubs as one reaches sexual climax. And that you can't have wild monkey sex on the floor of iTunes.

• •

Tommy

1975

Starring: Roger Daltrey, Ann-Margret, Oliver Reed, Jack
Nicholson, Tina Turner, Elton John, The Who
Dir.: Ken Russell

★ ★ ★

**Plot: War child witnesses murder of father by stepfather and
goes deaf, dumb and blind. Gets abused by all and sundry.
Becomes world pinball champion. Is cured. Becomes
messiah. Mom and stepdad slaughtered. But then, they
asked for it, so, fair enough, really.
Key line: 'Do you think it's alright? To leave the boy with
Uncle Ernie ...'**

Watching *Tommy* for the first time in over 30 years was one of my
weirdest recent experiences. As the opening credits rolled I was
immediately transported to the north London cinema – either the
ABC Turnpike Lane or the Gaumont Wood Green, I can't be sure
which – where I saw it with my mum in 1975. Sam and I would go
to the pictures at least twice a week, where she would happily
smuggle me into X- and AA-rated films I shouldn't see – I was a
tall, heavy-set kid. Rock and pop was my number two obsession
after football, so *Tommy* would have been a must-see for my 12-
year-old self. It had The Who. It had Elton. It had something new
and boy-impressive called 'quintaphonic sound', which actually
meant quadraphonic sound with a speaker directly behind the
screen for the singing. Plus it was a rock opera, which sounded
deep and meaningful and LOUD. Plus the papers had said it was
sick and rude, which always meant it had sex in it. I'm sure
there's a wealth of good psychological reasons why 12-year-old
boys shouldn't go and see this sort of thing with their mothers. But
it didn't do me any harm. Nope. No harm at all.

Anyway ... it's now 2009 and I'm watching *Tommy* on DVD

with my wife (see? No harm at all. Really. I'm fine), who pretty much hates everything that smacks of 1960s/1970s hippy-derived film-making and I'm expecting 106 minutes of cringing, laughing and possibly crying about just how perfect a symbol a Ken Russell-directed rock opera is of all the reasons why we desperately needed punk rock and *Star Wars* to wash all the misogynist pseudo-mystical hippy scum off the streets. And for the first 30 minutes or so, that's where I was, patting my 12-year-old self on his innocent, curly head, and telling him that the Sex Pistols were just around the corner, and that in two years' time I'll be sitting watching a film called *Taxi Driver* with my mum and my parameters of good taste in proper films will be reset in order to make sure I never, ever have to watch Oliver Reed ever again and pretend that he's good.

And then something weird happened. I started to enjoy *Tommy*. So did Linsay. Perhaps my mother is to blame.

Or perhaps this is the film equivalent of Guilty Pleasures, the nostalgic 40-something pop trend which swept the UK in 2006, reviving the careers of such overlooked musical titans as Randy Vanwarmer, Marshall Hain and Jarvis Cocker, and providing an unexpected economic boom among Islington baby-sitters, as previously sane and respectable media professionals with children found themselves rushing out to 'rave' to Supertramp as often as once a month. Amidst this giddy rush of middle youth hedonism, there was an actual cultural truth behind Guilty Pleasures . . . which was that punk rock was so powerfully dismissive of its various cultural *bêtes noires* that all of us of that easily bullied generation refused to allow ourselves to enjoy things that weren't cool. And it wasn't just punks who fell for that. A jaded self-consciousness swept British culture so insidiously and successfully during the 1980s that Johnny Rotten ceased to have any connection with its ubiquity, save for absent fatherhood.

So, I 'fess up: for 30 years I'd dismissed *Tommy* as bloated, unwatchable excess without even giving it a second viewing. The Who film you had to love was *Quadrophenia* (see p. 220) because it was down-to-earth and unpretentious . . . after a fashion. Rock opera, by its very nature, was ridiculous.

Well ... rock opera *is* ridiculous. But ridiculous has its charms. If you watch Russell's garish grab-bag of vaguely transgressive images expecting a profound philosophical message, of course *Tommy* is shite. Compared to your standard rock movie, though – or your standard 2009 rock video – *Tommy* is imaginative, memorable, funny, offensive, bizarre, risky, vivid, technically impressive ... and entertaining.

Ploughing through the plot of *Tommy* in detail is pretty pointless ... not only because it's enormously silly, but because Russell clearly agrees. His lack of interest in the story of a traumatised war-child who becomes a failed messiah is reflected in the film's lack of camera movement; *Tommy* is almost entirely comprised of montage and is best viewed as a series of eccentric pop promos. In that sense, Russell stays true to the original 1969 *Tommy* album, which made absolutely no sense as a story without the many Pete Town-shend interviews of the time telling you what it all meant. It transformed The Who from a failing hooligan pop group into one of the biggest acts in the world precisely because its blend of Jesus symbolism, musical bombast, anthemic singalongs, vague mysticism and depoliticised themes about grown-ups being really, really bad was perfect for the times. Youthful hippy optimism was already dying along with the 1960s, and *Tommy* provided a comforting post-hippy mix of rebellion without politics, intellectualism without meaning, religion without rules, and a repulsed attitude toward sex. The critical and commercial acclaim *Tommy* received invented the double concept album, prog rock and Andrew Lloyd Webber. It's not one of my favourite Who moments, all things considered. But it made The Who millionaires.

Russell's movie does attempt to lighten up about the sex. But, being the 1970s, it's in an entirely misogynist and homophobic framework. Dolly birds in bikinis appear during an air-raid for no other reason than so Russell can laugh at them and bond with us lads in the audience; Keith Moon's Uncle Ernie doesn't molest the senseless Tommy because he's a monster, but because he's been reading *Gay News*; and the best pop star cameo is interrupted by a bizarre manifestation of the director's fear of women. Get this: one of the various attempts to cure Tommy involves him being taken by his stepdad to see the Acid Queen, a hooker-cum-drug dealer played by Tina Turner. She's fantastic … the very essence of powerful and uncontrollable female sexuality … until she is very abruptly turned into a robot which Daltrey's Tommy has to climb into and become imprisoned within while being pumped with scary drugs, thereby revealing, with the total absence of subtlety which was Russell's career USP, the director's terror of the vagina with a side order of desperation to climb back into the womb. Puts a whole new spin on Russell's freakish toddler tantrum at the expense of Jade Goody in *Celebrity Big Brother*, doesn't it just?

But what makes the *Tommy* freak-show watchable is great bits: bullying torturer Cousin Kevin, played by future *Just Good Friends* cheeky chappy Paul Nicholas, portrayed as a prophecy of punk: a proto-Sid Vicious in leather jacket and Nazi Iron Cross necklace. The entire 'Pinball Wizard' sequence, with Elton John on stilts as the ultimate glitter-hooligan, at the front of an extraordinary shot stretching back to encompass a theatre full of screaming teens. Tommy's cure, as Mom pushes him through a mirror until he is falling into the bluest water in the world and 'I'm Free' makes you go unavoidably goose-pimply. Jack Nicholson as an impossibly handsome doctor. Tommy's hapless mom Ann-Margret dreaming about the telly exploding and covering her in foam, baked beans and what I'd prefer to think is chocolate. And the Best Bit Award goes to … the Sally Simpson sequence, where a teenage girl goes to a Tommy evangelical meeting, is scarred for life by stage security, and ends up marrying a teen rock star who looks like a Frankenstein monster version of Elvis. The song ends with the girl, still a child, pushing a pram at her husband's show, yawning, jaded, spent. It's the film's only thought-provoking scene, and you suspect that this is because Townshend's little sub-plot just about sums up what Russell really feels about rock, religion and sex. Sally was played by Russell's daughter, Victoria.

And the *Tommy* triv just keeps on coming. Bowie was originally chosen to play the Acid Queen. Who drummer Keith Moon was really pissed off that the stepdad part went to Oliver Reed, and not him. Russell was much criticised for using real footage of the burning Southsea pier. The Theatre Royal in Portsmouth, where the 'Pinball Wizard' sequences were filmed, also burned down during filming. The sounds of screaming teens accompanying 'Pinball Wizard' are from the *A Hard Day's Night* (see p. 49) soundtrack. Russell was also slagged off, can you believe, for using actual disabled people to play disabled people. Fuck me ... the 1970s.

Hmmm. 'Fuck Me ... the 1970s' is a *great* name for a cheap TV show. Anyone got Ken's number? Sorry ... always touting for work, you know how it is.

So ... *Tommy*. It's a movie with a message. Two, actually. First, 1970s rock stars all looked a bit like Jesus ... coincidence? Second, all mothers are cunts. This was thought-provoking stuff for 12-year-old me. But then my mum bought me chips on the way home, so I forgave her.

● ●

Saturday Night Fever

1977
Starring: John Travolta, Karen Lynn Gorney, Donna Pescow
Dir.: John Badham

★ ★ ★ ★

Plot: Disco, class struggle and the eternal appeal of the young, dumb and full of cum.
Key line: 'Dancing can't last forever. It's a short-lived kinda thing.'

It's a film that begins with a bridge to nowhere, two pairs of shoes, and a walk. But no-one remembers the bridge or the shoes.

The thing about Travolta's infamous strut down a street in Bay Ridge, Brooklyn in time to the rhythm of the Bee Gees' 'Stayin' Alive' is that it's very, very funny. Director John Badham and his star Travolta realised that the clothes and hair of the time were medallion-man ludicrous, and that if Travolta took his character Tony Manero's stud status too seriously, then one of the best films about both pop and class anxiety would have been entirely skewered. You had to like Tony, and if Travolta didn't play him subtly for laughs, he would have been despicable. The walk kick-started one of the most iconic careers in modern cinema, and it deserved to. The boy was charm personified.

But before any more about 'the quintessential disco movie' (that's what it says on the DVD box, and what a backhanded compliment!), a reminiscence that hopefully explains why it's way better than that. Every time I watch *Saturday Night Fever*, I'm reminded of the discos at the city centre swimming pool in Peterborough around 1978, the first adult club I ever went to. Well, kind of adult ... the reason that they were so popular is that they had a somewhat liberal attitude to serving alcohol to minors, and were therefore packed with 15-year-olds like myself.

The swimming pool discos had their very own Tony Manero. His name was James Horn. He was a handsome and hard-looking black guy who danced like Fred Astaire and Michael Jackson all rolled into one. When he turned up, he would disappear immediately into a dark corner with a harem of gorgeous girlies. He would finally deign to hit the dancefloor once, maybe twice in a night, and everyone would stop to watch. Whichever girl he was dancing with would literally disappear, just as Karen Lynn Gorney's Stephanie disappears when she dances with Tony in this film. I have a vague memory of the smoothness of the way he rolled his body, and the way sudden flurries of his feet would seem to make him float and defy gravity completely. But I mainly recall his face, and a smile/sneer that knew that everyone in the room wanted to fuck him or be him. It was the first time I felt that I was in the presence of a true star ... someone who transcended their surroundings and made you feel privileged to breathe the same air while simultaneously making you feel like a total klutz in comparison. James Horn was simply Better Than Us, because he could dance.

I saw him in a disco-dancing competition a couple of years later.

He won. It was funny because every other contestant tried so hard
. . . there was one tiny, pretty Italian guy who threw himself around
the stage so hard that the maroon dye in his wedged hair ran all
over his face and clothes. James strolled onstage after that, rolled
his shoulders, essayed a few casual moves and blew everyone away.
It was like watching Italy go one-nil up against San Marino or
someone and just defend for 85 minutes without breaking a sweat.
The boy just didn't have to be at his best. He just sneered that
sneer and *knew.*

But once I stopped going to disco dance-offs and discovered
hipper clubs, I never heard of James Horn again. In fact, I never
heard of James Horn in any context *except* at a disco. It was as if it
was the only place where he existed. Maybe he worked in a hardware
store, like Tony Manero. Maybe he still does. Or maybe he became a
professional dancer. But I suspect not. I suspect that those moments
when he was King of Peterborough Disco were the peak moments
of his life. One of the (many) reasons why *Saturday Night Fever*'s
1983 sequel *Staying Alive* was one of the worst films ever made is
because it gave Tony Manero a dancing career . . . and that simply
didn't happen to working-class disco dancers from the boondocks.
Their star burned brightly in dark rooms, and died, and they
became fat bitter guys with too-soon families and shitty jobs. It's
that probability that makes the unresolved ending of *Saturday Night
Fever* the right ending for a marvellous movie, and makes the
peacock sexual display of dancing in a club so much more resonant
and multi-dimensional and spontaneous and real and bittersweet
than the all-smiling physical jerks of pro dancers. It's why I always
think of James Horn when I see *Saturday Night Fever*. It's why
I adore this movie.

If you haven't seen it . . . *Saturday Night Fever* is based on a
magazine feature about the disco lifestyle by rock writer Nik Cohn.
Tony is a working-class Italian-American bridge-and-tunnel 19-
year-old with a mundane bottom-feeder life. He still lives with his
parents. His Dad's unemployed and his Mom's obsessed with
Tony's saintly brother, because he's a Catholic priest. They shout
and hit each other at the dinner table. He sells paint and charms

the hardware store customers into spending more money all day for peanuts and a boss who seems nice but, like all petit bourgeois, won't pay him what he's worth. He runs with a crowd of queer-bashing, pill-popping, woman-hating racists who worship him and is relentlessly pursued by the neighbourhood slut (the wonderful Donna Pescow as Annette). His saving grace is being the Ace Face at 2001 Odyssey, the local disco. He spends what little money he has on Cuban heels, crotch-bulging flares, hair product and cheap bling. He's the archetypal mod hero, albeit in less tasteful clothes. He's choosy about who he fucks, not because he's worried about STDs or pregnancy or waiting for the right girl, but because 'If you make it with some of these chicks, they think you gotta dance with 'em.' He's a narcissist, but a narcissist with a keen sense of priorities.

He meets the pretty but snotty Stephanie, an aspirational woman who works in Manhattan and dances to sophisticated Latin jazz and classical, and who, despite being revealed as pretentious by her thick Brooklyn accent, represents escape from his dead-end world. He persuades her to be his partner in a dance competition and edge towards a relationship. Meanwhile, his everyday life slides inexorably into the kind of chaos which makes working-class small-town life feel like prison, including a family scandal, racist gang fights, a rape, an attempted rape, a death, an unwanted pregnancy and sundry humiliations and frustrations. He and Stephanie dance together at the competition, but their big rivals are this Puerto Rican couple, and ... *that's* really not the point of the tale at all, which is why I'm not going to spoil the ending.

Suffice to say, *Saturday Night Fever* is only tangentially a film about disco. In fact, the deluge of foul-mouthed dialogue in a movie largely aimed at teens made it feel much more like a punk film at the time. It has a smart, ribald take on all of the key youth cultural talking points of its era. It's enlightened but real about race, and its sexual politics is occasionally breathtaking in both its crude wit and sly subversion (Tony: 'What are you anyway? Are you a nice girl or a cunt?' Annette: 'I dunno. Both?'). The Stephanie role *is* essentially thankless, the butt of a joke about getting ideas above your station *and* the dance partner who is just a skinny prop for Travolta's peacock thrustings, but Gorney makes a great job of it. Especially in the first date between Tony and Stephanie in a diner – a comedy-of-embarrassment masterpiece of bullshit, emasculation and bad manners in which you can see each of the pair's bad points from an entirely equal perspective. But the purely romantic bits don't work. The chemistry fails to ignite. She's just too ordinary for him. She's a representative of the teenage girls watching the movie. She's there to look up at Travolta, awestruck, during the dance scenes, and happily bathe in his aura of studliness.

Nevertheless, the dialogue zings. Most of the gags work. Some of the acting is weak but Travolta's so good it rarely matters. There's some neat symbolism with bridges that don't get crossed and priestly garb that doubles as a noose. Ooh ... and Curtis Hanson and Eminem's *8 Mile* (see p. 364), that least disco of films, is entirely in hock to *Saturday Night Fever*'s suburban traps, gangs of lost boys *and* undercuttings of the winning mentality.

But really, *SNF* is all about class – who's trapped by it? How do we define it? Can we change our class through who we sleep with or where we work? If you succeed, can you keep the parts of your background that make you what you are, or must you reject it all? Can you make any real difference to your class status unless you join with your proletarian comrades and seize control of the means of production? That sort of thing. It is a fairly un-American movie in terms of its worldview, yet it became one of the quintessential American hits of its era. Much of this is down to the dancing, which is iconic and was copied step-for-step in discos all over the world, and the music, which is mainly by the Bee Gees (and don't even get me started on 'Disco Inferno' by Trammps) and is altogether sublime. But it was also because of the adorable nice/nasty gaucheness of Travolta's Manero, and the resonance of the story at a time when youth tribes were at their peak of influence and the West was at the cusp of a change in attitude towards class and upward mobility. *SNF* is unique: its grimy *mise en scène*, knowledge of and affection for working-class life, and critique of capitalism are pure 1970s. But the gloss and glamour of the dance sequences and its prophecy of what we'd come to call 'the yuppie' are pure 1980s.

Take out all the music and dancing, and this would still be a politically acute and emotionally satisfying drama that says a great deal to future generations about the 1970s/1980s transition from liberal consensus to the brutal social Darwinism of Reaganomics.

But you can't dance to dem apples, and you can dance to *Saturday Night Fever*. A great many films attempted the social realist music-youth tribe-class conflict study in the wake of this film, and only *Quadrophenia* (see p. 220) matched its edgy balance of social commentary and pure pop entertainment. An absolute rites-of-passage teen classic.

• •

Abba: The Movie

1977

Starring: Abba, Robert Hughes, Tom Oliver, Bruce Barry, Stig Anderson
Dir.: Lasse Hallström

★ ★ ★

Plot: Hapless radio DJ follows Abba around Australia to get in-depth interview with the enigmatic Swedes.
Key line: 'I'm nothing special. In fact, I'm a bit of a bore' (from 'Thank You for the Music').

There are two especially famous quotes that dismiss the very idea of music journalism. One, attributed variously to Frank Zappa, Elvis Costello and US actor/comedian Martin Mull, is: 'Writing about music is like dancing about architecture.' The other, definitely attributable to Zappa, is: 'Most rock journalism is people who can't write, interviewing people who can't talk, for people who can't read.' Both are pretty funny, but I'd like to suggest an Exhibit C for the prosecution, from *Abba: The Movie*, which cuts through to the futility of my job like laser surgery, and has the added weight of being a completely innocent remark from a child.

The fictional premise that provides the spine for this Abba on-the-road documentary concerns a geeky country and western radio DJ called Ashley (played superbly throughout by Aussie TV actor Robert Hughes) chasing the Ab-Fab Four around Australia in order to get an interview. He is also charged with talking to Abba fans about the group's appeal and recording their answers on his trusty old-school tape recorder for his radio station's proposed Abba Special. At one point, he is in a school asking children about why they like Abba. 'What do you like about Abba?' he gently asks one tiny sprog. 'I like the songs and it's really good.' A pause. Ashley/Hughes tries again. 'What do you like about the songs?' The kid looks at him like he's a total moron. 'The parts that are good', the kid insists.

Abba: The Movie is a sly essay about the utter futility of our worship of pop. From our fascination for its makers, through our desperation to know them when it's patently obvious that few of us even truly know the people we live with, to the pointlessness of the media's search for deeper insight into pop summed up in the scene quoted above. In Abba's one foray into the world of feature film, they are little more than cardboard cut-outs, as made explicit in the 'I'm a Marionette' sequence. They smile, smoke, greet hundreds of fans, politely answer dumb questions from journalists, and are nothing. They walk out onstage and kick into 'Dancing Queen', and suddenly they are three dimensional ... and one of the greatest pop groups of all-time, as a bonus. Swedish director and co-writer Lasse Hallström, who directed most of Abba's videos and went on to make a career out of whimsically surreal movies including *What's Eating Gilbert Grape?*, *Chocolat* and *The Cider House Rules*, understood the gap between the mundanity of pop life and the transcendent glory of pop music, and made a whimsically surreal little gem out of the unpromising premise of Abba touring Australia. This makes *Abba: The Movie*, if not one of the best, then certainly one of the most honest and insightful of rock movies.

One of Hallström's genius masterstrokes throughout is an ability to take things the cultural hipster would define as middle-of-the-road – like Abba, of course – and illuminate their oddness – like Abba, of course. The film opens with a tortuously banal pop-country record backdropping tourist ad shots of the Australian countryside ... bushes, lakes, kangaroos, naturally. It's an immediate weird-out. And once the DJ-chases-Abba-for-interview premise is set up, we are very quickly eavesdropping on an Abba press conference at Sydney airport, which at first seems nothing more than dull, but is actually where the film's major themes and running jokes are introduced.

The group are asked whether they enjoy touring, and Bjorn Ulvaeus takes it upon himself to be honest. 'It's a bit of a [sic] asocial life on tour. You just eat, sleep and go onstage, and nothing more. It kills creativity in a way that I don't like.' And with that we embark on a 90-minute testimony to a touring life so dull that Hallström has to invent an outsider's quest to make it watchable. People are still under the misapprehension, I suspect, that rock stars become drug/booze/sex addicts on the road because they're crazy motherfuckers climbing aboard the Helltrain to oblivion in order to fulfil gargantuan desires or feed the extremes of experience needed to be creative geniuses. This is all bollocks. They're just bored. You'd do the same.

Back to the press conference, and Abba are asked whether they do booze and drugs. They smilingly dismiss the possibility of a family pop group doing drugs, but insist, 'We're not clean.' This is mocked throughout the movie, as Ashley repeatedly approaches middle-aged Abba fans and finds that their number one reason for liking Abba is that they're 'clean'. One even goes so far as to call them 'clean and tidy'. Apart from how agreeable Abba's gentle self-mockery is, these scenes are also a reminder of just how much the pop discourse has changed these past 30 years. Maybe 21st-century pop fan adults who bond with their kids over Westlife or Leona Lewis feel exactly the same way. But we're all too knowing about the rules of cool now to express it in this quasi-fascistic way.

The press conference question that brings the most laughs concerns the plump and fulsome arse of Agnetha Faltskog. Some context for younger readers: for reasons that remain shrouded in the mysteries of why the public will merrily follow a media obsession if it's repeated often enough, people of the 1970s were obsessed with the Blonde Girl out of Abba's arse. She won awards for it, repeatedly, until Felicity Kendall butted in. Agnetha's behind was the kind of behind that, nowadays, would be printed on the front of Heat with the headline, 'Look at the Size of that Big Fat ARSE!!!' But in the 1970s popular feminism had made inroads into the unconsciousness of the masses, and Agnetha's plump booty was somewhat iconic. A journalist asks Agnetha if she thinks she has the finest arse in the world. 'I don't know,' she grins modestly. 'I haven't seen it.' Much polite hilarity ensues, but, again, Hallström makes the sexist trivialisation of a great singer and beautiful girl into a running joke, sketching a great scene in a hotel room that suggests that Agnetha's vocal partner Anni-Frid Lyngstad is jealous of the arse attention, and a truer one when a taxi driver (played by future *Neighbours* star Tom Oliver, who also plays a barman and Abba's bodyguard) goes into an outraged rant about how Agnetha's arse is perfectly fine to display to 'red-blooded males', but not to 'the wife and kids'.

The film's cynicism – in another strong scene, DJ Ashley is stuck in a traffic jam missing yet another opportunity to get his interview and notices that everyone on the street is wearing another piece of tacky Abba merchandise – is so subtly but strongly shaped that, by the time an audience of fans are singing along to 'Fernando' at a concert, their worship of the band takes on a darker, almost fascistic hue. Admittedly, much of this is blown away by the first few bars of 'Dancing Queen' in a live performance that purveys the sheer joy of the universally loved pop classic as wonderfully well as anything in this book. But even 'Dancing Queen' . . . superficially happy song – desperately sad melody, innit?

And there is a genuine best-scene-in-rock-movie contender here, too. At the film's end, Ashley, who has failed to get his interview and has resigned himself to unemployment, bumps into Agnetha, Anni-Frid, Benny and Bjorn in a lift. He asks for an interview, they agree happily, but . . . the lift door shuts on us, and we find ourselves hurtling down through a kind of sci-fi lift-shaft into the video for the sublime 'Eagle', the song that inspired the Human League's 'Don't You Want Me'. The video is trippy, uplifting, melancholic and, because the camera, lest we forget, really adored Anni-Frid and Agnetha, deliciously sexy. 'Eagle' glides to a close, the lift door opens, and we learn that Ashley has got his dream interview where Abba tell you the intimate truth about who they really are . . . and we haven't heard a word of it, and aren't going to. And you absolutely know the truth of the fact that nothing that these four people could say – about their troubled marriages, their choices of stimulants, nor whether Anni-Frid was really jealous of Agnetha's sumptuous bum – could tell you as much about what is crucial to human life as the music and visuals of 'Eagle'.

Ashley gets to his radio station, whacks on his Abba doc just in time, and reclines happily as one of the children he interviews says, on tape, 'There's nothing really special about them. They're just human beings.' Those opening lines from 'Thank You for the Music' – 'I'm nothing special. In fact, I'm a bit of a bore' – ring out, establishing the out-of-the-mouths-of-babes truth of Ashley's journalistic angle. Abba's plane departs, like any other plane, to a place where Abba will live exactly the same 'asocial' life as they did in Australia. End of film. Why only three stars for such a smart and occasionally beautiful movie? Because everything that I haven't picked out in this chapter is pretty boring. Hallström didn't lie about that. And neither did Abba.

• •

Grease

1978

Starring: John Travolta, Olivia Newton-John, Stockard Channing
Dir.: Randal Kleiser

★ ★ ★

Plot: The ultimate teen sex pop movie.
Key line: 'I got chills. They're multiplyin' (from 'You're the One that I Want').

The Wife: (as Stockard Channing as the black-shirted Rizzo emerges from a pink car). Oh my God, isn't she cool? I have loved Stockard Channing from that moment onwards.

Me: And she is what my theory about *Grease* revolves around. That *Grease* is perennially popular with each new generation of women because it's the first great feminist pop film. The first nightmare that every adolescent girl has to deal with is that she'll be frustrated to the point of illness if she doesn't indulge her hormonal desires, and treated like a leper by both men and women if she does. In Rizzo, we have a character who does indulge her hormones, takes the abuse, and not only ends up a heroine, but helps to teach the good girl how to indulge her desires, too. The story proves that she's right to be a slut. And she has all the best lines and all the best clothes, too.

The Wife: It's a good theory. But I don't know if that's why I like the movie. What came into my mind when you were saying it was ... that I loved it because it was about young people who weren't children. I loved the songs and the clothes and the jokes. But you're right about Rizzo. When I was at school there were slutty girls like Rizzo and there was definitely two camps. They were hard and scary and they didn't talk to girls like me and I didn't talk to them. Seeing a character who was like them but was also quite nice and smart did feel good. It goes the other way, too. At one point Danny attempts to become a jock. It's about everybody getting to be a bit rounder.

Me: That's all a bit learning and growing.

The Wife: Yeah ... although I didn't think about that at the time. I think I was very attracted to the fact that they all looked so old and seemed so sophisticated. I was 13 at the time and thought that when you got to 16 you automatically got a car and nice cardigans. I think teen comedies went downhill once they started putting young people in them.

Me: What did you feel about Olivia Newton-John as Sandy?

The Wife: Too good to be true. Why would you want to be like her when you could be like Rizzo? ... Oh my GOD! I've only just realised that Danny and Sandy are telling two completely different stories in the words of 'Summer Nights'!

Me: But isn't that the whole point of the song ... the differing viewpoints of sexual encounters between boys and girls and the peer pressure that leads to them?

The Wife: Well ... the subtitles help. Don't make me sound like Bobo the Fool. Actually, I'm realising that most of this was incomprehensible to me when I was kid. Sneaky Pete? USO? What did I think these things meant?

Me: I know. What's 'fongool'?

The Wife: It's an Americanised Italian swear word. A sly way of saying fuck. I didn't understand Rizzo's 'defective typewriter' gag ('I feel like a defective typewriter. I skipped a period') at the time. I knew what missing your period meant. But I didn't know that Americans called full-stops periods.

Me: It's no wonder that our education system has become increasingly Americanised. Movies set in British schools are grim, even good ones like *Kes* ...

The Wife: ... whereas this and all the American high school movies that followed are all Disney colours and bonfires and people who drive cars to school. Exactly. They brainwashed us. American youth just seemed bizarrely glamorous. Drive-ins! The Prom! Even sleepovers ... wearing a baby-doll nightie and having sleepovers with your mates ... who knew that could happen? Now kids do that all the time.

Me: I remember being really shocked by the sexist language in 'Greased Lightning'. 'We'll be getting lots of tit'; 'It's a real pussy wagon.' It wasn't the language – there'd been a load of 'cunts' in *Saturday Night Fever* – it was the context. I mean, this was a film aimed at 12-year-olds . . .

The Wife: I think their attitude was 'mumble it and no-one will notice'. Except those of us who were looking for it.

Me: Do you still like *Grease* as much as when you were a kid?

The Wife: I'm really enjoying it. I love the big production numbers, especially 'Greased Lightning' and 'Beauty School Dropout'. They're just old-school musical numbers so I'm always going to love those. And it's much cleverer than I remember. The bit at the beginning where Sandy just announces, for no reason, 'I'm no stranger to heartbreak.' Very sly. When I was kid I liked the romance, but now I realise that the romance has no plot at all. It's a film completely made up of trimmings. Which is fine for me.

Me: Now *that* guy . . . the sleazy judge at the dance contest: he's Ed Burns. He played Kookie in *77 Sunset Strip*.

The Wife: Never heard of it . . .

Me: It was my mum's favourite TV show when she was young. An American teen show. He was the heart-throb hero. It was an in-joke for adults who'd taken their kids to the movie.

The Wife: There's a whole thing in the dance contest about 'no lewd or vulgar moves'. This is the fifties and the school is a whole society built on denying sex. But the kids' lives revolve around nothing else. Do you remember, at the drive-in, there's some really phallic action on screen behind Travolta singing 'Sandy' with a cartoon hot-dog jumping in and out of a bun? Here it comes . . .

Me: Oh. My. God. How could I not have noticed that? I was only 15. I hadn't lost my virginity yet.

The Wife: 'There are Worse Things I Could Do' . . . this is such a dignified song. Stockard Channing lends this whole movie a kind of dignity.

Me: It's a classic. Should've been longer.

The Wife: What should've happened is that Sandy decides to get her slut makeover after hearing Rizzo's song.

Me: Instead of after watching the race ...

The Wife: ... which doesn't make any sense.

Me: Maybe to be a full-on feminist polemic, Rizzo needed to have an abortion and still be loved and accepted by Kenickie and the gang ...

The Wife: Maybe she does. I mean, she agrees to marriage in seconds at a fairground. It hardly smacks of a firm and lasting decision. The natural couple in *Grease* are actually Danny and Rizzo. It's made clear that they've been together before. They've both been with everyone. They're doing their little version of *La Ronde* with their friends. Just one question – why the flying car? And 'We Go Together' is a terrible song.

Me: So you're saying that your favourite childhood film is a work of genius marred by a bad ending?

The Wife: A bad last third, really. It's a great opening and some brilliant set-pieces.

Me: So my theory that *Grease* is a pop-feminist polemic is bollocks. The reason that generations of girls love this movie is that it's about sex?

The Wife: Yeah. And what it has to say about sex and being a teenager is a lot more honest than something like *High School Musical*. *Grease* seems more cynical on the surface. But *Grease* is cynical in the telling, while *High School Musical* is cynical in the making. Everything is perfectly packaged and controlled, which *Grease* isn't. And one of the major reasons for me is because *Grease* has older actors playing the kids. It isn't selling youth. That's why it endures.

● ●

The Buddy Holly Story

1978

Starring: Gary Busey, Don Stroud, Charles Martin Smith
Dir.: Steve Rash

★ ★ ★

Plot: The day the music died. I never got that.
Key line: 'I have to confess we thought you were a negro group.'

One thing I'm learning in the process of writing this book is how accurately you can judge the quality of a film by its first scene. This seminal biopic is a case in point. I hadn't seen it since its release over 30 years ago. Yet every detail of its opening in an ice-skating rink had stuck with me, and came flooding back, image by image, sound by sound.

It is Lubbock, Texas in the mid-1950s. Gary Busey, as Buddy Holly, is leading bassist Ray Bob Simmons (Smith) and drummer Jesse Clarence (Stroud) through a show at their local ice rink. Fresh-faced soda-pop bobbysoxers skate round happily to the strains of Buddy & Co.'s mellow hillbilly balladry, largely watched by their parents and, in some cases, what appear to be their teachers. If the scene were any more wholesome you'd be able to smell the soap and toothpaste coming right out of the screen. Bizarrely, this humble small-town show is being broadcast live on local radio, and Buddy crouches stage-side to fiddle with the broadcast gear and check things are OK with the DJ.

After finishing the country ballad, the trio have a short discussion and elect to play one of their own songs, with some relish. The band slam into 'That'll Be the Day'. Heads snap to attention. Kids gawp. Oldsters wince. The bespectacled singer becomes a kind of geek Elvis, doing a strange bandy-legged dance and holding his guitar like a rifle. Delighted bobbysoxers stop skating and slurping and rush over to the bandstand to watch and bop along. We cut to the intrigued DJ in his studio. He is both enjoying it and looking worried. He takes an irate call and is soon reluctantly pulling the broadcast as the show's sponsor is threatening to pull all of his advertising.

Back to the rink. Flushed, excited kids. Horrified parents. The guts and punch of the sound echoing around this cavernous venue. Busey's epileptic Chuck Berry portrayal of Holly's performing style. You know everything about Lubbock, Texas and the period and the conflict and the dawn of change and the threat of miscegenation and the effect of early rock on 1950s youth from this beautiful scene.

As *Walk Hard: The Dewey Cox Story* (see p. 406) amusingly points out 30 years later, the following scenes of this key rock flick, where 'That'll Be the Day' is accused of being civilisation-destroying 'jungle music' by a stereotypical southern hellfire preacher, seem somewhat laughable now, after three decades of increasingly profane musical stylings and our own palettes being jaded by internet porn and comedy so dark you don't know whether to laugh or barf. But one has to assume that that's what our doomed and bespectacled hero and his fellow rockers had to go through, to win our right to chuckle at Eminem and mosh to Anal Beard. After all, Rash's loving tribute to Holly and his band the Crickets was the first successful modern rock biopic, and you can't set a template without reporting the fact, no matter how tiresome, that electric beat music was once considered, by goobers and reactionaries, as third only to the atom bomb and communism as the harbinger of Judgment Day. *The Buddy Holly Story* starts from that premise and then manages to make a story that really only has a dramatic ending into a compelling and enjoyable drama.

Aside from that, it's the rags-to-riches biopic story you know so well. Except that this was the first attempt to tell that story using the cinematic language of the post-1960s American movie brats – naturalistic acting, unglamourised settings, *vérité* sound design, music played by the actors themselves, and real people presented as neither angelic heroes nor exaggerated bad guys – but normal, flawed humans. It takes its 1950s period cues and general *mise en scène* (and the lovable nerdiness of Charles Martin Smith) from George Lucas's *American Graffiti* (see p. 132), and presents a solid entertainment that you can believe in. The film's mix of nostalgia and drug-free tragedy was so successful that it was pretty much remade in 1987 as *La Bamba*, starring Lou Diamond Phillips as Holly's fellow crash victim Ritchie Valens, and managed to be even more successful.

What *The Buddy Holly Story* does do well is the little rock biz details. Racist Nashville record producers. Pressure put on owners of small radio stations to only play 'white' music. Holly's first hit recorded live without his knowledge. Holly winning the right to write, perform, arrange and produce his own material. Except that, in its rush to anoint Holly King of Indie, the film actually lies about Holly's career. Missing completely from the film is Texan songwriter/producer Norman Petty, who served as Holly's mentor and manager until months before Holly's death. Holly split from Petty and moved to New York to escape the clutches of a man who had successfully conned Holly into giving him songwriting credits on several of his most lucrative songs, as was the accepted business practice at the time. The final irony that makes Petty's omission from the story somewhat unforgivable? Holly reluctantly signed up to the tour that killed him to raise money that Petty had tied up in litigation. *The Buddy Holly Story* isn't actually the Buddy Holly story at all.

The makers' avoidance of this vital component in Holly's life and death was probably inspired by fear of litigation: Petty was still alive at the time. But there are other serious flaws to Steve Rash's film. Much of the acting is poor aside from the three principals, and Maria Richwine is especially awful as Holly's wife. The gags largely fall flat, despite Busey's natural comic talent. The dialogue often can't make up its mind whether its old-school exposition or naturalist banter. But the major flaw is that, the closer the film gets to the unhappy ending we all know is coming, the more trite and hagiographic the film gets, as if Rash suddenly decides to remake *The Glenn Miller Story* after all. A long medley of Holly hits performed (badly) by Busey with an orchestra replacing the Crickets puts the audience in a position where we're waiting for the guy to get on with it and get on the plane. Except that he doesn't. Rash makes the bizarre decision to replace the drama of the crash (that also famously killed fellow rockers Ritchie Valens and the Big Bopper) with this bland facsimile of his last show. Though it's admirable that the script completely avoids portentous lines about mystical rock death, the fudged ending is still a bizarre loss of nerve that keeps the film entirely grounded.

So why is this a good movie at all? It's partly down to its moral gusto. Rash has a lot of fun ripping the piss out of American racism, with the certainty of one those metropolitan liberal types who has deluded himself into thinking it was all sorted by 1978. But for Rash and screenwriters Robert Gittler and Alan Sawyer, this story is all about race: whites not allowed to play black music, whites not allowed to play with black musicians to black audiences, whites not allowed to date Latin women, drummers (it's always the drummer) making cracks about 'dark meat'. It's the film's upbeat attack on racial segregation, and promotion of Holly as a depoliticized but determined crusader for integration, that gives a slight story an unlikely substance.

And then there's things like the show at the Harlem Apollo where Holly is bottom of a bill comprising – get this – Fats Domino, Chuck Berry, Sam Cooke, Clyde McPhatter and the Drifters and Laverne Baker. Of such nights, the modern world was made. The scene where Buddy and the Crickets have to win over the Apollo's horrified all-black crowd with their hillbilly sounds should be as corny as fuck. But this is where Rash's masterstroke of hiring three actors who could play the songs live hits paydirt. The punk rock ferocity of the opening version of 'Oh Boy' forces you to believe the fairy-tale, the 'music-breaks-all-barriers' silliness of it. This incendiary two minutes is one of the most stirring performances in rock film.

But mainly, it's all about Gary Busey, and a performance so casually memorable and dominant that you suspect that the eccentric Texan is a better Buddy Holly than Buddy Holly. His goofy charisma and edge of darkness lends dimensions and enigma to

Holly that you quickly realise are not in the script. Busey was nominated for an Oscar for the portrayal and his performances in this and the same year's surf classic *Big Wednesday* marked Busey out as one of the potential heavyweight character actors of his era. Instead, erratic behaviour, cocaine addiction and brain damage resulting from a 1988 motorcycle accident has led to a recent career as an all-purpose rent-a-loony for reality TV and shows like *Entourage*, where he plays himself as a self-obsessed nutcase.

All of which makes *The Buddy Holly Story* a dodgy but enjoyable and influential film about a man who had it all and lost it in a cruel twist of fate. And Buddy Holly.

The Last Waltz

1978
Starring: The Band, Bob Dylan, Van Morrison, Joni Mitchell, Neil Young, Eric Clapton, A Beatle, A Stone ... erm ... Neil Diamond ...
Dir.: Martin Scorsese

★ ★

Plot: The biggest mutual back-slap in rock history ... until Live Aid, anyway.
Key line: 'We tried to call ourselves the Honkies. Everybody kind of backed off from that, you know?'

The Last Waltz is a film of the Band's farewell show from Thanksgiving Day 1976. Of course, it isn't just a concert film, because it's made by none other than Martin Scorsese, who was right in the middle of filming *New York, New York* and was pretty much at his peak. It is therefore beautifully shot by cinematographers including Michael Chapman and the great Laszlo Kovacs, has crystal clear sound, and has the members of the Band – Robbie Robertson, Garth Hudson, Rick Danko,

Levon Helm and Richard Manuel – talking about their history. It also has almost anyone who was anyone in the late 1970s roots-rock establishment turning up to ... shudder ... *jam* with their great mates. I've avoided this movie like the plague since it was first released, and fully expected to hate it with a passion, due to my severe aversion to the entire notion of 'proper rock' that it symbolises. But, actually ... it's bearable.

Or it might have been, if the Band didn't keep rudely interrupting things to play their *horrible* music. Stodgy, bland, *faux*-Americana – 'cos they're Canadian, apart from Helm, lest we forget. My favourite rock writer, Greil Marcus, is almost as obsessed with analysing and re-analysing the Band as he is with Bob Dylan, and I think of myself as relatively eclectic in my tastes ... but I'm baffled as to how a critic who understands the political and sexual deviance of Brit punk and post-punk better than anyone can hear anything worthwhile in this aggressively sexless middle-aged hetero sludge. They do a version here of Bo Diddley's 'Who Do You Love?' with their former mentor Ronnie Hawkins which contrives to transform the most visionary piece of electric voodoo eroticism ever written into a blueprint for Dire fucking Straits. It's rock with all danger and imagination and velocity and frustration surgically removed and replaced with dragging beats, musak keyboards and dahn-the-pub bonhomie.

The concert took place at Winterland, San Francisco ... the same venue where the Sex Pistols played their last show just 14 months later. You couldn't get two shows that said two more polar opposite things about rock. The Band are all technique and sharecropper beards, and smiles and community and nothing illuminating to say about anything. The Pistols' show is a nihilistic black hole that took the simple act of going onstage and playing guitar rock as far down as it could go. It's hard to believe that the two shows are from the same era, and that that era could sustain two such mutually exclusive but potent rock-historical symbols. If you attempt to cross the two, you probably get Oasis. Liam even has the beard nowadays.

The film's major saving grace is guitarist Robertson, who you can tell, right from his conversation with Scorsese at the beginning of the film, has decided to play the part of a charismatic young rock star making the best of some actually rather dull we-paid-our-dues anecdotes. This is a good thing 'cos the truth that we rock journalists never tell you is that rock musicians are murderously fucking dull when they're just being themselves. They're only engaging company when they start playing whatever role they used to establish their image. Oddly, musicians from other genres – pop, rap, jazz, punk, reggae, whatever – are exactly the opposite: tedious when hiding behind their image, fascinating when they start being themselves. Anyway, Scorsese concentrates all his non-music focus on Robertson, and his knowing but boyish enthusiasm stops one from falling asleep. The rest of the Band seem like a bunch of *Beavis and Butthead* dicks. This is put into some kind of perspective when you realise that Robertson is the only Band member credited as producer. Interestingly, Robertson has gone onto a successful career as a music business guru.

Scorsese also does us a favour by making the performances stand alone without being interspersed with voiceover or skits or exciting visual experiments of any kind, so you can just fast-forward straight through 'em. You might wanna stop for Dr John doing 'Such a Night' (he looks like a star and not even the Band can entirely ruin a song that good), Muddy Waters doing 'Mannish Boy' (ditto), Joni Mitchell being casually unique, Van Morrison for the terrible clothes, and Dylan for managing to make corkscrew hair and a scraggly beard look cool ... but your life won't be the poorer if you don't. They're just musicians, playing some tunes, in a can't-possibly-dance-or-shag-to-it way. Well, apart from Waters. I mean, you can't *dance* to Mannish Boy, but ...

The big finish sees Ron Wood and Ringo join the gathered throng of Rock Greats for a crowd scene version of 'I Shall Be Released'. It comes and it goes and finally, I am released. But not before the Band do a staged performance of a waltz called 'The Last Waltz'. Man, these people are literal.

My trusty *Radio Times Guide to Films* gives this *five stars* (and these guys only gave *Harold and Kumar Get the Munchies* three stars, so you can see how strict they are) and insists that *The Last Waltz* is 'a masterpiece of pop cinema'. Well, maybe it is. In which case, *Dirty Dancing* is a grim but provocative study of urban alienation from the Golden Age of Czechoslovakian neo-realism.

• •

The Rutles – All You Need Is Cash

1978
Starring: Eric Idle, Neil Innes, John Halsey, Ricky Fataar
Dir.: Eric Idle and Gary Weis

★ ★ ★

Plot: Monty Python's Life of Beatles.
Key line: 'Their first album was made in twenty minutes. The second took even longer.'

There's no disputing the seminal nature of this made-for-TV Beatles parody. It was the first full-length piss-take of the rock world. Its mock-doc format was nicked wholesale by the makers of *This Is Spinal Tap* (see p. 264). Its pastiches of Beatles songs and familiar visuals from their career are brilliantly conceived. And it's an enduring cult amongst the kind of anal, college-educated rockbloke that writes rude letters to *Mojo* magazine when they print something about the music made by women, the young and black people … a sort of *Hitchhiker's Guide to the Galaxy for Grumpy Old Dadrockers*. But beware of the man (and it will be a man) who tells you that it's a pants-wetting work of genius – because it's a 70-minute waste of time for anyone who isn't obsessed with the Beatles. And, contrary to popular belief, that would include most of us.

Written, co-directed and starring Monty Python 'nudge-nudge' merchant Eric Idle … *All You Need Is Cash* is a sixth-form revue re-telling of the Beatles' story made into something a bit better by clever recreations of the Fab Four's most infamous screen appearances and former Bonzo Dog Doo Dah member Neil Innes' bravura twists on Beatles songs. The likes of 'Cheese and Onions' ('A Day in the Life'), 'Ouch!' ('Help!'), 'Hold My Hand' ('I Want to Hold Your Hand'), 'Love Life' ('All You Need Is Love'), 'Piggy in the Middle' (I Am the Walrus'), 'Let's Be Natural' ('Dear Prudence') and 'Doubleback Alley' ('Penny Lane') are touched by genius, altering the originals often by virtue of one chord or key change and a parodied lyric, and performed and produced with sincere musical artfulness and attention to detail.

What makes the film dated and somewhat tiresome is the smugness. The story is told by Idle's Alan Whicker-like narrator, a conceit he finds so hilarious that he dispenses with writing himself any jokes. The script is all sniggery schoolboy puns, barely disguised old music hall skits and lame gags like the replacement of LSD with 'tea' . . . the Beatles admit they've taken 'tea', inspiring thousands to experiment with 'tea' . . . geddit? No? Good for you.

The self-congratulatory tone is reinforced by the star cameos: Mick Jagger, Bill Murray, Paul Simon, Dan Ackroyd, John Belushi, Michael Palin, Ronnie Wood, Bianca Jagger and George Harrison himself all make appearances which are deemed to be funny by their very presence. The basis of both the film's cult appeal and myriad flaws is the laziness of the celebrity in-joke . . . 'Look, a star's laughing at another star, and therefore, themselves! If I get what jolly good sports they're all being, then it's like I'm in their star club! Must laugh. *Must laugh* . . . HAHAHA!!!' . . . and so on. If, on the other hand, you think comedy is funny because it's well-written and performed, you'll find the Rutles irritatingly half-baked.

A couple of skits stand out, though. The best early joke is a visit to New Orleans where blues singer Rutling Orange Peel claims to have invented the Rutles' music, before his wife interjects angrily, suggesting that every time a documentary is made about a white musician he does the same thing. And the only laugh-out-loud segment is inspired, predictably, by the arrival of Yoko Ono in the tale. She's parodied here as moustachioed Nazi stormtrooper Chastity, 'A simple German girl whose father invented World War 2.' Admittedly, ripping the piss out of John and Yoko's bed-ins and art happenings phase – not to mention blues singers with amusing names – is the satirical equivalent of kicking a cripple.

But the major irritation is the film's reluctance to match the implication of the title . . . that what you're about to see is an attack on the god-like aura around the Beatles, a reminder that all those symbolically counter-cultural acts their fans obsess about actually made them rich. Despite being made before Lennon's death, *All You Need Is Cash* is too busy wanting to be mates with the Beatles to say anything controversial or pertinent about them. It's a silly film by Beatles trainspotters, for silly Beatles trainspotters. The makers of *This Is Spinal Tap*, in sharp contrast, took their amalgam of different Brit-metal bands and located an attack on pretension and machismo that someone who'd never heard a metal record could understand and laugh at.

Satire bites. Parody licks arse. This film's tongue is a nasty shade of brown.

• •

Rockers

1978

Starring: Leroy Wallace, Jacob Miller, Gregory Isaacs, Burning Spear, Richard Hall
Dir.: Theodoros Bafaloukos

★ ★ ★

Plot: Carry On Rasta.
Key line: 'Dem t'ief mi bike!'

The opening scene is a masterpiece of iconography for counter-culture boys. Eleven Rastafarian musicians crushed into a small space in a shot designed to look like a painting. The space looks like a treehouse, and the only instrument that isn't percussion or vocal is an acoustic guitar. Ganja is being imbibed from a bulbous bong. The men positioned at the front of the shot all look like pillars of mystical and ancient wisdom, with their beards and dread-locks, and their faraway, pensive expressions.

An African percussion rhythm begins to slowly build and lock into a groovy, low-tempo stomp. As the dope smoke swirls, there are sudden unison chants of 'Jah Rastafari!' and the guitarist begins to play a reggae riff. Suddenly, this random jam is a song, a beautiful one, carried entirely by harmony vocals. 'There is a land, far far away', it croons plaintively, because it is a version of the reggae roots and displacement classic called 'Satta Massagana' performed by the Abbysinians and Ras Michael and the Sons of Negus. The man standing 'stage' left walks away from the musicians, sits in front of the camera and begins to address us. He is thin and shirtless, and his beard and dreads make him look like the old man of the hills, even though you can see that he's roughly in his 30s. He wishes us 'Greetings and love', and welcomes us into the film with a bunch of spiritual platitudes which are inclined to sound deep and substantial when spoken in thick Jamaican patois. The patois is entirely uncompromised by the need to be comprehensible to non-Jamaicans, so the love 'n' peace gibberish is helpfully translated by subtitle, as is the rest of the movie. He returns to his former position, and the band plays on.

From this scene onwards, you might think that you are going to be treated to a self-consciously authentic reggae movie so raw and *vérité* it makes *The Harder They Come* (see p. 128) look like an ad for the Jamaican tourist board. But *Rockers* actually becomes a daft, ambling comedy designed to showcase Jamaican music at its late 1970s peak. Its story – a ridiculous half-story which only exists as an excuse for the music, the male rebel poses and the depictions of rasta lifestyle – concerns skinny rasta rude boy Horsemouth (Wallace) and his attempts to become a music biz hustler by way of distributing records on his motorbike and being a hotshot drummer. Along the way he meets characters played by real-life reggae stars Miller, Isaacs, Robbie Shakespeare, Big Youth, Dr Alimantado, Leroy Smart, the Mighty Diamonds and Burning Spear aka Winston Rodney, and we get to see some of them perform in evocative, humble settings. The nightmarish poverty and ugliness of the Jamaican ghetto is given a dignity and beauty by the subtly roving camera, and women exist to look after babies and give their shiftless men food and money.

The music, which is all from the conscious, militant sphere of the reggae spectrum as popularized by Bob Marley, explodes from the soundtrack with irresistible force and an ebullience that transforms a potential vision of Hell into a vibrant portrayal of survival under heavy manners. We get to watch natty dreads play football, make and sell records out of the sexiest record stores of a rockboy's dreams, dance like strutting peacocks, smoke dope, act the fool and talk bollocks and are forced to accept that they do look pretty cool while doing it. None of the actors can act for shit, and that's what keeps the film real.

Greek director Theodoros Bafaloukos was still a photographer by trade when he wrote and directed *Rockers*, and his interest here is in the look and sound of Jamaica and its underclass. There is a scene at an outdoor soundsystem dance which is an unforgettable chaos of flash clothes, crazy dance steps, random play-fighting and stolen motorbikes which makes you feel like you've been dropped in the middle of a riotous alien planet. While *The Harder They Come* is interested in politics, corruption and thriller conventions, Bafaloukos rejects all that in favour of trying to encapsulate the folk-art of reggae music, the romance of making records, and the constant chatter and frantic activity of the Kingston shanty towns. While the two films share portrayals of music biz moguls as Americanised and obscenely rich tyrants, Bafaloukos seems too charmed by reggae's streetwise exuberance to care about the slave overseer. This should be the downfall of *Rockers*, but the film is distinguished by its absence of white liberal attempts to simplify and trivialize a nation's complex economic and racial history. It's simply a snapshot of a culture and an era and its people, shot with both imagination and flair, which cleverly passes over the usual obsessions with repression, stardom and money in favour of a plot based around a motorbike ... a symbol of freedom and self-sufficiency in a small and cluttered world, used as a MacGuffin for a reggae-fied comic heist.

When Whitey does turn up in *Rockers*, he consists of a comically middle-class couple staring with bemusement at a performing reggae band in a touristy restaurant and saying, 'Hey! That's no calypso!' in 1950s BBC English. The slyly self-parodic tone builds throughout *Rockers*, as Horsemouth responds to being pushed to the ground by a bigger man with a comic lecture to camera about rasta non-violence, and incidental extras start chewing on gigantic watermelons. It's this eccentricity that mitigates against the awful acting and editing, as we suddenly find ourselves at a gospel baptism, or at a garish diner playing disco which inspires a roots reggae DJ siege.

Undercutting *The Harder They Come*'s death or glory theme, *Rockers* portrays rebellion as consequence-free, Robin Hood fun. All of which makes *Rockers* the reggae version of *Woodstock* (see p. 97) and *Rude Boy* (see p. 233) – a document of the roots of a pop culture tribe and the reasons why it was appealing enough to become big business.

• •

The Kids Are Alright

1978
Starring: The Who
Dir.: Jeff Stein

★ ★ ★ ★

Plot: TWANG! SCREE! CRASH! BOOM!!! *KER-CHING!*
Key line: 'Rock 'n' roll's never ever stood dissecting and inspecting at close range. It just doesn't stand up. So shut up.'

Jeff Stein was an American Who fan who produced a Who photo book around their 1970 tour at just 17 years old. In keeping with that kind of youthful precocity, Stein had no film-making experience whatsoever when he approached his favourite rock band with the idea of making a cinematic film out of nothing but clips of live shows, TV appearances and interviews. The end result is a unique movie; a visceral mix of documentary, biopic and montage that proves that The Who are a unique group. There's simply no other band violent, funny, tricksy, analytical, slapdash, charismatic and self-deprecating enough to present as a thought-provoking 90-minute entertainment without chronology, voiceover, captions or contextual interviews. *The Kids Are Alright* just chucks The Who at you and stands well back.

The tone is set perfectly in the opening clip: a legendary 1967 appearance on American TV show *The Smothers Brothers Comedy Hour*. It sums up everything about The Who that is brilliant – and self-damaging – in five hilarious, thrilling minutes.

We join the show as The Who finish playing 'I Can See for Miles'. They look both stylish and incongruous in their fab Beau Brummel gear, all ruffled shirts and hair caught somewhere between street-fighting 1966 mod and flowered-up 1967 hippy.

Comedian Tommy Smothers, youngish, clean-cut and slick in

his preppy suit, has the job of attempting to introduce a band who are still some way off of American success to the watching millions, and finds himself in a world of pain. The four give him an unsettling mixture of too much and not enough, throwing him off balance. The viewer can't tell whether the band like him or despise him, and you suspect that the same is true for Smothers himself, even when Keith Moon cuts him dead with a waspish: 'My friends call me Keith. But *you* can call me John.' Smothers makes lame attempts to return the mocking but only makes himself look less in control of the situation.

Finally, he leaves the stage and The Who crash into a great version of 'My Generation', completely live and completely stunning in its controlled violence, with Daltrey making especially good use of his stammered taunting of the old and in the way. Bassist John Entwistle is the unlikely star; the calm, comically distracted eye of this storm, his fingers a dizzying rush on the high-speed bass solos, his head and body perfectly still and utterly disinterested.

Smothers has already intimated that something unusual is going to happen, so there's no surprise for us or the programme-makers when Townshend and Moon begin to violently smash their gear as the song dissolves into its end chaos. But Moon has come up with something that no-one – not even the rest of the band – is prepared for. He has planted a bomb in his drum kit. It explodes with a deep, frightening BOOM!!! For a moment, Pete Townshend's hair is on fire and he is apparently rendered temporarily deaf. This is a significant moment; Townshend has suffered from tinnitus ever since.

The stage is a circus of billowing smoke, crashing instruments and human debris. The bewildered Smothers tries to restore authority by creeping on with an acoustic guitar in hand – he was obviously all set to top the instrument-smashing with a scripted musical joke. But the poor guy is lost and scared. Every time he seems ready to talk, another piece of Moon's kit crashes to the floor with expert comic timing.

Finally, Pete spots the acoustic guitar, wrestles it away from the hapless host, and smashes it to pieces. Smothers is humiliated. Game over. Roll opening credits.

Keith Moon, famous for destroying hotel rooms, driving cars into swimming pools, and drowning in booze and drugs and thereby inventing the rock 'n' roll cliché, died of an overdose of anti-alcohol drug Colmethiazole in September 1978 at the age of 31 and made *The Kids Are Alright* into an accidental epitaph. And, although there are plenty of Moon's madcap antics in the movie, Stein is to be applauded for avoiding any sentimental acknowledgements of the drummer's demise. You're left to decide whether Moon was a hilarious maverick or the world's most irritating office clown, while being left in no doubt that his endless negation of Townshend's intellectualism and introspection was vital to the creative tensions surrounding The Who. They were never a great studio band again after his death.

Guests that wander into The Who's on-camera history include Melvyn Bragg, Ken Russell, Ringo Starr, Jeremy Paxman and Steve Martin, but all are small beer compared to the band themselves. Take their first US TV appearance on a pop show called *Shindig*. Whether the presenter's announcement that it's the last-ever *Shindig* is anything to do with what follows we don't know. But the young, whiplash-thin and fabulously moddy Who are a sight to behold. And especially Daltrey, who does a super-stylish James Brown shimmy before fixing camera and audience with a look of glassy-eyed, speed-freaked, come-and-have-a-go fury that predicts Johnny Rotten with eerie prescience. The Who that perform 'I Can't Explain' here are monochrome, spotty, and look like they want to take the whole of America outside for a scrap.

From there, we cut immediately to a later Who appearance from Britain's Russell Harty chat show, another Townshend amp smashes to the ground, the hyper Moon is a camp barrow-boy and makes a lame joke about 83 Pakistanis living in the now horizontal gear. And then, Bang! It's now a 1978, pre-Moon overdose Who performing 'Baba O'Reilly', and they may (except Daltrey) look older but are still imperious and define how to make hard rock without being punk or metal.

This crash-edit refusal to shilly-shally soon pulls us into even more interesting territory, as various bits of extraordinary footage are used to paint a picture of these four unholy fools. Chat show interviews are cut with clips of early pre-fame shows and strange skits like Moon being interviewed about his public image while dressed in full leather-masked fetish wear and being half-heartedly flogged. Again, here is the set text for Malcolm McLaren's Sex shop outrages and the queasy use of fetish wear for his and Julien Temple's *The Great Rock 'n' Roll Swindle* (see p. 206)

But anything about The Who is, inevitably, mainly about Pete Townshend. At one point, Melvyn Bragg asks a tortuous question on some arts show about Woodstock (see p. 97), finally managing to end with: 'What did it change?' A bored Townshend quickly answers, 'Well, it changed me. I *hated* it.' Many of the film's most entertaining moments come from Pete's self-flagellating denunciations of everything cool – including a sneering trashing of the Beatles – and he and Moon's double-act, which reaches a peak on a Harty clip when, in response to a question about tensions within the band, the pair launch into a perfectly timed routine where both talk over the top of each other with Moon virulently gainsaying everything Pete has just said a second beforehand.

At one point, a very young Townshend says this to an interviewer: 'You have to resign yourself to the fact that a large part of the audience is sort of thick, you know, and don't appreciate quality ... The fact is that our group don't have any quality. It's just musical sensationalism.'

Man ... I love that. Can you imagine any current rock or pop star saying anything like it now, when musicians are so conditioned to lick consumer arse that they're virtually ready to give us all their home phone number and a quick one off the wrist if we'll only love them in return? He's echoed by Daltrey, who seldom speaks, perhaps because he can't resist saying things like 'Rock 'n' roll's got no future' and calling The Who the worst rock 'n' roll band in the world. This undercutting of The Who's art and impact is also apparent in Stein's sly running joke: a frustrated Townshend's recurring insistence that The Who must stop being a gimmicky live band – and them never, ever stopping being the most gimmicky live band of all time.

I found myself prevaricating over the star rating for *The Kids Are Alright*. Because it's obvious that, if you don't like The Who and have no interest in 1960s guitar bands behaving badly, this movie won't be your cup of tea at all. But I plumped for four stars in the end because the film is a perfect idea, perfectly executed.

Stein never directed a cinematic feature again, going on to American television including writing and production for popular 1970s sitcom *Barney Miller*. Bruce Springsteen commissioned him in the 1980s to direct the promo for *Dancing in the Dark* and then sacked him ... and it's hard to believe that anyone could make a worse video than the one Springsteen did use of him dancing really, *really* badly. But Stein's one rock shot is unique, thrilling and a great time-capsule reminder of when snotty bands smashing up stuff was still shocking, big and clever.

● ●

Jubilee

1978

Starring: Jenny Runacre, Little Nell, Toyah Willcox, Orlando, Jordan, Wayne County, Richard O'Brien, Adam Ant, Helen of Troy
Dir.: Derek Jarman

★ ★ ★

Plot: Elizabeth I visits the 1970s to witness punk end civilisation as we know it.
Key line: 'As long as the music's loud enough, we won't hear the world falling apart.'

A bewildering, occasionally tedious, unapologetically pretentious and strangely compelling jumble of art-punk images and nihilistic slogans, the debut film from celebrated British *auteur* Derek Jarman is a product of a specific time and place. That time and place is the

King's Road, Chelsea in the mid 1970s as Malcolm McLaren and Vivienne Westwood created the Situationist petri dish from which shocking little Sex Pistols could grow and infect the world with visions of no future in England's dreaming. In Jarman's imaginary England, law and order has been abolished, Myra Hindley is a role model, and gangs of punks marshalled by a chubby Toyah rule the streets by force, destroying passers-by in order to create ... um ... well, nothing, actually. Sex shop acolyte Jordan gets to do ballet in a rubble-strewn bombsite next to a masked man with a huge penis, fellow Pistol friend and little person Helen gets some practice in for *The Great Rock 'n' Roll Swindle* (see p. 206) as Liz's lady-in-waiting and a pre-stardom Adam Ant gets an 'introducing' credit. *Jubilee* chucks together the concerns of the Pistols, Jean-Luc Godard (*again!*) Andy Warhol and Ken Russell (Jarman began his film career as Russell's set designer) with the gleeful mania of a man who believed that sets crammed with satirical detail, gorgeous, pouting boys, characters called Chaos, Mad, Crabs and Amyl Nitrate, and the epic sweep of classical music are much more interesting than mundanities like script, acting or plot. It's one of the key benchmarks of that part of punk that just wanted to be as contrary and transgressive as possible before it inevitably became just another layer of rock orthodoxy ... the bit that wore swastikas, glorified random violence, formed bands called Raped and the Moors Murderers and was never explained cleverly enough by the art schoolers to achieve anything else but inspiring the bully-boy quasi-fascist OI! scene. In *Jubilee*'s case, this translated as lots of swearing, fetishistic murder, burning Union Jacks, breaking Winston Churchill mugs, ugly shagging, stunningly bad acting and a mime.

There isn't really a story. England – which means London – has become an anarcho-fascist war zone, Elizabeth I creeps among the ruins in a fruitless search for Albion's former glory, and a gang of punks do naughty stuff in various dank rooms and bombed-out streets. Very early punk bands crop up – Siouxsie and the Banshees and Chelsea on a fake *Top of the Pops*, a pre-panto pop Adam and the Ants, naturally. Toyah ends her song by gobbing on us. New

York punk's token tranny Wayne County (later Jayne County, post-op) is a scream performing 'Paranoia Paradigm' in her living-room with curtains like my mum used to have, before being murdered.

Like many an early punk intellectual, Jarman obviously hated punk music and interrupts the mayhem to make Adam go look at statues of Mozart and Bach. But still, killing Chelsea's male model singer by suffocating him with a plastic sheet and dumping him in mud next to the Thames probably wasn't a bad idea, in hindsight. And the song performances do look pretty tame compared to cops with monster cocks (are you detecting a theme here?) having violent sex with each other at blood-soaked punk-disco orgies before the Slits dismantle a Ford Anglia. Who needs people playing when you can have psycho feminists on the rampage? Certainly not me.

It all gets going when Jordan does a cod-reggae version of 'Rule Britannia' as the United Kingdom's Eurovision entry, resplendent in cavalier helmet, *Aladdin Sane* make-up, hooker lingerie and a Union Jack apron. She's being sponsored by a bug-eyed cackling old queen called Borgia Ginz who has bought the entire global media (and Buckingham Palace). Julien Temple definitely took some notes on the theatre pastiche of Jordan's performance before filming Sid Vicious' version of 'My Way', and McLaren copped the (very funny) music for the Black Arabs' disco-Pistols sequence in . . . *Swindle*. Jordan's grotesque parody of a porn star is pretty fabulous, too, and much smarter than poor Mary Millington's turn in Temple's film. One's suspicion that Jarman is heavily influenced by Peter Watkins' brilliant *Privilege* (see p. 64) is reinforced by yet another rocked-up version of Blake's 'Jerusalem', still the greatest song about England, Sex Pistols notwithstanding.

One of the best scenes looks like a happy accident. Sphinx (played by Karl Johnson) takes Adam's fledgling pop star Kid off at one point for a short tour of grey, grim London by rooftop, and starts in on a classic, cliché-ridden punk-era rant about tower blocks and social conformity . . . and Adam can't look at him for laughing. Could be in the script, but considering Adam is to acting what Ant Rap was to hip hop, you suspect the laughter's very real, and the way Johnson keeps selling it to him like a stand-up is very endearing.

It's also a glimpse of just how quickly punk protest had become a joke among the punk inner circle, while we naive provincial Everykids were still taking it all desperately seriously.

Future *Chariots of Fire* star Ian Charleson plays an incestuous brother and we get to see his willy, too. But Jenny Runacre is a strange choice to lead the cast, playing both QE1 and psychopathic gang leader Bod. Devoid of the goofy charisma of Toyah, Jordan or Adam, yet no better an actor than them, she seems like the film's big missed trick, the blowing of an opportunity to give such a scattershot movie a watchable focus. All the *faux*-Shakespearian Elizabethan intrusions fail to reveal any point to their presence here, and she and the perennially annoying Richard O'Brien (and the fucking mime!) are chief among the reasons why. But every time *Jubilee* threatens to get too up its own arse, someone screams 'No Future!' while chucking a molotov cocktail, or ironically references pop TV show *Rock Follies* as post-coital chat, or tightrope walks across a washing-line while singing Edith Piaf's 'Je ne regrette rien'. *Jubilee* is too busy mocking itself to insist upon itself, and arguably does it better than *The Great Rock 'n' Roll Swindle*. Arguably, mind.

Jubilee is one of those movies that requires a certain readjustment of the brain before enjoyment can be had. The first ten minutes are so pretentious and baffling that no-one would be blamed for flipping over to *My Madeover Fat Kid Ate a Masterchef* and having done with it. But stick with it and you enter a psychological zone where two old ladies at the bingo saying, 'They threw the toaster in the bath and she was electrocuted. What do you expect with millions unemployed?' seems both logical and quaintly amusing. Toyah's stage-school hamming and bouncy cartoon androgyny becomes particularly wonderful, in an 'ooh, I can barely watch' sort of way. She pulls off the idea of Mad as meta-punk by way of sheer enthusiasm.

If Jarman was trying to tell us that, by 1978, we English all spoke in clichés and were totally desensitised to violence . . . well, I actually have no idea whether that's what he was trying to say at all. But his way of saying it looks like no other rock movie – no other movie, period – that I've seen, and that's always something to treasure. I suspect that the best way to watch *Jubilee* is on a big screen, at a club or party, with the sound down. The extraordinary run of grainy, ugly-beautiful images will give party-goers some surreal sex and violence to watch while they chat about house prices and decide whether to dance. One always needs an icebreaker when one is entertaining.

• •

The Punk Rock Movie

1978

Starring: Sex Pistols, The Clash, The Slits, Siouxsie and the Banshees, etc.
Dir.: Don Letts

★ ★ ★

Plot: London's early punk scene shot on 8mm by rasta DJ and scenester
Key line: 'Don't film me! I look awful!'

As punk percolated in West London in 1975/76, a Jamaican shop assistant found himself the right man in the right place. From his stall in the Acme Attractions mini-market in the Kings Road, Chelsea, Don Letts sold reggae records and dope to the scene's hip young things. He became everyone's best black friend, which gave him unrivalled access to the roots of a counter-cultural movement. So, when the Roxy club opened for 100 days in 1977 to give a venue to the endlessly banned bands, Letts was asked to be resident DJ. And when the boy decided that his ambitions lay in film-making, he bought himself a cheap camera and pointed it at his infamous mates. The results were a film that looked and sounded exactly like early punk rock – ramshackle, amateurish, childish, cacophonous and strangely compelling.

There is no narration nor interview in Letts' documentary. He simply points his camera at the leading punk bands from London and New York while they play at the Roxy, or rehearse and record at tiny studios, or wait to perform in scruffy dressing-rooms, or lark about on the tour bus. The sound quality is appalling, which means you can barely make out what anyone's saying, and the tinny distorted recordings of live songs are occasionally replaced by the studio versions . . . which is annoying and feels like a cheat. The most memorable musical moments are provided by the Slits and Siouxsie and the Banshees, playing stunning hooligan art music long before they were signed and acquired a modicum of professionalism. Otherwise, the stand-outs are telling little incidents that Letts stumbled upon along the way: a giggly Topper Headon of the Clash riding a child's play-car outside a service station until a shop assistant threatens to call the police; more boys in blue forcing a display of severed body parts (made out of plastic) to be removed from the King's Road's Boy boutique; future Pogue Shane MacGowan pogoing; the lead singer of Eater serenading a pig's head before beating it up and throwing it into the crowd; former Clash and future PiL guitarist Keith Levine and friends shooting up in the Roxy bogs; an anonymous boy turning his torso into a red and dripping pin-stripe suit with the aid of a razor-blade; the Slits playing a children's show; a girl with a swastika on one cheek and a safety-pin through the other complaining about being sacked from her job in a shop; an uncredited Jamaican bloke teaching Alternative TV how to play reggae; New York's Heartbreakers, led by former New York Doll and professional junkie Johnny Thunders, being a proper, professional cock-rock band, which suddenly cuts to a fresh-faced and beautiful Banshees taking vitamin pills in a dressing-room while listening to Donna Summer. London 5, New York 0.

The big reason the film works is Letts' clever decision to not ask the punks to explain themselves. In the similar but inferior *DOA*, Lech Kowalski's shambolic 1980 account of punk and the Sex Pistols in America, the technical inadequacies of the film-making are made yet more embarrassing by Kowlaski's trite attempts to give punk a political context. When both London and America's punks tried to talk about why this all mattered, all that ensued was platitudes and boredom. By keeping schtum and barely making what anyone says audible, Letts conjures up a feeling of what it all was – a directionless anarchy, accidentally manufactured by weird, bored outcast kids, behaving like hyperactive and cheerfully wicked infants who've somehow bunked into the big boys' playground. It becomes hypnotic, and whether the band playing are any good or not also becomes irrelevant, as it should be.

And then there's the Sex Pistols. It's only when you see footage of the Pistols at their best that you realise just how much Johnny Rotten dominated the band visually, how he really was the only unconventional thing about them. See him, in a white dress shirt and bow tie, whippet-thin and beautiful, blurring the lines between rock iconography, cartoon anger and slapstick comedy. The DVD features an oddly irrelevant 1983 interview with Lydon by the film's Australian executive producer Peter Clifton, in which Lydon cheerfully and fiercely states his refusal to do all the shitty, boring, sell-out things that he inevitably went on to do over the following 25 years. It's pretty depressing. *The Punk Rock Movie* itself, however, is a wonderful, modest slice of cultural history which reminds you just how young, dumb, smart, brave, annoying and doomed punk's stars were at the beginning, and makes you want to forgive them all their later sins.

• •

The Great Rock 'n' Roll Swindle

1979

Starring: Sex Pistols, Malcolm McLaren, Helen of Troy, Ronald Biggs
Dir.: Julien Temple

★ ★ ★

Plot: How Malcolm McLaren killed Bambi.
Key line: 'Malcolm McLaren came up here. Beautiful ear. He should have been the singer.'

The Great Rock 'n' Roll Swindle is one of the most audacious spin jobs in British cultural history. Having failed to keep control of the career of the most important band of their generation, Sex Pistols' manager Malcolm McLaren made a movie that presented the entire world-changing adventure of the Pistols – the accidental triumphs and the mistakes that led to real tragedies – as a masterplan designed to expose and defeat the rock industry. In the bonus interview on this DVD, McLaren's partner in this endeavour, director and screenwriter Julien Temple, says that the film set out to 'enrage the fans' by undermining the Pistols' status as – and therefore the phenomenon of – Rock Gods. 'The myth had to be dynamited', he recalls. Which would be more heroic if . . . *Swindle* hadn't successfully replaced it with another equally vapid myth . . . that McLaren hadn't just manufactured the Pistols and their shock value, but had deliberately manipulated the entire British establishment. Because . . . *Swindle* didn't enrage the fans at all – it just convinced us, in our Bambi-like innocence, that the band that had changed our lives and given us a glimpse of a potentially better Britain had actually just been one big joke. No-one came out of the cinema and rioted. They just became cynical and jaded and perfect fodder for the nihilist 1980s.

To be fair to Temple, he was a young film student who had literally stumbled onto his path in the movie industry when he'd chanced upon the early Pistols rehearsing in Rotherhithe and, detecting 'a sense of theatre in the room which you didn't get in rock and roll at that point', convinced them to let him follow them around with a camera. That made Temple exceptionally prescient but still no match for the older, wiser McLaren, who bullied Temple mercilessly through the making of the film. Temple admits, on the DVD director's commentary, that *The Filth and the Fury* (see p. 339) was 'the film I owed the Sex Pistols after making this'. Throughout the commentary Temple sounds embarrassed and reticent about his first film, often having to be prodded into saying anything by accompanying journalist Chris Salewicz. But none of this makes ... *Swindle* a worthless film. It is, at times, brilliant, and even when it isn't, it puts its finger on a whole bunch of peculiarly British cultural hypocrisies, neuroses and lies, often by virtue of its own clumsy dishonesty. It's also a great example of how a control freak can be his own worst enemy, in light of the long and bloody court case which saw the band members wrest all control of the Sex Pistols' legacy from McLaren in 1986.

The film is based around ten, somewhat spurious lessons in how to swindle the music industry, mainly told by McLaren to Little Person and original punk Helen of Troy. The Pistols' history is then hung around this loose structure using archive footage, animated sequences and Jean-Luc Godard-inspired surreal fictional sequences, most of which consist of Pistols' guitarist Steve Jones, in a detective's trenchcoat and titfer, trying to track down McLaren and the Pistols' money – the chief irony being that the Pistols' money had been spent on the film, which had been McLaren's obsession since he'd first approached US trash *auteur* Russ Meyer (see p. 93, *Beyond the Valley of the Dolls*) to make a somewhat different movie called *Who Killed Bambi?*

This mockumentary's twisted reflection of the Pistols' reality is unavoidable ... the first two-thirds of the film features the real Sex Pistols with Johnny Rotten aka John Lydon as lead singer, and is thrilling and funny and hugely entertaining. The last third of the film features the fake Pistols *sans* Rotten and is silly, prurient and boring, apart from the brilliant Sid Vicious trashing of 'My Way', and Tenpole Tudor's insane performance of an orchestral comic song called 'Who Killed Bambi?' How McLaren must have hated Rotten, who virtually stopped the country in its tracks by just singing in that voice and looking at us with those eyes that seemed to see straight through everything. Without him, McLaren is reduced to Eddie Cochran cover versions, and following charmless and gormless Great Train Robber Ronnie Biggs around Brazil and hiring someone to play minor Nazi Martin Bormann; getting Jones to call the elderly and much-loved character actress Irene Handl a cunt; getting porn star Mary Millington, who would soon commit suicide, to fake giving Jones a blow-job . . . all to (fail miserably to) shock a constituency that had already had its ideas of shocking radically rewritten by how savagely Britain had turned on the Pistols for telling a few home truths, and how the marketing of Sid Vicious as the ultimate junkie loser had actually ended up with two sordid deaths. Incidentally, it really is Sid's mother Anne Beverley that he 'shoots' first in the comically violent climax of 'My Way'. A few months later, she would give her son the smack that killed him.

The film ends with tabloid headlines about the murder of Sid Vicious' girlfriend Nancy Spungen, and the doomed bass player's subsequent death by heroin overdose. I'd always thought it was the most gratuitously unpleasant move on Temple's part – tacking tragic reality on the end without comment or context after 100 minutes of gleeful trivialisation of violence and nihilism. But Temple reveals on the commentary that he was forced into tacking on the tabs by the British Board of Film Censors – still powerful and patronising enough in 1979 to insist that even the most mischievous movie carried the right 'message' . . . i.e. don't try this punk rock at home, kids. In that context those headlines become a perfect encapsulation of the mind-numbing stupidity of the old British establishment, and how the Sex Pistols seemed to expose this stupidity by their very existence. The Thatcherites couldn't have changed Britain so radically without the Pistols as their stalking horses. And it's the good and very, very bad of that that makes *The Great Rock 'n' Roll Swindle* an important cultural artefact and a cowardly, brave and provocative film.

• •

Hair

1979

Starring: John Savage, Treat Williams, Beverly D'Angelo
Dir.: Milos Forman

★ ★

Plot: The dawning of the Age of Aquarius? Aw . . . you missed it, man. Bummer.
Key line: 'Gliddy glup gloopy nibby nabby noopy la la la lo lo/Sabba sibby sabba nooby abba nabba lee lee lo lo/Tooby ooby walla nooby abba nabba/Early morning singing song!' (from 'Good Morning Starshine').

Hair began its cultural life as the very first 'rock musical'. Written by American actors James Rado and George Ragni and much-sampled composer Galt McDermot, *Hair* opened in New York theatre in October 1967 (the Autumn of Love?) and ran on Broadway and in London's West End for well over a thousand performances. Its major selling-points were its controversial depictions of sex, drugs and anti-war American flag desecration, a racially integrated cast, a nude scene, hit songs 'The Age of Aquarius', 'Good Morning Starshine', 'Let the Sunshine in' and 'I Got Life', an odd little song which has remained popular due to Nina Simone's stirring version, and an invitation to audiences to come onstage and take part in a 'Be-in' at the show's finale. Strange, then, that it took 12 years and the largely unmourned death of hippy culture before a film version of *Hair* finally hit the cinemas. Stranger still that the job was given to heavyweight Czech director Milos Forman.

Forman was still riding high on the back of his seminal adaptation of Ken Kesey's beatnik rebel novel *One Flew Over the Cuckoo's Nest*, and his early satires had all been sympathetic, pro-freedom studies of the rebel outsider. So perhaps *Hair*'s draft-dodging hippy commune did seem a natural fit. But none of his films hinted at any potential flair for the presentation of stage musicals. Which is probably why *Hair* is so enjoyably, embarrassingly awful, and an entirely fitting way to treat both freeloading hippies and the enduring horror that is musical theatre.

The film was well received and it and its star Treat Williams even nabbed Golden Globe nominations. But sanity prevailed among us civilians. The film bombed and has become quietly forgotten. It's almost impossible to comprehend that this unintentionally hilarious smorgasbord of shite was made by the same feller that directed ... *Cuckoo's Nest* and *Amadeus*.

At least, one assumes that the savaging of *Hair*'s reputation was unintentional. The stage hit's co-writers Rado and Ragni weren't convinced. They hated the movie so much that they insisted that a film of *Hair* is yet to be made, complaining, with much justification, that Forman had made anti-war hippies look like 'oddballs' and an 'aberration'. Which is exactly what happens when you base an entire film around the most unlikely looking hippies on Earth living to scrounge, take drugs and make each other pregnant in New York's Central and Washington Square Parks while dodgy hoofers from the Twyla Tharp Dance Foundation do comedy dance duets with policemen on horseback. These hippies are so smug, work-shy and useless that you find yourself cheering on the Vietnam draft board.

The plot, which was also different from the stage version, goes like this: semi-autistic redneck mumbler Claude (the appalling Savage) gets on a bus somewhere and ends up adopted by hippies due to his ability to leap tall horses in a single bound. Said hippies, led by the unbearable Berger (the painfully miscast Williams), all seem inordinately proud of their vile unpleasantness but look like extras from *Murder, She Wrote* who've had shaggy wigs plonked upon their heads. We eventually learn that Claude is from Oklahoma and has come to New York to join the army and go to Vietnam. The hippies teach Claude a valuable lesson, but someone dies anyway.

In and around this, there are songs. Terrible, *terrible* songs, with no tunes. They are punctuated by gymnastic dance routines that exaggerate the hippy freak-out cliché to surreal degrees which are made even funnier by that over-emoting, po-faced, professional dance twat way in which they're performed. It occasionally looks as if Forman has torn up the script, raided the local am-dram group, dragged them into a park and paid them a dollar to do their Movement, Music and Mime workshop while he points a camera at them and sniggers.

What makes you wonder most about Forman's agenda is the lifestyle and behaviour of the main hippy group. Their world is based around surrounding everyone who comes near them and asking them for free stuff in a pathetic but still threatening way, so much so that even the Rich – we know they're the Rich because they have horses and wear proper horse-riding gear and look down their tiny, titchy WASP noses at everyone – engage the viewer's sympathy, and you're urging the police to round the scruffy, scrounging leeches up and take them to Guantanamo Bay. But the NYPD seem powerless in the face of, I dunno, mass not-washing, or something. No wonder New York elected Rudy Giuliani.

Admittedly, I've never seen the *Hair* stage musical. But, as it was inspired by their own crazy, counter-cultural New York lives, I'm assuming that this wasn't the effect that the authors were going for.

This is exacerbated by Forman and screenwriter Michael Weller's tricksy plot rewrites, which dump a ridiculous *deus ex machina* in an army base at the movie's end, effectively destroying the original musical's attempt to debate the theme of 'you can't beat the system'. But Forman was surely scuppered from the start. Hippy protest culture was kitsch by 1979. Vietnam was over. Forman was in Czechoslovakia trying to escape a *real* brutally repressive regime while young America was being encouraged to get high and muddy at Woodstock (see p. 97) and watch tits jiggle in *Hair* at the theatre. Of course he had no feel for the hippy/rock/anti-war alliance of late 1960s America, and no contemporary context to feed upon.

Still, Rado and Ragni get what they deserve. These are, after all, the men who wrote: 'When the moon is in the seventh house/And Jupiter aligns with Mars/Then peace will guide the planets/And love will steer the stars' ('The Age of Aquarius'). They are, undoubtedly, the worst lyricists in musical history, and they made big money out of it. They must surely accept, with their deep knowledge of all matters spiritual, that they were due a little bad karma.

But why, Garry ... why oh why is such a bad *and* forgotten movie in here? And why does it get two whole stars? Well ... because it's fun to laugh at. So much so that it's rarely boring, even though it's far too long and fails so badly to contrive an ironic yet uplifting ending. If you are one of the many who think that much of what 1960s hippy-rock culture said and did was a shameful load of banal money-making on the back of a youth culture that only wanted a revolution because their favourite rock star said revolution was cool, then *Hair* is the movie for you. Every prejudice you have against hippies, from bad hair and clothes to self-serving misogynist politics, is reinforced in this 116 minutes of jaw-droppingly bad film-making. And, to be scrupulously fair, the song 'Hair' *is* a bit funny, in a meant-to-be way, as is the 'Black Boys/White Boys' routine, which takes the provocative piss out of the army, latent homosexuality and 'jungle fever' quite nicely.

And, as I mentioned before, *Hair was* the first rock musical and its success is therefore directly to blame for Andrew Lloyd-Webber, which makes this film of historical value and a must-see for those interested in pop culture in all its wonders and horrors. Every mainstream pop musical money-spinner, from *Jesus Christ Superstar* to *Mamma Mia!*, finds its origins in *Hair*'s relentless crassness and misguided feelgoodery, which means I don't have to watch or write about any more of them. Thank you, *Hair*! Thank you so bloody much.

● ●

The Rose

1979

Starring: Bette Midler, Alan Bates, Frederic Forrest, Harry Dean
Stanton
Dir.: Mark Rydell

★ ★ ★

Plot: Sometimes it's hard to be a woman.
Key line: 'You don't think she's drinking too much, do you?'

When *The Rose* begins, it looks like it's going to be a right old dog
of a movie. Loosely based on the life and death of Janis Joplin –
very loosely – it immediately hits you with a bunch of 1970s shock-
rock clichés: hysterical heroine who is obviously destined to die
because she likes sex; portrayal of the rock biz as a highly paid slave
system where the star has no power to say the word 'no'; dreadful
gig scenes where the music bears no real resemblance to actual
rock music; and, worst of all, Alan Bates playing the stereotypical
bully manager with a Dick Van Dyke mockernee accent and a
distinct lack of interest. In the film's opening scenes you're supposed to feel sorry for heroine Mary Rose because Bates' manager
Guy Rudge won't let her take time off. What you actually feel is
enormous sympathy for Bette Midler, trying vainly to bring some
believable drama to the awful dialogue while Bates hams and shams
his way through their scenes. So, for the first half an hour or so,
you're just hoping for a so-bad-it's-funny movie experience. But
then ... something happens that changes the film in an instant.
And reminds you that when you've had the foresight to cast
Hawaiian-Jewish cabaret force-of-nature Bette Midler in your
dodgy movie, then you've just given yourself the opportunity to
light the blue touch paper and stand well back.

The scene in question stars Harry Dean Stanton as Billy Ray, a
pompous, conservative country singer and songwriter, and it's in
his confrontation with Midler that *The Rose* suddenly kicks into

focus. They meet in a room full of people ... Billy Ray's band, both their managers. He is her hero and she's recorded one of his tunes for her new album. But Billy Ray's a country purist with a quiet hatred of women ... he cruelly humiliates her, asking her to cease and desist on the cover version front. He is condescending and sadistic and Harry Dean Stanton convincing, and Midler is right there with him, a well of childlike hurt and vulnerabilty.

There's a key thing here, in this scene, about the Quest for Authenticity, and even the most commercially successful star's desperation to be accepted and approved of by the credible authentic artist, and the way Stanton and Midler carry that weight in what is a relatively short scene is impressive. What's more, Rose is no straight heroine and her pain is soon an ugly anger. She bottles a redneck who asks her to sit on his face. Now, this film is getting somewhere.

Enter the eternally underrated Frederic Forrest as the small-town chauffeur and errant soldier Houston Dyer who becomes her Sir Galahad. Suddenly the dialogue's great – 'I hate this mushy love stuff, man! Wake me up when the killing starts'; 'I didn't come back for some hoochie-coochie woman to blow my mind!' – and there's a great little scene in a diner ('We don't serve hippies') where you feel Midler's ability to hit any hostile environment like a whirlwind. Then the girl takes her Texan ingenue to a tranny bar. One for Ms Midler's gay following, for sure, but by now the film's hard to predict. You think she's gonna do a song – boo! – but instead she gets impersonated by a drag queen, and they duet. It's hard to imagine a night out with Janis Joplin being quite so much fun.

Director Rydell – who went on to two major successes with 1981's *On Golden Pond* and 1984's *The River* – may not have been able to drag a serious performance out of Bates, and obviously has no interest in rock 'n' roll. But he has moments here. The best comes when a particularly awful 'live' song ends with Bette doing a scarily supple gymnastic-type fall to the floor, which is enough to spark a stage invasion. As chaos ensues, Forrest/Dyer rescues her. We follow the pair as he carries her offstage and past various very accurate backstage arguments and huddles. The moving camera pokes its nose into all of them, and scuttles away, subtly exposing the distance between Rose and the one man that cares about her, and the various music wonks and lackeys who are only there to make money and/or bask in her glory. The noise subsides slowly and we're in Rose's dressing room. She and Dyer start to get it on but over Forrest's shoulder – blink and you miss her at first – a prim blonde is watching them, silently. This is *proper* film-making.

And nicely odd film-making, too. When Rose finally sees the blonde, they kiss hello a little too passionately. Poor old Dyer looks like Bambi. Turns out he's not turned on by the sudden arrival of lesbo shenanigans and hits Rose. But, in this film, this is not a cue for a woman-as-victim scene. She hits him back harder, nearly cripples him.

There's a haunting take on the past and loss here, too. As Rose travels to the big Homecoming show that provides the film's climax, she drives through her old neighbourhood. She points out her childhood home, confirms that the two goobers in the yard are her parents . . . and then hides as they go past. There's also a very neat running motif about being fucked by men on football fields, the nearest the film gets to the study of misogyny that just wasn't *de rigeur* in 1970s Hollywood. Whereas male dead rock stars always get the whole 'too sensitive for this cruel world' legend attached to their name, Janis Joplin's 1970 drug overdose has gone down in social history as the desperate act of a woman unlucky enough to be both promiscuous and homely. No Jesus analogies for Janis. Just a very male fear and loathing of women who achieve anything in a male world. *The Rose* attempts to redress at least some of the balance, even if it fails.

But everything good about the film is really about Bette Midler. She makes every scene tick . . . an entirely unpredictable ball of wildly differing emotions. Like most big stars actually are, she's irresistible and infuriating, a walking, screaming, crying and kissing headfuck. *The Rose* is nowhere near the best film featured in this book. But it might just feature the best lead performance in a rock movie. It wouldn't be a 'might', if it wasn't for her music – a terrible, pub-standard white version of Stax soul with extra dull funk-rock bits. The stage performances go on and on and on and on for what feels like forever. You can't help feeling that Midler would be the legend her obsessive fans think she is if only she'd never convinced herself that she could sing.

But Midler's lack of vanity in other matters is key here. By the movie's end, her extraordinary face is a totally unglamourised version of utter dissolution ... running mascara, snotty nose from the tears, eyes insane with the pressure of teetering on the verge of the abyss. She is 'Unpretty', as TLC sang it, and it's beautiful.

Midler's performance teeters on the edges of both comedy and grotesquerie, and she deserved her Oscar nomination. Indeed, Courtney Love appears to have based her whole life on the way the doomed Midler/Rose looks as she arrives at the stadium for her last show ... if that's a recommendation of any kind. But the death scene doesn't cut it, perhaps because Rydell has been so confused by the conflict between rock and the defiantly non-rock Midler that he can't make up his mind whether to go for camp melodrama or gritty realism. The film dies like Rose ... with an apologetic whimper, instead of a big, old-fashioned bang.

● ●

Rock 'n' Roll High School

1979
Starring: P.J. Soles, Vincent Van Patten, Mary Woronov, Paul Bartel, Clint Howard, Dey Young, The Ramones
Dir.: Allan Arkush

★ ★ ★ ★

Plot: 'A classic confrontation between mindless authority and the rebellious danger of youth!'
Key line: 'People say your music is loud and destructive and lethal to mice. But I think you're the Beethovens of our time.'

Bald, beardy Mr McGree solemnly lectures a high school class of sullen, slovenly Seniors about the delights of Beethoven. But when he goes to play the fifth symphony, the turntable's gone! Cut to the school grounds, where the wonderful P.J. Soles as Riff Randell is placing a record with a Sire label on said stolen turntable. Bang! 'Sheena Is a Punk Rocker' by the Ramones. Crash! The entire student body starts dancing. Wallop! The words *Rock 'n' Roll High School* in lurid red letters tilt across the screen. We're in Roger Corman B-movie exploitation territory, and bad taste fun is assured.

At Vince Lombardi High School (named after a legendary American football coach, a symbol of old-school winning-is-everything values), new principal Evelyn Togar has the looks of an irresistible Amazon dominatrix and the values and dress sense of Margaret Thatcher. To make this work, all legendary cheapo movie producer Corman and director Allan Arkush have to do is hire Bad Taste Queen Mary Woronov, an actress blessed with the unique gift of being comically frigid and utterly filthy at the same time. No-one else can infuse the line, 'Every time a teacher isn't in the room the entire school erupts in a shameless display of adolescent abandon!' with the same levels of frisky innuendo as Ms Woronov.

Elsewhere we have Tom Roberts (Van Patten), the blonde football captain who can't get the usual jock quota of chicks because he's so dull; Kate Rambeau (Young), the nerd who loves him; chubby sex-obsessed hall monitors in scout uniforms; innocent mice blown to smithereens by exposure to the Ramones' 'Teenage Lobotomy' at high volume; and Eaglebauer (Howard), the money-mad school fixer of fake IDs, stolen test answers and sexual problems.

Before long, Ms Soles, who played less light-hearted variations on the wide-eyed schoolgirl crazy in *Carrie* and *Halloween* and later married Dennis Quaid, is bursting into ebullient Ramones-song while young girls jump up and down . . . in a knowingly clean-teen, beach party movie manner, I might add. Corman's form of bad taste, like early punk rock, goes against the grain of the sexism and barely legal obsessions of your average Hollywood gross-out comedy. So while we're not encouraged to leer at adolescent girls, and songwriter Riff's nemesis is an evil groupie, we also get Eaglebauer using an inflatable doll to show the virginal Tom and Kate how to get to first base. The sexual values of punk were kinky but benign, and so is *Rock 'n' Roll High School*. When Joey Ramone serenades a bikini'ed Riff in her bedroom, it's in the full knowledge that the geeky beanpole was the least likely sex symbol in American history. With a saturated Dee Dee playing bass in the shower, it's goofily funny and sort of touching, too.

The plot, such as it exists, revolves around Riff's need to go to this week's Ramones concert in order to meet them and sell them her songs. But how can she and the other punk-loving kids of Vince Lombardi High cut class to get tickets without bringing down the wrath of the clearly insane Ms Togar? This is basically an excuse for gags like the one where a Native American suddenly turns up at the ticket queue, threatening kids with his tomahawk. One boy looks quizzically at his friend. 'Scalper', he informs him. *Scalper!!!* See ... scalper is the American word for ticket tout, and Indians used to scalp ... oh, please yourselves.

It's also an excuse to revisit the anti-rock 'n' roll mania of 1950s adults without going all *American Graffiti* (see p. 132). Just to make this clear, Chuck Berry joins the Ramones, Nick Lowe, Devo, the Velvet Underground and ... erm ... Wings on a soundtrack that makes you want to pogo, twist and shout while you watch. Although nothing about *Rock 'n' Roll High School* is to be taken seriously, it is interesting to note that this is the only movie that makes the obvious links between 1950s rock and 1970s punk outrage.

When the Ramones finally arrive, they play in a car and on the street. It's brilliant, as is the concert footage of the quartet. No run-through of their new album or a dodgy new soundtrack. Just 'Blitzkreig Bop'. 'Teenage Lobotomy'. 'Pinhead'. 'California Sun'. By a band at the end of their peak years.

A gleeful parade of bad acting, worse jokes and dumbass sight gags at the expense of traditional post-1950s high school movies, the film operates as the visual equivalent of a Ramones song: a fast, cheap, irreverent, smart-dumb pastiche of American mores. *Animal*

House without the leering, *Grease* without the family values, *Hair-spray* without the budget. The set-up is perfect, the aesthetic spot-on ... but there aren't quite enough good jokes, and Woronov, Soles and Bartel aside, the cast don't possess the necessary goofy charisma. Corman probably should have put his money where his bad taste mind was and hired John Waters (see *Hairspray*, p. 281) or Russ Meyer (see *Beyond the Valley of the Dolls*, p. 93). Instead, he makes do with an entertaining curio and the only movie that captures the side of punk that wasn't about angst-ridden politics, but a return to catchy, stoopid pop songs about teen life played fast and loud.

So that would make this an average movie ... until a final 20 minutes of genius. Ms Togar proposes 'the final solution' – a ritual burning of rock 'n' roll records. Anti-fascists to a boy and girl, the Ramones and the students occupy the campus, riot, terrorise the staff (apart from cool teacher McGree, played by cult director and Woronov's creative partner Paul Bartel), face down the police and finally blow the school up, to the strains of MC5, Alice Cooper and the Ramones' brilliant title song. It's a ridiculous and uplifting cartoon version of every anarchist student's fantasy – the college occupation that ends in revolution; like the Paris 1968 insurrection, but directed by the Monkees ... or maybe just monkeys. If the rest of the film had had the same level of madcap anti-authoritarianism, *Rock 'n' Roll School* would have been a masterpiece. Or banned. Or both. It's the great ending that ensured that it was the cult hit it was intended to be, and a remake is in production, funded by veteran US shock jock Howard Stern.

• •

Quadrophenia

1979

Starring: Phil Daniels, Leslie Ash, Philip Davis, Mark Wingett, Sting, Toyah Willcox
Dir.: Franc Roddam

★ ★ ★ ★ ★

Plot: Portrait of the mod as a young punk.
Key line: 'You cunts! You killed me scooter!!!'

The first thing to understand about *Quadrophenia* is that it's a punk rock movie. Yep, it's set in the early 1960s. And its central characters are mods. And it revels in the details of mod clothes and lifestyle. And it's based upon a double-concept album about the mod scene by The Who. But the resulting film seethes with the energy, violence, outsider glamour and fuck-everything rebellion of the most visible pop culture tribe of the late 1970s. It both fed and fed off of a mod revival in Britain, but, like the mod revival's ace faces The Jam and The Specials, it took its anger and aesthetic from punk's nihilistic approach to rock culture. As such, *Quadrophenia* looms large as a *fin de siècle* document, marking the logical end of the key run of pessimistic and brilliant British rock movies that kicked off 20 years earlier with *Expresso Bongo*, as well as the beginning of the end of British youth tribes and rock and roll as legitimate symbols of rebellion.

The original 1973 album/rock opera saw Pete Townshend analysing the disintegration and rebirth of a young mod called Jimmy Cooper. Franc Roddam and his fellow screenwriters Dave Humphries and Martin Stellman cram this into the last 20 or so minutes of their script, and use the original Jimmy's fleeting memories of better times as the meat of the movie. We see Jimmy (Phil Daniels in a career-defining performance) living the mod life in Shepherds Bush, west London in 1964, causing trouble with his mod mates, battling his nagging parents, doing a shitty 9-to-5 as a runner at an ad agency (a very similar upper-class, youth-hating establishment to the agencies that exploit the young and powerless in *Catch Us If You Can* [see p. 57] and *Slade in Flame* [see p. 147]), necking pills, dancing to soul and British beat, obsessing about suits, parkas, Levi's and scooters, chasing Leslie Ash's *femme fatale* Steph … all in preparation for a bank holiday weekend in Brighton where rival tribes of mods and rockers stage a mass riot.

After Jimmy is arrested for affray with King of the Mods the Ace Face (a luminous Sting … no, really), he returns to London and quickly loses home, job, girl, friends, scooter and mind. He catches a train back to Brighton, the only part of his recent life where life made sense, where he was somebody. When he sees that the Ace Face is actually a humble bellboy at a posh hotel, Jimmy loses it completely. He steals Ace Face's scooter and drives it off a cliff at Beachy Head.

For many years there's been a doubt over the ending … is it just the scooter that plunges to its death, or is it Jimmy too? But if you're concentrating the puzzle is cleared up in the film's opening scenes, as we see Jimmy striding purposefully away from a cliff's edge, in order to … well, who knows? The only mystery is in what Jimmy did next, and it remains unusual that neither Pete Townshend nor Roddam contemplated a sequel. Does he start a band? Go to Uni in Brighton? Go travelling? Join a kibbutz? Or go home and beg Mum, Dad and mates to give him another chance? Whichever way, we can be pretty sure that he won't be waiting for mod or any other youth movement to sort his life out any more.

Quadrophenia was the perfect 1979 film. Presenting tribal rebellion as both a working-class lad's dream and nightmare, in Jimmy it also gave us a character who seemed to be Johnny Rotten, Paul Weller and The Specials' Terry Hall all rolled-into-one. Daniels' urchin face encapsulated the adrenaline rushes of sex, drugs, music and violence, *and* the childish agonies when the aimless teen realises that all of these glories are fleeting, and that when they can't be bought or stolen all that is left is toil and conformity and parents, peers and authority figures whose inability to understand that agony leaves you feeling cripplingly lonely. Jimmy ends up there, on the edge of everything. But only once he's entirely alone can he see through the mod con ... or the idea that consumerism, no matter how stylish and urgent, will lead you to any kind of promised land.

This could have been patronising hippy preaching. But Roddam's insistence on tinting England a sepia-toned grey, employing the roughest, realest language (there are so many 'cunts' in *Quadrophenia* that you stop noticing the word after half an hour or so), and employing a cast of working-class kids that were exactly who you went to school or football or the youth club with, cut through the potential liberal hand-wringing and hit us hard in the heart. And it has continued to, down the years, as it has slowly overtaken the far inferior *Tommy* (see p. 164) album, stage show and film in popularity, and finally been revived as a successful stage musical.

There are flaws. The script could have been wittier. There are storylines hinted at that never develop, particularly Jimmy's friend-ship with rocker Kevin (played by Ray Winstone); a potentially tear-jerking love triangle between Jimmy, Steph and Toyah's adorable Monkey; and the lack of reprisals when Jimmy and mates smash up a gangster's Jag in a scene that gives real-life dodgy geezer John Bindon his second key rock film performance after ... erm ... *Performance* (see p. 89).

But if *Quadrophenia* had been technically perfect, it just wouldn't have been *perfect*. Ms Ash wouldn't have launched a million teen boy fantasies with the notorious knee-trembler in a Brighton alley. The riot scenes wouldn't have felt so visceral and celebratory. The scene where Jimmy's Dad (played by Michael Elphick) slags off The Who on *Ready Steady Go* wouldn't have so accurately summed up the discomfort of watching punk-era *Top of the Pops* with my punk-hating mother. And the scene where Jimmy applies eye-liner in a ladies' loo on that Brighton train, and fixes us with a look – of terror, of sexual come-on, of drug-induced psychosis – that sums up every English boy who ever played publicly with his sexuality in order to cause outrage and express his fear of what is expected of a 'real man', wouldn't have been quickly and quietly understood and accepted by every entirely straight lad who has ever seen *Quadrophenia*.

And at the centre of all this is Daniels, finding the exact location where the wide-eyed, chin-out snarl of the hooligan meets the vulnerability and defeat of the crying child. It is the face of the punk; defiant, despised yet really only wanting to be loved.

When he dashes that scooter onto the rocks, Jimmy trashes all youth culture's false promises. And we hate him for it. But we know he's right.

1980s

Babylon

1980

Starring: Brinsley Forde, Karl Howman, Trevor Laird, Victor Romero Evans, Brian Bovell, Mel Smith
Dir.: Franco Rosso

★ ★ ★ ★

Plot: The reggae *Quadrophenia*.
Key line: 'This is my fucking country, Lady! And it's never bin lovely! It's always bin a fucking tip!'

This *vérité* slice-of-life drama pulls off a feat that no film-maker matched until Menhaj Huda and Noel Clarke's excellent noughties pictures *Kidulthood* and *Adulthood*: an accurate depiction of urban black British life that neither exploits nor preaches. But unlike Clarke and Huda, Franco Rosso builds his film around music in the shape of the vibrant reggae sound system scene of the early 1980s, when militant reggae was at its peak of hipness and influence.

Set in a beautifully grim, sinister and frantic Brixton, *Babylon*'s storyline also serves as a setting out of the issues that saw the south London area burn in riots just a year after the film's release and again in 1985. Brinsley Forde, leader of Britain's biggest reggae band Aswad and former star of children's TV hit *The Double Deckers*, plays Blue, a garage mechanic and reggae toaster/MC whose preparations for a sound system battle against the legendary Jah Shaka crew are relentlessly interrupted by lack of funds, demanding mother, Bad Dad, errant kid brother, girl troubles, police harassment, vile white neighbours, threatening criminals and the particular misfortune of having a hippy-haired Mel Smith as his racist boss. The best of the era's Brit and Jamaican reggae, led by Aswad's own legendary horns 'n' dub call-to-arms instrumental 'Warrior Charge', bolsters the soundtrack, and aids the movie's spot-on blending of Jamaican and Cockney language and culture.

Babylon's credentials as an early British *8 Mile* (see p. 364) are impeccable.

Rosso's biggest achievement in *Babylon* is his accurate capture of the look and atmosphere of Brixton while seeing the unlikely beauty in the way it had been fucked up by successive town-planners. The cramped high street, the insane market, the railway arches where Blue's crew store their sound system and hang out, the blank and sterile public buildings ... all give me a shot of nostalgia for the area I lived in through most of the 1980s, as Rosso sets his camera to turn the ugly and anonymous into somewhere exciting and genuinely cinematic.

Unlike its Jamaican twin *Rockers* (see p. 192), *Babylon* is packed full of accomplished actors and rarely tips into whimsy. It balances its comic and optimistic moments with harsh realities, content to tell as true a story as it can without pursuing an agenda other than black Britons are good and bad in equal measure like anyone else, and that, as The Specials' 'Ghost Town' warned the following year, 'The people getting angry' with their underclass lot as Thatcherism and monetarism declared class war. On the other hand, the movie could do with some of *Rockers*' imagination and sense of the ridiculous, especially when Blue gets beaten up by racist coppers from Central Casting and the film threatens to become dull and worthy.

While Forde's Blue is the nice guy we all root for, the contrast in different characters' reaction to the relentless pressure and claustrophobia of inner city life are carried by Beefy (Laird), a raging black explosion waiting to happen, and Ronnie (Howman), the sweet, stoned token white boy who represents a new generation of working-class whites who look at the cool of black culture with an aspirational awe.

While the gang of male friends who lead *Babylon* are rounded characters and lovable company, somewhat predictably the women in the film are not given credit for the possession of three dimensions. But Rosso stops well short of the full-scale sexist abuse of 1970s film-makers, and while *Babylon* possesses many elements of the hard-bitten male-orientated 1970s docu-drama, there is a generosity of spirit here which makes it very much a movie that heralds a 1980s change of emphasis as far as gender (and even gay sexuality) is concerned. The scene where two of Blue's acquaintances run a violent rent-boy scam on an older white man is just another example of the wickedness of *Babylon*, that white-ruled font of all Rastafarian evils.

In that sense, Blue is a close relative of *Quadrophenia*'s Jimmy (see p. 220), a boy too thoughtful and independent to accept the flaws of his tribe and environment. *Babylon* is obviously heavily influenced by the previous year's big British youth culture hit. Like the Roddam landmark, it presents a vision of working-class youth overwhelmed by ignorant, out-of-touch parents, violent tribal rivalries, ribald male-bonding, concrete jungles and cheating girlfriends, a place which stamps upon the sensitive. Indeed, watch *Quadrophenia*, *Babylon* and *Kidulthood* in quick succession, and the only conclusion you can come to that neither environment nor rules of engagement have changed in council estate London between 1966 and 2006. Only the shop-fronts and brand logos. Just to push the point, the latest Dizzee Rascal album, 2009's *Tongue 'N' Cheek*, features 'Can't Tek No More', a rousing, witty protest song entirely inspired by a scene, dialogue, and music from *Babylon*.

But *Quadrophenia*'s Jimmy The Mod never learned to chat on the mic, and therefore couldn't focus his woes by chanting them in a room full of revellers over a fiery, irresistible rhythm. This leads to a magnificent ending to the film: a visual question that would be answered by the residents of Brixton and Britain's other flashpoint black ghettoes over the next 12 months. It's the final reason why *Babylon* stands as the last great British rock movie of its era; made before music stopped mattering, and the British film industry stopped caring about its nation's young, poor and pissed-off.

● ●

The Blues Brothers

1980

Starring: John Belushi, Dan Aykroyd, Kathleen Freeman, James Brown, Aretha Franklin, Cab Calloway, Ray Charles, John Candy
Dir.: John Landis

★

Plot: How blue men invented the whites.
Key line: 'The Blues Brothers? *Sheeeeit!***'**

The Blues Brothers is one of the Holy Trinity of late-night, dress-up cult cinema perennials, along with *The Sound of Music* and *The Rocky Horror Picture Show* (see p. 155). Its popularity and main-stream shelf-life is such that, in most British city centres on most Friday or Saturday nights, you'll see gangs of men in dark suits, shades and pork-pie hats who have chosen *The Blues Brothers* as their stag night or birthday booze-up theme. In the year of its release only *The Empire Strikes Back* put more bums on seats, and the movie continues to sell on video and, now, DVD. The film's lead, John Belushi, died of a drug overdose two years after the movie's release, and *The Blues Brothers* is the film that cemented his cult hell-raising comic genius reputation. The Blues Brothers band had a life both before and after the movie, and the 1978 Blues Brothers album *Briefcase Full of Blues* went to Number One in the US and went on to sell 3.5 million copies. By any criteria, the Blues Brothers, and the film the concept spawned, are a bona fide popular culture phenomenon.

So why the fuck is it such a pile of fetid shite?

You can't blame the plot, which is fine for dumbass comedy purposes anyway. Jake (Belushi) and Elwood (Aykroyd) Blues are besuited Chicago brothers who used to front a rhythm 'n' blues revue band. Their career was rudely interrupted when Jake was imprisoned for five years for, well, we're not sure. When Jake is released the pair find that their old Catholic school owes five grand in back taxes, and, in search of redemption for their sins, they decide to raise the money in the required 11 days. So they re-form the band, meeting many black music legends and smashing many things with many cars along the way. And . . . that's it. The rest is the most blatant and banal white co-option and castration of black culture since Pat Boone butchered Little Richard's 'Tutti Frutti'.

This is actually quite an achievement. To have James Brown, Aretha Franklin, Ray Charles, Cab Calloway, Chaka Khan, John Lee Hooker and Steve Cropper and Donald 'Duck' Dunn from the Stax label house band at your disposal and still make such desperately terrible music (and equally dreadful, minstrelish filmed performances) must have taken serious work on the part of director John Landis and his soundtrack producers.

It doesn't matter who you have playing or singing; if you take any kind of black music, play it too fast, turn the rhythm section down, and turn a bunch of over-slick session horn players up to 11, you're going to rip the guts – or, more accurately, the sex and politics – out of that music, even before you decide to ignore all the confrontational songs in 1960s soul culture. Suffice to say, Aretha is not performing 'Respect' here, and James Brown's happy-clappy preacher is designed to make you forget that this is the man who hollered 'Say It Loud – I'm Black and I'm Proud', while black America set fire to its ghettoes in the late 1960s.

But hey – it's a comedy, right? A no-brain escapist laugh about men doing funny dances and car chases in ill-fitting suits. No-one expects nor wants Hendrix doing 'The Star-Spangled Banner' (see *Woodstock*, p. 97) or the collected speeches of Eldridge Cleaver. Fair enough. But surely you've got a right to expect some jokes. And, believe me, there isn't one decent gag in the entire, interminable 127 minutes.

So why do many millions of people over the last 30 years love this film with something approaching a passion? Sadly, for exactly the same reasons that anyone with an ounce of taste in film, music, comedy or left-liberal politics sees it as bad bordering on offensive. Because none of the weaknesses I've mentioned above are accidents. Jon Landis was third only to Lucas and Spielberg in terms of commercial movie success in the early 1980s. He made some great films (*National Lampoon's Animal House, An American Werewolf in London, Trading Places*) and directed Michael Jackson's 'Thriller' video, a superb short film that had the same enormous impact on pop that *Star Wars* had on film.

He and co-writer Aykroyd knew exactly what they were doing here, in the sense that they both understood that much money could be made from 1960s nostalgia – especially if you could separate the pop culture of that decade from the social upheaval that provided its context. As a movie like Lawrence Kasdan's *The Big Chill* explained both eloquently and annoyingly, the 1960s generation of middle-class whites felt desperately guilty for having grown up and sold out in the 1970s. Not only did they want the pop and fashion of their youth revived without being reminded of their more embarrassing radical affectations – they wanted the black music that they had felt enlightened for enjoying to literally *belong to them*. After all, black Americans had moved on to funk and disco, and by 1980 were on the cutting-edge of electronic music in the shape of hip hop, electronic soul and the electro-disco that would soon morph into house. But surely ... the soul and blues of the Motown, Stax and Atlantic labels ... *that* was *real* black music. Hell ... white people were now more authentically black than black people! I mean, you didn't see Aretha Franklin playing sidekick to Chic or this new upstart Prince. Yet there the Queen of Soul was, playing the humble sixth banana to two fat white comedians in suits! It was the baby-boomer dream come true, just in time for Ronald Reagan to make them rich and convince them that the 1960s had just been an experimental phase involving cheap drugs and hairy armpits.

Just in case any of the film's intended audience pick up on the defeatism and cultural theft of this whole scenario, it dumps country-loving rednecks and even throws a Nazi party into the mix, making sure that the crowd that have arrived to protest against the Nazis is largely white. They're almost as angry and righteous as the hippies who battled against Mayor Daley's Chicago police at the Democratic Party convention in 1968. But much cleaner. And no need for a scrap either, because Jake and Elwood solve the problem by driving a car at the Nazis. If only things had been so simple back in 1968, when America responded to watching their kids having the shit kicked out of them by voting for Nixon. And the moral superiority of *The Blues Brothers* might be a little more convincing if the Nazis' first appearance hadn't immediately followed a Belushi paedophile 'joke'.

The white desire to be black without having to endure the inconvenience of being seen as second-class citizens never dies. Each generation of white middle-class British kids talks, walks and dresses a little more black than the last. And let's not forget, this is a film that reduces ARETHA fucking FRANKLIN to the status of nagging but powerless spoilsport harpy, and where the only other featured females are a nun and Carrie Fisher, who has to kiss the hideous Belushi before letting him throw her into a pool of mud. So the appeal of a film that trades on the non-existent joke of two ugly sexist white blokes being the Kings of Soul endures.

I don't know if anyone ever asked Ricky Gervais what David Brent's favourite film is, but I bet you it's *The Blues Brothers*. A film that goes all out to convince the most oafish and deluded of white men that he is cool, and especially when he dances like a twat.

• •

Rude Boy

1980
Starring: The Clash, Ray Gange, Johnny Green
Dir.: Jack Hazan and David Mingay

★ ★

Plot: A handy guide on how not to make a rock movie.
Key line: 'I wish that more black guys would come to our gigs'.

David Mingay: 'The real meaning of the sub-plot in *Rude Boy* is ... if you set out to be an anarchistic group who try to overthrow the state, who try to mislead the youth, who support drug-taking and who create anarchy, you'll make a million ... if you are white. If you are black you'll be arrested for stealing a pound. And you'll be put in jail and kept there for many years. That is really what the message was intended to be.'

Well bugger me ... sometimes it really is worth watching the DVD extras before you watch the movie. How else was I to know that this notorious member of the Bad Rock Movie club had actually been a sly satire at the expense of the bands who misled innocent youths like me into a life of drug-taking and anarchy, when I'd been under the impression, for almost 30 years, that it was the kind of ill-conceived shambles that inevitably happens when you let elitist middle-class liberal documentary makers indulge their contempt for a culture they don't understand?

Rude Boy has always been universally seen as a definitive film of two halves. One half is, very possibly, the greatest live rock 'n' roll footage ever shot, as expert cameraman Jack Hazan caught the Clash at the peak of their relevance and at the cusp of change from chaotic punk band during the On Parole tour to the hard rock machine of the Sort It Out tour. The other half is an almost unwatchable embarrassment. And that includes the 'sub-plot'.

The 'Rude Boy' is Ray Gange, a record-shop worker and friend of Joe Strummer's who Mingay selected to play Ray Gange, moronic Clash roadie. Gange is also interviewed for the DVD extras and confirms what we thought when we saw it; that the poor amateur had been given no idea of what the film was about and was asked to improvise his scenes like a veteran, and failed to see the consequences of playing a horrible character with his own name. It was the beginning and end of Gange's acting career, but it was presumably enough to see the guy judged to be a reactionary oaf by thousands of strangers.

The footage of the Clash and the fictionalised accounts of Gange being an annoying twat are further confused by (brilliantly shot, again by Hazan) early footage of contemporary social unrest, battles between hideously malformed National Front runts and heroic anti-Nazi demonstrators, with the police seeming to enjoy their role of protecting the racists' right to spread their nauseating bile in the middle of communities full of non-Caucasians. If the film had just been the Clash playing, plus these scenes that remind oldsters like me just how truly ugly the late 1970s were, it would have been a socio-historical classic. But documentary makers Mingay and Hazan decided that they wanted to establish some storytelling credentials.

Like *Babylon* (see p. 227), *Rude Boy* chooses Gange's manor of Brixton as the geographical symbol of British underclass discontent. But while *Babylon* director Franco Rosso illuminated the area's ugliness with arresting camerawork and an edge balanced by vibrancy, Mingay and Hazan are content to just show Gange shambling along to the dole office repeatedly.

So the movie quickly settles into a pattern. A 'political' conversation between Gange and Joe Strummer that is so wince-inducingly mutton-headed that you start to wonder why you ever liked this band of fools; quickly followed by the Clash playing a version of 'Garageland' in their rehearsal studios that reminds you that Strummer performed rock 'n' roll with a charisma and intensity that imbued the music with power and meaning that made the bogus political ideologies of the time crumble and fall; then you're watching Gange getting a blow-job in a bog, and feeling embarrassed and strangely itchy, and wondering what point the scene is trying to make.

The best I can do with all of the Gange scenes is guess that a point is being made about white punk rockers trying to ape the legend of the black 'rude boy', the uncontrollable outlaw killer of *The Harder They Come* (see p. 128), and how they lack both the desperation and courage to carry it off (and, perhaps, the charisma to carry it off aesthetically). As the Clash used so much reggae music and imagery as part of their MO, the band themselves are being criticised for their rebel pose. Which is maybe why, according to the DVD extra interviews, Mingay and Hazan were not being entirely forthcoming about the film they were making, leading the Clash to become increasingly suspicious of their presence. Strummer dealt with the very same theme of the gap between white and black rebellion in the lyrics of 'White Man in Hammersmith Palais', 'White Riot' and 'Safe European Home', and Mingay also points out in interview that the film was a critical hit in France because the subtitles of Clash lyrics made the film make more sense. In other words ... the Clash made far more sense of their own flaws than these people could.

Because it's glaringly obvious that no script has been written and that no-one, including Gange and the Clash, has the slightest clue of what they're doing or why they're doing it. What could be subversive and interestingly satirical becomes inept and, at over two hours, stupendously boring.

The thing is ... there was a great warts-and-all documentary here if Mingay and Hazan could've spotted it. There is, for example, a section concerning bassist Paul Simonon and drummer Topper Headon's arrest for shooting pigeons with air guns in 1978. While the Clash were marketing themselves as revolutionary guerrillas with guitars, the members themselves were actually sniggery lads getting arrested for cruel schoolboy pranks rather than revolutionary acts. Their defence counsel? David Mellor. I know ... you couldn't make it up.

Film them for a year, without ludicrous fictionalisations, and the Clash would probably have made all Mingay and Hazan's points for them, just by being themselves. Luckily for the Clash's myth and reputation, the film-makers' painfully contrived attempts to intellectualise the contradictions that were always part of the Clash's art simply made Mingay and Hazan look like the pseuds.

Consequently, *Rude Boy* is only of interest to committed Clash fans who have got the stomach to sift through the shite for the pearls. The stunning versions of all your early Clash faves, which, even with extensive overdubbing long after the shows, are still deliciously ramshackle. Mick Jones's unintentionally amusing, long-haired rock star poses. Joe getting the words comically wrong in 'I'm So Bored with the USA', and talking with self-aggrandising relish about his night in jail after fighting with bouncers at a Glasgow show. The band's habit of following self-righteous lectures to fighting fans and bouncers by playing, of all things, 'White Riot'. The footage of urchin Clash gig-goers, which disproves the theory that it was middle-class lefties who were most devoted to the band, but also confirms the theory that all Clash fans were boys.

Then there's the very odd day when Jimmy Pursey of Sham 69 led the Clash in a version of 'White Riot' at the huge anti-Nazi league concert at Hackney's Victoria Park ... a British countercultural happening (the concert, not the Pursey guest spot) which *Rude Boy* doesn't seem to grasp the significance of. And the best moment: when a furious Jones interrupts a performance to roar 'Get off the fucking stage!' at us. This extraordinary few seconds sums up what's wrong with *Rude Boy*. It was completely unscripted, a spontaneous reaction to Hazan's intrusive camera. Bizarrely, Mingay and Hazan decide to make it look scripted by cutting in later footage of Gange fiddling with equipment. Something real and powerful almost made into meaningless throwaway comedy, as if the directors were more interested in appearing to be in control than in making a good film.

The only fictionalised scene that works hinges around a one-liner. Gange is watching Strummer wash his onstage clothes in a hotel sink. He asks what Joe's T-shirt says and Strummer says, 'Brigate Rosse ... it's the name of a pizza restaurant', with a smile full of knowing self-deprecation. T-shirts bigging up distant terrorist organisations like the Italian Red Brigade were a key part of the early Clash's revolutionary posturing, 'turning rebellion into money' (their own famous line from 'White Man in Hammersmith Palais') by making all those student Che Guevara posters into an all-pogoing, eight-legged pose machine. On the completely other hand, no major label band ever treated their fans with as much love and made as little real money while they were together as the Clash. Film-makers with this much access at such a key time in the Clash's career could have answered a lot of questions about the band's contradictions and motives, and fulfilled any anti-punk agenda they fancied at the same time.

When you do that sifting for pearls thing I mentioned earlier, the one thing you won't be finding is Mingay's suggested film about black oppression. That must have fallen down the back of a sofa. His quote does make some sense of the sudden appearance of scenes where some black pickpockets get nicked by CCTV-spying coppers. But . . . these 'rude boy' ciphers are stealing from ordinary people (at least, I think they are. The CCTV scene is baffling). And that is worse than shooting pigeons or trying to protect your fans. And as these guys aren't given any character or back story, then we can't relate to them anyway. What we do get instead is a long Margaret Thatcher anti-crime speech and a whole lot of confusion about what this film is trying to say.

At *Rude Boy*'s end, the Clash are a slick uniformed rock band playing 'I Fought the Law' ('and the law won', of course), black men are going to jail after forced confessions, Gange is a jobless loser again and Thatcher gets elected. I mean, I get it, but . . . like so many of us at the time, Mingay and Hazan are just projecting too much convoluted sociological theory onto a bleeding pop group, and the entire enterprise becomes almost comical in its sweeping generalisations about the System. Thankfully, the DVD has a bit called 'Just Play The Clash!' where you can, you know, just play the Clash. You should do exactly that.

● ●

Breaking Glass

1980
Starring: Hazel O'Connor, Phil Daniels, Jon Finch, Jonathan Pryce
Dir.: Brian Gibson

★ ★

**Plot: Punk rock stardom revealed as a lousy, hollow sham.
Key line: 'Arse!'**

It begins with a godawful song on a London tube train. It sounds like something one of those social worker bands take around youth clubs. Everything that Hazel O'Connor recorded is like X-Ray Spex as reinterpreted by Crème Brûlée and the cast of *Rock Follies*. In essence, *Breaking Glass* is a film version of 1970s TV serial *Rock Follies*, which concerned three unlikely girls (Julie Covington, Rula Lenska and Charlotte Cornwell) trying to make it in a music biz which turns out to be, like, all about making money. For shame!

The music of *Breaking Glass* is the worst music found anywhere in this book. Worse than the Cliff movies, worse than *The Rose*, worse than pissing rain on a winter's night, worse than possibly anything, barring war, famine and pestilence. Rather astonishingly, the music was 'directed and produced' by Bowie/Bolan production Godhead Tony Visconti, and one Dodi Fayed was the film's executive producer. The story of how people like these conspired to make someone like Hazel O'Connor a pop and movie star for six months or so in 1980 remains untold, and I suspect it would make a far better music biz story than *Breaking Glass*. Fact is stranger than fiction, and all that.

Because Ms O'Connor was rubbish. She could look hot, in that androgynous, hard girl, pale and sick-looking punk rock way. Or she would have, except that every time she's onstage in *Breaking Glass* she puts on Siouxsie make-up that makes her look like Leo Sayer doing *The Show Must Go On* and stares like she's mental and does these marching robot spazz movements. Her singing voice is like Patti Smith being throttled with a hose. Her acting is beyond the valley of the execrable. Ms O'Connor must have been who they were thinking of when they did those Kit-Kat telly ads in the 1980s which starred Terry out of *Eastenders* as a nasty A&R man listening to the demo of a tragic band. 'You can't sing. You can't play. You look awful . . . you'll go a long way.'

What *Breaking Glass* also is, though, is a screaming laff-fest, of the so-bad-it-smells variety. The Ken Loach/Mike Leigh/Alan Clarke approach to *vérité* film-making was all the rage in Blighty at the time, but writer/director Gibson's take on it is so hysterical and clumsy that *Breaking Glass* just looks like a long, bad episode of

Grange Hill. His vision of the London rock world was five years out of date already, a riot of feather cuts, mullets and pop as the enemy. The bit where strugging biz hustler Danny (Daniels) first meets wannabe mockney punk star Kate (O'Connor) and makes her sing to him – 'YOU'RE A PROGRAM!!!' – is the kind of toe-curling embarrassment that just can't be contrived by conventional film-making.

Gibson shoehorns in every hot topic from the onset of Thatcherism – rising unemployment, petrol rationing, violence at gigs, *Sieg-heil*ing skinheads, squatted housing, strikes, fashisht oppression from the pigs – but his awful dialogue and cliché-ridden view of class makes it all seem like comedy. Absolutely nothing rings true, about the state of the nation or the music biz. But . . . it does provide an oddly endearing snapshot of the concerns of the inept, bandwagoneering end of punk and new wave as personified by Toyah, the Boomtown Rats, Sham 69, Tom Robinson and dear old Ms O'Connor herself. The bit where she performs a song about kicking Big Brother up the arse-arse-arse-arse-arse is absolutely priceless. And Gary Tibbs is doing jerky robotics on bass! You remember 'Ant Rap' by Adam and the Ants! You don't? It went 'Marco! Merrick! Terry Lee! Gary Tibbs and yours true-lee!' No wonder kids of today have come to their senses and gone crazy for that post-punk sound! Music was just so much better when I was a nipper.

Unfortunate Brit bit-part actors whizz by – Charlie out of *Casualty*, Richard Griffiths, a bloke from *The Bill* whose name escapes me, Jonathan Lynn, even Jim Broadbent! – and poor old Jonathan Pryce slums it as the sax player who looks like a 1960s supply teacher, literally doing the bare minimum to pick up the cheque.

But, in defence of *Breaking Glass* . . . there are a fair few boys of my generation who hold the film in cultish affection, simply because there were no other contemporaneous fictionalisations of punk. It was enjoyable, watching People Like Us in the cinema, running the gauntlet of random violence at gigs and saying really trite things about anarchy. And some of the film was actually based on truth, ludicrous though it seems. Teams of promo wannabes really were employed to go to chart shops and buy records into the charts (might still be, for all I know or care). And the scene where the record company suggests changing the lyrics of 'Big Brother' so a kick up the arse becomes a punch in the nose is an echo of an incident at *Top of the Pops* where the producers insisted that a Gang of Four lyric referring to 'rubbers' be changed to 'rubbish' (the band refused and never appeared on *TOTP*).

So maybe Hazel O'Connor was only bad because this bad film demanded badness. There's a bit where she and Danny finally and inevitably get it on on a train which is actually very sweet and quietly sexy because both manage to pull off vulnerable and good-hearted. Maybe the iconic Daniels – never a great actor, but always an indisputably great Phil Daniels – just brings it out of a girl.

Plus ... I fancy Hazel O'Connor. I know. I know. It's just plain wrong, in every way. But my nostalgic punk chick fetish is so chronic I still have unwanted thoughts and feelings about Toyah Willcox. The therapy's going well, cheers for asking.

The central conceit of Kate's inevitable crash and burn is authentically weird. A protest show under the Westway at Notting Hill turns into a race riot, and she watches a boy die. Cue recording sessions interrupted by uncontrollable weeping and the record label feeding her drugs so she can keep working, and her being shipped off to a country mansion to record with super-suave producer Bob Woods, played by a neatly oily Jon Finch. Bob knows kung-fu, which can only mean the end for Danny. In true punk fashion, the fact that Kate's now recording ballads and getting a video made is the end of everything good and decent. People start staring into the middle-distance. It's very distressing.

It's the same plot, essentially, as *Stardust* (see p. 141), *Glitter* (see p. 358) and *The Rose* (see p. 213), but with straighter trousers and uglier actors. *Breaking Glass* was the last in the line of bleak, *grand guignol*, Rock-Is-Hell British pop movies. Both film and soundtrack were moderate commercial successes. But the awfulness of the film exposed the fact that no-one believed that rock was important enough to be Hell or Heaven or anything extreme enough to cause such violent misery. It was the 1980s, everyone was well on the way to accepting that rock was just showbiz, and satirical, critical ideas that had felt relevant in the times of *Catch Us If You Can* (see p. 57), *Privilege* (see p. 64) and *Slade in Flame* (see p. 147) had reached their real-life conclusion in the furore surrounding the Sex Pistols. It is darkly funny when a distressed Kate gets mobbed at a signing, and you realise that the version of 'Big Brother' soundtracking the scene has changed 'kick him up the arse' to 'pinch him on the nose'. But, in the wake of Thatcher and Reagan and a real class war, no-one sane could possibly find themselves caring about the compromises of ambitious youth, or the significance of continuing to say 'Arse', or fictional pop gods who'll do anything for money and fame and come to a sticky end. I mean, all these rock movie victims could always do what Slade did in *Flame* (or what John Lydon did to the Sex Pistols) and say no, yes?

Breaking Glass is a bad film because it thinks rock matters more than the failing England it's set in. To all intents and purposes, the Great Dark British Rock Movie ends here, a busted flush.

• •

The Loveless

1981

Starring: Willem Dafoe, Robert Gordon, Marin Kanter, J. Don Ferguson
Dir.: Kathryn Bigelow

★ ★ ★ ★

Plot: The *nouvelle vague* biker movie the French never got round to making.
Key line: 'We're going nowhere. Fast.'

The opening of this cult arthouse biker gem is as sexy and satisfying as anything in post-1960s film. A tough, prowling rockabilly tune called 'Relentless' is playing, and the credits give way to a tight shot of the gleaming chrome of a motorcycle shaded inky blue by the night. Legs in leather walk into shot. The camera moves slowly and lovingly up, over thighs, crotch and torso, until we're watching a whiplash-thin leather boy combing his greasy hair into a perfect DA. He is posing, heavily conscious that he's being watched. He looks down, pouting, and the camera rises until we see a bush and know he is in the countryside.

He puts away his comb, sighs and does up his thick belt. The music fades. As he prepares to mount his Harley-Davidson, the camera backs off into a crane shot, and we slowly see the full picture from our vantage point above; enigmatic, leather-clad man-boy with enormous red and chrome machine between his skinny, shiny black legs.

Willem Dafoe – for the biker is he, in his first film role – takes an age to do up his gloves, put on shades, check the bike ... and finally kicks it into throbbing action. The bike starts, and so does the same vampy rockabilly tune ... 'I'm the source of all sorrow ... I'm here and gone tomorrow/I never leave a trace ... I'm relentless/I'm never satisfied ... You better look out, cat! I'll kill ya twice ... '

As Dafoe pulls away from this lay-by, the camera sweeps to its left and reveals a highway, a lake and a lush sunrise. A huge yellow car glides by and lets us know immediately that this is America in the 1950s. The bike follows the car into the distance, and then the scene melts until we are in front of Dafoe, watching him ride. The sun has risen now and he looks so fucking *Wild One*/*Scorpio Rising* cool that you just wanna ... well ... you just wanna.

The song fades again, the shot switches to a low shot of the open road, and, as a voiceover, Dafoe says, 'I was what you call ... ragged ... way beyond torn up ... I weren't gonna be no man's friend today.' The bike appears, as a speck on the horizon, and thunders, inevitably, deliciously, towards us. It's coming straight at us! It's ... it's ... well, it goes past us, actually. Dafoe mumbles, with self-conscious poeticism: 'And to me, this endless blacktop is my sweet eternity.' And he speeds away from us and we sigh with pleasure.

Leather-clad boys. Postmodern homoeroticism. The American road. Thug existentialism. Violent rockabilly. Willem Dafoe. What can possibly go wrong?

As it turns out, nuthin'. *The Loveless* is a visual feast of sumptuously stylised rock 'n' roll existentialism. The music is constant and brilliant, with Robert Gordon's meta-rockabilly joined by rock, pop, blues and jazz hits from the decade where music and teenagers reinvented the Western World. No-one sings a song or plays an instrument, although Gordon plays Dafoe's boisterous buddy Davis. It's not about a band or the music biz. But it's a perfect representation of what the fantasy of rock 'n' roll means: sex and sin, nihilism and speed, smirking amorality and doomed boys. In *The Loveless*, the music is a star character; an erotic idol bleeding from radios and jukeboxes and earning the right for Bigelow to point her camera at iconic pose after iconic pose in a stream of lurid tableaux. You know from the outset that things are going to go really, really badly in this anonymous southern backwater, and you also know that it will be painless and beautiful, with no annoying 'real' people getting in the way. This is a film about the American 'live fast, die young' part of the American dream, and why dreaming about it is so much easier than living it. It's film about art, as opposed to art film.

The plot is nasty, brutish and short. It's 1959, and Vance (Dafoe) is the leader of a biker crew travelling to Daytona for a race. But a broken chain on one of the hogs means they're forced to stay in one of those sinister one-horse towns, swaggering, pouting, throwing flick-knives at each other, sexually taunting housewives, shagging adolescents, and heading towards an inevitable confrontation with the repressed and insular townsfolk and the sweaty, sinister Tarver (Ferguson).

The Loveless meta-movie aesthetic may be nicked from the French New Wave; the homoerotic iconography from Kenneth Anger; the basic plot from *The Wild One*. But Bigelow's bravura shooting style is pure John Carpenter; every angle of every shot feels like a portent of violence. The homoerotic leather fetishism gay men saw in *The Wild One* and adopted as clone standard is made gleefully apparent here by Bigelow, who seems to instinctively understand the sensual appeal of hard bikers better than any gay male director.

The hilarious dialogue is purloined from beatnik poems, Tennessee Williams-style melodramas, girl-group records and bad teen movies ... but deadpanned as if it's the most meaningful conversation ever uttered. It's what Tarantino did later, but without the ironic winks and frat-boy swearing, which is probably why *The Loveless* bombed like Enola Gay.

The ending revolves around the abuse suffered by Vance's boyish underage conquest Telena (Kanter) and her tragic revenge. It is manic, hysterical and brilliantly staged. Unavailable and unloved, *The Loveless* is a magnificent, unashamed celebration of both rock 'n' roll and movies that was released at a point when art movies just weren't fashionable. Like *Privilege* (see p. 64), its re-release and reappraisal are long overdue.

• •

Ziggy Stardust and the Spiders from Mars

1982
Starring: David Bowie, Mick Ronson, Angie Bowie, Trevor Bolder, Mick Woodmansey
Dir.: D.A. Pennebaker

★ ★

Plot: The cold-blooded murder of glam-rock, caught on CCTV.
Key line: 'You're just a girl. What do you know about make-up?'

The first shot of this document of 1972's legendary final Ziggy Stardust show, as Bowie looks into a mirror while having his hair done, reminds you what a genuinely odd-looking guy he was during the glam-rock years. The sickly pale skin. The skeletal cheekbones. The eyes that gave him his alien credentials – one with a normal pupil, the other constantly dilated, as if the right half of him was always getting fondled somewhere exciting. The lustrous auburn feather-cut. The thin lips and crooked teeth that gave away his working-class background and lent his smile a sinister, Artful Dodger quality. In another life, Dave Jones was a razor-toting Sarf London hooligan who gave you chilling evils in the pub or on the bus. It's that edge of griminess that lent his carefully constructed camp a fag-stained earthiness that working-class boys could relate to. But the guy is still wearing a leotard, and few urban Bowie clones had the balls to do that on a night on the town.

Pennebaker's eye for striking images in dark places is immediately evident in the pre-show build-up, as we cut to an elderly, grey-haired, bespectacled man tuning the piano on the near-black Odeon stage. It seems an unlikely preparation for a flashy, trashy rock show, Pennebaker reminding us that, glam-rocker or not, the musicianly Bowie wasn't Alvin Stardust.

Curiously, the last-ever Ziggy Stardust show was billed, on the Odeon's billboard, as 'From 8pm We're All Working Together with David Bowie'. We know this because we're now standing outside the venue, in the bright sunshine, with the fans. They wear tank-tops, loons, platforms, garish bum-freezer plastic jackets, clown make-up, awesome mullets, Aladdin Sane zig-zags and gold stars on their faces, and they are almost all heartbreakingly young. We guess it must still be hours until showtime but anticipation is defeating their boredom. The buildings, flyovers and loud, busy roads that surround the Odeon – now the Hammersmith Apollo – are exactly the same as they are today; this otherwise grey and anonymous corner of West London where Bruce Springsteen played his legendary 'The Future of Rock' first London show and Steve Jones and Paul Cook stole the Sex Pistols' first guitars and amps.

As we survey the fans, Pennebaker treats us to the sound of Bowie's introductory announcement later that night, and that reminds us that this very smart self-publicist actually told the press that Ziggy's last show was actually Bowie's last show – ever.

The fans mob Bowie's wife Angie as she arrives, and there follows a somewhat embarrassing scene in hubby's dressing-room, as she fakes a posh accent and tries to drag Bowie into some sort of comedy routine. Instead, David and his make-up man pompously critique her cosmetics skills.

We want more of this fly-on-the-wall stuff, but, instead, we're very abruptly watching the show. And the first surprise is how poorly shot Bowie and the band are; often out-of-focus with chaotic camera movement from all five cinematographers. The opening 'Hang on to Yourself' shows how much British punk owed to Bowie, with guitar legend Mick Ronson's coruscating guitar lines savagely dominating the sound far more than they do on the record. Cue a great, but, again, poorly shot moment where, over the opening notes of 'Ziggy Stardust', Bowie stands, arms stretched out, framed in spotlight. Two girls sneak on in the dark and pull away his blue, black and red, almost superhero-style costume, revealing a yellow kimono dress affair, with thigh-length yellow boots.

From there, it's a face-off between a wonderful, historic show and utterly rubbish film-making. As Bowie and his best band mix material from *Ziggy Stardust* and *Aladdin Sane* with surprises like a very silly 'Space Oddity' and a truncated but towering version of 'All the Young Dudes', bringing the curtain down on the glam era that made Bowie a superstar, it's both fabulous and endlessly frustrating, like looking at the Sistine Chapel through a keyhole. The sound recording isn't much better, either. All of which probably explains why it took ten years and the early 1980s surge in Bowie's popularity before anyone decided that this was good enough to put on a cinema screen. Reviews at the time expressed disappointment at such a botched job, and they weren't kidding.

Considering that many believed that this was Bowie's last show, you might expect some dramatic theatre after the final song – 'Rock 'n' Roll Suicide', naturally. But no. An interview with Bowie about why or if he was quitting? Nah. How about some reaction from fans who must have been either distraught or disbelieving? Too much effort, presumably. It's all such a missed opportunity.

What even Pennebaker can't help but capture is a performer so charismatic and subversive that he introduced a generation of men to the pleasures of being gay or feminine or both, irrespective of whether they actually wanted to have sex with other men. Influential enough, too, to make sure that an already established rule that rock stars should be slim became a neurotic obsession with the unhealthily thin. Swingers and roundabouts, I guess.

I'm glad someone captured something so precious for posterity. But, if Marc Bolan's *Born to Boogie* (see p. 124) is anything to go by, Bowie should have hired Ringo.

● ●

Pink Floyd – The Wall

1982

Starring: Bob Geldof, Christine Hargreaves, James Laurenson, Eleanor David, Kevin McKeon, David Bingham, Bob Hoskins
Dir.: Alan Parker

★

Plot: Walls are bad. But women are worse.
Key line: 'Oh Babe/Don't leave me now/How could you go?/When you know how I need you/To beat to a pulp on a Saturday night.' (from 'Don't Leave Me Now')

I don't like Pink Floyd. Worse than that, I'm a typical punk-era rock journalist . . . I like the early, funny ones with Syd Barrett, hate everything since. So loathing the band's one foray into film is a given. Except . . . that I had this persistent memory from going to see . . . *The Wall* when it first came out. I took my girlfriend at the time . . . let's call her S . . . and she was very quiet as we were bombarded with 90 minutes of images of war, blood, masculine self-pity and man-eating vaginas. And then we left the cinema and, after a few steps down the street, she stopped … and vomited, copiously.

So this memory kept playing around my head and I figured that I had to give *Pink Floyd – The Wall* credit for two things. One is for being the world's worst date movie. But also; anything that can produce a reaction that physically powerful in anyone must have something going for it. I should put my loathing of the music and everything Pink Floyd stand for aside, and be objective.

So that's what I did. Stood back from my punk loyalties. Looked positively at the flamboyance and total commitment of director Alan Parker. Admired the elegant animation stylings of cartoonist Gerald Scarfe. Gave silent props to the acting debut of former Boomtown Rat and future Sir, Bob Geldof, who had to make a character out of Pink while largely staring silently and without expression at a television screen. After all, it's 27 years since this movie came out, and I should have got over my childish affiliations to long-defunct teen tribes and trend-hunting dismissals of progressive rock. Be mature. Be objective. Yup. Objective old me.

Oh, fuggit, what I really want to say is … this film is the rancid toenail clippings of fetid rotting dogs. The thing that comes out of a gorilla's arse after feeding it raw laxatives and hanging it upside-down by its balls for an hour. It's a film of inane metaphors about walls and fucking mincing machines and teachers that made you eat your school dinner and the terrible, terrible pain of being a million-selling stadium rock star which, according to *The Wall*, actually equates to fascism and dying in wars and having real mental health problems. Can you believe? … the idea of *The Wall* came from a Pink Floyd stadium show in Canada where Waters reacted to not having a good time on tour by spitting at a fan. Most would've given themselves a stiff talking-to and then booked some shows at smaller venues. Not Roger Waters. The guy makes a huge-selling double concept album, the worst British Number One single of all-time ('Another Brick in the Wall, Part 2') and a fucking film out of a bad hair day! Suddenly, we're all covered in his phlegm.

The story, as far as one exists, revolves around rock star Pink (Geldof), who is having a breakdown because ... um ... well, because that's what alienated rock stars on drugs do, innit? The 'songs' provide a whinging, unintentional comedy backdrop to his life-story – Nazis killed his Daddy in the war, Mummy, wife and groupies keep leaving him to face thousands of adoring fans alone, the bitches. Even the teacher that beat baby Pink only did it because his stone-faced missus was making him eat his dinner.

The key line quoted above from 'Don't Leave Me Now' is meant ironically, but Parker and Scarfe seemed to have missed this, and in case we miss their issues, Scarfe helpfully does a cartoon where two flowers morph into a penis and a vagina and then the vagina eats the penis. Pink Freud. Fuck me.

And then there's this pesky wall. It's the one we all build to protect ourselves from the pain of life, which then keeps us from connecting to each other. If the alternative means connecting with Roger Waters and his Godawful music then I want one of those walls you can see from Outer Space.

While the film's rock opera construction and fatherless war-baby angst is entirely stolen from *Tommy* (see p. 164), the gig-as-fascist-rally ending is cribbed from Peter Watkins' awesome *Privilege* (see p. 64), a debt that nobody involved admits to. While Watkins was simply positing the idea that mass entertainment might be a useful agent of control in a totalitarian society, and understood the humour in that idea, Waters' vision (he wrote the screenplay, incidentally) infers to me a loathing of the fans who go to see his band's sullen parade of flying pigs and bank clerk guitar solos.

The film's final scenes are entirely meaningless.

But in the interests of fairness, I did track down my ex-girlfriend S to ask her why *Pink Floyd – The Wall* had produced such a visceral reaction, way back in 1982. She did vaguely remember the night. Turns out she'd had a dodgy prawn.

• •

Wild Style

1982

Starring: 'Lee' George Quinones, Sandra 'Pink' Fabara, Frederick 'Fab Five Freddy' Braithwaite, Grandmaster Flash, Rock Steady Crew, Busy Bee, Double Trouble
Dir.: Charlie Ahearn

★ ★ ★

Plot: Rap, scratch, bomb and break: THE cinematic record of the early New York hip hop scene.
Key line: 'Watch out for the third rail, baby. That shit is high voltage!'

Wild Style is a film where none of the actors can act, the storyline is foolish, the music is recorded so badly it sounds like someone just put a cheap mic next to a radio, and where the tiny shooting budget is all over the screen. Yet it's a thing of great beauty, especially to anyone who has ever loved a hip hop record, or, more importantly, believed in the ideal of underground working-class art. Charlie Ahearn may have had little technical talent as a director, but when he pointed a camera at the Bronx in 1981 he captured a broken New York in all its scrapyard glory, and gave us a crucial document of the birth of what would become the most successful and influential pop culture movement on Earth.

But *Wild Style* is not, principally, about rap music. Out of the 'four elements' (rap, turntablism, graffiti and b-boying aka breakdancing) of original hip hop culture, Ahearn chooses to focus upon graffiti. Real-life 'bomber' Quinones plays Ray aka Zoro, a Latin proto-Banksy who is refusing to join with his fellow graffiti artists and get paid to make legitimate graffiti for commissioned murals or on canvas in galleries. He believes in the outlaw code of bombing, making his art on trains and the walls of his slum environment in the dead of night, using a crumbling South Bronx as his canvas. *Wild Style*'s footage of kaleidoscopically tagged trains snaking through the shattered remnants of ghetto New York is peerless.

And Zoro's dilemma is a clever opening gambit. The film was made just as the downtown NY art scene leaders Jean-Michel Basquiat and Keith Haring were networking with the uptown graffiti kids, making bombing cool for the cognoscenti. The downtown world is represented here by Virginia, a white, platinum blonde journo played by Patti Astor in one of the all-time bad acting performances. Virginia is beautiful and fearless but ultimately stupid and ambitious, and is the sharp class and colour contrast to the Bronx kids. This gives an opportunity to lampoon the whole class-clash element of the uptown/downtown cultural exchange, as we bounce quickly from Virginia and Ray, almost getting shot by Bronx thugs, to the pair and hustler Phade (played by future Clash collaborator and Yo! MTV Raps presenter Fab Five Freddy) at a downtown gallery party, explaining graffiti and hip hop culture to the bohemian suits as if picking their way through a perilous linguistic maze. Just to punch the point home, one of the wealthy and mature female art patrons pays the young Ray an advance for an art-piece and then fucks him. At least, we think she does. As their conversation becomes sly innuendo, the camera switches to the Manhattan skyline, leaving you to guess. You're reminded of that great Joe Strummer line from the Clash's 'Death or Glory': 'He who fucks nuns will later join the church.'

Journalist Virginia's resemblance to Debbie Harry is an in-jokey reference to a real cultural milestone, when the Blondie heroine accompanied Fab Five Freddy to a Bronx hip hop club and was so impressed that she invented white rap on the seminal 'Rapture', complete with shout-outs for Freddy and Grandmaster Flash. 'Rapture' brought hip hop to mainstream America, and *Wild Style* captures the culture on this cusp as the Blondie hit plays on the car radio while Phade and Ray make their literal and symbolic journey downtown. Blondie's Chris Stein, by the way, provides *Wild Style*'s incidental music.

The lack of cinematic guile (and of styled stars and designer clothes) lends excitement to the scenes in tiny Bronx parties, where you feel like you're smack dab in the middle of the action as nerdy-looking MCs chat their Sugarhill Gangish rhymes over the sparse funk of the DJs. This hits paydirt in the legendary scene where the rival Cold Crush Brothers and Fantastic Five crews hold a beautifully choreographed freestyle rap battle while shooting hoops on a neighbourhood basketball court, serenaded by all-rapping females.

Hip hop was inevitably conquered by four more powerful elements – cash, sex, champagne and conspicuous consumption. And the prophecies of that are all here too, as MC Busy Bee wins a rap competition, and treats Ray, Phade and three girls to a limo ride and a night at a hotel. But the hotel is cheap and the implied orgy is the model of fresh-faced innocence in comparison to the megalomaniac porn fantasies that sustain rap now. Ahearn emphasises the youthful optimism of the fledgling scene in his attempt to sell its positive side. And watching a hip hop film that doesn't drip with cynicism and misogyny is what makes *Wild Style* an enduring pleasure after all these years.

This inspiring belief in the young, the poor and their creativity reaches a peak in the scenes where the community prepares for a big rap show at an amphitheatre in the park. The montage cuts between Phade watching the legendary Grandmaster Flash cut records, Ray working on his art, some extraordinary B-boy dancing, and a bunch of neighbourhood kids transforming the faded grandeur of the amphitheatre into a gleaming palace of street art. The prowling bass-heavy electro-funk of the *Wild Style* theme backdrops the scenes, and it feels like a glimpse of a socialist Utopia, as everyone works for the common good, to make their hellish environment beautiful, to create an event accessible to everyone in a community that can't help but be exclusive. The rich aren't here because they're scared of the poor, and when the cat's away, the mice work hard and play harder. You feel both an enormous pride in what this scene went on to achieve, and the sadness in all that it lost as it made big money for everyone but the neighbourhoods it came from and those few who invented it. Still ... let's not get grumpy. The dignity of labour is an exciting reality in *Wild Style*, and that's something that few movies can boast.

The climactic show reminds us of a few other key facts. Hip hop was better dressed at the beginning, before it discovered a uniform of baggy jeans and rubbish jewellery. The gangstas didn't invent posing onstage with guns. Hip hop legends like Ramm-ell-zee, Grand Wizard Theodore, Grandmaster Caz, DST and Crazy Legs actually existed. And hip hop was, originally, a two-tone movement ... black and Hispanic. The basis of this rich and omnipresent culture was not one race or another, but the American working-class. It's always a class thing, and the best things in life are always invented by the poor.

Wild Style doesn't qualify as a four- or five-star docu-drama because, although the docu is extraordinary, the drama is a bust. If just one ounce of care had been taken with acting, dialogue and plot – not to mention camerawork which falls apart every time a conversation ensues – *Wild Style* would have been a bona fide classic. As it is, it's a flawed but much-loved cult history lesson which has been happily embraced by each successive generation of hip hop fans who want to get beyond corporate rap's banal surface and discover the roots of an all-embracing culture. Hip hop, in all its elements, has always been caught between keeping it real and getting paid, and *Wild Style* clumsily but endearingly debates the wrongs and rights of that conflict while wryly predicting hip hop's future as the ultimate in packaged rebellion.

• •

Footloose

1984

Starring: Kevin Bacon, Lori Singer, John Lithgow, Dianne Wiest, Chrisopher Penn, Sarah Jessica Parker
Dir.: Herbert Ross

★ ★ ★ ★

Plot: Rock 'n' roll, dancing and Kevin Bacon vs God. He never stood a chance.
Key line: 'It's not just about a dance. Not any more.'

While putting together the list for this book, I decided I had to include a representative of the modern dance movie genre that has such enormous popularity among women, children and gay men. It could've been *Fame, Flashdance, Dirty Dancing, Strictly Ballroom* or *High School Musical.* But in the end it was this passionate little movie with an unlikely storyline. If you've never seen it, it's a film about a small American town that has banned dancing, specifically to rock 'n' roll. It was a huge hit, not just because it's fun, but because it says morally right things in a simple, punchy way, with characters you can believe in and actors, in Lithgow, Bacon, Penn and Wiest, who give a potentially silly film a great deal of subtle substance.

Kevin Bacon plays Chicago boy Ren, who has been moved by Mom to a tiny rural Christian backwater called Bomont after Dad abandoned them. The opening scenes are a vivid depiction of the hysterical misanthropy and stultifying boredom of fundamentalist Christianity . . . and any film that goes out to teach kids that lesson is a friend of mine. But, despite initial appearances, the squeaky-clean Aryan Stepford kids are actually walking outta church and straight into gleeful and profane discussions of teen pregnancy and the wisdom of buying diaphragms by mail order, before performing death-defying stunts involving straddling two cars and a high-speed truck. And that is just the girls. Godless American youth – don't you just love 'em? *Footloose* does.

But poor city slicker Ren is a cool, sexy and well-read kind of boy who likes heavy metal, and is quickly realizing that he's been moved to a full-on, book-burning, shag-hating fascist fiefdom, the kind of place that bans Kurt Vonnegut books, the word 'fox', and, most pertinently, dancing. No wonder, then, that the Kids are driven to distraction by the up-tempo synth-rock sounds of Kenny Loggins. And it ain't just the Kids. The sounds of a dodgy Prince impersonation through a tinny beatbox even send the adult staff at the local diner into a frugging frenzy, inducing smiles of such pearly-toothed and goggle-eyed enthusiasm that the very boundaries of the act of smiling must be immediately re-assessed in relation to this new and slightly disturbing information. God equals grumpy, pop equals ecstasy, in this microcosm of the fundamentalist Bible Belt. So Ren persuades his fellow pupils that they must be allowed to have an all-dancing Senior Prom. He takes his fight all the way to City Hall, putting himself in direct opposition to hellfire preacher Reverend Moore (Lithgow), who also happens to be the father of the Bad Girl Ren falls for.

Footloose is part of a great American film tradition – irrational fear and loathing of the American small town, and the insistence that the city (where all film-makers live and work, obviously) is where all freedom and enlightenment resides. Thank fuck these liberal Nazis never lived in Peterborough. They would been so traumatized by the lack of macrobiotic Sushi bars, African per-cussion workshops and Woody Allen seminars they would probably have had a whip-round for an atom bomb and wiped everywhere but Los Angeles and New York off the map for good. The most meaningful insult thrown at a character in a script full of teen 'banter' comes when love interest and tough girl Ariel is told by her hick boyfriend, 'You're as small town as they come.' From then on, her coupling with Chicago boy Ren is as sure as farts follow beans.

But in spite of that, there are many reasons why *Footloose* is magnificent. Obviously, I can't call it a masterpiece or anything, because it doesn't have any bits where Oscar wannabes stare grimly into space and nothing happens for ages, giving the cinephile an opportunity to marvel at the camera angles, the subtle use of lighting and the emotional repression. But if you prefer smart things like fun and metaphor, then *Footloose* rawks, Dude.

First, it's a blatant attempt to tap into a pre-1960s milieu where rock's racial and sexual blendings were revolution without the messy and difficult realities of having to educate, agitate and organise. But most film-makers – even John Waters (see p. 281) – would have made a 1950s/1960s period piece. By making *Footloose* contemporary to the 1980s, Herbert Ross and screenwriter Dean Pitchford tap into pre-1960s innocence and youth rebellion while also making a point about Reagan-era values and the way that freedoms that its youthful audience took for granted could be lost if not fought for. *Footloose* turns back the clock because American power was trying to turn back the clock.

Second, it's a teen high school movie, and teen high school movies are better than any other genre of film. High school is a universally understood microcosm of society, with its arcane rules and customs, social hierarchies and useless and morally bankrupt authority figures. But one thing is always to be counted on ... the jocks, beauty queens and privileged kids will end up humiliated; the aliens, victims and poor kids will always triumph, and lessons about social justice and judging other humans by the content of their character will always be learned as an essential rite of passage. This is played out against a backdrop of the only things that matter when you're a teen – sex, friendship, style, music and sex. Telling kids all this in entertaining stories is a social and philosophical service, because, after 20 or 30 years of wasting too much time on work, money, conforming and acquiring life-threatening addictions, you find that all that actually does matter in life is sex, friendship, style, music and sex, with the only potential added useful element of being a good parent; that is, a parent who teaches their kids the wisdom of all of the above.

Third, Kevin Bacon, and that lovably rat-like face which always looks like its going to cry, even when it's smirking triumphantly.

Fourth, tasteless 1980s dancing and even more tasteless 1980s hair and clothes.

And fifth ... by tapping into the entire basic point of dancing as a publicly acceptable form of sexual display, and then having young people dancing wildly to win the day, you get to make a message film in a right-wing era about how healthy it is for young people to have sex without making something obscene or disturbing the Forces of Reaction, who are always too thick to get symbolism. Metaphor, innit?

Among all these Big Ideas, any teen film worth its salt needs funny, pop culturally referential dialogue that tells you quickly what kind of character is talking, and reflects the vitally important bollocks that teen discourse consists of. Thankfully, Pitchford duly obliges with stuff like this: Ren: 'Do you like Men at Work?' Willard (played by Chris Penn): 'Which men?' Ren: 'Men at Work'. Willard: 'Where do they work?' Ren: 'No. They don't. They're a music group.' Willard: 'Yeah? What do they call themselves?'

Pitchford's script is sly all round. This being a farming community, his version of the *Rebel Without a Cause* 'chicky run', a traditional teen movie staple, uses tractors rather than hot rods. To Bonnie Tyler's 'Holding Out for a Hero'. Priceless.

The dancing doesn't truly kick in until around 35 minutes in, when an alone and pissed-off Kevmeister opts to dance away the heartache using the warehouse he works in as a gigantic partner. And, Boy ... is his dancing gay. Nope, not camp. Truly, truly gay, in a way that only 1980s dancing can be, with its hyperactive mix of ballet, Michael Jackson, the pogo and the *Jane Fonda Workout*. It's also pretty obvious when the routine gets to a hard bit, and we suddenly cut to a stunt dancer. I've actually just got through writing, in the entry on *The Rocky Horror Picture Show* (see p. 155), that I don't get so-bad-it's-good. But *Footloose* is helping me with my kitsch deprivation problem, because this segment is toe-curlingly bad ... and I frigging love it. Maybe this scene defines the subtle differences between camp and kitsch. Or maybe I just like *Footloose* a lot, and refuse to let logic in at this late stage.

In other business, it's interesting to see a young Sarah Jessica

Parker being completely unremarkable in every way, unknowingly establishing her credentials as a future post-feminist megastar. But *Footloose* is a part of the 1980s revival of strong female roles after the whores and victims of the 1970s, and Lori Singer's excellent Ariel is anything but a bog-standard love interest. She's another throwback, a revival of the terrifying Jennifer from 1960s B-movie classic *Beat Girl* (see p. 35), albeit with a nice side. In perpetual love/hate revolt against her Bad Dad Reverend Moore, Ariel plays out her angst by being sexually promiscuous and, in a scene that closely resembles one of the best scenes from *Beat Girl*, doing death-defying things with motorized vehicles that emasculate the pretty boy who wants her. When Bad Dad tries to bully her, she simply looks him square in the eye and refuses to be controlled. 'It doesn't get much better', she hisses at him, an oddly sexualized way to describe yourself to your father. It's Ariel who provides the substance to win the argument over the prom, giving Ren quotes from the Bible, using her father's obsession against him.

You've got to admire a movie that takes on Reaganism, not with the scowling pessimism of 1980s socialism, but with the all-shagging, all-bopping equivalent of Mickey Rooney and Judy Garland exclaiming, 'Let's put the show on right here, in the barn!' But *Footloose*'s most heroically futile gesture is its attempt to give rock back its rebel cachet, at the very time that the co-option of punk had finally made rock the conservative showbiz cash cow we know and love/loathe it as today. Like any kids desperate to dance would put on rock in 1984, when disco, electro, R&B and hip hop existed? Hence, *Footloose* has an oddness to it, summed up by Kevin Bacon gyrating and whooping in his entirely gay way in a redneck bar to utterly undanceable rock records . . . and fitting right in.

Footloose is a cult movie among gay men, enduring enough to form the basis of an episode of *Will and Grace*. The reason, perhaps, is because the movie accidentally presents a gay teen fantasy. As the strains of 'Let's Hear It for the Boy' by Deniece Williams blare tinnily out of the soundtrack, Ren teaches Willard (Chris Penn) how to dance . . . in montage, naturally. Willard is the essence of the guy at school who would kick the shit out of anyone potentially un-hetero, with his cowboy clothes and his dumb hick accent. But here, he is the hyper-enthusiastic aper of his pretty friend's gyrations. Alone together in their tight jeans, they horse around, happily, with no homophobic hang-ups, exchanging loving looks.

We even get a beefcake shower scene earlier in the movie, yet nowhere in the film is Ren or anyone else accused of being a fag for wanting to be different or show off their bodies – except by one kid, a one-line extra, who shouts, 'Only fairies dance!' before walking right out of the film. Ren is a gay hero in disguise, bringing civilization to the heathens by way of uptown style, sensitivity to women, a pop culture aesthetic and a perfect butt in unfeasibly tight jeans. He makes these uptight boys feel good about themselves by getting them in touch with their feminine sides, represented by ostentatious dance moves and a better rapport with their girlfriends. He makes men feel good about their bodies.

The easiest thing to sneer at about *Footloose* is the yawning chasm between the wet pop on the soundtrack and the extremes of good and evil that this 'rock 'n' roll' is supposed to inspire. But there's some context for that, too. *Footloose* is actually based on real events. A small town called Elmore City in Oklahoma really had banned public dancing from the moment it was founded. In 1980, a group of high school students really did agitate for a senior prom. They really did take their argument all the way to the town council, and they really did win the day. They themed their first-ever dance party around … 'Stairway to Heaven' by Led Zeppelin. How long before actual dancing broke out in Elmore City is not a matter of public record, but I think we can safely assume that Kraftwerk, James Brown and Run DMC were not on the original dance card.

Footloose is a short, sharp, culturally enlightened and beautifully made argument against repression hiding beneath the veneer of a lightweight pop dance movie. Considering that Herbert Ross was a jobbing director whose next big hit was *Steel Magnolias*, he deserves a lot of credit for pulling off a genuinely subversive film that was a big enough hit to inspire a forthcoming remake starring Zac Efron. Let's hear it for the boy.

● ●

Stop Making Sense

1984
Starring: Talking Heads
Dir.: Jonathan Demme

★ ★ ★ ★

Plot: A nerd in a big suit gets fonky.
Key line: 'Thank you! Does anybody have any questions?'

The finest concert movie ever made builds from almost nothing. We begin by watching feet in white shoes walking across a grey floor. A voice says, 'Hi. I wanna play you a tape', and a beatbox is placed upon the floor. A sparse drum-machine plays a rhythm.

The camera travels up a thin body in a grey suit. We eventually get to the body's head, and we're looking at an American Bible salesman from the 1930s. He seems terrified, with a skull-face and huge eyes on stalks. But he's not here to warn you of the coming apocalypse. He is David Byrne and he's here to play you a song called 'Psycho Killer' on acoustic guitar.

The stage is undressed, ugly and chaotic. There are bare walls and exposed pipes.

The beatbox begins to improvise, and the Bible salesman gets thrown around the stage as if punched or shot or electrocuted. He finds a camera – us – at stage left, and begins to play to us confidently. He's a funky dancer, for such a geek.

Stop Making Sense was pieced together from three Talking Heads shows at the Pantages theatre in Hollywood in December 1983. The director, Jonathan Demme, was some way away from his greatest successes – 1991's *Silence of the Lambs* and 1993's *Philadelphia*. But he had already made six critically acclaimed low-budget features by the time Byrne asked him to make a different kind of concert movie. The cinematographer was Jordan Cronenweth, who had enabled Ridley Scott to show us a wet, claustrophobic, neon future in *Blade Runner*. His camera behaves differently from the normal filming of a rock show. No senses-pummelling quick edits. No dull shots of hands strumming. Instead of being impressed by musicians, you are watching music.

Byrne devised these live shows to be filmed, rather than simply asking a director to make something visceral look multi-dimensional. As Byrne and Weymouth perform a guitar and bass version of 'Heaven', the stage is literally being set up around them ... drummer Chris Frantz is next. The camera is almost as inter-ested in people pushing things around as it is the performers, and you realise that Byrne's staging and Demme's carefully choreo-graphed cameras have turned a concert into a story, where you wonder what's coming next. They're also deconstructing the myth of the magic of showbiz, of course, but you're having too much fun to stroke your chin over all that. The title is from a line in a song called 'Girlfriend Is Better', but it's also about the irrational physicality of music, its ability to overwhelm intellect and confound reason. Stop making sense. If only we could.

As the quartet – fourth member Jerry Harrison is with us now – play 'Found a Job', you also wonder at how four fresh-faced, collegiate white middle-class musicians got so effortlessly funky. A stunning version of the gospel-tinged 'Slippery People' adds two black female backing singers and congas, and the show becomes a disco, complete with the girls impersonating Byrne's geeky guitar heroics.

By now there is more typical concert lighting and staging, which does seem to have emerged as if by magic, and more black musicians including Funkadelic keyboard legend Bernie Worrell. There are wonderfully bandy-legged, jogging dance routines for 'Life During Wartime'. What *Stop Making Sense* captures for posterity is the fact that Talking Heads weren't just a cerebral, art-pop experience. At their peak – which was right about here – they were a big old daft ecstatic sweaty dance party. Which doesn't stop a bank of red screens at the back of the stage suddenly flashing up random words: Onions. Facelift. Pigs. Or the stage being turned into a living-room by the addition of one lamp for 'This Must Be the Place (Naïve Melody)', and Byrne using the lamp as a romantic dance partner.

Or Byrne becoming a bespectacled professor hit by out-of-body voodoo in an awesome 'Once in a Lifetime'.

Bassist Tina Weymouth's pleasure in comically acting out the emotions of songs with her eyes makes her post-punk's cutest Soccer Mom. Which only makes it a better surprise when the leader of the band departs and Tina leads a version of her and Frantz's Tom Tom Club hit 'Genius of Love' that is only slightly ruined by Frantz's insistence on rapping. There's a bit where hard strobes flash and Weymouth and the two backing singers just dance, and it looks so beautiful I cry a little.

It's all a diversionary tactic, of course, for the arrival of the visual image that David Byrne will always be most associated with – the Big Suit. One of the most simple and effective pop performance ideas of all-time, it's all the better because no-one can copy it without blatantly plagiarising. And anyway, it's Byrne that makes the suit: the slicked-back matinee-idol hair; the tiny head; the popping eyes; the diamond-cutting cheekbones; the bizarrely long, thin neck, making him look like a giant, besuited turtle. It's the perfect visual expression of Talking Heads' major theme – the anxious and repressed white Western everyman, imprisoned by inhibition, dwarfed by conformity.

This isn't just the best concert film of all time. It's a film of one of the very greatest live acts of all time, fusing the muso side of black and white music with such effortless swing and lack of wiggerness that it makes similar attempts by the likes of Bowie look silly in comparison. The musicianship is ridiculously accomplished and the arrangements complex and sophisticated. But there is absolutely nothing clinical or smooth about this broiling, tactile, epic music. It's about energy and pleasure. Eighty-seven minutes shoot by and, when it's over, you still want to dance.

• •

This Is Spinal Tap

1984

Starring: Christopher Guest, Michael McKean, Harry Shearer, Rob Reiner
Dir.: Rob Reiner

★ ★ ★ ★ ★

Plot: The best mockumentary ever made.
Key line: 'I heard a band that, for me, redefined the word "rock 'n' roll". I remember being knocked out by their exuberance. Their raw power. And their punctuality.'

If you've bought an entire book about rock movies, then it's extremely unlikely that you haven't seen *This Is Spinal Tap*. The most acclaimed, adored, referenced, quoted and influential rock film of all time, it's also up there amongst the best comedies and the best mock documentaries of any genre. Christopher Guest, who plays guitarist Nigel Tufnell and who co-wrote the sparkling script, has gone on to a career making brilliantly observed and affectionate spoof documentaries including *Waiting for Guffman* (amateur dramatics), *Best In Show* (dog shows), *A Mighty Wind* (folk musicians) and *For Your Consideration* (the Oscars), all of which are unique and great, and none of which are as funny as *This Is Spinal Tap*. Director Reiner's gift with actors and set pieces led him to direct a number of blockbuster hits, including *Stand By Me*, *When Harry Met Sally*, *Misery* and *A Few Good Men* . . . none of which are as good as *This Is Spinal Tap*. It forged the template for *The Office*, rendered all other pop spoofs superfluous and introduced a string of phrases – 'What's wrong with being sexy?', 'Well – it's one louder, isn't it?', 'It's such a fine line between stupid and . . . clever', 'There's too much fucking perspective now', 'This piece is called "Lick My Love Pump"', 'Hope you enjoy our new direction' – into the cultural discourse. But you know all this, don't you? Of course you do. But just in case you don't . . .

A maker of commercials called Marty DiBergi (Reiner) decides to follow fading British metal band Spinal Tap on their US tour to promote their 1982 album *Smell the Glove*. But it becomes increasingly clear that their label has barely released the album in America. With sales and crowds plummeting, relationships between singer and guitarist falling apart, a Yoko competing for the guitarist's attentions, and their increasingly outdated and preposterous stage schtick hitting technical problems, DiBergi gets a better story than he bargained for.

And that's it, plot-wise. The devil is all in the detail, which is piled on with such relentless accuracy that it suggests that Reiner and Guest had had many dealings with many idiot rock bands who, I can confirm, have all seen this film since its mid-1980s release, yet all still behave in the same ludicrous way, without a hint of irony, to this day. And not just the metal bands, either.

But then, this is because ... *Spinal Tap* is not just about rock bands. Everyone who sees ... *Spinal Tap* gets the joke, whether they have any interest in rock or not. Women especially. Because it's a film about something that everyone on the planet experiences on an almost daily basis – men who refuse to grow up. Or rather, deluded, egomaniacal men who refuse to grow up. That's how the characters of Tufnell, David St Hubbins (named after 'the patron saint of quality footwear') and Derek Smalls invented David Brent, because they are all one and the same ... a man of average intelligence, talent and charm put in a position of power which allows their delusions of genius to be indulged at the expense of everyone around them. And the reason this is funny, rather than annoying, is because none of these men are bad people. The characters are written by men who are well aware of their own stupidities, and they are therefore not judged too harshly. They're decent, underneath it all. They've just – like so many men in a patriarchal world – been given far too much rope.

Once that's understood, it's all about your own personal fave scene. The two that are usually cited are the bit where the band head onstage in Ohio and find themselves lost in a labyrinth of corridors, and the bit where they perform their prog-rock masterpiece 'Stonehenge' – played against the backdrop of an 18-inch Stonehenge with dancing dwarves because Tufnell has drawn the wrong stage set dimensions on a napkin. The song is the best on the soundtrack – a spot-on parody of early 1970s progressive rock-folk, conceived with obvious love and care. Ooh . . . and there's the bit where bassist Smalls gets stuck in an onstage pod . . . very funny.

But my personal highlights are all smaller ones . . . like the bit where Tufnell patiently explains to DiBergi why women don't like Spinal Tap: 'Really, they're quite fearful. They see us onstage with tight trousers . . . We've got, you know, armadillos in our trousers. It's really quite frightening . . . the size. And they run screaming.'

And then there's the running gag of an endless number of Tap drummers inevitably dying in mysterious circumstances, topped by this discussion of the demise of second drummer Stumpy Joe. Small: 'The official explanation is that he choked on vomit.' Tufnell: 'It was actually someone else's vomit.' Small: 'They can't prove whose vomit it was. They don't have facilities at Scotland Yard.' Tufnell: 'You can't really dust for vomit.'

And then there's the performance of 'Jazz Odyssey', the legend that is Fred Willard as Lieutenant Hookstratten, the sharp pastiches of 1960s beat and hippy pop, Patrick Macnee as the head of Polymer records who is later knighted for founding 'a summer camp for pale young boys', the mimes including Billy Crystal serving canapes at the label party, and the masterpiece of smut that is the Queen/AC/DC-lampooning 'Big Bottom': 'My baby fits me like a flesh tuxedo/I'd like to sink her with my pink torpedo.'

Dirty jokes aren't funny without the context of an uncynical heart, though, as anyone who's sat through a Russell Brand stand-up set will readily attest. And it's another small scene – perhaps the only one not completely played for laughs – that gives . . . *Spinal Tap* that heart. Di Bergi asks Nigel and David about the first song they wrote together, at the ages of 'eight or nine'. It's a skiffle song called 'All the Way Home'. They sing it together a cappella . . . and it's really sweet. Possessed of all the innocence and authenticity that Spinal Tap are obviously incapable of. The Biz has corrupted the two young boys who, at some point many years ago, had a simple musical talent. No preaching, though – Reiner and Guest head straight back to the jokes without milking the moment.

I'd love to be at least a little iconoclastic about *This Is Spinal Tap*. But I can't, 'cos I just can't lie that well. This is one of the few films in existence that is absolutely faultless. One has no choice but to get down on one's knees and lick its love pump.

• •

Purple Rain

1984
Starring: Prince, Apollonia Kotero, Morris Day
Dir.: Albert Magnoli

★ ★

Plot: A $6 million tribute to Small Man Syndrome.
Key line: 'Are you sick? How many girls have you done this to?'

I must have been a huge Prince fan. I was just one of the millions who rushed breathlessly to the cinema to see the Minneapolis Midget's debut film . . . and I convinced myself to love it. Twenty-five years later and I'm watching it for only the second time and wondering what kind of gormless twerp I was at 21. *Purple Rain* isn't just a bad movie. It's an offensive bad movie, dripping with so much misogyny it makes your average Snoop Dogg record sound like Patti Smith reciting Simone de Beauvoir. Maybe I just wasn't the right-on boy I thought I was.

Buoyed by the cross-over success of the soundtrack of the same name, *Purple Rain* grossed $70 million dollars at the box-office. Pretty good, for a film with no script, no characters, no actors, no story and a pathological loathing of 50 per cent of its potential audience. These were the dark days of the mid 1980s – Reagan getting his second term, full-on backlash against 1960s radicalism, Live Aid and the privatisation of economic justice on its way. In that sense, *Purple Rain* is the ultimate mid 1980s product: style over substance, flash over talent, fashion over morals, men over women. There is a cruelty and egomania in this Prince vehicle that has never emerged in his music, and especially not in the mid 1980s when he was at his creative peak. But, commercially, this shit worked so well for Prince that it catapulted him into the megastar category with Michael Jackson as his only serious commercial rival. Hard times make us sado-masochistic and keen to laugh at the humiliation of others.

As the Reagan 1980s was an attempt to wipe out the 1960s, it's fitting that *Purple Rain* is a throwback to the traditional backstage musical about the soapy perils of showbiz. Prince's The Kid is a little man with big hair and the Next Big Bandleader Thang in his Minneapolis hometown, but he has to vanquish Kid Creole copyist rival Morris (Day) and his bad, wife-beating Dad (Williams), while also torturing ... sorry ... wooing new all-singing, all-dancing girl in town Apollonia. This he does by taking her into the countryside on his enormous phallic motorbike and forcing her to strip off and jump into a lake while he watches, leering and laughing. It drives her crazy with lust as, in this movie, women of all colours live only to be slapped around, dumped in skips and ritually humiliated by laughably unattractive black men.

But, no matter how fucked up the Western World was in 1984, this film would not have been an enormous hit if it didn't have things going for it. And *Purple Rain* has two pretty substantial elements in its favour. The first is Prince's music. The second is a gloriously over-the-top look, with special mention going to cinematographer Donald E. Thorin and costume designer Marie France.

The style that accompanied Prince's rise was an extraordinary blend of the 'new wave' – America's take on Britain's New Romantics; all wedge haircuts, beauty spots, headbands and pantaloons – with bits and pieces from the 1940s zoot suit era, Little Richard's pompadour camp, Rolling Stones dandyism, Sly Stone's hippypimpisms, Bowie/Bolan glam and ruffled flourishes all the way from the Edwardians. This eye-popping mix of lurid styles is not confined, in *Purple Rain*, to the lead players or musicians. In the club scenes at Minneapolis's First Avenue, where the real Prince played his early shows, every single extra who accidentally fills a frame is decked out in peacock finery, giving the film an insanely decadent look that defines the bad-taste excesses of the 1980s while also qualifying as a fully formed fashion statement.

To add to this, Thorin is unapologetic about making the film look like one long rock video, capturing a wealth of dry ice and sumptuous colour and making the performances of Prince and The Time look appropriately timeless. Set designer Anne McCulley packs every frame with gold lamé, junk-shop curios, tacky neon and vintage chic, until you figure that the best way to watch the film is with the volume down for the talking and up to 11 for the songs.

But the film's big winner, when all is said and done, is the music. *Purple Rain* just beats out *Quadrophenia* (see p. 220) as the best rock movie soundtrack of all time, and whether being performed by Prince and the Revolution on stage, or blasting out as Apollonia is biked through the country towards the watery death of her dignity, the songs just make you want to jump out of your seat and dance like a pillock.

This explains why OutKast's recent star vehicle *Idlewild* is such a prize turkey. The duo have always been in hock to Prince as composers and musicians. So it figures that they just pinched his one hit movie wholesale. Got it right, in many ways … rubbish script, embarrassing dialogue, glossy cinematography, misogyny masquerading as comedy, an over-emphasis on clothes and not one person in the cast who can act. Sadly, they forgot that commercial success did not make *Purple Rain* an enduring classic, and the fact that the two not dissimilar Prince follow-ups, *Under a Cherry Moon* and *Graffiti Bridge*, were such putrid stinkers that they belong in lists of worst films ever, right up there with *The Swarm* and the collected works of Ed Wood. But mostly, they forgot that they didn't have incandescent songs like 'When Doves Cry', 'The

Beautiful Ones', 'Take Me with U' and, of course, 'Purple Rain' itself to distract the viewer from the emptiness of the exercise. *Purple Rain* essentially wastes 85 minutes of your life getting to the nub of the crux . . . a beautifully staged, gratuitously melodramatic, cynicism-shredding performance of the title song which stands as one of the best-ever rock movie scenes . . . the very essence of Pop Corn. Baffingly, having hit paydirt, the movie still elects to serve up another 15 minutes of anti-climax.

Prince fanatics – an especially sad breed of insane celeb-stalking obsessive-compulsive – will probably point out that the story provides get-out clauses for its loathing of birds. Abusive father, blah blah blah; The Kid learns and grows blah blah blah; he gives the women in the band their props blah blah blah. It's all far too banal to redress the balance. The point here lies in how often the male viewer is encouraged to laugh at and get off on the weakness of the female characters, and that Prince and the screenwriters obviously believe that female viewers will go all weak at the knees as they watch themselves being bullied by tiny men with comedy facial hair. The *Purple Rain* soundtrack is an ageless thing of beauty. The *Purple Rain* movie is a relic from dark times best forgotten, but never forgiven.

• •

Sid and Nancy

1986

Starring: Gary Oldman, Chloe Webb, Andrew Schofield, David Hayman
Dir.: Alex Cox

★ ★ ★ ★

Plot: Love's young nightmare.
Key line(s): Sid: 'This is just a rough patch. Things will get much better when we get to America. I promise.'
Nancy: 'We're in America!'

Now ... I realise that Alex Cox was never setting out to make a biopic of the Sex Pistols. He wanted to re-cast a lurid tabloid scandal as an unlikely romance. But that's the problem when you use real characters and shoot in a *vérité* style. It looks like you're dealing with facts. And so much about *Sid and Nancy* is so wrong.

The major reason that Sid Vicious got to join a band and publicly self-destruct was that the Sex Pistols were already infamous, and that was largely down to the charisma and talent of manager Malcolm McLaren and singer Johnny Rotten. Hayman and Schofield are so awful and dull and unpleasant it's almost as if Cox went out of his way to find the two least appropriate actors in London. As far as I know, Rotten aka John Lydon's appeal didn't hinge upon saying the word 'boring' over and over again and encouraging Sid to smash Roll Royces and attack helpless dogs. He and Sid didn't stumble upon Nancy Spungen in a posh flat – Lydon actually introduced Sid to Nancy, to his eternal shame. She wouldn't have said, 'I've got all your albums' ... because they hadn't made any. The Pistols did play one show in a Soho strip club, but McLaren didn't have to stand outside ironically pretending that a band weren't playing, and the inside was unlikely to have been smothered in punk graffiti. And the lead singer of X-Ray Spex didn't look like a Goth porn star. And calling journo Nick Kent 'Dick Dent' and having Sid assault him with a bass guitar (it was actually a bicycle chain in real life) right before he plays his first gig ... it's just embarrassing in its desperation to shoe-horn every early Sid legend into seconds of screen-time.

And this is just the first eight minutes.

But it's one of the many things Cox got wrong that saves this curious tribute to junkies. Gary Oldman and Chloe Webb are way too talented and charismatic to be the real Sid and Nancy, and it's their energy that saves *Sid and Nancy* from being completely unwatchable. Unusually for any film, the most convincing scenes are when the two are making love ... and I mean, making love, rather than fucking.

To get anything else from *Sid and Nancy*, you have to disengage credulity in the same sort of way as you would for anything directed by Michael Bay. Accept this world where the Sex Pistols drank in pubs where mulleted rock bands hang out, where they throw darts at their drummer who's a little fat bloke, where Johnny Rotten looks every day of 40, and where Sid Vicious is actually a Sir Galahad, saving the useless but harmless Nancy from groupie abuse. You remember Cox's debut film, a brilliantly original, bad-taste B-movie pastiche called *Repo Man* that managed to corral American punk, sci-fi and Harry Dean Stanton into one weird and wonderful place. You start to notice things here, like Sid, Nancy and a mate walking down a street oblivious of a gang of children smashing every car on the road with sticks and clubs. You realise that you're watching a caricature of what outsiders thought punk was, and that that could be a funny idea.

But, at the same time, it's unavoidably about a woman who was murdered and a man who killed himself. It's about a young boy offered an extraordinary opportunity who meets a junkie groupie and becomes a dead junkie instead of a live rock star. Real people, real tragedies, and loved ones left behind. And, to add insult to injury, the crucial context of being in a band so loved and loathed that they became a national obsession is almost entirely removed, as if being Public Enemy Number One and effectively banned from actually playing wouldn't be any kind of factor in someone barely out of their teens wanting to escape into smack. Not to mention Sid's abusive, junkie mother and lousy upbringing. So, when the drug scenes veer between repulsive and romantic, rather than unsettling black comedy, *Sid and Nancy* just feels like a film that can't make up its mind what it is – except for a self-indulgent two fingers to everyone who was involved with the real Sid Vicious and Nancy Spungen.

But *Sid and Nancy* overcomes all of this because Cox finds so many moments of cinematic beauty in the most unlikely situations. One real-life Pistols moment depicted is the Silver Jubilee boat trip fiasco on the Thames, when an attempt to launch the 'God Save the Queen' single by sailing by the Houses of Parliament ended in violent police raids. While comic chaos ensues on the embankment, Sid and Nancy walk through it, rendered untouchable by love, as a swelling synth drone drowns out the noise of the arrests. It's a truly memorable representation of first love's 'nothing exists but us' syndrome.

And this sets a tone. Every time Cox deals with the Pistols or punk or 1977, it's dreadful. Every time he deals with Sid and Nancy in a hermetically sealed drug bubble, it's great. Webb is spectacular as the wildly over-the-top Spungen, greeting a plea to do the washing-up with a New York roar-whine that forces the henpecked punk to do it himself. Sid and Nancy as parallel universe sitcom couple, or alternative Hollywood romance, or a dark twist on any-stock-screen-couple-you-choose, is an inspired idea that Cox fully exploits for both touching romance and surreal comedy. He remodels the pair as anarchic children amongst disapproving adults that include the rest of the Sex Pistols. It's cute. And then you pinch yourself and remember the skag, and the stabbing, and the overdose . . .

Which is all here, along with a theory on the mystery of whether Sid did or didn't kill Nancy. Cox has little interest in the Sex Pistols, so it's difficult to understand why he didn't just make a film that began with the band's split, packed full of Oldman falling through glass doors and Webb screeching. Cox has fun recreating Sid's 'My Way' promo as Sid and Nancy's blood wedding, and it's the final act dealing with the pair's swan-dive towards oblivion in New York's Chelsea Hotel that provides the meat of the movie, including a tragic-comic imagining of what taking your boyfriend Sid Vicious home to meet the folks might be like.

From there on in, the dissolution is horribly believable, a mutual apocalypse. If you want to turn your kid off drugs, the last 40 minutes of *Sid and Nancy* might just do it.

• •

Superstar: The Karen Carpenter Story

1987

Starring: Gwen Kraus, Bruce Tuthill (voices)
Dir.: Todd Haynes

★ ★ ★ ★

Plot: Karen Carpenter's life and tragic death, acted out by Ken and Barbie dolls.
Key line: 'Karen and Richard Carpenter – just a couple of kids-next-door.'

In 1987 budding gay movie director Todd Haynes and writer Cynthia Schneider decided to tell an overlooked story from the annals of rock death. Karen Carpenter, the lead singer and drummer of Californian brother-sister MOR pop duo the Carpenters, died in 1983 of a heart attack attributed to the disease, anorexia nervosa, from which she had suffered since her teens. She was 32 years old.

Although Karen's death made headlines and inspired greater awareness of eating disorders amongst young women, it has not been accepted into the pantheon of Great Rock Deaths. Whether this was because she was a woman, or not rock 'n' roll enough, or because starving is not as exciting for ghouls as planes, drugs and automobiles, the tragedy and its causes were quickly forgotten. But not by Haynes and Schneider. They decided to make a film which stands as both the angriest and artiest rock movie ever made. The life and death of a pop star, told using Barbie dolls.

If you haven't seen or even heard of the debut film by the 'New Queer Cinema' prodigy who went on to make *Velvet Goldmine* (see p. 326), *Safe, Far from Heaven* and *I'm Not There* (see p. 413), don't beat yourself up. The film made liberal, unauthorized use of the Carpenters' music and was withdrawn from circulation in 1990 after legal action from Karen's brother Richard. Considering the film depicts him as a self-serving tyrant and implies that he is a closet homosexual it's not entirely surprising that he didn't give Haynes the big thumbs-up.

I was lucky enough to see it when it was first released in 1987, and then track it down, in rough bootleg form, on good old YouTube. It's as shocking and powerful now as it was 20 years ago.

Made as a parody of a portentous and melodramatic TV documentary, *Superstar* ... knocks you flat by going – in 43 brief and brilliant minutes – from what seems like a smartarse ironic joke to a furious indictment of misogyny, the music business, suburbia, American capitalism, the family and a world too busy exploiting talent to care if it lives or dies. By employing (largely unanimated) dolls and non-actorly voices, Haynes jars the viewer out of their preconceptions about both squeaky-clean showbiz and the emotional manipulation of the standard true-life tragedy, and creates a biopic that makes all others seem shallow and compromised. The early scene where the Karen and Richard dolls' successful meeting at A&M records slowly curdles by way of atonal music, a hand bathed in shadows, queasy camera angles, the slowing-down of the A&R man's voice until his reassuring platitudes become warped and terrifying, and, finally, a shock split-second shot of a Holocaust victim being shovelled into a grave ... well, it should be ludicrous overstatement. But it isn't. It's disorientating horror that makes Haynes's anger apparent in seconds, and removes the film's potential for camp laughs in an instant.

A major coup of the film involves the 'performances' of Carpenters songs. This is, after all, two entirely static dolls doing nothing while a song plays. Somehow, Haynes makes these scenes move and moving, forcing the viewer to concentrate on the effortless depth and balmy stillness of Karen's extraordinary voice; a voice that conveys fathomless despair while seeming to simultaneously smile. I became a Carpenters fan after first seeing *Superstar* ... having never noticed, as a noise-loving, rebelworshipping rockboy, the layers of interpretive power in both

Karen's voice and Richard's glossy, harmony-laden arrangements. Like Abba, the Carpenters' muse was dominated by heartbreakers that conveyed a very adult and feminine kind of loneliness and disappointment, where the superficial lightness of the music perfectly suited the repressed emotions of women who had been convinced that anger and tears amounted to hysteria and emotional blackmail.

Haynes uses old newsreel footage and narration to give the Carpenters' success its context – an early 1970s America bombarded by Vietnam, internal conflict and angry noise, where the silent majority desperately wanted something that spoke of 'wholesomeness and easy-handed grace'. This switches to pictures of laxative pills and calorie-free food and dry facts about anorexia nervosa as Karen begins her obsession with her weight after a reviewer calls her 'chubby', and her singing voice tells us she's 'On top of the world looking down on creation'.

Karen goes to the White House and sings for Nixon, who has just carpet-bombed Cambodia. A caption points out that the Carpenters' superficially soothing sound reached its peak of popularity as Watergate forced Nixon to resign. Haynes and friends appear playing pundits talking to camera, explaining how the Carpenters 'epitomised the return of reactionary values in the seventies ... I never trusted them'. The other side of the equation is represented too, but all in the language of the media intellectual dismissing her as a person while recreating her as a cipher for various personal interests. This was a girl singing fluffy pop and suffering from an acute mental illness brought on by her inability to deal with stardom, yet both right and left were projecting enormous responsibilities and symbolism upon her, regardless. Everyone's to blame for this tragedy.

As each detail of her condition is revealed, each song becomes more emotionally devastating. 'Rainy Days and Mondays' sounds less like a lovelorn ballad and more a scream for help that all of us were too stupid to hear.

As well as the Carpenters' music, great, darkly ironic but incidental use of other big soft-pop hits of the era – by the likes of

Elton John, Gilbert O'Sullivan and the Captain and Tennille – adds to the feel of an America attempting to drown savage realities in treacle.

Karen's final straws are an apartment of her own, the pressure she felt to keep working and a short, failed marriage to a man she thinks is her brother when she first sees him. Yeah ... no sick implication left unimplied. So I don't suspect we'll be seeing *Superstar* ... made available again anytime soon. Track it down on YouTube before it's inevitably removed, and I hope your computer is better equipped to deal with the quality than mine. Because, along with the political and emotional weight of Haynes's debut, the magnificence of the miniature sets – all constructed so that the dolls fit – are a marvel in themselves. And so is the Karen doll, which Haynes makes smaller and thinner as Karen slides inexorably towards oblivion.

• •

Moonwalker

1988
Starring: Michael Jackson, Joe Pesci
Dir.: Colin Chilvers and Jerry Kramer

★ ★

Plot: Before the fall, a portrait of the artist as singer, dancer, icon, God, car, alien, robot, spaceship, baby-sitter, vigilante and fifth Beatle.
Key line: 'Your success is an American dream come true.'
(Ronald Reagan)

Michael Jackson's one attempt at a cinematic movie vehicle was made when he was at the peak of his popularity. His appearance had changed, but not to the point where he had yet become freakish. There'd been no dubious marriages, flop records, financial disasters nor hard evidence of illnesses nor drug problems. Neverland was still being built. Elizabeth Taylor had yet to dub him 'the King of Pop'. His *Moon Walk* autobiography had been a Number One bestseller, he was making $125 million dollars a year and most of the general public felt that the first 'Wacko Jacko' stories were probably media lies. Most pertinently of all, the first accusation of child abuse was five years away. *Moonwalker* captures the biggest star of our era at the highest point of his staggering success, but teetering on the edge of the abyss. Which should make it a major voyeuristic experience at the very least. The truth is ... it's just routinely weird.

The relationship between Jackson and MTV was key to the rise of both in the 1980s. And *Moonwalker* is an MTV idea of a feature film ... a messy, narrative-scrambling, self-referential montage of pop promos, sprinkled with some techno-sci-fi fairy-dust, and given some visual gusto by *Celebrity Death Match*-style animation.

The movie begins with a stadium performance of 'Man in the Mirror', intercut with glimpses of the atom bomb, JFK, Lennon, Gandhi, Reagan and Gorbachev and sundry other defining images of the 20th century. In short, Jacko is making it clear that he is the equal of any world-changing event or iconic figure of recent history. What inspires far more shock, however, is the sight of Michael Jackson, singing, dancing, sweating, relating to a live audience and still looking on this side of human. This is followed by audio clips from the more newsworthy moments of his career, including the somewhat chilling tribute from Reagan quoted above.

This leads to the best part of *Moonwalker* ... a montage of video clips covering Jacko's career from the first Jackson 5 TV appearance through the hit promos, and including the performance from the *Motown 25* TV special that changed him overnight from pop star to global obsession. It is here that Jackson showcased the Moonwalk to the planet – but it's the short clips of the Jackson 5 that are the most extraordinary and heartbreaking moments in the movie. It's difficult, even now, to imagine how a child could be as talented and beautiful as the pre-pubescent Michael. And the evidence proves that he was a better singer and dancer when he was kid, notwithstanding anything on *Off the Wall* or *Thriller*. Whatever really

↑↑↑ 'Bleedin' gangsters in dinner jackets' – Noddy Holder lends an ear to the reality of the rock biz in *Slade in Flame* (p.147)

↑↑ Having taken too many drugs on the set of *Easy Rider*, a hideously mutated Jack Nicholson makes his comeback in *Tommy* (p.164)

↗ Relax, girls – he's taken. Richard O'Brien in *The Rocky Horror Picture Show* (p.155)

↓ Jill Gascoine and a pair of tits in *Confessions of a Pop Performer* (p.159)

↓↓ David Essex goes mad in a bath in *Stardust* (p.141)

↑ 'Energy, violence . . . and fuck-everything rebellion'
- the mods rock Brighton in *Quadrophenia* (p.220)

→ 'Bring me sunshine . . .' The comedy stylings of Travolta and Karen Lynn Gorney in *Saturday Night Fever* (p.168)

↓ Too cool for school – Rizzo and the gang get pretty in pink in *Grease* (p.178)

↓ 'You Boy! What's the square root of 16?' 'ONE-TWO-THREE-FOUR!!!' The Ramones invent math-rock in *Rock 'n' Roll High School* (p.216)

↓↓ Original pirate material – publicity poster for *The Great Rock 'n' Roll Swindle* (p.206)

In the '80s, Tottenham's exotic 3-3-3-and-an-enormous-mural formation confounded opposition managers . . . *Wild Style* cuts a rug on p.251

CARPENTERS

Living Doll – Barbie
Karen eats to the
beat in *Superstar:
The Karen
Carpenter Story*
(p.274)

↓ Willem
Dafoe models
the Moss
Bros Gay
Biker range in
The Loveless
(p.242)

↑ Michael
Jackson goes
through a
lean period in
Moonwalker
(p.277)

➤ Heap Big
Hokum – Val Kilmer
and dance partner
fail to impress the
judges in *The Doors*
(p.289)

⇈ The world's only Cold War transsexual rock'n'roll self-help comedy . . . John Cameron Mitchell in *Hedwig and the Angry Inch* (p.362)

↑ It ain't him, babe – Cate Blanchett as Bob Dylan in *I'm Not There* (p.413)

↑ DiGging a hole for themselves – The Brian Jonestown Massacre in *DiG* (p.381) happened to the boy who was Michael Jackson, it started when his balls dropped.

The montage is a significant reminder of an easily forgotten fact; all of his transcendent specialness came from his ability to sing and dance better than anyone on the planet. Otherwise, the boy Jacko was a normal – and handsome – young black man.

At this point, it appears that *Moonwalker* is simply an immaculately assembled full-length argument for Jacko's coming assertion that he is the undisputed King of Pop. One so winning that it can even cope with the gargantuan egomania of his Jesus complex. But then, in true Jacko style … it goes mental.

First, we get the 'Bad' gang-fight video re-enacted by children. Then the kid who is being Baby Jacko makes self-mocking jokes about Bubbles, Prince and the self-reference of this movie. Then he walks through some dry ice and becomes full-grown Michael with entourage, and we're still on a movie set, but he gets spotted by some fans on a guided tour, some of whom have giant puppet heads, and they chase him, and there is *Wallace & Gromit*-style puppet fun. He puts on a rabbit head and becomes a cartoon rabbit, and a bicycle becomes a motorbike, and the jolly Disney-type soundtrack music becomes a Jacko song. Occasionally, Rabbit Jacko morphs suddenly into someone like Sly Stallone or Tina Turner. It's actually quite entertaining, and has a surprising self-mocking tone, among the predictable pandering to the children.

The film only wanders, inevitably, into troubling territory, when, around 35 minutes in, Jacko whisks us off to a Never Never Land where he keeps … yikes … entertains … no … plays with … shit … looks after happy children, and begins to indulge his post-*Thriller* penchant for mild peril. The true horror arrives when you cop that the mild peril comes in the shape of Joe Pesci as Mr Big, a child-bothering drug dealer who Jacko obviously has to save every innocent baby in the world from. So … pub debating point: who would you rather have babysit your kids: a drug dealer, Tommy out of *Goodfellas*, or Michael Jackson?

Jacko spends much of the film running away … he's a cod-psychogist's dream, really. And little Joe doesn't look that embarrassed about being in a film where he has to react convincingly to Michael Jackson turning into a flying car, *Home Alone* having given him plenty of practice at being humiliated by weird child prodigies. *The Goonies*-meets-*Bugsy Malone*-meets-*Transformers*-at-Mr Byrite schtick of this whole sequence gets very wearing though, and you understand why we've never heard of the two directors since. Thankfully, 'Smooth Criminal' turns up and saves the day, Michael's childlike muse safe again in the land of the all-dancing pop promo, where his King of Popness essentially resides. As a final gambit, Jacko makes good use of guest kid Sean Lennon and his ownership of the rights to Beatles songs by performing a version of Lennon's 'Come Together' ... a great version, incidentally.

As I wrote the above, Jackson was gearing for a shock run of 50 shows at London's O2 Arena. We all know what happened next. The surrounding publicity has left me even less clear-headed than usual about the crimes against children that he's been accused of, not to mention the weird marriages and kids dangled off balconies, the blown fortune, the Bashir documentary, the drug problems, the truth about his appearance. I know that I feel that he was, until the end of the 1980s, the greatest entertainer of his generation and also feel that that doesn't matter a damn if he really was a paedophile. Every entirely innocent scene in *Moonwalker* where Jackson leads a child through somewhere spooky and unknown makes your stomach turn ... but is that down to Jacko or my own polluted mind?

I also know that *Moonwalker* proves one thing ... that the only great potential Michael Jackson movie would be one that just collects all of his TV appearances and promos up to and including 'Earth Song', and plays them start to finish, one after the other. His self-image was simply too delusional and contrived to do anything well, other than sing and dance.

But instead, we are left with an honest Michael Jackson cinematic product for future generations to ponder – a mixture of the very best and the very worst that American culture has to offer. His success *was* an American dream come true. Why do they always become nightmares?

• •

Hairspray

1988

Starring: Ricki Lake, Divine, Sonny Bono, Deborah Harry
Dir.: John Waters

★ ★ ★ ★ ★

Plot: How rock 'n' roll and working-class teens made Martin Luther King's dreams come true.
Key line: 'Wilbur ... it's the times. They're-a-changing. Something's blowin' in the wind. Fetch me my diet pills, would you, Hon?'

In the greatest of all the Waters movies, rock 'n' roll, anti-racism, dayglo colours and a gleeful embrace of straight-baiting bad taste are all part of the same subversive view of the Baltimore of his youth.

It is 1963 in Baltimore, Maryland and working-class teen life revolves around *The Corny Collins Show*, where local kids get to display their mastery of the latest rock 'n' roll styles and dance moves on prime-time TV. Our heroine is a pre-chat show Ricki Lake as the rotund and ravishing Tracy Turnblad, who has to battle racists, body fascists, snobbish blonde bitches and parental disapproval to be the star of the *Collins Show*, win Miss Auto Show 1963 and bag the cutest guy in Baltimore to boot. Not easy, when Mom is Divine aka Harris Milstead, two-ton transsexual and a bad taste icon ever since he/she ate dog shit onscreen at the end of John Waters' early cult hit *Pink Flamingoes*. Divine also plays the entirely male racist head of the television company, finding just as much camp gusto there as he/she does for Edna Turnblad.

Hairspray was a moderate hit on release. But critical acclaim gave the movie a cult following on video, and it was eventually transformed into a cleaned-up but hugely popular Tony Award-winning Broadway musical in 2002. The stage musical inspired a 2007 remake starring John Travolta, Michelle Pfeiffer and Zac Efron, which I do not include here – not because it's not very, very good – but because show tunes replace rock originals, and the racial integration angle is intentionally divided from the rhythm 'n' blues, girl-group and deep soul that Waters saw as the frontline troops against Jim Crow. Travolta is a particular revelation in the Divine role. But the recent *Hairspray* simply isn't a rock movie.

The original *Hairspray*, however, lays a strong claim to being the finest rock 'n' roll movie of all. Funny, scabrous, enlightened, angry and anti-conservative on every radical front you care to mention, *Hairspray* explodes from the screen with a vigour and shamelessness that perfectly encapsulates why apparently trashy pop was and is always more anti-establishment and daring than dreary old bloke-rock. A delighted perviness permeates every scene without a single cruel joke or shred of nudity, and Waters understands his *mise en scène* so exquisitely that he gets greater good-natured comedy from the sight of Divine and Lake walking into a shop called Hefty Hideaway than exists in every Adam Sandler vehicle rolled into one.

My favourite scene involves super-suave (and super-liberal) dreamboat Link (Michael St Gerard) taking Tracy and her best friend Penny to a Mom and Pop record store in the black part of town owned by local black DJ legend Motormouth Maybelle (Ruth Brown). Penny's racist mother follows and 'rescues' Penny at knife point, symbolising the xenophobia of all ignorant rednecks while a shop full of beautiful black kids laugh their heads off. Waters is no subtle polemicist, but there is an incredibly rousing ferocity to the campaign to de-segregate Corny's show that feels more useful and sincere than more self-consciously adult anti-racist films. This is because, with the soundtrack of tough R&B classics, the gorgeous group dance routines and the fabulous fashions, Waters is constantly reminding us how vapid white culture would be without everything it took from African-Americans. Even the crazy beatniks – short cameo roles for Pia Zadora and Ric Ocasek of The Cars – worship at the altar of reefer and black folk singer Odetta.

Considering Waters' past reputation as a maker of low-budget bad taste fests, he creates a film here that is utterly beautiful to look at. The colours, the clothes and the faces of his actors transform garishness into a lush aesthetic fit for a dream. And a dream is what *Hairspray* is, in a sense, as these kids desegregate the whole of Baltimore, winning every political battle with sheer moral force. Waters pokes fun at both teen naivety and wet liberalism – Tracy: 'I wish . . . I wish I was dark-skinned!' Link: 'Oh Tracy! Our souls are black!' – but makes you understand that it's far better to mean well, no matter how guilelessly, than to be a well-read reactionary. The absolute good faith of Waters' intentions enables him to do the impossible and play a race riot for slapstick laughs.

Debbie Harry, incidentally, plays Velma Von Tussle, pushy racist mom of Tracy's sworn enemy Amber (Colleen Fitzpatrick). And seeing Harry in both this and David Cronenberg's 1982 sci-fi weird-out *Videodrome* leads inevitably to the conclusion that the Blondie icon was no loss to acting. The same cannot be said, however, for Ricki Lake, who is so adorable in *Hairspray* you just want to take the girl home and marry her. But perhaps the chat show route was a fine idea in hindsight, for who else but Waters is going to cast a fat girl as the neighbourhood sweetheart?

All this pro-plumpitude is sadly undercut by the demise of Divine. A week after the release of *Hairspray*, the corpulent cross-dresser died of an enlarged heart, aged just 42. Remember him/her this way, fabulous and funny in such a wonderful movie, rather than eating doggy do for the weirder amusements of John Waters.

• •

Leningrad Cowboys Go America

1989
Starring: Matti Pellonpää, Karl Väänänen, Nicky Tesco, Jim
Jarmusch
Dir.: Aki Kaurismäki

★ ★

**Plot: Jim Jarmusch meets Spinal Tap meets the Blues
Brothers.
Key line: 'Go to America. They'll put up with anything there.'**

The Leningrad Cowboys are a punk rock Gypsy-folk band who
appear to live on a farm in Finland. They, and everyone they know,
have unfeasibly big quiffs and wear unfeasibly long winklepickers.
Their bassist has just frozen to death. Unable to get a gig in their
native land, they go to America. Their dictatorial manager Vladimir
keeps his charges in check by tweaking their noses and feeding
them raw onions. He forces them to learn English and rock 'n' roll
('study this book') and takes us on a whistle-stop of New York,
Memphis, Texas and, finally, Mexico. The Cowboys are followed
around America by village idiot Igor, who wants to join the band
but can't because he is too bald to grow a quiff. Igor asks a barber
to attach a bush to his head but he sings him a hillbilly folk song
instead. They take their dead bassist along too, in a wooden crate.
Their attempt to give him a funeral lands them in jail.

Fans of art-house trashabilly director and Nick Cave dop-
pelganger Jim Jarmusch will love this movie. Kaurismäki is so in
hock to his stylised deadpan comedy, 1950s visual references and
aimless conversations that he does the decent thing and gives his
hero a cameo as a used car dealer. And the Cowboys themselves
are entertaining – an inspired take on what it might be like if a
group of brilliant musicians who had never heard of rock might
look and sound like if they took their cue from the 1950s. Absolutely
right, yet absolutely wrong, with their jerky dance movements and

harsh accents. But this one joke is simply not enough to sustain a movie, and the 75 minutes eventually drag. Much like Jarmusch's early films, come to think of it.

Despite being a surreal comedy, it's the film's visual beauty that hits home hardest. Kaurismäki points his camera at the poorest and ugliest parts of America and gives them a wonderful grandeur. Ghettos, swamps and dilapidated backstreet bars combine to form a vivid vision of America from the perspective of a European who is fascinated by the Great American Underbelly.

But this doesn't explain the unlikely cameo appearance of Nicky Tesco, the diminutive former lead singer of English new wave band the Members and now a music journalist. Nick plays a long-lost cousin who gets elected singer and saves a gig in a biker bar by leading the Cowboys through a stirring rendition of Steppenwolf's 'Born to be Wild'. Definitely one of the oddest cinematic moments in this book, but an altogether agreeable one.

Leningrad Cowboys Go America is here because of its impeccable art-house credentials, and because it was enough of a cult success to spawn a 1993 sequel, *Leningrad Cowboys Meet Moses*. The group even did successful tours, like a proper band. But really this is just a sixth-form revue skit that happens to have been filmed in visually arresting places by a technically gifted director. It's somewhat typical of a style of 1980s art-house film-making whereby the likes of Jarmusch, Wim Wenders and Alex Cox would make films for male student types that appeared to be one big, smug in-joke among cast and crew. And, like all of these kind of movies, *Leningrad Cowboys* . . . is not really very funny. It's just tiresome.

1990s

The Doors

1991

Starring: Val Kilmer, Meg Ryan, Kyle MacLachlan, Kathleen Quinlan
Dir.: Oliver Stone

★

Plot: Twat stops shaving and dies.
Key line: 'You killed my duck!'

This is a story about the coolest rock star that ever lived! You probably haven't heard of him, 'cos you probably like R&B or chav music or rubbish like that. But this director called Oliver Stone, like, knew him really well, when they were both in the 'Nam. His film about Jimmy Hendrix Morrison leaves out the 'Nam but apart from that it's really good and now I've seen it I'm going to put Doors songs on my Rock Star game and rock out! Although some of the songs are a bit slow and don't have as many guitar solos as the Halen and Metallica. But, like, those bands are still alive so my friend Pongo reckons they're not keeping it real, like what Jimbo did.

What happens is that Jimbo is a little boy and sees an Indian dying on a motorway. Not, like, a real Indian but one of those Alternative Americans who cowboys shoot. And then, quick as a flash, Jimbo is Val Kilmer from *Batman* and he's hitch-hiking and you know he's deep because he's holding a book. Val Kilmer's really good-looking and good-looking guys don't read, normally. It's little things like that that Mr Stone notices and are really cool so I should probably get those *Naturally Born in July* and *Killer on the Wall Street Platoon* movies out next, because Pongo reckons they tell you who killed the Kennedys in the 'Nam, and that the reason those huge films are not in Blockbuster is because the government don't want YOU to know the TRUTH!

Anyway, some writing on the screen tells you that it's 1965 and that Jimbo is on Venice Beach, which is the Italian bit of California. And he's in his swimming trunks but he still has a book so he's still deep. And he climbs into a garden and gets Meg Ryan to kiss him in 29 seconds, so she's now his wife. When he climbs in to the garden Meg says, 'You got a problem with Doors?' And Jimbo answers, quick as a flash, 'Waste of time'. And that's why his band will be called the Doors ... see?

And he makes a film at college with dancing bears and Nazis and the other students don't get it 'cos it's too deep but one guy with glasses on says it's 'Godardian' which is French for 'Godlike', but Jimbo's a true rock rebel and leaves school and takes Meg out instead and they have a mad conversation about how that band the Shamen invented sex and Jimbo wants to die 'cos they're ON ACID!

Then Jimbo sings a song to the speccy guy from college and he says, 'Those are great fuckin' lyrics, man ... Let's get a rock and roll band together and make a million bucks!' So they do and this smarmy record company guy is wearing a suit and says that they should sound like something called Herman's Hermits, which is this weird type of music they liked before the Doors and Elvis and the Halen started rockin', and Jimbo says, 'I don't like a man who wears his soul on his face,' which is deep when you think about it.

So the band play more shows and Jimbo stands on a car and says, 'I'm the Lizard King! I can do anything!', and to prove it he takes the band and Meg Ryan to the desert and they do crazy dancing and talk of snakes. ON ACID! And then a bald Indian arrives on a horse and takes him to a cave where he sees the dying Indian from his childhood and a really quick picture of a man in a bath. Now, you could miss this if you, like, go out for a cup of tea or start thinking about something else. But the man in the bath is *really important*. I mean, this isn't like a Chick Flick or something. This is like a really brainy director and if you don't concentrate, you'll just be surprised by everything that happens and then where would you be?

So Jimbo plays another cool show where he sings that song he wrote for *Apocalypse Now* and says he wants to kill his father and fuck his mother. And haven't we all felt like that? I know I have. So an old guy tries to beat him up but these other old guys say Jimbo's a hot new star, and he makes a whole album in a week and Jimbo's the most famous man in the world. People follow him to San Francisco and he makes the women take their clothes off and the men play the bongos, such is Jimbo's power over the Kids. And then they all get mobbed at an airport and when someone asks Meg Ryan who she is she says her name's Pam and that she's 'an ornament'. And she's really happy and smiling about that and Pongo says that the reason girls are so angry these days is because they don't know their place and if they could just all be more like girls in the old days before Maggie Thatcher and Beyoncé then we could all be having sex without getting hung-up about money and kids and rights and boring stuff, like, now. ON ACID! Pongo, like, *gets stuff*.

Then Jimbo's watching TV and lots of people are burning stuff because that's what they did in the swinging sixties and Jimbo says, get this: 'No wonder "Light My Fire" is Number One!' 'Cos the Doors had this song called 'Light My Fire' which was Number One and what he's saying there is that he's really caught the mood of the times in this really deep way, although the gimpy guitarist actually wrote that song. And the double joke is that Jimbo's going to be on TV, on a show by some old dude called Eddie O'Sullivan, and he and the producer are wearing suits so you know they're gonna say something really old and safe 'cos they don't get it, and what they say is that Jimbo can't sing the word 'higher', 'cos it's about ACID! But Jimbo does and the rest of the band are really shocked 'cos even they don't get how rebellious Jimbo really is and then you can see Jimbo's huge penis through his leather trousers and there were riots in places like Watts and Harlem because no-one in America had seen a penis before, even though the Shamen had invented sex. The show's really famous, Pongo says, but I've never heard of it before.

But then it all goes bad for Jimbo, who is just too much of a poet and a rebel for The Man. He meets a witch who makes him drink blood and then he has two wives and they keep saying to him, 'Don't worry ... it happens to every man sometimes', and I don't really know what that means but I think it's because girls don't really understand that his penis is huge and his love is free. And then he starts drinking whisky and Meg Ryan burns a duck and this big gig goes a bit mad when he pretends to show the crowd his willy and then does the conga, and the pigs arrest him and take him to court and he grows a beard and gets fat. It's the getting fat part that lets you know that things are really bad, because you can't be fat *and* rock. Everyone knows that.

So Jimbo is now Jumbo (I made that bit up!) and then he leaves the band and they're sad 'cos they know that without this fantastic poet-Lizard-King guy, they probably would just have to play in pubs like Pongo's uncle's band, the Blues Swankers. And Jimbo goes to Paris and the bald Indian comes and the next thing Jimbo's dead in a bath. See, I told you that was important. And what it's saying is that Jimbo was, maybe, like a god or an alien or something, and could see his own death. Especially ON ACID! And that's what made his music, so, like, different, like when he made songs like 'Strange Days' – because he was strange – and 'People Are Strange' – because people are strange – and 'Love Me Two Times' – because he two-timed all his women.

And then we're in a graveyard and see all these tombstones with the names of smart guys from ancient days like Chopin and Wilde and Sarah Bernhardt, but the only tomb with cool graffiti all over it is Jimbo's, 'cos his fans are rebels, just like him.

The Doors is the best film about music I've ever seen and Mr Stone really made me think about deep stuff like how hard it is to be a poet in this cruel world, and how to juggle da bitchez, y'know what ah'm sayin', Homes? You should watch this because you would realise that the music of today is, like, really meaningless compared to Jimbo and his organ-based rock sound. Jimbo's name begins with 'J' and like another famous 'J' who died young, his hair was just too long for this world.

• •
The Commitments

1991

Starring: Robert Arkins, Michael Aherne, Angeline Ball, Maria
Doyle, Dave Finnegan, Bronagh Gallagher, Felim Gormley,
Johnny Murphy, Andrew Strong, Glen Hansard
Dir.: Alan Parker

★ ★ ★ ★

Plot: The smaller they are, the easier they fall.
Key line: 'Today – St Bridget's Community Centre. Tomor-
row – oblivion.'

The Commitments was a big commercial hit, written by peak-time
TV veterans, directed by a mainstream director, and based upon a
bestselling novel by a popular storyteller. So it's easy to ignore the
subversive qualities inherent in the comic tale it tells. Because *The
Commitments* turns the conventional pseudo-Icarus rock band story
on its head; this is about a band who get their wings burned and
fall back to Earth, having achieved . . . absolutely nothing. Even the
late, half-hearted stab at an uplifting message as the film's hero
trudges disconsolately into a night of broken dreams is yet another
knowing joke about the gap between real life and the bullshit the
world's wannabes console themselves with when confronted with
their own limitations. It could be a bitter little movie. But it's the
exact opposite because, unusually for any film concerning pop
music, it doesn't fall for the idea that stardom is either the best or
the worst of all possible worlds. The secret, one suspects, lies in
the hiring of TV sitcom giants Dick Clement and Ian La Frenais,
who defined the tragicomedy inherent in the pessimistic stoicism
of the British working-class male in *The Likely Lads*, *Porridge* and
Auf Wiedersehen, Pet, and, in collaboration with Irish novelist Roddy
Doyle, transported that profound and profanely bitter survivalism
to the streets and sink estates of southside Dublin here. Add several
short-sharp, hilarious knockabout set-pieces and the Irish ability

to multiply the power and humour of any given swear word by ten, and you have the best dialogue in this book, barring the speed-contempt of *Expresso Bongo* (see p. 27) and the deadpan rock-satirical idiocy of *This Is Spinal Tap* (see p. 264)

Set in an ugly, vibrant, rambunctious and nostalgic Dublin, *The Commitments* concerns the formation and mercurial 'career' of an all-white soul band, playing covers of Stax, Atlantic and Motown classics. The catalyst is Jimmy Rabbitte (Arkin), a skinny, smart-arse, rockabilly-styled small-time music hustler ... so small-time that his most lucrative sideline pre-Commitments is selling recorded-off-TV videos of the Hothouse Flowers to kids on the bus into Dublin. Arkin, one of a whole cast of Irish unknowns dis-covered by Parker, carries the movie, representing hope, street smarts, ambition and the audience, who know, as he surely does in his heart of hearts, that the bunch of eejits he's stuck with are never going to make his fortune. He's a sexier and more believable version of Phil Daniels' Danny Price from *Breaking Glass* ... a mouthy, charming pop manager-in-waiting. As guitarist Outspan (Hansard) puts it, as he and sax player Dean take time out from a deliciously awful wedding to chat Jimmy up: 'You know everything about music, Jimmy. You had that Frankie Goes to Hollywood album before anyone had ever heard of 'em. *And* you were the first to realise they were shite.'

Every young wizard needs his Dumbledore, and Jimmy gets ancient pony-tailed hornman Joey 'The Lips' Fagan (Murphy), who talks about the prospect of Irish soul and his part in it as if he is the John the Baptist of pub-rock. 'The Lord sent me. And the Lord blows my trumpet.' It's the mysterious Joey who does the most to give the motley crew enough hope to work at becoming a decent band, while also doing his damnedest to sabotage it with his blithe blarney and the apparently irresistible charms of his dick.

The early scenes of present-day Dublin quickly establish it as a rough-and-tumble city, rooted somewhat in a quaint, tough-but-friendly past where there's a horse at the market and buskers sing the Everly Brothers. All this is played out to the music we'll be hearing – a feather-light, bleached-white, pub-standard version of

1960s soul and rhythm and blues ... that ultimate musical short-hand for down-home authenticity.

Parker, whose many commercial triumphs include *Bugsy Malone*, *Fame*, *Midnight Express*, *Birdy* and *Angela's Ashes*, is a director who is generally uninterested in art in favour of bums on seats. *Pink Floyd – The Wall* (see p. 248) is an exception, and it fell foul of audiences and critics. In *The Commitments* he goes for what he knows – show what the world we're dealing with looks like, with high production values and plenty of detail. Then get on with the plot, the jokes and the songs. This is perhaps why he always worked so well with amateur or inexperienced actors: appealing faces who say the lines with a natural enthusiasm, and who wouldn't know how to indulge themselves, even if Parker allowed it. None of the film's stars went on to movie careers because none of them (Arkin aside) can really act at all. For a movie like *The Commitments* you just need believable *people*.

The Commitments is also a movie that takes an unusual delight in the minutiae of pop, at least for a mainstream film. When various Dublin wannabes audition for the band by standing on Jimmy's doorstep and telling him their influences, the contrast between their tribal clothes and hair styles and the unlikely bands they name makes for instant, charming comedy. Wings, Joan Baez, Barry Manilow, Soft Cell and Bachman-Turner Overdrive come out of the mouths of both the likely and unlikely candidates, and the scene says pinpoint accurate things about the pretension and frustration of trying to form a band in little more than seconds of screen-time. The musicians' front-room auditions are even funnier, sourcing everything from the Sweet to Slayer to Cajun music to get knock-about laffs. Parker's often been accused of being a philistine populist because of his lack of interest in developing a personal, *auteur*-ist style. But *The Commitments* gives its audience enormous credit for depth and breadth of musical and cultural knowledge, knowing full well that the jokes won't be funny and the forming of the band won't make sense unless the viewer has a working knowledge of the Smiths and Procul Harum, while also knowing that Clarence Clemmons is Bruce Springsteen's sax player. The film's packed with music criticism, the kind of snarling, snobbish invective aimed at bands or genres that music fans really do spout at each other in pubs ... or when they're forming bands. One of the reasons why *The Commitments* was so successful is that it flies in the face of the British post-1980s 'mission to explain' – the polite term for assuming that your audience are as thick as its thickest member. Parker's string of big hits stems from his refusal to believe that he's smarter than his audience. He likes us. He suspects that the working class read.

From around half an hour in, the film becomes more of a musical – as well as gigs and rehearsals, various band members burst into song on buses, the back of trucks, in tumbledown backyards festooned by washing-lines. The music of *The Commitments* is ... not awful, like the majority of music for musicals, but stolidly mediocre, exactly as a white pub band are. The public disagreed, making *The Commitments'* soundtrack a huge commercial hit, and flocking to see various Commitments line-ups in sizeable venues for the next few years. The similarities to *The Blues Brothers* (see p. 230) phenomenon are there for all to see, a disturbing enthusiasm among casual music fans for black music that dispenses with the scary alien characteristics of actual black people. It's a genuinely weird person who would rather listen to some dodgy white singers and average session musicians perform 'Nowhere to Run' than Martha and the Vandellas.

But in purely cinematic terms, the music fits. This is a story about a bunch of enthusiastic but limited dreamers who don't get beyond playing Dublin pubs. If Parker had insisted on finding a collective who could tap into the freaked, dark, mystical 'Celtic Soul' visions of Van Morrison and Dexys Midnight Runners, he would have immediately transformed *The Commitments* into some sort of magical realist art film, which is not what Doyle wrote in his novel, nor what Parker wanted to do in his film. Crucially, though, unlike the hideous *Blues Brothers*, *The Commitments* makes no attempt to colonise and patronise black cultural history until it's convinced the white middle classes that it now belongs to them. By having no black people in the movie at all and comparing, no matter how self-mockingly, the Irish working class with black Americans, *The Commitments* comments cogently on the 'wigger' impulse while making no attempt whatsoever to suggest that The Commitments' music is actually black. It finds common cause with black culture, but from a good-natured, removed and somewhat awestruck perspective. We understand the essential ludicrousness of The Commitments' venture from this exchange between sax player Dean and Jimmy at his toytown Malcolm McLaren best.

'D'you not think, er . . . well, like . . . maybe we're a little white for *that* kind of thing?'

'D'you not get it, lads? The Irish are the blacks of Europe. And Dubliners are the blacks of Ireland. And the northside Dubliners are the blacks of Dublin. So say it once, say it loud – I'm black and I'm proud!!!'

Andrew Strong is a good soul shouter compared to 99 per cent of the planet's white people. But the film knows he's terrible compared to soul's legends, and doesn't pretend otherwise. We Brits will always have a soft spot for stolid mediocrity because it makes us feel better about our own. *The Commitments* taps into that with knowing efficiency.

From then on, the bittersweet comedy draws from a little-known truth about bands: no matter how big or small they are, they usually break up over sex. If the band is unisex, as The Commitments are, then eternal triangles break out all over. If the band are single-gender, two or more members will inevitably fall out over one member's dominant seduction skills, or girlfriend/boyfriend who wants to take over the band, or one member nicking another's lover, and so on. Musical differences? Pah. More great bands have split over the lead singer and guitarist's repressed homosexual desires for each other than anyone's sudden impulse to go in a Balkan death-metal cabaret direction could ever manage.

The other key element is one never made explicit by the script, but which hits the viewer early . . . if the band were fronted by the beautiful, charismatic, stylish and fiendishly clever Jimmy, rather than Strong's oafish Deco, then dreams might come true. But life is rarely like that, which is why we love our favourite pop groups where life turns out to be exactly the way you want it – fascinating sex-muffins at the front, frog-faced labourers at the back, safely behind the drum-kit. Admittedly this doesn't explain the Kaiser Chiefs, but you get my drift.

The inevitability of a non-triumphant ending also hails from Deco, a horrible loser who is nevertheless the best thing about the band, and knows it. So it's fitting that the film's most enduring images belong to Strong, and the strange, punch-drunk and agonised facial tics he manifests as he sings.

But it's the script that's the clincher. Every time the story even edges towards 'Let's do the show right here!' corniness, the earthy, foul-mouthed dialogue and cruel working-class humour keeps it real. Every everyday situation – Catholic confessional, a conversation about Elvis, an Isaac Hayes-backed shag – is a trigger for another ribald gag about sex or music. The first Commitments gig in a church hall of grannies, kids and Boy George clones is a wonderful set-piece, an affectionate, exquisitely timed and only slightly exaggerated version of local-gig chaos that proves that Parker should have made far more straight comedy than he has.

Despite being set in Ireland, *The Commitments* created a market for further, hugely popular, ribald but romantic movies about the British working class. *The Full Monty* and *Billy Elliot* took their cue from *The Commitments* and reflected Thatcher's defeat of unionism and class war, adopting an Americanised view of living with poverty, unemployment and terrible living conditions ... that our ability to sing and dance, and remain stoical, and concentrate on individual achievement, will allow (a few of) us to transcend our environment and regain our dignity. Kitchen-sink Frank Capra, so to speak. And, in the context of a small dark world of ghetto estates and drab community centres, the Commitments *are* a magnificent band – musically exotic, and full of pride in their anti-punk musicianship and achievable glamour in their tuxes and sexy black dresses. They shine, despite their shortcomings.

The Commitments is awash with images of grey estates, overcrowded dole offices, under-fed kids, cramped homes and broken streets. But no-one complains about it ... they just laugh, dream and sing, and enjoy the fact that they live more authentic and vibrant lives than their economic betters. If you think I'm going to say that these films are part of the evil conspiracy against the poor, filling our addled heads with a deluded opiate of moral and creative superiority when we should be organising a revolution ... uh-uh, no way. They made us feel better about ourselves for a few hours. Or, to paraphrase Joey 'The Lips', films like *The Commitments* raise our expectations of life. And we all need comfort food, especially when it's dirty and sweet.

● ●

Wayne's World

1992

Starring: Mike Myers, Dana Carvey, Tia Carrere, Rob Lowe, Lara Flynn Boyle
Dir.: Penelope Spheeris

★ ★ ★ ★

Plot: Not!
Key line: 'He wants us to be liked by everyone. I mean, Led Zeppelin didn't write tunes that everyone liked. They left that to the Bee Gees.'

If this much-loved cult pastiche of teen movies had had nothing else going for it at all, I might well have given it four stars for the 'Bohemian Rhapsody' scene. On paper, this scene consists of four 30-somethings pretending to be metalhead teens, singing along to the Queen classic in a car, and then nodding their heads during the guitar break. But on screen, it ecstatically encapsulates the enduring pleasure rock 'n' roll has given to men since the dawn of rock time. It is split into two parts ... a charming taster five minutes in, and, once the four friends have picked up a completely wasted extra passenger, a full-on assault on the funny bone after six minutes, when bad singing, worse miming, air drumming and head-banging come together in a spectacular celebration of every moment of idiot fun that big, stupid songs and heavy guitars have ever provided. The goofy faces of Mike Myers (Wayne) and Dana Carvey (Garth), both hilariously ugly yet beautiful in their knowing immersion in a moment of innocent slapstick hedonism, are the faces of every boy of any age who has ever forgotten to be self-conscious and just blissed-out to rock's mock-aggressive power. It makes me laugh but it also always reminds me why love of rock 'n' roll overpowers critical reason, even when you're a critic, and why I never want to lose that ability to reject all dignity in favour of freaking out to the joys of inarticulate riffage. The scene entirely explains why, as I write in 2009, the console games Rock Band and Guitar Hero are beginning to out-sell rock records.

There are better films than *Wayne's World* in this book. But if I had to show one scene from a movie that explains the exhilaration of rock 'n' roll to that proverbial alien or cave-dweller, then 'Bohemian Rhapsody, from *Wayne's World* is the One.

If you *have* had an unfortunate life situation involving a cave since 1992, *Wayne's World* is a rock teen comedy based on a *Saturday Night Live* skit conceived by Myers and performed on the influential US show by Myers and Carvey. It was a huge commercial success on release, remains a cult favourite, and introduced an astonishingly large set of catchphrases into Western culture, some of which have stuck ('Party on, Dude!', 'Are you mental?', 'We're not worthy!', 'He shoots, he scores!', 'Not!', 'Denied!'), and some which are only familiar now to *Wayne's World* obsessives ('Schwing!', 'And monkeys might fly out of my butt', 'Fished in!'). It took the initial export to the world of American teen 'dudespeak' begun by the previous year's *Bill & Ted's Excellent Adventure* (the movie that made Keanu Reeves a star) to the next level and forged a change in hipster slang that paralleled the spread of hip hop-derived 'ebonics'. It's the first movie to do a now familiar cake-and-eat-it gag where characters talk about not selling out to sponsorship while ostentatiously holding or wearing brand names. The film constantly breaks down the 'fourth wall' and has the main characters explain the action to camera, but rarely feels smug or patronisingly postmodern. There probably isn't another rock movie which has been more quoted or been more directly influential on popular culture. Yet, like most comedies, teen movies, rock movies and celebrations of the ordinary geek, it's rarely given the acclaim as a seminal classic that it deserves.

The story concerns two best friends from a small town called Aurora, Illinois who do a show for local cable access TV from Wayne's parents' basement. They are obsessed with heavy metal, babes, dudespeak catchphrases and taking the piss out of the adult world. When they are cool-hunted by Rob Lowe's oily TV executive and put on primetime, they find that their ramshackle but inspired show has been turned into bland corporate entertainment. What's more, Lowe's Benjamin Oliver has designs on Wayne's ridiculously cool, kung-fu fighting, Asian-American rock chick girlfriend Cassandra (Carrere). The dumb and dumber duo must somehow wrest back control of their lives from The Man.

The joy comes from how cleverly writers Myers, and Bonnie and Terry Turner and director Penelope Spheeris balance childish humour with pin-sharp pop satire. The deluge of gags cut between the moronic and the intelligent with a speed and respect for the smarts of the viewer that set a template for the likes of *The Simpsons* and *South Park* as well as much recent MTV output. In many ways, *Wayne's World is* a cartoon, where everything any of us recognise from our teens is exaggerated for visual effect and every actor plays their character like a comment on *that sort of character* from other, less clued-in movies. Lowe is a particular revelation as the dashingly handsome bad guy whose every blithely charming 'Yes' conceals an entirely self-serving agenda, a character which pokes fun at Lowe's looks and reputation as much as every empty vessel that successfully cruises the choppy waters of modern media. Lowe enables *Wayne's World* to carry an anti-money, anti-corporate 'message' without doing anything as dull as preaching, hugging or learning.

The movie's other heroic performance comes from Dana Carvey. His Garth is a feast of nerd neuroses and gleeful ugliness, like a giant, walking zit. Yet his good nature has you rooting for him from the first moments, so wonderfully does Carvey convey the kind of meekness that really should have inherited the Earth by now. Garth approaches everything as if it's a naughty secret, making the viewer feel like they've been let into a real private world that is funnier and kinder than the real one. And that is the essence of cult art.

The hiring of Spheeris is also key. The New Orleans director had made her name with punk and metal documentaries *The Decline of Western Civilisation* Parts 1 and 2 and sadly forgotten teen alienation drama *Suburbia*. In short, she knew, understood and loved the white suburban culture *Wayne's World* celebrates. The movie subtly subverts the usual Hollywood/New York contempt for and fear of the American everytown, presenting the empty-headed pursuit of harmless kicks as an essentially benign and lovable product of the suburbs, rather than evidence of hick-town ignorance. Spheeris's use of metal here works perfectly, infusing what was seen, in 1992, as a dead culture with a new hipness that counter-balanced the dark, nihilistic appeal of Nirvana and grunge. In *Wayne's World*, metal and hard rock are shallow fun that only takes on meaning when shared with the rest of your rock-worshipping tribe. The movie punches the point home with cameos from Meat Loaf and Alice Cooper, but neither adds anything that isn't there on the soundtrack, or even the tuneless one-chord 'theme' of the *Wayne's World* show.

The prominence of Cassandra's Crucial Taunt as the local metal bar's best band – and the fact that her babelicious appeal to all men is to do with her talent and toughness as much her looks – even roots out much of metal's traditional misogyny. If you've noticed how much women and gay men love the *Guilty Pleasures* phenomenon, and also how many of the records that it's revived are crass-but-great cock-rock records, you can trace their acceptance back to the success of *Wayne's World*'s inclusive vision of the rock scene.

Although, actually, Crucial Taunt aren't really metal and kinda suck.

When the whole non-misogyny thing is being somewhat undercut by the presence of 'psycho hose beast' Stacy (Boyle), a stalking comedy ex who flags up Wayne's unlikely success with women, the nastiness is blown away when Wayne and Cassandra have a conversation in Cantonese that deconstructs Wayne's collusion in Stacy's neediness and the destructiveness of labelling. Again, *Wayne's World* is a paragon of cake-and-eat-it film-making, whereby you can do lazy, cynical things as long as you wink at the audience and make them feel good about noticing. This only becomes self-defeating towards the end of the movie, when the plethora of false endings and self-referential comments on the mechanics of formula plot devices spirals out of control. Unlike *The School of Rock* (see p. 377), *Wayne's World* doesn't wholly believe in its own good-heartedness, so therefore continually breaks into a sneer. Myers, you suspect, is the weak link. His brittle over-confidence and desperation to establish his own cleverness isn't a joke; a feeling continued in the humourless horror of the Austin Powers movies.

Nevertheless, Myers is humble enough to admit on the DVD's cast and crew interview that, when the movie was first screened, he could only see the jokes that didn't work. And he's right ... plenty don't. Thankfully, there's enough that do. *Wayne's World* is less a coherent comic narrative than a series of sketches, and the best ones – 'Bohemian Rhapsody', Carvey's magnificent sexy mime of Jimi Hendrix's 'Foxy Lady', the *Wayne's World* shows, the Cantonese scene – make the film hilarious and memorable. Many of the best scenes rely on the chemistry between Myers and Carvey, and nowhere is this more apparent and appealing than in the skits where the pair travel to the nearby airport to lie on the hood of their car, get buzzed by incoming planes, and talk and fight. Suddenly, a genuinely touching film about male friendship briefly emerges, reinforced by Myers' enthusiasm for handing Carvey the best lines: 'If she were a President she'd be Baberaham Lincoln' and the inspired, 'Did you ever find Bugs Bunny attractive when he put on a dress to play a girl bunny?'

Nevertheless, helpless belly laughing is induced by the most puerile lines – and the winner is Wayne sniggering, 'I'll have the cream of Sum Yung Guy' when he orders Chinese food – while the postmodernism is designed to make us feel all right about the irresistible delights of men being childish. You could say exactly the same thing about the best heavy metal, and you would be spot-on.

● ●

In Bed with Madonna

1992
Starring: Madonna
Dir.: Alex Keshishian

★ ★

Plot: To some, a behind-the-scenes doc of Madonna's Blonde Ambition tour. To others, a big old fake.
Key line: 'I'm so desperate.'

The one and only cinematic Madonna documentary kicked off a bad phase of her career. Flop film roles, the ludicrous misadventure of the *Sex* book, the badly received *Erotica* album ... all followed this self-consciously fruity behind-the-scenes look at her 1990's world Blonde Ambition tour. Truth was, the girl convinced herself that she'd become a sex symbol and learned, with the career rebirth of the 1997 *Ray of Light* album, that she was really just another manufactured pop star who had made some really good song, video and hair choices. There's a reason why Madonna's fan-base remains dominated by gay men first, straight women second. It's because she's not that hot.

So if an almost-terminal self-regard had set in by the turn of the 1990s, it's fitting that *In Bed with Madonna* is a performance film and absolutely nothing to do with us getting a peek at the star's 'real' self. The backstage scenes where Madonna delivers potted insights on her work and withering denunciations of friends and foes alike are immaculately lit, obviously planned and immaculately acted by Herself. The interesting thing is the version of Madonna that she chooses to give to the world ... a prize bitch and control freak who embarrasses herself over men like Antonio Banderas and Warren Beatty. As she endlessly worries away at her face – make-up deserves a Best Supporting Role Oscar here – Madonna coolly and cruelly dismisses her worshipful co-workers ('I think I've unconsciously chosen people that are emotionally crippled in some way') and famous people ('That's another reason not to live in Chicago. Aside from the fact that Oprah Winfrey lives here'), pausing only to humiliate her (admittedly sleazy) brother and accuse a childhood friend of finger-fucking her.

Twinned with Keshishian's grainy, deliberately vintage mono-chrome, the effect is like one of those old movies where a Dietrich, Davis or Crawford would effortlessly command the screen and forge the template for diva bitchiness, making the viewer fall in love with their frosty, Medusa-like power over all men and contempt for weaker, nicer women. This Madonna is a waspish fag-hag dominatrix who repels and attracts in equal measure, and who flies in the face of the usual pop star obsession with being loved. It seems heroic; especially in 2009 when even scruffy 'alternative' pop stars are so desperate to ingratiate themselves, especially with other famous people. Madonna appears to have no standard career neur-oses about the dangers of publicly humiliating the rich and power-ful. She came out of her 1980s golden period utterly convinced that she wouldn't be meeting any of these people on the way down, because there would be no down. You've got to admire the woman's big brass testes.

Which brings us neatly to the mutual love affair between Madonna and gay men. Here, she goes out of her way to present herself as mother to her group of male dancers, fulfilling every diva fantasy of her loyal gay following. But even when they all dance together in a hotel room, Madonna is careful to put herself in the centre, an object of deference, a Queen among queens. The dancers themselves are overbearing in their adherence to the stereotype of pretty young gay male dancer . . . shallow, needy, effeminate, bitchy and willing to concede authority to their godmother in every given situation. It's like spending 113 minutes in a homophobic joke. I'm happy to admit that I find these men dislikeable and find myself wondering if gay men are happy to see themselves constantly por-trayed as ditzy Himbos; especially for the benefit of a straight woman.

The onstage performance scenes are shot in a lovely, muted colour. Whether they're fabulous or not depends entirely on your enthusiasm for the elaborately staged, all-dancing, cast-of-thousands, band-of-session-musos pop show which Madonna did more than most to establish and develop. As someone who prefers inspired musicianship and the kind of singing that reveals the innermost feelings of the singer, the songs here are my go-make-a-cup-of-tea moments. Bad enough that we're all so impressed and oppressed by empty spectacle. But post-1980s live pop spectacle is so ... unspectacular. Madonna is one of those to blame, with everything performed as if it's a military exercise, a voice incapable of peaks and troughs, all emotions choreographed so that messy, real emotions can't go around causing trouble. On record, at her best, Madonna is an art-trash disco magpie. Live, she's pop as aerobics. We're supposed to be impressed by the hard work of it, as if magic can be measured by physical jerks-per-minute.

But back to the story ... sorry ... completely unscripted reve-lations. One of Madonna's dancers has a reunion with his dad, and she sings a song that mentions fathers, so now we have a mini-theme. Madonna is, in the end, behind that tough exterior, just an insecure little girl in need of Daddy Love. This neatly leads to the arrival of Warren Beatty, the legendary Hollywood actor-renaissance man (see *Bulworth*, p. 330) and seducer of A-list totty who was Madonna's 53-year-old boyfriend at the time. Beatty appears to be the embarrassed male escort, moving between fear of and contempt for Keshianian's camera. But Beatty has made an acting career out of frozen, mirthless smiles that you can't exactly read. You feel that you're being given an insight into the inevitable failure of an unlikely relationship because Beatty appears to find his toy-girl's moaning and attention-seeking sadly funny. But is he just playing the role of jaded Hollywood veteran and misguided father-figure Warren Beatty, written, of course, by the very woman he's patronising? Or maybe by Beatty himself? Hell ... maybe their entire 18-month relationship was a Beatty–Ciccone co-production. And the Oscar *doesn't* go to ...

As for her real Daddy, Madonna brings him onstage at her Detroit hometown show and frets about performing her tediously rude version of 'Like a Virgin' in front of him. 'I crave my father's approval' is not an exciting theme.

One inarguably great *In Bed with* ... moment concerns a backstage party packed with celebrities, largely because the variety of types and levels of celebrity that get access to a superstar like Madonna is very, very weird. I mean, yeah, Al Pacino, fair enough. But Olivia Newton-John? Lionel Richie?

This leads to the movie's best and most talked-about scene. One of the well-wishers is actor Kevin Costner, at that time the biggest box-office draw on the planet. He enters, looking oddly dweebish in his Gap blazer, mullet and round specs. He meets Maddy and tells her that her show was: 'Neat ... really neat.' He mentions a 'deal' that isn't going to happen. 'What ... not *neat* enough for you?', Madonna grimaces. Costner turns to leave. Madonna waves insincerely, turns almost towards us ... and puts her fingers down her throat in a 'makes me want to vomit' gesture. The world cheered. Costner's career never really recovered from being made to look so uncool by a working-class girl.

In America the movie was called *Truth or Dare*. It's not as good a title but it's a more accurate one about the film's aim, which is to knowingly make the viewer wonder whether anything here isn't entirely scripted. Even the bit where the police try to force her to tone down her show seems theatrical, and too well-written (Madonna: 'So what's considered masturbation?' Flunkey: 'When you stick your hand in your crotch'). If we accept that the incident is real, you do get a nice idea of how it feels when someone lends your cheesy bit of packaged soft-porn real, pro-free speech rebel cred. The woman seems so excited that masturbation would appear her only option.

The most painful scene involves her meeting with an old hometown girlfriend Moira. Basically ... she humiliates the woman with insincere kindness and 'go away' body language. Again, it's interesting that Madonna wants us to see her contempt for those who are not famous or creative ... she must know that even fans will be unsympathetic towards the scene. It's the only part of the film that makes you wonder if Madonna's worldview has been corrupted by fame, and that she perhaps thinks that she's been perfectly nice to Moira. But, like everything else in *In Bed with Madonna*, you can't quite put your finger on how much is Madonna and how much is Keshishian, how much is real and how much is staged, whether she's putting us on or playing it straight. The result is that, when the film begins to deal with personal problems around the tour – press gossip, the homophobia of the one straight dancer, a date-rape, artist Keith Haring's death, Madonna's own pro-gay agenda and pre-show prayer Earth Mother crap – it just seems like scripted soap. Unconvincing scripted soap. Watching Madonna and actress/comedian/what-exactly-*does*-she-do Sarah Bernhard act out a 'conversation' in a self-absorbed orgy of lame bad-girlness is just plain sad. But not as sad as hearing Madonna proclaim that she's a 'provocative and political' artist. The only people she ever provoked were the kind of reactionaries that live to be provoked.

The one moment when you unconditionally love Madonna and unconditionally believe what you're seeing involves a birthday party for Madonna's assistant Melissa. Ms Ciccone reads out a comic poem about Mel in a Bronx accent, and it's funny, and Mel's reaction is the kind of emotion one can't fake. Admittedly, a whole film of Madonna being lovable probably would have been dull and might have damaged the controversial rebel-slut image that she was desperate to promote in the early 1990s. But there's a glimpse of a genuine, quite clever and demanding, but ultimately reasonable boss of a business here that you suspect conveys some kind of truth.

Another one comes out of the mouth of a pissed black female backing-singer, ragging on her boss behind her back: 'Mother-fuckin' world tour, year 2025 ... ' She howls, before rubbing her tit like a porn star and singing, 'Like a virgin!' That *is* the embarrassing reality we have to look forward to, it seems.

When *In Bed with Madonna* was first released, it was naughty fun, watching her force a dancer to get his dick out, continually embarrass the unfortunate hetero dancer Oliver, melodramatically confess that Sean Penn was the love of her life, and deep-throat a bottle. But after all these years, this over-long and rather dull movie has dated because its star has dated. The ravages of having worked all the softness and charm from face and body have already set in here. You watch and sigh, and wait for the damn thing to end, and wish she'd go away and leave us with our memories of dancing to great pop records in discos. But Madonna has never understood that *our* experiences and memories are what great pop is about. She still thinks that it's her, and her ambition and work ethic, that we're worshipping when we sing along to 'Into the Groove'. And that delusion starts here.

● ●

Tina: What's Love Got to Do with It

1993
Starring: Angela Bassett, Laurence Fishburne
Dir.: Brian Gibson

★ ★ ★ ★

Plot: Vengeance is Tina's.
Key line: 'Nam myoho renge kyo.'

Any movie that transforms its biographical subject from corporate pop veteran into global feminist icon has to be packing some powerful mojo. Screenwriter Kate Lanier's account of Tina Turner's suffering at the hands of violent husband Ike may not be a great work of art, but it is one of the great examples of Hollywood's mastery of emotional manipulation and one of film's most effective arguments against domestic abuse, bullying and misogyny. The cliché insists that Hell hath no fury like a woman scorned. If Ike Wister Turner had had any inkling that the woman he was beating down would eventually make his name into a worldwide two-word shorthand for wife-beating scum ... but then again, forethought didn't seem to be the guy's strong point.

It's impossible to consider the merits of *Tina* ... without some questioning of whether the film's story is accurate or not. In his autobiography *Taking Back My Name*, Ike Turner denied that he ever raped his wife in the pair's home studio or pulled a gun on her. But then, he would, wouldn't he? What casts far more doubt is a factual inaccuracy that alters the context of the story entirely.

The movie strongly implies that the former Anna Mae Bullock was a virgin when she fell in love with Ike. We infer this partly because she has her first two children with him. In real life, she had already had a child in 1958 to a man called Raymond Hill.

Did the film-makers honestly believe that we would have had less sympathy for the plight of a woman trapped in a violent marriage if she had been revealed as a sexually active teenage mother before she met the monster? I was genuinely shocked when research unearthed this fact, and suddenly a film I had been entirely convinced by seemed completely suspect. What else here is a lie? And why does a film made from a feminist standpoint dump a set of outmoded Christian values on its main character; do they think that *we'll* think that a slut would have deserved what she got?

We know that Hollywood values often stink. But this is a man's reputation – and our sympathies – that the makers were playing with. Let's face it ... there's no way this man's reputation could recover from the graphic horror of the rape scene in this film. And he's dead now, and loathed by thousands who never met him. What if this simply never happened?

But, but, but ... I don't think there's much doubt about the violent nature of the marriage as a whole. It's not as if the guy sued. And *Tina* ... remains an immensely powerful argument both against male violence and for female independence, carried by the two most powerful and committed acting performances in this book. Laurence Fishburne, who was initially reluctant to play Ike, gives a selfless commitment to dark villainy and creates one of the most convincing and repulsive of all screen monsters. And Bassett is extraordinary ... her muscular body and muscular character get the point over that it isn't just weak women or willing victims who find themselves trapped in a cycle of violence.

There are things to talk about, both good and bad, outside of the film's main theme. There was, of course, no dirtier female singer than Ms Turner, and Bassett captures that with a surprising intensity, sticking out that ridiculously perfect butt and saying even more with her eyes than Tina does with that rasping, rude voice. Strange to consider that the part was originally given to Whitney Houston, who withdrew because she was pregnant.

On the downside, there's Stanley Clarke's schmaltzy, bland incidental music. When dealing with old music stars, particularly from the south, the soundtrack composer's job appears to be hiring some pony slide guitarist to noodle away atmospherically while keeping his own finger on the synth-drone button and the knob marked 'reverb'. It's shit.

There's also a disease that afflicts anyone who decides to film the life of an Afro-American musician. An Oz-like hue descends over the screen, every black person got rhythm and dresses like a fashion-plate, overacting is sold as a celebration of blackness. *Tina* ... actually invented much of that inverted racism. But there's no arguing with the energy, joy and eroticism of the scenes in the St Louis club where Ike and Tina meet. Fishburne passes the mic around to women as part of his act, and Bassett sings and tears the roof off, and gets the gig ... so far, so predictable. But Fishburne's stud arrogance and Bassett's charisma and vulnerability are a shock (Bassett mimes to Tina's re-recorded vocals. Fishburne does his own). That's the tough and great trick of the biopic – to make you feel like you're there when, say, Tina Turner first sings with Ike and forms a partnership that will make some of the greatest soul and rock 'n' roll records. Gibson pulls this off and then some.

Gibson also has a flair for interiors. The scene where we see Anna Mae rehearsing in what looks like a ramshackle studio only to find, as the camera moves with Ike, that it's his house, crammed with instruments and people, is a graceful, evocative reveal.

But mostly, this *is* a film about a beaten woman and the domestic violence scenes are horrifying. After 50 minutes of being made to believe that Fishburne and Bassett *are* Ike and Tina, the first attack is brutal and shocking and you *feel* the blows breaking Tina's face. It's a brilliant piece of script-writing, that the first attack we witness is provoked by Tina telling Ike that all his songs sound the same. Ike and Tina Turner's songs really did all sound the same.

Except for one. The reconstruction here of the recording of the Greatest Record Ever Made – that would be Phil Spector's production of Tina singing 'River Deep, Mountain High' – is enough to make a pop romantic burst into tears, which I nearly did. The film reminds you that this work of art only exists because Ike Turner accepted Spector's demand that he had no involvement in the record. Throughout the movie, the point is made that Ike's bitterness about the success and talents of others is as draining and dark and relevant as his penchant for sexism and violence. The movie lies (again!) about the record's commercial success in America – famously, the failure of what Spector considered his masterpiece in the US sent the midget maestro into a depression he never fully recovered from – but you buy the idea that Ike was sent psycho about how much better his wife was without his input.

The film becomes something a little different – and somewhat laughable to us heathen sceptics – when the Ike problem gets solved by Buddhist chanting. But people find their own ways out of nightmares, and if that worked for Anna Mae Bullock, then Amen to that. The moment when Tina finally hits Ike back in the back of a car is one of the very greatest get-up-and-cheer moments in cinema, and you're hit again by just how selfless Fishburne is, playing the pathetic coward every bit as realistically as the marauding bully. When they both stagger into the hotel lobby covered in blood it's the film's one wink at black comedy. Could've done without the terrible power-ballad guitar when she finally makes her escape, but, by now, you're forgiving Gibson anything.

By the time of Ike Turner's death of a cocaine overdose in December 2007, there had been some re-acceptance of the guitarist and composer. In the same year he won his first Grammy for his *Risin' with the Blues* album. His 1951 'Rocket 88' hit with Jackie Brenston and his Delta Cats is still the track most often credited with being the first ever rock 'n' roll record. And Damon Albarn hired him to play piano on a track on the Gorillaz' massive *Demon Days* album.

But the world never entirely forgave a man who admitted, in the aforementioned 2001 autobiography: 'Sure, I've slapped Tina ... There have been times when I punched her to the ground without thinking. But I have never beat her.' Let the full repercussions of that quote sink in, and you understand why *Tina ... What's Love Got to Do with It* stands as one of the most empowering and necessary acts of revenge in the history of the struggle for women's rights.

• •

Backbeat

1993
Starring: Stephen Dorff, Ian Hart, Sheryl Lee
Dir.: Iain Softley

★ ★ ★

Plot: The story of the Fifth Beatle. The one who wasn't Pete Best. Though he's in it, too.
Key line: 'We're gonna be too big for Hamburg. We're gonna be too big for Liverpool. We're gonna be too big for our own bloody good.'

This low-budget curio charms early. Rather than opening with anything to do with the Beatles, we get nostalgic, grainy, evocative images of late 1950s Liverpool, a bluesy instrumental by Don Was, of Was (Not Was) fame, and an introduction to two artsy Scouse smartarses getting beaten up outside a working-men's club. Almost every line is the kind of one-liner that you can absolutely imagine a young John Lennon amusing himself with, and you immediately feel that you've been invited into a rarity ... a post-1970s rock movie with rough edges and a sense of history beyond a fascination with famous people. *Backbeat* wasn't a big hit nor a critics' rave, but it was good enough to get a shout-out in 'Wonderwall' by Oasis, and it's easy to see why.

The story stars American actor Stephen Dorff in a study of Stuart Sutcliffe, the original Beatles bassist who never came back from the group's legendary pre-stardom sojourn to Hamburg, Germany. An artist rather than musician by trade, the pretty, somewhat alien Stu fell into the Beatles through his friendship with Lennon (the excellent Lennon specialist Ian Hart) rather than any rock star ambitions or musical talent. When he falls for photographer and counter-culture beauty Astrid Kirschner, and the decadent art and jazz lifestyle of her intellectual friends, and then starts to get really bad headaches, he ensures that we never get to extol the virtues of a Fab Five, and that Paul McCartney will always be known as a bass player.

Key to the success of the movie is the innovative soundtrack. With no need to license Beatles songs for a story set before they wrote any, overseer Bob Last (founder of indie punk label Fast Product and discoverer of the Human League, Gang of Four and Fire Engines) recruited an American punk super-group including Dave Grohl of Foo Fighters/Nirvana, Thurston Moore of Sonic Youth, Greg Dulli of Afghan Whigs and REM's Mike Mills to play the rough-arsed covers of rock 'n' roll and rhythm 'n' blues hits that a club on the Reeperbahn required to fill the gaps between strippers. Even though Hart and Co. mime, the effect is effortlessly incendiary, conveying the speed-fuelled primitivism that prefaced both the beat boom and punk rock ... though neither music nor vocals sound anything like the Beatles. This is interspersed with tough blues and rock originals as incidental music to create a soundtrack to cherish.

Which is handy. Because even though the period detail and

atmosphere of impending change is present and correct, the movie doesn't entirely ignite. Hart is superb, but Dorff is pretty and nothing else, and the rest of the Beatles are barely there. The script occasionally indulges itself with self-conscious Beatles winks, as when Lennon tells the soon-to-be-cuckolded Klaus Voorman (the future bassist on the *Imagine* album) that the constant gigging is 'a hard day's fucking night' (actually a Ringo remark, according to legend, and Pete Best still occupies the drum stool here). Paul McCartney didn't like the movie, and you can see why when the script gives Lennon all of the Beatles' best ideas, jokes and jealous temper tantrums, as if Paul and George were just bystanders in their own story. Harrison is the comedy baby ('I can't take scones … I'm in a rock 'n' roll group, Mum!'), McCartney just the moaning Minnie putting professionalism before camaraderie. Which could've have been as true way back then as it was by the time the Beatles reached *Let It Be* (see p. 109). But it doesn't feel entirely convincing here.

Nevertheless, *Backbeat* is solid pop entertainment, with an edge of seediness and spontaneity reminiscent of *Slade in Flame* (see p. 147) mixed with the easy amiability of *The Buddy Holly Story* (see p. 182). And it's fun meeting Beatles that wear fabulous Ted-meets-beatnik styles, make their first unlikely record backing appalling pop crooner Tony Sheridan, and who are already rehearsing for those comedy press conferences and the bitter split. The film looks and sounds good enough to make you forget the non-performances of Dorff and Sheryl Lee as Astrid, and the somewhat shallow characterisations. It gets across both the romance and squalor of being European rock's frontiersmen: drinking, drugging, scoring and whoring as boys away from their families will do, but also paying the musical dues that made them into the most influential pop group ever formed.

The film plays with the implication that Lennon was in love with Sutcliffe without convincing itself to really go for it. Hart played that Lennon in the previous year's *The Hours and Times*, a watchable but pretentious art film that obsesses about whether Lennon and gay Beatles manager Brian Epstein had a shag in Spain, which

I didn't include here because it has little to do with the Beatles or their music.

But *Backbeat* doesn't need that, in the end, to pack an emotional punch when Stu goes to see his band being brilliant without him, and Dorff does find a look, full of nostalgia and pride and regret, that makes you wonder exactly what it might feel like to pass up the chance to rule the world.

The end comes swiftly and tragically and is neatly contrasted with the Beatles' triumph, and the film works hard to bring some tears to the eyes. It feels like a cultural footnote has been given an importance it richly deserves.

• •

That Thing You Do!

1996

Starring: Tom Everett Scott, Liv Tyler, Tom Hanks, Johnathon Schaech
Dir.: Tom Hanks

★ ★

Plot: 1960s rock according to Forrest Gump.
Key line: 'It's a very common tale.'

Why Tom Hanks opted to debut as screenwriter and director with a nostalgic rock movie is anyone's guess. But it is entirely fitting that, just like Hanks' performances in *Philadelphia* and *Forrest Gump* and *Apollo 13* and *Saving Private Ryan*, *That Thing You Do!* is a film that looks good at first but is essentially empty at its core. As a director, he's obviously professional, reliable and technically proficient. As a writer, he sucks, and you suspect that it's not because his original script was a mess, but because various money men kept tweaking it and worrying at it until, inevitably, anything that might offend anyone whatsoever had been successfully removed, and replaced with banal compromise and a story that manages the unusual feat of being moronically simple and utterly befuddled at the same time.

Set in Hanks' hometown of Erie, Pennsylvania in 1964, the (in)action begins when drummer Chad (a criminally under-used Giovanni Ribisi) breaks his arm arsing about like a big kid, forcing budding Beatle-esque popsters the Wonders (originally spelt Oneders, which cues a lame running joke) to ask jazz drummer Guy (Scott) to provide the beats at a local talent show. Guy jumps at the chance of some respite from the stifling conformity of working in his father's electrical appliance store, and the band win the contest with their self-penned pop nugget 'That Thing You Do!', largely because Guy forces them to play it at twice the usual speed. Enter paying gigs, a following and, eventually, cold-eyed Svengali Mr White (Hanks) and overnight pop success.

For the first 30 minutes or so, *That Thing You Do!* is good-looking and smart enough to draw you in. Shot in smooth, glossy colours, it involves lots of Cadillacs, Art Deco coffee bars, smooth haircuts and all that post-*American Graffiti* (see p. 132) pre-hippy teen ephemera that makes everyone feel instantly nostalgic for a world uncomplicated by modern things like racial equality and upward mobility. The original songs are clever pastiches of early 1960s pop, but with enough subtle modernity to give away the fact that someone hoped these songs would be contemporary hits. The title song upon which the plot revolves is actually fabulous – but the story requires it to be played almost identically so many times that it becomes a major part of the film's many problems. Again, you detect the cynicism of producers who think we'll buy anything as long as it's sledgehammered into our brains by repetition.

Liv Tyler plays band girlfriend/mascot/manager/cheerleader (not groupie – this is a chaste antidote to the rockpig movie) and is adorable. Hanks clone Tom Everett Scott as Guy seems an agreeable enough chap, but who wouldn't be agreeable with Charlize Theron on their arm? Theron doesn't get as lucky as Tyler, though, having been stuck with the stereotype bitch-princess role. Her Tina simply disappears a third of the way through, having only been employed to make Tyler and Scott seem even nicer.

The early part of the film also offers affectionate pastiches of worthy folk revivalism, black girl-group pop, suave Bobby Darinesque MOR and trashy beach movies. And the Wonders themselves are unusual rock movie heroes; based more on half-forgotten US beat boom bands like the Rascals, Paul Revere and the Raiders, Tommy James and the Shondells, etc. than any of the Classic Rock Pantheon. It also does a better job than most rock movies of conveying the simple, ecstatic pleasure of playing your first packed-out successful show, of hearing your record on the radio for the first time, of realising that people love what you do. But . . .

The film sets up potential conflict after potential conflict, but instead of telling a story it just runs away to another pastiche of 1960s Americana. Lead singer Jimmy (Scheach) starts to prefer aging chanteuse Diane Dane to Liv Tyler's Faye, and then . . . nothing. Hank's Mr White looks, for one scene, like he's going to seduce Faye, and then . . . nothing. It's almost 90 minutes in before we suddenly get to the point – gorgeous, pouting and earnest lead singer Jimmy thought this was all about his songs and creativity; Mr White makes it clear it's about manufactured pop and cover versions. The band splits after one mild row, with a long-telegraphed Hanks punchline about the band being 'one-hit Wonders'.

Interestingly, the preceding scene has seen Jimmy being so beastly to Faye that we're manipulated into taking the record label's side . . . further evidence, perhaps, of Hanks' essential conservatism. But the band split is so abrupt and lacking in any real conflict or context that even this pro-corporate attitude could be as much mistake as worldview. If we're left with any message, it's that jazz is better than pop anyway, and that – sigh – black people, in the shape of imaginary jazz man Del Paxton, are the symbols of authenticity and an almost mystical integrity.

The felony is compounded by the final scenes, which dispense with the previous 90 minutes completely and become sappy, sexless romance, backed by cheesy musak pianos. As a final insult, a black hotel porter suddenly breaks down 'the fourth wall' in what has been a deeply conventional movie and looks knowingly at the camera, before the film ends with the *American Graffiti* conceit of captions about the futures of its imaginary characters – an unearned attempt to lend Hanks' specious vanity project some form of historical resonance.

So the real stars of the movie are art director Dan Webster and set decorator Merideth Boswell. Their *mise en scène* is a joy to watch, and it feels as if Hanks is so desperate to make their efforts look good and impress as a technical director that he can't let his baby out of the buggy. The film's feel obviously tries to tap into the same sense of a no-pain past as *Almost Famous* (see p. 342), and, if it's less smug and dishonest, it's still stuck somewhere between nostalgic comedy and bland drama, until it settles for being pleasant and nothing else. Significantly, *That Thing You Do!* appears to be the sum total of Hanks film-making career, a victim of its lack of heart, courage, sex, balls, story, point . . . all those things he didn't do.

● ●

Kurt & Courtney

1997
Dir.: Nick Broomfield

★

Plot: A documentary about a man boldly going where bad documentaries have gone before.
Key line: 'It's also a story that some people have not wanted told, and the various attempts to control the journalists, writers and film-makers that have tried to tell it. This control I discovered made even the financing of this film very difficult.'

How has London documentary maker Broomfield contrived to make Kurt Cobain's story dull? After all, this is the classic story of the emotionally disturbed and physically frail high school nerd who was reinvented by rock 'n' roll, became a rock star and a global icon for alienated youth, married a fame-hungry junkie-feminist ex-groupie, took a ton of smack and blew his brains out. A story not dissimilar to much of the most entertaining fiction discussed in these pages. Yet, in Broomfield's hands, all is tedium and cod-psych 101. He's so busy trying to pin a murder rap on someone that he is utterly uninterested in Cobain, Love or any of the film's interviewees as people.

Which is a shame, because Broomfield does get some unusual background material. He visits Cobain's Aunt Mary, who plays him recordings of a happy two-year-old Kurt trying to sing the Beatles' 'Hey Jude'. She's put the recordings through an echo effect, and it sounds suitably spooky and sad when you know where the giggly toddler is going to end up. She reveals that, even at age 15, Kurt refused to do his first recording with his auntie on digital equipment, already seeking purity and integrity. We don't get to hear these first recordings because, as Broomfield portentously informs us, Courtney Love has threatened him with legal action. He makes great play of Love not giving him permission to use Nirvana songs on the soundtrack, and of Love's lawyers pressuring his film's co-funders to pull out of the project. But if someone I'd never met was picking through my past looking for dirt to put onscreen, and I had good lawyers, I'd do the same thing. The movie's big finish revolves around testimonies about Love's physical and verbal attacks on journalists, contrasted with her special guest appearance at an American Civil Liberties Union dinner. It makes a good point about Hollywood hypocrisy. It hardly makes Courtney Love into Charles Manson. Moreover, it makes what the paying punter thought was a film about a famous doomed marriage into a film about Broomfield's heroic crusade for free speech . . . a favourite self-justification tactic of those who make a living out of tabloid scandal.

Those who've seen 2002's *Biggie and Tupac*, Broomfield's other failed attempt at a hard-hitting music documentary, will know that his favourite device is filming the reactions of people when he turns up with a film crew to ask questions. This isn't just irritating, it's narcissistic – Broomfield's process is more fascinating to him than his subject – and disingenuous. If someone turned up at your home or workplace with a film crew in tow and stuck a camera and a mic in front of your face without prior warning, wouldn't you react with a degree of hostility and paranoia? In Broomfield's world this device is used to suggest to the viewer that everyone he meets is hiding something. So even when they do talk but don't give him the sensational info he's after, this simply becomes part of the conspiracy of silence he uses to replace his failure to find the story.

Still, in Broomfield's defence, if any one person on the planet could make an objective journalist go on a character assassination rampage, then it is Courtney Love. Her issues may have something to do with her father, Hank Harrison, a former Grateful Dead roadie who responded to his son-in-law's death by writing two cash-in books and who can't wait to imply that his own 'deranged' daughter could be a murderer on camera by reading out one of her dodgy old poems. This is when Broomfield is at his best . . . simply pointing a camera at someone and allowing them to hang themselves. If *Kurt & Courtney* (and *Biggie and Tupac*) are about anything other than Broomfield, it's how low some will go when someone they know becomes rich and famous.

But how can you take a film-maker seriously whose idea of analysis of Love involves reciting voiceover garbage like, 'She then moved into the world of rock 'n' roll . . . and got into the glamour of drugs!' As the key line I've picked out at the beginning of this entry shows, he's so desperate to tell you how fearless he's been, and to make what he's got fit his shock-horror agenda, that he can't even be bothered to make his empty portentousness grammatically coherent. In the absence of any contribution from Love or a member of Nirvana, Broomfield is forced to dig around for minor players in the saga, who are only too happy to get just a little reflected glory and an opportunity to spit bile at those who moved onward and upwards and left them way behind. Again, *Kurt & Courtney* will tell you plenty about the bitterness of the rejected wannabe, but nothing conclusive about the people whose names are selling the film. The major players may have refused to take part because they don't want to incriminate themselves.

I'll save you 90 minutes of your time. The evidence that Love was involved in her husband's death amounts to several people who don't like her seeing her inherit Cobain's millions and feeling that this is unfair. Maybe they're right. But this doesn't make Love capable of murder or powerful enough to get the powers-that-be to whitewash it on her behalf. If Cobain had stayed alive and divorced her, she would have still taken half of the money and he'd still be making more records to make more money out of. It seems an awful lot of trouble for someone who, the same people insist, is obsessed with her own attempts at stardom. Her accusers pretty much define the term 'unreliable witness'.

Here's what I think the real story is. A man who was worshipped by millions was so estranged from his friends and family that he could escape from a rehab clinic, lock himself in his home, shoot up, kill himself and decompose for four days before anyone found him. He left a daughter who will never be allowed to forget this by everyone she meets for the rest of her life, and who will spend that life believing that her Daddy didn't love her enough to stay alive for her. When someone wants to make a film about that, it will be worth watching. Maybe it will even have a Nirvana soundtrack.

• •

Spiceworld: The Movie

1997

Starring: The Spice Girls, Richard E. Grant, Alan Cummings, George Wendt, Roger Moore, Sundry Ageing and Desperate Hacks
Dir.: Bob Spiers

★ ★

Plot: Girls powerless.
Key line: 'It's probably the sad anti-climax. It's all over. Back to reality.'

Within five minutes of the beginning of the Spice Girls' only cinematic vehicle, the viewer has been hit with two things that sum up the very best and the very worst of 21st-century manufactured pop. On the horror side, the five are walking down a corridor after performing a song, and they bump into ... Elton John. There is no reason for this meeting, and writer Kim Fuller can't be arsed to actually write anything for either side to say as they swap hideously fake hugs and kisses. The makers of *Spiceworld* just want the suckers who've paid to watch this 88-minute commercial to know that the Spice Girls know Elton John. The definition of celebrity is knowing another celebrity. If ever there was an unconscious admission of a pop group's lack of talent or staying power, this is it.

But on the glorious side, Fuller follows that with a perfect pop idea. The Spicesters travel everywhere in a Union Jack bus which is basically a Tardis. The interior is an enormous baby doll paradise of leopard-skin seats and red quilted leather walls and loft conversion scaffolds and platform shoes and weights for Sporty. It is what every pop group should live in, and it sums up the cartoon appeal of the Spice Girls better than anything except, maybe, 'Wannabe'.

The embarrassment of each passing cameo – Meat Loaf,

Jonathan Ross, Jools Holland, Barry Humphries, Bob Hoskins, Hugh Laurie, Stephen Fry (actually pretty good), Geldof, an utterly fucking terrible Michael Barrymore, Elvis Costello, Bill Paterson, Jennifer Saunders, Richard Briers, Richard O'Brien, Dominic West for God's sake!!! – is surpassed only by the Happy Shopper tackiness of the *Spiceworld* premise. Alan Cummings is a bloke hired to make a film about the 'energy and the chaos' of the Sex Pistols ... sorry ... Spice Girls. Wendt (Norm out of *Cheers*) and Roger Moore (a piss-take of Spice Girls manager Simon Fuller) are evil overlords trying to ... sorry ... nodded off. Every now and again someone says something like 'Can you imagine you lot having kids?', and then we get a *Scrubs/Spaced*-type cut to said imagining. If they'd hired the future writers of *Spaced* or *Scrubs* this might have been brilliantly ahead of its time. But instead, they hired the manager's brother, so these scenes are very poor indeed.

And it's all supposed to be ironic. And that's about it.

As pop star thesps go, the girls themselves are the best thing about their own film. You suspect that if they really had just got a documentary maker to follow them around before a gig they would have made a much better film. Especially when the poor bitches were forced to make their acting debuts opposite Useless E. Git, a man still dining out on *Withnail and I* and making a bad smell while he's eating.

But which Spice Girl is the best actress? That would be Ginger, closely followed by Scary, with Baby managing a surprisingly charming third. Then Sporty. And no surprise that the worst is Posh, a woman who has proved that the best way to do the impossible and become a bigger solo brand than your band is to marry well and make the *least* of what you've got. But, as Wendt's Hollywood mogul observes, 'Who cares if Monroe could act, as long as she stayed in focus?' Which I'm sure the Fullers would like to tell us is irony, but isn't because everything about the Spice Girls' career – and the entire *X Factor* world they spawned – shows that this is what these kind of asswipes believe.

Or is it? Because, occasionally, right out of the blue, there's the odd moment of comic clarity and accidental good taste. Is the bit where *Daily Event* proprietor Kevin McMaxford (Humphries) plots the downfall of Girl Power and a thunderstorm ensues in his office really a reference to Samuel Fuller's classic 1963 loony bin *noir Shock Corridor*? Does Mel C really come out when asked about boys ('Doesn't ring a bell') just before Mel B gets a really filthy one-liner about knob-cheese? Isn't the bit where the Spice Girls get accused of saying that the Pope isn't a Catholic both a nice parody of the Beatles' 'bigger than Jesus' furore and a pretty cogent summing-up of the tabloid press? And isn't the running motif of the nice, non-famous, pregnant Spice Friend Nic (played by a pre-*Torchwood* Naoki Mori) being ignored and humiliated by everyone around the group actually a subtle plea for the End of Celebrity? Maybe. Possibly. Probably not.

And it gets stranger. They do a cover of a Gary Glitter song, complete with comically hunky dancers. It's supposed to be a parody but is actually great pop campery. Roger Moore keeps being quite funny. An alien feels Mel B's left tit. The film's inept, self-referential, plotless madness is endearing in its refusal to make the mistake of pretending that the Spice Girls matter. But it's exactly the same lack of belief in itself that makes much of it unwatchable. Every time the girls themselves begin to charm you, their Svengalis push them aside in favour of another second-rate celeb whose lack of cinematic talent is only matched by their contempt for the whole affair. The scene where Stephen Fry as a fantasy pop Judge sentences them to 20 years of doing chat shows in Taiwan feels less like jokey postmodernism and more like Simon Fuller giving them their P45s.

But *Spiceworld* does provide ample evidence of why people once loved the Spice Girls. There are various small, apparently insignificant scenes of them dancing in clubs or chatting in the bus ... and they look gorgeous (not in a *phwoaar* way, but in a cute and charismatic mates way) and you wish you were hanging out with them. It looks like fun. If they really did all hate each other, then they're really good actresses. Ones that deserved better than being made to hold a newborn baby and say, 'Now that's what I call Girl Power.'

● ●

Velvet Goldmine

1998

Starring: Jonathan Rhys-Meyers, Ewan McGregor, Toni Collette, Eddie Izzard, Christian Bale
Dir.: Todd Haynes

★ ★ ★

Plot: A walk on the Wilde side.
Key line: 'Well I think it's a disgrace. Parading around all ponced up like a pack of bleeding woofters.'

The opening scenes of Todd Haynes' florid tribute to the glam and glitter 1970s must have made Morrissey wet his pants. The baby Oscar Wilde getting beamed down from the sky like a leper messiah. A munchkin Wilde with Jesus hair announcing, in a dour public school classroom, 'I want to be a pop idol.' A caption saying, 'One hundred years later.' And cut to a boy in a school that can only be in 1960s England getting beaten up for being too pretty, weird and sensitive, which leads the victim to find a talismanic brooch mysteriously handed down from Wilde himself. Three minutes that sum up the romanticised origins of the entire history of sexually ambiguous English pop boys who are just too special for this cruel world full of frightened, intellectually stunted, normal people. One thing you can never accuse Haynes of is not understanding the context and emotional aesthetics of his chosen subjects. What he goes on to do with that instinctive grasping of cultural resonance is an altogether more erratic proposition.

Velvet Goldmine should be brilliant. A provocative, pro-gay study of the background and impact of 1970s glam-rock, based around the relationship between thinly disguised versions of David Bowie and Iggy Pop. Lots of the best music from Bowie, Iggy, Roxy Music, Brian Eno, Marc Bolan, Cockney Rebel ... even Slade. Michael Stipe among the production team. Immaculately and affectionately recreated versions of 1970s England and its glitter-associated fashion mistakes. Decent cast. Lovely cinematography. Some sly jokes. Intellectually driven, pop-art script. Lots of very 1970s surrealist grandstanding. So ... what goes wrong?

Before we get to that, the basics: Jonathan Rhys-Meyers is Brian Slade is David Bowie is alter-ego Maxwell Demon is Ziggy Stardust, who, at his last show in London with Venus in Furs (who are the Spiders from Mars) in 1974, lives out the Rock 'n' Roll Suicide idea and gets assassinated.

Or does he? In the crowd is teen glam fan Arthur Stuart (Bale) who, as a grown-up journalist working in a nightmare dystopian America ten years later, is forced to go and search for Slade, who isn't dead at all. As he does the detective work, he uncovers, for our delight and delectation, weird scenes from inside the velvet goldmine which largely concern the dysfunctional love affair between Brian and Ewan McGregor is Curt Wild is Iggy Pop with a smidgeon of Lou Reed. By the end, we find out what Slade's Rosebud was, as all good *Citizen Kane* fans will probably have guessed.

Exaggeration or lack of authenticity aren't what keeps *Velvet Goldmine* grounded. Haynes hasn't attempted a Bowie/Iggy biopic, nor a potted history of glam-rock. He is attempting to explain why he feels glam was hugely important; its effect on kids who felt alienated and unusual; its ability to conjure a fantasy world of alien polymorphous perversity, its skill at scrambling fixed identity and its seductive suggestion that the individual could be anyone or anything they wanted to be ... lessons learnt well by Johnny Rotten and Siouxsie Sioux and Uncle Tom Vicious and all. Its splash of reckless colour in a dour and ugly Britain. Its rejection of the hippy scene's sexism and homophobia. Its promotion of the false over the true, the artificial over the authentic, its ability to pastiche every past period of glamour and remake/remodel it for a young generation who found political rock both boring and hypocritical. If you're thinking, 'that seems an awful lot to sum up in two hours', you're getting the picture.

What the too-young-for-glam Haynes does do is use Arthur to expertly recreate the pain and pleasures of being a pop obsessive in the 1970s. The joy of buying a new album on vinyl, locking yourself in your bedroom with a music paper and placing the record on your record player for the first time. The excitement and fear of seeing people who dress like you and wanting desperately to be their friend.

Bale is wonderful here, and it's telling that his very introverted, ordinary boy blows the two 'rock stars' off-screen. Much of *Velvet Goldmine* flounders on the simple fact that McGregor and Rhys-Meyers aren't talented or charismatic enough to recreate Iggy or Bowie. The film is hugely dependent on the individual viewer's love and knowledge of the era's music and imagery. Anyone who isn't a fan of the glam gods will simply wonder why these comically camp performers were so influential.

Jonathan Rhys-Meyers is a disastrous piece of casting. Not being Bowie is forgivable ... I mean, Bowie has failed to be Bowie on screen on many occasions. But this guy is utterly useless, chosen for his prettiness and nothing else. That bloody immovable pout ... Jeez, even Prince managed three facial expressions (leer, sulk and 'aren't my eyes limpid pools?') in *Purple Rain* (see p. 267). Making your lead character a cipher of gay male fantasies seems a move designed to leave your movie bereft of substance.

There is an offhand unpleasantness, too, as a baby Brian accidentally witnesses nasty adult sex and immediately becomes a mod paedophile, all to the strains of Gary Glitter's 'Do You Wanna Touch Me?' Is this a tasteless joke, or Haynes' disturbing fantasies about what glam-rock was based upon? One fantasy that Haynes definitely overcooks is his vision of glam's rebel qualities. In truth, glitter-rock just wasn't that controversial. Sure, there were a few sniffy tabloid headlines and I'm sure a few boys in make-up had to endure some homophobic stick. But glam's more transgressive effects were based on the fact that blokes in dresses *were* accepted by the cultural mainstream, which made a whole bunch of us feel better about exploring our sexuality and experimenting with clothes and make-up. It was a pop trend, albeit a better one than most. In Haynes' mind it was a social scandal on a Sex Pistols scale. The Beatles and the Stones had already got the older generation used to girlie boys acting up for fun and profit. Glam was just the mid 1960s taken to funnier and artier extremes.

Of course, we do get a full-frontal of McGregor's impressively huge knob, and Haynes has fun recreating various 1960s and 1970s rock legends, and even finds time to pay homage to his own *Superstar: The Karen Carpenter Story* (see p. 274) with an earnest conversation between dolls. Much of his flicking about from story to fantasy sequence to pastiche rock video (the original songs by the likes of Pulp and Shudder to Think are seamlessly authentic) is reminiscent of Ken Russell's *Tommy* (see p. 164), and this sense of low-attention-span madness is always entertaining and frustrating in equal measure. Izzard is irritating, Collette is wasted, and the whole enterprise becomes nothing more than technical brilliance without soul or emotional centre … a bit like the music that glam-rock was battling against, ironically. You find yourself impressed, but alienated, and, as with Haynes' Dylan flick *I'm Not There* (see p. 413), struggling to see what the point of it all is.

• •

Bulworth

1998

Starring: Warren Beatty, Haile Berry, Paul Sorvino, Don
Cheadle, Oliver Platt, Amiri Baraka
Dir.: Warren Beatty

★ ★ ★ ★

**Plot: Ancient 1960s stud-muffin produces, writes, directs
and stars in screwball satire that somehow defines the
meaning of hip hop, the decline of American civilisation,
and everything.**
**Key line: 'Rhyming. He's talking in rhymes. It's very, *very*
disconcerting.'**

In *Bulworth*'s opening scene, Californian Democratic Senator Jay
Bulworth sits slumped and alone in his office, endlessly rewinding
and running the mind-numbing conservative images and platitudes
of his latest electoral campaign ad. He is surrounded by mem-
orabilia: photographs of Martin Luther King meeting Malcolm X,
and of himself as a young hippyish man alone and with Robert
Kennedy. These latter shots are real archive shots of *Bulworth*'s
writer, director and star Warren Beatty, who, as the dashing icon
of the late 1960s New Hollywood, had campaigned for Kennedy's
presidential run before his assassination in 1968. Beatty also worked
for the presidential campaigns of George McGovern and Gary
Hart, both controversial failures, and would himself be approached
to run as Democratic candidate in 2000, and as California governor
against Schwarzenegger in 2006. It is this sense of personal failure
and disillusion, you suspect, that drives this passionate and heavily
propagandist political satire. More surprisingly, the child of 1960s
rock chooses hip hop as his fantasy vehicle for reaching a fantasy
American public.

When we finally see Beatty/Bulworth's face, he is crying. And
not quiet, stoical tears of disappointment, but the inconsolable sobs

of a man at the edge of his tether. From there, the opening ten minutes swiftly and wittily establish the reasons for the strange journey Jay Bulworth is about to take. First, that everyone involved with Democrat politics in 1996, as Clinton runs for his second term, talks the same right-wing, racist and money-obsessed language that we usually associate with Reagan–Bush Republicans. And, second, that all the policy wonks and lobbyists and campaign managers that surround Bulworth are so wrapped up in their own frantic, business-as-usual agendas that they can't see that the frontman for their ambitions is refusing to eat and spending every spare moment staring at a silent, channel-hopping television. The hive of fast-talking hyper-intelligence is similar to that which we came to know and love during the course of *The West Wing* TV show. But whereas President Bartlett's brilliant team were all basically good people under pressure, Bulworth's political entourage are a bunch of noxious slimeballs.

But Bulworth is smarter than he looks. There are good reasons why he doesn't attract attention to himself. Because the depressed Senator has arranged a ton of life insurance and has hired a hit man to assassinate him. Once he gets to the arranged hit spot in Los Angeles, he freaks out, changes his mind, and ends up on the campaign trail in, of all places, South Central LA. As he prepares to speak in a Baptist church, he begins the usual meaningless speech ('We stand on the doorstep of a new millennium ... '), pauses, discards his notes and asks for questions from a room full of angry Afro-Americans. And then he answers them ... truthfully. Not the uplifting, it's-all-their-fault, we-shall-overcome 'truths' of old Frank Capra movies. But simple, brutal confessions of his own culpability in a morally bankrupt system. We tell you what you want to hear and once you've voted we discard you. We take money in campaign contributions from corporations to buy policy and legislation that makes your lives shit. Democrats do nothing for black people because they know black people won't vote Repub-lican. And, magnificently, 'If you don't put down your malt liquor and chicken wings and get behind somebody other than a running back who stabs his wife – you're never gonna get rid of someone like me.' Bulworth's campaign manager, played by the reliably oily Oliver Platt, presses the fire alarm. But too late ... a TV crew have got it all and the damage is done. As they leave the church, young black girls volunteer for his campaign, Bulworth spots Haile Berry's Nina and leers and even attempts to do a cool hand thing while saying, 'Yo'. He is a man who has relocated his penis with his self-respect. Bulworth is on his way to giving us 100 minutes of a whole other kind of American Dream – that one where those in power tell us the truth. Oh ... and the one where an old rich white bloke can get in touch with his inner poor young blackness, and make it funny and relevant and moving, rather than the usual self-loathing wigger thing.

Meanwhile, there is still a hit out on our loose cannon, causing him to dive to the floor when motorcycles backfire as the increasingly stunned TV crew record every bizarre moment. He finally breaks his depression fast by buying a bucket of KFC. He then lays casually into a mansion full of Jewish film-makers in what must be a very personal act of Beatty revenge, before being continually accosted by a hobo poet (Baraka) spouting mystical verse.

It's all mad and brave and great, and Beatty is deftly and goofily hilarious. But I guess you're wondering what the hell this has to do with rock movies. Well, it's simple really. In order to hit home his truths, Jay Bulworth becomes a rapper.

The story pivots around the scene where Bulworth follows Nina to an underground hip hop club full of both gangstas and gangsters. Obviously, for comic effect, the mad old white guy has to smoke dope, dance, scratch and learn to rhyme. If Beatty gets the tone of this scene wrong, Bulworth becomes just another egomaniacal, racially paranoid colonisation of black culture. But Beatty nails it, being rakishly charming and oafishly square in equal measure, never suggesting that the Bulworth character would be either especially good nor especially bad at blending in, overcoming the implausibility of the situation with good faith and spot-on soundtrack choices from the likes of the RZA, Cypress Hill, Ice Cube, NWA, Public Enemy and Nas. It's the polar opposite of something like, say, the black club scenes in 1978's otherwise very funny

National Lampoon's Animal House, which take the liberal terror of the black man to unapologetically racist extremes. It's always unwise to project too much onto things one likes, but, the fearless, adult way that a hit film like *Bulworth* deals with race feels like a white America reaching its way towards being mature enough to, I don't know, elect a black president within ten years, or something.

The one problematic part of these scenes is the strong suggestion that Beatty and Berry are inevitably going to get it on, which would suddenly make this whole thing as much about a wrinkly old fella dusting off his stud reputation for one more distasteful indulgence with one of America's most beautiful young women as it is about the state of the nation. Except that the old buzzard turns that particular American WASP male fantasy on its head, too.

Bulworth's first rap to a room full of corporate backers is brilliantly constructed; his rap skills start off bad and stay there, but what he says becomes increasingly transgressive ('Let's hear that dirty word! Socialism!'), prescient (a prophecy of the second Iraq War) and politically incorrect ('I like the pussy/The pussy/I like it really fine/And when you be a Senator/You get it all the time'). It ain't the medium, it's the message. Hip hop becomes the ultimate in anti-spin.

Aside from the messages, *Bulworth* is a masterclass in mainstream Hollywood film-making. Twists, *deus ex machinas* and sub-plots come thick and fast without distracting from the Big Picture of this big picture. There are occasional, lovely visual flourishes, like the moment when a dying man turns slowly green as he slumps into the light reflected from a green sofa. And, while Beatty may beat himself up for not standing for office, he makes up for it here by putting his own convincing and intellectually driven policy ideas into the mouths of Bulworth and other characters without ever taking his eye off the screwball comedy ball. Beatty gives the viewer so much hard political information – right down to the numbers when he makes a debate speech about how much government pays insurance companies to run an unjust healthcare system – that you do think he's preparing to run for office. Except that the film itself is simultaneously explaining why he'd have no chance of winning.

When Bulworth borrows hip hop garb to walk alone through the mean streets of South Central, his beanie hat and big shorts give a good hard kicking to every single one of us who've ever convinced ourselves we can carry off gangsta style. The kids with guns who confront him get bought off with his offer of ice cream, allowing a scene of LAPD humiliation that sorts the right- from the left-wing viewers in an instant. By now, Bulworth is confronting death and performing heroic deeds. Except that Beatty has already undercut this predictable Great White Hero proposition by pointing out that Bulworth is not choosing to be brave. He's simply and clearly going completely insane.

Bulworth is one of those movies that feels utterly convincing while you're watching, but falls apart somewhat once it's over. It deals in Big Gestures. Its plot is plainly ridiculous. And the ending blows the carefully constructed atmosphere of tragic inevitability both by getting pretentious and finally allowing Beatty's ego to run wild.

But it's still a great satirical script, which is lent further depth by the subsequent emergence of Obama. Bulworth's urgency comes from the kind of despair that assumes that nothing in American politics is going to get better; and this is a film made before Dubya's two terms and 9/11. At one point, Bulworth and Nina are talking in a car, and the exhausted Senator asks, somewhat rhetorically, 'Why ain't there no more black leaders?' Berry's Nina, tired of playing the Bulworth stooge, replies: 'Some people think it's because they all got killed. But I think it has more to do with the decimation of the urban manufacturing base.' Her amusingly well-informed rant continues, but it serves as a reminder that Obama wasn't seen as the candidate of the dispossessed American working class, and had to fight perceptions that he was too elitist to understand the problems of the ordinary urban family. It also reminds us that many thought America was so fucked up by both race and fear of change that Obama wouldn't live to win or lose. He survived and thrived by being the anti-Bulworth – conciliatory, careful in his language, and grounded in his ambitions, apart from his stress of the word 'hope'.

But the reason why *Bulworth* is a key film in this book is Beatty's use of rap. Hip hop has been so poorly served in the movies you'd think it was some minor cult, rather than the most popular music genre on the planet. *Bulworth* may be a white liberal's attempt to find rap's meaning, but it's also a very successful one, capturing something real and true about rap's status as a global purveyor of unpalatable truths. *Bulworth* wouldn't have worked – as either comedy or political propaganda – without hip hop.

2000s

The Filth and the Fury

2000

Starring: The Sex Pistols
Dir.: Julien Temple

★ ★ ★ ★ ★

Plot: Ever get the feeling you've been cheated?
**Key line: 'You don't write "God Save the Queen" because
you hate the English race. You write a song like that because
you love them.'**

I first saw this Sex Pistols documentary at a preview screening in a
small West End viewing room. I have a vivid memory of being
pinned in my seat by the opening montage of 1970s British horrors
spliced with Laurence Olivier's Richard III and his 'winter of our
discontent' soliloquy and John Lydon's powerful voiceover. No
rockumentary has ever worked so hard in its first five minutes to
grab the viewer by the balls and make them understand that what
they are about to watch is about far more than a rock band. The
other thing I remember is crying at the end and having to wait in
my seat at the end so that I wasn't seen by my jaded colleagues in
the arts media.

The Filth and the Fury is, first and foremost, an extraordinary
feat of research and editing. Temple pulls visuals from thousands
of different sources, most directly applicable to the story, some
random and abstract. He then edits slivers of these brilliant, vivid
images together to dramatise the story told by the band themselves,
very rarely settling for the usual talking head addressing the camera.
Even when he does, Temple pulls another masterstroke, filming
the present-day Pistols in shadow so that their middle-aged faces
don't interfere in the tale of reckless, innocent, confrontational,
thoughtful and unthinking youth, because the story of the Sex
Pistols is explicitly about teen working-class boys who are in the

moment and too young to understand the consequences of their actions.

We learn that Lydon's role models for the character of Johnny Rotten weren't rock performers, but Olivier's Richard III, the Hunchback of Notre Dame, and comedians Tommy Cooper, Arthur Askey, Ken Dodd and Norman Wisdom. 'What people don't understand about the Sex Pistols', he says, in that unique, camp, Peter Cook sneer, 'is that we are Music Hall ... there's a sense of comedy in the English. That even in your grimmest moment – you laugh.'

Grim laughter here comes from an unlikely source. It was fey junkie music journo Nick Kent, rather than any of the Pistols, who sent a ripple of hilarity around the preview audience that day. He stands out here as punks originally did, provoking embarrassment and antipathy by his very manner. It's a perfect journo-as-failed-rock star moment when Kent insists that a legendary assault upon him with a bicycle chain led to the former John Ritchie being re-christened Sid Vicious, before Lydon confirms that it came from Sid being bitten by his pet hamster.

It's also fascinating to see the infamous Bill Grundy incident in full, analysed by those who were there. To recap, in December 1976 the Pistols were interviewed by a drunk and hostile Grundy on London tea-time magazine programme *Today*. They swore and became an instant tabloid obsession, going from hip London band to national anti-stars literally overnight. Rotten was actually somewhat embarrassing on the show, a naughty but chastened schoolboy. It took fan Siouxsie Sioux to goad Grundy into being pervy, which in turn provoked guitarist Steve Jones into calling him a 'dirty fucking rotter'. Grundy is entirely in control ... and then very suddenly isn't. The encounter ended Grundy's career and changed the course of history. Funny thing was, the Pistols were last-minute replacements for Queen, of all people. And *Today* was usually hosted by genial Irish *This Is Your Life* presenter Eamonn Andrews. If the Grundy incident had never happened, the Sex Pistols would have been a cool but obscure cult band, like the Stooges or the New York Dolls. How different would the world have been? All accounts insist that Malcolm McLaren was stricken with terror over Jones' swearing. His fear of the classic spontaneous moment reveals the lie of his Machiavellian *Great Rock 'n' Roll Swindle* (see p. 206)

With the Pistols having always been cast in the role of monsters or heroes, it's great to get detail about who these scourges of society really were. Lydon reveals that he and Sid Vicious had a pre-Pistols career as buskers: 'Me on violin, Sid on a tambourine or maybe a broken guitar. We did Alice Cooper songs – "I Love the Dead" was our favourite. That would get us the most money: Just, please, shut up. Here. Take the money. Go somewhere else.' This is followed by the revelation that Sid's Dad was a Grenadier Guard who could have been being all ceremonial at Buckingham Palace while the Pistols signed their ill-fated A&M contract outside.

It's the picture painted of normal boys with normal friendships that sets up the shock of big bad Johnny Rotten bursting into tears as he talks about Sid's sordid death. 'You can't get more evil than that, can you, Julien?', he sobs to director and interviewer Temple, who couldn't have done any more to right the wrongs of his previous Sex Pistols film than highlight the real cost of the kind of infamy the band guilelessly wandered into.

The Filth and the Fury takes me back to times that shaped me, and makes me feel inordinately proud that my country and generation came up with things as important and exciting as the Sex Pistols and punk rock. Because the major thing that *The Filth and the Fury* proves is that the Sex Pistols were organic. This is what the music biz and the rent-a-shock style magazine set miss – they believe the rock and roll swindle and believe you can contrive something like this. But what you need, always, is people with ideas that are infused with art and politics, and an environment where those ideas are nurtured. The reason it worked is because the control freak lost control early. All you've got to do is act naturally.

● ●

Almost Famous

2000

Starring: Patrick Fugit, Billy Crudup, Kate Hudson, Frances
McDormand, Jason Lee
Dir.: Cameron Crowe

★ ★

Plot: Schoolboy rock journalist follows band on tour. Valuable lessons learned.
Key line: 'Adolescence is a marketing tool.'

'Rock stars have kidnapped my son!', exclaims the great Frances
McDormand around halfway through this semi-autobiographical
whitewash-hogwash, and a whole different, better film briefly
dances in front of you, teasing you with its possibilities of true rocky
horror. But McDormand is playing the Mom of the man who wrote
and directed *Jerry Maguire*, so you know this moment of surreal
humour is a mirage before the real business of sentiment, fudge
and compromise continues. The success of the foul *Jerry Maguire*
gave former music journalist Cameron Crowe the power to write
his own creative ticket, and the guy came up with what might be
the ultimate mainstream Hollywood vanity project. Did you know
I was *Rolling Stone* magazine's youngest ever contributor? That
I was a teen prodigy? That legendary gonzo critic Lester Bangs was
my mentor and that I met Led Zeppelin and Dylan and Bowie and
... um ... all those other great 1970s rock bands? That beautiful
groupies took my virginity? That I married a member of Heart?
And – and this is the Big One – that I was more sensitive, intelligent
and goddam mature than all of those crazy but lovable loonies put
together?

Must have been some pitch meeting. 'I think the Big New Theme
that could really capture the imaginations of the millions of fans of
mainstream Hollywood movies is ... music journalism.' Ha! Man,
those Dreamworks execs must have taken some serious drugs in

the early 1970s to buy that one! But buy this dog they did. The end result is like *Abba: The Movie* (see p. 173) remade with a huge budget, but without the irony, truth and great live music. The 'Making of . . .' documentary included on the *Almost Famous* DVD neatly captures that key Hollywood belief (encapsulated perfectly in *Jerry Maguire*, actually) that boundless positivity will just carry the dumb old masses in its wake. It turns out that fictional band Stillwater, which includes *My Name Is Earl* star Jason Lee as singer Jeff and Billy Crudup as guitarist Russell, learned to play like a real band under the tutelage of Peter Frampton (and if you've just read that name and thought, 'This film sounds like punk never happened', then a big hit, nail and head shout-out to ya). And we must believe, despite the evidence of the terrible sub-Free blues-rock in the *actual* film that we can *actually* hear, that they became a truly brilliant group. Crowe's wife Nancy Wilson finds herself exclaiming, 'People are gonna be asking, "Where can I get my Stillwater tickets?!"' These people presumably lurk in the same dimension where Alan Titchmarsh is Elvis, Sooty and Sweep wrote the Beatles' many classics, and anyone went to see *Almost Famous*.

Crowe's 'love letter to music' (his words), or love letter to himself (they would be mine) falters at the first hurdle. His fictional self, William Miller, is played by the unprepossessing Patrick Fugit, who spends most of the film staring at somewhat dull events with big puppy eyes. The one thing that stops *Almost Famous* being a total one-star bust is Billy Crudup who, as Stillwater guitarist Russell, really does convey that dangerous mix of dreamboat, 'gotta love me' vulnerability and utter selfishness that so many male rock musicians carry as their calling-card to the world. He lights up the screen whenever present, despite Crowe's lack of interest in character. The script keeps telling us that Russell is too talented for Stillwater, but nothing onscreen shows us why.

There are two great set-piece scenes in *Almost Famous* – the bit where band and entourage climb out of a bad vibe on the bus by singing along to Elton John's 'Tiny Dancer', and the near-plane crash where they all confess their darkest secrets and inter-band betrayals while we *know* that the plane *won't* crash. But the film doesn't earn the right to these fake climaxes, so neither is as uplifting or funny, respectively, as they ought to be. That's the difference, as much as anything else, between an artist and a craftsman ... or a hack, actually.

Which is why McDormand and Philip Seymour Hoffman do their best by the characters of William's mother and the late Lester Bangs, but are scuppered by having nothing real to work with. Bangs, who died of an accidental drug overdose in 1982 at the age of 33, and is pretty much the Bill Hicks of musical journalism – genius, hysterically funny, right about almost everything, but difficult to know and ultimately doomed to go way too early – is portrayed here as a curmudgeonly uncle who only exists to give young William/Cameron soundbite advice like, 'Be honest. And unmerciful!' If only the fucker had taken it. We might have been spared ten years of Tom Cruise's leer.

Indeed, the cake-and-eat-it shamelessness of using Bangs's cred leads to dialogue so at odds with Crowe's work that you wonder if the lines are the unconscious reflex jerks of a guilty conscience. He casts Bangs as prophet, in one early scene, proclaiming the death of rock and its descent into becoming 'the industry of cool'. As if working for *Rolling Stone*, writing *Fast Times at Ridgemont High* and making *Almost Famous* weren't key parts of that process! And before that, this exchange, which had me thinking, for a moment, that this film might get good later on. Bangs: 'So, what, are you, like, the star of your school?' William: 'They hate me.' Bangs: 'Don't worry. You'll meet them again on the long journey to the middle.' Self-justification? Or a cry for help? Trying to care. Failing miserably. Do know that you'll glean more truth about love, music and teenage rites-of-passage from an episode of *Hollyoaks* than you will from these two hours of half-hearted narcissism.

• •

Rock Star

2001

Starring: Mark Wahlberg, Jennifer Aniston, Dominic West, Timothy Spall, Timothy Olyphant, Dagmara Dominczyk, Jason Flemyng
Dir.: Stephen Herek

★ ★ ★

Plot: *Spinal Tap* meets *The Brady Bunch*.
Key line: 'Isn't the rock star fantasy thing something you're supposed to grow out of at, like, around 14?'

Set in 1980s Pittsburgh, *Rock Star* begins with a present-day Chris Cole (Wahlberg) explaining that, as a kid, he had no choice but to 'live the Dragon'. The Dragon is Steel Dragon, a British poodle-metal band (based, apparently, on Judas Priest) whom Chris worships by forming a tribute band called Blood Pollution that plays entire Dragon shows note-for-note, pose-for-pose. This involves bickering with lead guitarist Rob (Olyphant) over his tendency to improvise, going to Dragon shows and singing better and louder than Dragon frontman Bobby Beers (Flemyng), and having fistfights with rival Dragon tribute bands in the stadium car park after pointing out that the rival singer has the wrong colour lapels on his Bobby Beers jacket.

Blood Pollution is a family affair, with girlfriend Emily (Aniston) managing and Chris's parents their biggest fans. The only dissenter is big brother Vince, a cop who thinks, not unreasonably, that Chris ought to grow up and get his own life together, rather than wishing he had someone else's.

To make ends meet, Chris works in an office fixing photocopiers, his wayward locks tied back into a tidy pony-tail, dealing with suits who get all weird and unnecessary when they notice he's wearing mascara. Make-up is a big part of *Rock Star*, with explicit sex scenes between the very cute Wahlberg and Aniston replaced by the girl doing his make-up and piercing his nipples. Chris is such a New Man sweetie that when he approaches hot slutty Steel Dragon groupies, it's to ask them to hand out fliers and tell them how awesome they look, with a strictly platonic beam. There's a quite fabulous scene where Chris and Emily are practising with their church choir ... told you this wasn't the usual rock film ... and Chris can't stop himself unleashing his 'Hallelujah' as a strangulated metal wail.

Rock Star is to standard rock movies what *Bambi* is to *The Deer Hunter* ... although the *Radio Times Guide to Films* goes for 'a leather pants-clad *Cinderella*'. However, modernised fairy-tales seldom feature spoof porn titles on a grubby cinema billboard – 'My Favourite Rear', 'All That Jizz', 'Das Bootie' – and a male character saying, about the application of make-up, 'I just put this shit on until I want to fuck myself.' *Rock Star* is not a fairy-tale or a kids' movie, but an odd, good-natured, subtle spoof ... of metal, of Satanist rock fans, of cynical rock movies and of the 1980s. It's no surprise that it bombed. It resists niche at every turn and refuses to give the typical adolescent male rock fan what he wants ... rebellion, gross-out humour, panto nihilism. It puts metal in its proper place ... light entertainment.

Shit has to happen, though, and it does. Chris gets chucked out of his own band for taking being Bobby Beers too seriously. As it happens, this coincides with Beers himself leaving Steel Dragon. See where this is going?

The band-splitting onstage argument between Chris and Olyphant's angry guitarist Rob is so knowingly silly that you can't tell whether the next, serious scene between Wahlberg and Aniston is serious or not. The entire movie is likeably like that. But once Dragon guitarist Kirk Cuddy (a wildly mugging and somewhat miscast Dominic West) has made all Chris's wildest dreams come true, the pair now have to contend with beautiful and predatory bisexual PRs, the revelation that Beers is gay and doesn't want to leave the Dragon, and the fact that Chris is expected to change his name to Izzy, fake an English accent and insist that all he does, when not singing, is eat pussy. *Rock Star* runs through plenty of the same jokes at the expense of Brit metal bands as *This Is Spinal Tap*, but isn't the same kind of spoof. The sly joke here is that Chris is rewarded for being completely unoriginal and bland ... which anyone who has actually hung around with mainstream rock stars knows is God's honest truth. The further irony piled upon this is that the music written and produced for Steel Dragon is authentic, excellent (if you like poodle metal, which I sometimes do) and sung shockingly well by Wahlberg, who really could have done this for a living. Maybe should have, all things considered.

The speech that Chris gives from the stage at his first Dragon show – all 'follow your dreams and they can come true' platitudes – is chillingly similar to the kind of guff that *American Idol* and *X Factor* contestants are forced to parrot. The implication appears to be that, despite rock's pretensions to authenticity and heaviness, it runs on precisely the same lines as talent contest MOR ... have a good singing voice, do as you're told and be grateful, help sell the losers the aspirational dream, and you're in. Meanwhile, Chris's former bandmates languish in jealous obscurity at home, their crime a desire to write their own songs.

Spall is reliably great as the repulsive road manager with a heart of gold. Boys – actually, girls, too – should be alerted to the aftershow party scene where Chris and Emily are seduced on a dancefloor, together and separately, by Tania the PR and an army of gorgeous androgynes. It's hot. And, again, not exactly the kind of thing you find in *Cinderella*.

This is also a remarkably enlightened film concerning women. Emily initially leaves Chris not because she's jealous about other women or wants babies – she wants a business and an independent life that on-the-road rock wives can't have. Then the boy goes off and has a great time doing rock star stuff that Herek injects new comedy life into. Chris screws up eventually, of course, but no lessons learned, no story.

Rock Star shares an attitude with the *Entourage* TV show, which Wahlberg devised and produces: an idea that the Boy's Own celebrity fantasy doesn't have to be cruel, deadly or misogynist ... maybe it can just be another harmless reason to laugh at the endless daftness of people, especially men. Like *Entourage*, it's good-natured, witty entertainment, and it makes a virtue out of laughing with the stupidity of corporate rock, rather than laughing at it and the people who love it.

● ●

24 Hour Party People

2001

Starring: Steve Coogan, Lennie James, Shirley Henderson, Paddy Considine, Andy Serkis, Sean Harris, Danny Cunningham, John Simm, Ralf Little, Peter Kay
Dir.: Michael Winterbottom

★ ★ ★ ★ ★

Plot: The tall-but-true tale of Tony Wilson, Factory Records, the Hacienda and why Manchester has so much to answer for.
Key line: 'May 21st 1982. The night the Hacienda opened. Everyone wanted to play ... Bowie, Queen, the Stones. I chose A Certain Ratio.'

By some distance the best British rock movie of the modern era – actually, take the 'rock' bit out of that hyperbolic opening sentence – *24 Hour Party People* concerns Manchester impresario and TV presenter Anthony H. Wilson's label, club and roster of bands that defined the 1980s for a significant amount of British 30- and 40-somethings. It's played as a black *vérité* comedy with surreal flights of fancy, and is led by a performance from Coogan as Wilson that makes you irrationally angry that Oscars only seem to go to actors in drag or playing disabled people. Not that Wilson – who died in 2007 of a heart attack at the age of 57 – didn't have a kind of disability. He was chronically unable to tell fact from fiction, allow logic to stop his best ideas, or work out how to make money from them. A northern Malcolm McLaren with the unfortunate trait of quite liking people, Wilson brought Joy Division, Happy Mondays and New Order to the world and acid house to the white mainstream, and left a trail of legendary anecdotes in his wake. Director Michael Winterbottom makes all this into the only movie in this book that's both achingly funny and historically useful.

Coogan's Wilson narrates his own tale himself, and begins by taking us to the infamous Sex Pistols show at Lesser Free Trade Hall in Manchester in June 1976. The Pistols played to 42 people, some of whom turned out to be Joy Division, their producer Martin Hannett, Buzzcocks, Mick Hucknall and Wilson himself. Legend has it that Mark E. Smith of the Fall and Morrissey of the Smiths were also there, but it's very much in the spirit of the movie that they are ignored in favour of a pogoing nutter called John the Postman. The hall is like a scout-hut: no lights or atmosphere, seats in rows, absolutely depressing and dead, but the device of using real footage of a very early Pistols performing 'No Fun' makes its point, as Coogan/Wilson says to camera, 'Every single one of them is feeding on a power, an energy and a magic. Inspired, they will go out and perform wondrous deeds.'

Wilson's initial wondrous deed was *So It Goes*, a Granada TV show that put on the best of punk while it was unofficially banned elsewhere. Manchester and its environs got to see the Pistols, Iggy, the Banshees, the Clash, the Jam, the Stranglers while the rest of us sat around in blissful ignorance waiting for the Bill Grundy show to make punk into tabloid outrage.

We see a young Shaun Ryder (Cunningham) and his brother Paul switch off the Stranglers in their front room, and swoon over yodelling MOR singer Karl Denver instead. Coogan/Wilson reminds us that the Ryders would go on to form Happy Mondays and sing with Denver on 'Lazyitis'. The device of splicing the real performances into the fiction works perfectly, and you already feel dead excited when Wilson and wife Lindsay go to see the grimy venue that would host Wilson's Factory nights. Peter Kay turns up as the owner of the Russell Club, and you realise that the chubby Bolton comic always looked ancient. He offers Wilson a 60/40 split, a crate of beer for the band, and Friday nights, and an empire is born. On the first night, Mark E. Smith – the real one, at the age he is now – turns up in the queue. Cute. (Rob Brydon, Simon Pegg, Keith Allen, Paul Ryder and Rowetta from Happy Mondays and various Manc rock luminaries all get cameos too.) Joy Division are the headliners and Ian Curtis (Harris) calls Wilson a cunt. When it comes to performance, Harris isn't as good an Ian Curtis as Sam Riley (see *Control*, p. 408), but John Simm and Ralf Little are ultra-cool as Bernard Sumner and Peter Hook, even though they look nothing like them. There's a running joke about John the Postman jumping onstage and bawling 'Louie Louie' a capella at every show that rings true about any and all insular, regional live music scenes.

I love all this. It reminds me of both going to and playing small shows when I was a kid. It also reminds me that, even though all these people went on to do wondrous things and me and my friends didn't, that it was still low-rent and smelly and just like everywhere else for them, too. But it felt like something was as stake, at the time. Rock wasn't just showbiz yet, and it had meaning-of-life qualities even in the least likely settings.

But the reason Winterbottom picked this story to tell is because it's full of everyday surprise. After the Joy Division show, Kay's Don Tonay congratulates Wilson with two hookers and a foursome in the back of a shag-carpeted transit van. No idea if it's true, but the moment is so bizarre and unexpected that you suspect that it is. Unlike *Control*, there just isn't any need to embellish this script with arty shots of people staring moodily into the middle-distance. Which is just one of the many reasons why *24 Hour* ... is an infinitely better film.

Another comes straight after the shag-pile transit van incident. And it's about the way that rumours become truth in pop scenes, and about how to play with that when mythologising people who are still alive, and how to make that funnier while also being respectful of people's reputations. Lindsay catches Tony getting his BJ, but walks away and lets him get on with it. Her idea of instant karma is tracking down Buzzcock and future Magazine genius Howard Devoto and shagging him in the Russell Club bogs. Wilson catches her, but lets her get on with it, too. As he walks out of the loo, we see that the cleaner is the real-life Devoto, in all his bespectacled and dome-headed glory. He turns to us and says, with some exasperation, 'I definitely don't remember this happening.' The frame is frozen and Coogan/Wilson, in voiceover, reminds us of the famous line from John Ford's Western masterpiece *The Man Who Shot Liberty Valance*: 'When you have to choose between truth and legend – print the legend.' If I had to make a list (Honestly, I haven't. No. Really) of my favourite individual scenes from rock movies, this would be the Number One.

So legends get printed. Wilson signing his first Factory label contract with Joy Division in blood as, quite wonderfully, lost glam classic 'Standing in the Road' by Blackfoot Sue plays on the pub jukebox. Wilson finding Martin Hannett (Serkis) recording silence on a hill, and finding himself paying the maverick producer £50 an hour to dismantle Steven Morris's drumkit and reassemble it on a roof. The Ryders feeding rat poison to 3,000 pigeons. The floppy-disc sleeve to New Order's 'Blue Monday' (the most successful 12-inch single of all time) that was so beautiful that it lost Factory and New Order five pence for every copy it sold. The Happy Mondays only becoming funky when an initially reluctant Bez climbed onstage and started dancing. Hannett's Phil Spector-esque drug psychosis and the blizzard of birds and narcotics that surrounded the Mondays. New Order manager Rob Gretton (Considine) trying to beat up Wilson because he'd spent 30 grand on a table for the Factory office. Gun-toting drug dealers killing the Hacienda and the whole peace and love acid house vibe. The Mondays breaking an already ailing Factory by recording the flop *Yes Please* album in Barbados on crack, but not before Shaun Ryder had had to snort his entire month's supply of methadone off the floor of the airport. According to this legend, Ryder then forced Wilson and Co. to buy the tape of the record back off them at gunpoint in the legendary Dry Bar. For £50. When they play it, it turns out there are no vocals on it. Actually, you really couldn't make this stuff up.

But the most predictable myth – that Joy Division's Ian Curtis was a misunderstood Messiah who was just too sensitive for this

cruel world – is undercut completely. In *24 Hour* ... he's an obnoxious Manc Johnny Rotten, gainsaying everything for the sake of it,
showing no emotions at all. The suicide is sudden yet mundane –
and all the more shocking for it. When it comes to printing the one
Factory legend that the mainstream wants to buy into, Winterbottom is utterly uninterested. Wilson pays tribute to Curtis by
getting a town crier he's doing a news item with to ring it out on
camera. I believe this gallows humour in a way that I don't believe
in a single thing that happens in *Control*.

24 Hour ... is a tribute to Manchester and a love letter to Manc
wit – sardonic insults delivered with dour deadpan accuracy and a
heavy dose of scattershot surrealism. Wilson is often the butt of the
joke and, consequently, the standard rock biopic is turned inside
out and upside down. The young cast of homegrown comedy and
character actors capture the gnarly spirit to a T, and make you feel
that these are guys you know and want to hang out with, rather
than icons to be worshipped. It captures the essence of everything
that was smart, funny and working-class bohemian about punk,
basically. It has the confidence in itself to be hilarious about stuff
that 99 per cent of movie goers will never have heard of, like the
scene where Wilson has convinced the cruelly underrated art-
funkers A Certain Ratio to wear shorts onstage. 'Have you seen
our legs? They're like fucking milk bottles!' 'I wouldn't worry about
it,' Coogan replies. 'Although, that reminds me ... I must get some
chicken drumsticks on the way home.'

Screenwriter Frank Cottrell Boyce, Winterbottom and Coogan
portray Wilson as a tentative, self-obsessed man, a sort of faint-
hearted egomaniac, fussing over whether someone else being called
Tony makes him Tony One or Tony Two. He has a chronic case of
what would later be called 'status anxiety', and endlessly reminds
those around him that he went to Cambridge. In short, being a
regional TV presenter hadn't satisfied his youthful ambitions (some
of the film's best comedy juxtaposes his adventures in cutting-edge
rock with the wacky news items he was forced to do in his day job)
and, at the relatively tender age of 26, punk showed him a way to
be the high-achiever of his dreams. Coogan probably gets sick of

this ... but there's more than a little Alan Partridge in his Wilson, as there is in all of his best work. Finding the missing-link between acid house and right-wing woolly jumper TV presenters from Norwich is something Coogan should be truly proud of.

Wilson may not have been Berry Gordy, but he undoubtedly was someone who understood the significance of a moment, and who knew how to announce it, exploit it and make it accessible to anyone who wanted it. It's fitting that Coogan narrates his own story, straight to camera, a mixture of newsreader and myth-maker, comparing himself to F. Scott Fitzgerald and acknowledging that the portrayals of the genuine tragedies of Curtis's death and his wife leaving him ('Obviously, this is a low point ... ') are recon-structions, just like the scene where the poisoned pigeons come raining out of the sky to Wagner's 'Ride of the Valkyries' ('No pigeons were harmed in the making of this film'). His delusions simultaneously forge a key strand of British popular culture while making everyone around him treat him like a moron.

Wilson's ability to spin disasters into triumphs is a constant delight. When the doomed A Certain Ratio complain that only 30 people turned up to see them open the Hacienda, Wilson reminds them of the 42 people at the historic Manchester Pistols show. 'The smaller the attendance, the bigger the history. There were 12 people at the Last Supper, half a dozen at Kitty Hawk. Archimedes was on his own in the bath.' How could you fail to fall in love with this guy? When he gets off with beauty queen Yvette you want to cheer for him. And so does he: 'And by the way, we're still together. So whatever you're thinking, you're wrong.'

Wilson was still alive (he inevitably turns up in a cameo, accom-panied by postmodern Coogan narrative, towards the end of the film) when 24 Hour ... was made, so you're wondering all the way through just what the ending is going to be. It turns out that it involves *literally* selling out, by way of a game show and a major label called, of all things, London. The comedy is still there, but it becomes painfully awkward tragi-comedy, a fitting end. Coogan/Wilson gives you the film's theme at its outset ... the ancient myth of Icarus flying too close to the sun. But that in itself is the joke – Wilson making his common or garden financial mistakes into the stuff of tragic heroism. It's a very British climax to a very British sitcom tale in the Tony Hancock mould ... the comic figure who attempts an ambitious, life-changing journey fuelled by hubris and ends up right back where he started. The irony is that that contract signed in blood at the beginning of the adventure means that Wilson can't sell out properly ... and he's hugely proud of that. In that context, the closing night of the Hacienda is the only kind of death the film could end with.

Afterwards, God visits our hero and bigs him up. 'It's a pity you didn't sign the Smiths. But you were right about Mick Hucknall. His music's rubbish and he's a ginger.' This confirmation that God is a music critic is just one of many moments of truth that make *24 Hour Party People* among the greatest rock movies ever made.

• •

Josie and the Pussycats

2001
Starring: Rachel Leigh Cook, Tara Reid, Rosario Dawson, Alan Cummings, Parker Posey
Dir.: Harry Elfont and Deborah Kaplan

★ ★ ★ ★

Plot: Subliminal voices in rock songs are real. The history of rock is a giant global conspiracy. But then, you knew all this when Pink got big.
Key line: 'You know, if I wasn't a key player in this whole conspiracy to brainwash the youth of America with pop music ... we could totally date.'

This undervalued teen pop satire, based on the 1970s comic book and cartoon TV show, begins with a neat skit at the expense of boy bands. A Backstreet Boys-ish pop combo called Dujour arrive at an airport and put on an impromptu show for their screaming (girl and boy) fans. The song, packed full of the dumb dance moves and crass post-R&B sex lyrics we love to love, is called 'Backdoor Lover'. The band, which includes Seth Green (Oz from *Buffy the Vampire Slayer*) and Donald Faison (Turk from *Scrubs*) board a plane and begin to bicker but are kept in check by posho manager Wyatt Frame (played by the excellent Cumming). Finally, one of the group ask Frame why one of the remixes of their new single appears to feature strange background noises. Frame promises to find out, enters the cockpit, tells the pilot of the private jet to 'Take the chevy to the levee', and parachutes out, leaving the plane to crash. 'Looks like we need a new band', he tells someone on his mobile phone.

Cut straight to credits and our introduction to the titular band, an all-girl trio who play that 21st-century corporate version of punk rock popularised by the likes of Green Day. They're playing at a bowling alley, wear leopard ears onstage and get ragged on by the local pink and vacuous prom queens. It's all like a cleaned-up version of *Beyond the Valley of the Dolls* (see p. 93) at this point. No dropping acid with the Principal here. But we do have Josie (Cook) practising looking cool in the mirror somewhat spazzily, failing to flirt successfully with cute guitar-playing best buddy Alan, and discovering, with the rest of the band, that Dujour's plane is missing just outside their home town of Riverdale and that MegaRecords have already put out the commemorative box set. Drummer Melody (Reid) suggests they have a bake sale to raise money for a search party. Like all drummers, she's the lovably thick one. The Pussycats are a modern girl-power-informed Monkees and everything here has the bright colours and pretty faces of classic post-*Buffy* high school comedy-drama.

But beneath the cuteness is an agenda, and that agenda is the scariness of teen consumerism. When Frame gets someone to play the posthumous Dujour single ('Ride on a motorbike with Dujour/Kickin' it in a Benz with Dujour') at the Riverdale Mall, toothy young things begin hysterically proclaiming orange the new pink and realising that they simply *must* bin their Reebok sweats for … um … Puma sweats. What the unfortunate Dujour had heard on their single is subliminal messages designed to make the young buy pointless stuff. *Josie and the Pussycats* is already becoming a fascinating exercise in good old corporate cake-and-eat-it with a Starbucks latte and an Egg McMuffin. Even as it revs up its anti-consumerist agenda, the onscreen product placements roll past your eyes . . . Ray-Bans, Diesel, Benetton . . . and Coke, of course.

A Goth girl wanders by insisting the song sucks. We get a crash-course in cool-hunting, as Frame smarms her into telling him what MegaRecords are doing wrong. Soon he's whispering, 'Smells like teen spirit' into his watch and Goth girl is being kidnapped in a van that only covers up the background MTV logo for a second or two. I've been hit by so many ironic cultural references in this first 20 minutes I'm feeling slightly seasick.

But that's the point. Each strategically placed logo looks increasingly obvious and evil . . . almost sci-fi in intent. Planes are Motorola. Fish tanks in aquariums are Evian. City skylines are dominated by huge McDonald's arches. The scene where Frame meets the girls – he almost runs them over, they're framed by Frame holding up a clear CD case sign saying 'No. 1 Band in the World', Meat Loaf is singing 'I've seen paradise by the dashboard light' on the car stereo – is genius, and when they get on the plane to stardom someone asks their manager's evil sister why she's there. 'I'm here because I was in the comic-book', she replies, reminding us what the film is based upon. This is self-reference and cross-marketing gone mad. And probably explains why the film didn't go down big with the impressionable young consumers it's cruelly lampooning. Kids are somewhat sensitive about having their gullibility thrown in their faces like this. But we adults get to laugh at them and convince ourselves that we were smarter, so that's alright.

From here, the plot is straightforward . . . the Pussycats must avoid being killed, eventually discover how they're being used and thwart MegaRecords' devilish plans. All is played strictly for goofy laughs. In all American teen comedies, no matter how waspishly satirical they might be, friendship always wins the day. Which is why the main plot device isn't the subliminal voices, or even the

MegaRecords secret bunker where black-clad operatives decide everything we'll say and do in advance. But the label's insistence that the Pussycats become Josie and the Pussycats. Make one person special, divide and rule. It's half-an-hour in and you've decided that the ending you most want is one where, wherever the band are, they're called the Pussycats again. It never happens.

The rest is surprisingly savage satirical detail about pop truths. Every pop death is a murder (Mel C and Geri Halliwell should watch their backs). Every record is made similarly sparkly and tight by pressing a button in the studio marked 'Megasound'. MTV presenter Carson Daly is just a hitman employed by The Man.

The makers don't spare themselves. Sardonic jokes are inserted into montage about the film's debt to *Charlie's Angels*. At one point, Josie interrupts the celebrations of the girls' pop triumphs to ask, worriedly, 'Does anyone else think it's strange that all this happened in a week?' Frame gives them the evil eye, gets out his mobile, is about to make the call that kills them. Finally, bassist Valerie says, 'No.' He clicks the phone shut and the girls get on with screaming with joy. But soon Valerie is getting her first non-invite to a party. She's the wrong colour. Cue a fake TV doc about the lost black member of the Captain & Tennille.

It's odd how similar the concerns of this movie are to the concerns of *Privilege* (see p. 64). But in 1967 you did it dark and grim, in 2001 you do it light and bubbly, and you find that, actually, neither way goes down that well with critics or general public. Man, I feel my own conspiracy theory coming on . . .

Parker Posey almost steals the movie as MegaRecords' very own Cruella de Vil. It turns out that the big subliminal message she wants to sell the world is that she's cool. She was bullied at school because she had a lisp. She just wants to be popular. In US teen screen gems this is always what everything is about. I sometimes suspect that every writer and director in Hollywood is endlessly playing out the horror of being labelled a nerd at school. The ludicrous ending of *Josie and the Pussycats* suggests that the makers agree, and are as bored with it as we are.

Over the last two decades subversive ideas in American screen fiction have increasingly become the preserve of teen product. *Buffy the Vampire Slayer*, *The Faculty*, *Ghost World*, *Juno*, *But I'm a Cheerleader*, *Bring It On* ... all based in the same superficially sunny high school milieu, all with an anti-establishment agenda and satirical integrity that has largely been lost to mainstream film. And most of these are based on strong female characters and take the pleasure part of their agenda from the joy of female bonding. *Josie and the Pussycats* is another in that line, and the corny bits and catchy songs are entirely justifiable in the context of the deluge of potshots it takes at American consumer culture. It's made with both a good heart and a good head, and deserves to become a future cult hit.

● ●

Glitter

2001
Starring: Mariah Carey, Max Beesley, Valarie Pettiford, Eric Benet
Dir.: Vondie Curtis-Hall

★ ★

Plot: Yet another rewrite of *A Star Is Born* produces the most reviled pop movie ever.
Key line: 'They didn't dig the "Woe Is Me" type thing.'

'Gruesome'. 'Excruciatingly inept'. 'Manifestly silly'. And that's just the edited highlights of the first three reviews of *Glitter* I can find online. To be honest, the first – and last – acting performance of Mariah Carey wouldn't have found its way into *Popcorn* if it wasn't for *Glitter*'s critical reputation. The abuse it's had puts it into the pantheon of the most infamous movie turkeys of all time, alongside *Cleopatra*, *Ishtar*, *Heaven's Gate* and *Showgirls*. The one thing all of those movies have in common is that, when one finally gets to actually *see* them ... they're not *that* bad. Even OK, in parts.

Yeah, you're right ... apart from *Showgirls* ... that really is fucking shocking. Meanwhile, *The Departed*, which is by some distance the worst film of Martin Scorsese's career, wins the guy his first Oscar! What is going on here?

Because *Glitter* is ... not *that* bad. Even OK, in parts. I mean, as long as you're not expecting *Citizen Kane* or *Battleship Potemkin* or somesuch, which, if you're sitting down to watch a bleedin' Mariah Carey vehicle, you're surely not. It has a lightweight and familiar plot, some dodgy acting, some bland dialogue and Mariah Carey songs ... all things that prevent it being the kind of movie I'd want to watch more than once. But it makes a kind of sense, the scenery doesn't wobble and considering Ms Carey was reported to be going through some kind of breakdown at the time ... I reckon the girl does all right as an actress. No worse than Jagger, Sting or Bowie, anyway, and nothing they've acted in has got the savage pummelling *Glitter* was treated to.

You know what I'm going to say ... but here it comes anyway. *Glitter* is a film aimed at women, written by women and starring a female superstar. The world loves nothing better than kicking a rich bitch when she's down. And as for who the movie was aimed at ... I've never done a focus group on Ms Carey's fanbase, but I don't think I'm reaching too far to assume that it's working-class women of all ages. Women who, after a hard day of being called 'Pramface' or doing some shitty job for a fraction of what a man would be paid for doing it, like to relax with the warbly romanticism of Ms Carey's pop-soul stylings, and imagine that they are beautiful and wealthy and having their heart broken by some gorgeous swine in a tux, rather than the bloke farting next to them and forcing her and her screaming brats to watch Rotherham vs Leeds in a vital Sherpa Vans Trophy match. Her films of choice, when enjoying the more civilised company of other women, would probably be *Ghost* or *Dirty Dancing* or *The Bodyguard*. Middle-class film critics, male and female, hate these women and their entertainment, and the unfortunate *Glitter* bore the brunt of their loathing because it didn't put bums on seats. So much so that (male) director Curtis-Hall hasn't been allowed near a movie camera again, despite getting the

Glitter gig by having made the deservedly praised *Gridlock'd*.

None of this excuses the second-hand rags-to-riches plot or some of the poorer acting (rapper Da Brat is especially awful as one of Ms Carey's 'dancers'). Just trying to get things in perspective.

The major problem with *Glitter* is that Hall is just too damn tasteful to get into the spirit of what should have been a knockdown, drag-out, tearjerker camp-fest. The story might be old-school melo-drama, but, when you're given a script that goes poor mixed race girl is put into care because her drug and drink-addled singer Mom burns down the house, but then gets the guy and the pop career of her dreams in a lovingly recreated 1980s New York disco milieu, and then loses guy through jealousy and hankers after Mom, and then has to bear a tragic shooting on what should have been the greatest day of her life before a tearful reunion ... you've got to swallow your film school pride and make *Lassie Come Home* with songs. But every time Curtis-Hall is handed an opportunity to send emotions spinning into orbit, he turns away and does something sensible instead. Give a straight man a gay man's job ...

For example, there's a bit when Billie Frank (Ms Carey) and her manager/mentor/lover Dice (Beesley) are in a cab and hear her debut single (which, oddly, appears to actually be 'Candy' by Cameo) played on radio for the first time. Billie stops the cab, bounds out of it in girlish joy, and you're waiting for the big musical number where she performs the song to the resulting traffic jam and everybody goes from grumpiness to dancing in the street in ecstasy and ... and ... she just goes and phones her mate. That's it. Noooo! And again ... Billie and Dice are estranged but pining for each other, and both start writing a lovelorn ballad about their feelings and stuff. But, even though they're both alone and many miles from each other in separate stylish apartments ... they're writing the same song! Brilliant! Now, if you're saying that your hero and heroine are so deeply in love that they have a quasi-supernatural spiritual connection that bends time and space ... you've got to have the buggers finish the song and start singing it, probably in split-screen, until they are singing it to each other, in perfect harmony ... yes? No! Hall just loses interest and goes back to the dodgy plot. And therein lies *Glitter's* failure – it's a musical that doesn't have the flights of fancy (or enough music) to be a proper musical. It's a fantasy that veers away from the fantastic. It's a pop star vehicle that drives really carefully and occasionally opens the door and kicks Mariah to the kerb. What's more, although Beesley's a decent actor in a pound shop Ewan McGregor sort of way, he's nowhere near sexy nor heavyweight enough to drag Ms Carey through the story's more dramatic moments. Our heroine is from the Joey Tribbiani school of acting – be happy (smiles), be sad (pouts), be confused (just be yourself) – and needs some chemistry and an actorly example to draw from.

Glitter is always accused of being unintentionally funny, but the only scene which really scores high on the so-bad-it's-good-ometer is the bit where Dice seduces Billie for the first time by . . . showing her his marimbas. This makes slightly more sense if you know that Beesley first came to prominence as a vibes player/bandleader on London's acid jazz scene. I've just read that sentence back . . . and no, it makes no more sense after you know that. But you've got to pity poor Mariah who, having had to play hard to get up to this point, now has to portray helpless lust 'cos this skinny bloke has hit some bits of wood with a stick.

So, no, I'm not trying, single-handedly, to revive *Glitter's* critical rep by insisting that it's a brilliant work that's been misunderstood by other critics who aren't as pop-obsessed and fond of women as me. But it's a decent TV movie matinee that whiles away 100 minutes in a gently pleasant manner. Compared to hapless bloke fests like *The Doors* (see p. 289) – or *American Gangster*, for that matter, which was so dull they had to give me smelling salts and high-grade PCP to get me out of the cinema (they were on hand; I wasn't the first) – it's a trailblazing work of art.

Now . . . where's that copy of *Shanghai Surprise*?

• •

Hedwig and the Angry Inch

2001

Starring: John Cameron Mitchell; Michael Pitt, Miriam Shor, Alberta Watson
Dir.: John Cameron Mitchell

★ ★ ★ ★

Plot: *Tommy* meets *The Naked Civil Servant*.
Key line: 'I had just been dismissed from university for delivering a brilliant lecture on the aggressive influence of German philosophy on rock 'n' roll, entitled, "You, Kant, Always Get What You Want".'

John Cameron Mitchell's film of his successful off-Broadway stage musical is a brilliantly realised thing that deserves a wider audience. It is, after all, the world's only Cold War transsexual rock 'n' roll self-help comedy, and it makes *The Rocky Horror Picture Show* (see p. 155) look like the tediously safe and straight view of sexual transgression that it so obviously is.

Hedwig is the East German transsexual singer of a trashy rock band called the Angry Inch. His/her backing singer and lover is a frustrated drag king called Yitzhak who wants to be in *Rent*. The only gigs the band get involve playing to bemused middle-aged diners in dodgy steak houses in Kansas. The 'Angry Inch' refers to Hedwig's mutilated penis – Hedwig had a sex change so he could marry a GI and move to America, but the op went wrong. And if he'd only waited . . .

What's more, a rock star called Tommy Gnosis, whom Hedwig mentored, has stolen all his/her songs, but no-one believes him/her. She/he's stalking him, which isn't helping the lawsuit.

Out of this bizarre scenario, Mitchell conjures a witty, surreal and deliciously camp deconstruction of what rock 'n' roll actually means. For Hedwig's life has been saved by real rock 'n' roll . . . the art and transgression and sexuality of Lou Reed, Iggy Pop and

Bowie ... and this movie is a hymn to glam and punk's effect on global culture, through its ability to give us weirdos and outcasts something to relate to, and give us permission to reinvent ourselves as anything we choose. Hedwig, after all, had a shitty start in life – 'Our apartment was so small that mother made me play in the oven' – taking in sexual abuse from his father, uninterested neglect from his mother, oppression from a Stalinist regime, and the small matter of genital mutilation ... and it's only the sleazy, poly-morphously perverse end of rock that has got him this far by letting him know that he's not alone. The songs – written by prodigiously talented Angry Inch member Stephen Trask – tread a bravura line between seriously great rock singles in a post-Alice Cooper style and the hysterical melodrama of Broadway show tunes. What's more, Mitchell as Hedwig looks like a blonde slut version of Rachel Griffiths from *Six Feet Under* and *Muriel's Wedding*. He/she's a wonderful thing, baby.

So why not a big old five-star rating, if it's that shit-hot? *Weeelll* ... it all gets a little in love with the melodrama and hugging and learning at the end, and suddenly you're thinking about Jack's one-man off-Broadway show in *Will & Grace* – 'JUST JACK!!!' – and sniggering. Which is ironic, because what the end of the movie does, in essence, is forgets to be funny. Hedwig only finds himself as a person and an artist when he accepts that he's 'just a boy'. Out go the wig and the false boobies, in comes a seemingly endless, quasi-operatic, self-realisation suite. You're reminded of one of the best lines from earlier in the film: we're watching a flashback to Hedwig's mentoring of future rock star Tommy. A neighbour is singing 'I Will Always Love You'. 'Do you think love lasts forever?', Tommy asks. 'No – but this song does,' Hedwig replies.

But before we get too sneery, this line heralds one of the movie's Great Moments, as Hedwig paints a silver star on Tommy's fore-head, then shows him his/her work in a mirror, holding it at such an angle that both their faces merge into one beautiful whole. But Tommy adjusts the mirror's angle so he can only see himself – a perfect visual explanation of the narcissism necessary to become a star at any cost.

Much of the central theme is about things being cut in half – people, countries, gender roles. Primitive animation occasionally pops up, illustrating a song. It's very dreamy and childlike ... almost *Juno*-esque. And the jokes are black, black, black. In one flashback conversation about religion between seven-year-old Hedwig and his blank, bitter Mom, she tells him off for mentioning the name Jesus. 'But he died for our sins!', exclaims the boy, plaintively. 'So did Hitler,' deadpans Mom.

The film is full of brilliant puns and brave jokes about paedophilia and teenage masturbation. It has a somewhat romantic view of sex with young boys, which is perhaps why it wasn't packing 'em in at the Multiplex. But ... it's easy to forget that this used to be a key part of rock and pop's job, questioning our most treasured moral viewpoints. People still ask why there isn't a new Sex Pistols. That would be because the Sex Pistols said things that people found horrifying and morally questionable, something that young musicians are either too scared or too dumb to do. You don't have to agree with all of it. You just have to feel the point, which is that certain art makes you feel that everything you take for granted is up for grabs. *Hedwig and the Angry Inch* taps into that most vital part of art and music effortlessly. It's everything The Who's *Tommy* tried and failed to be.

• •

8 Mile

2002
Starring: Eminem, Brittany Murphy, Kim Basinger, Mekhi Phifer
Dir.: Curtis Hanson

★ ★ ★ ★

Plot: The hip hop *High Noon*.
Key line: 'It's always easier for a white man to succeed in a black man's medium. Right, B?'

Right from the get-go, *8 Mile* stinks. We see Eminem aka Marshall Mathers as Jimmy 'B Rabbit' Smith limbering up, practising those all-important rap hand gestures in the mirror of a club's filthy backstage toilet, his silent moves in perfect time with the ominous subterranean funk of Mobb Deep's 'Shook Ones Pt 2'. The film has a sepia tone that bumps up against the modern setting and gives it a historical feel, and you quickly realise how cleverly *LA Confidential* director Curtis Hanson has manipulated you into imagining that you're somehow witnessing a key moment in the real pre-fame career of Eminem. If you boil *8 Mile* down to bare bones of plot, it's just the ancient potboiling cliché of talented-poor-boy-puts-the-show-on-right-here-and-wins-the-day ... an Elvis movie, fittingly, in a movie where calling the hero 'Elvis' as an insult is a running joke. But Hanson and writer Scott Silver find so many ways to give that old chestnut integrity and authenticity that *8 Mile* becomes a classic of the pop film genre, and an image-reinventing triumph for its enigmatic star.

Or it would have been, if he'd followed it up. Since *8 Mile*, there have been reports that Eminem had accepted separate roles as a boxer, a bounty hunter and in a horror comedy ... but nothing has emerged. A decent comeback album, *Relapse*, has come out in 2009. But no sign of a follow-up film.

Whatever reasons lie behind the absence of an Eminem movie career, we've become so used to celebrities dumping the day job when Hollywood comes calling that Mathers' refusal to conform is both admirable and baffling. Because, if *8 Mile* is anything to go by, Mathers as an actor is ... OK, with a future option on very good. Good enough to carry a good movie on his debut. Admittedly, someone must have told him he has pretty eyes just before shooting, 'cos his main acting chop involves sucking in those geometric cheekbones and staring dolefully past the camera, looking like he's just fixing to cry his baby blues right out of his head. But one thing Mathers really does capture is the white fear of blackness. And this must be a tough thing from his past for him to confront, because rap is so much about not admitting fear of anyone or anything. This isn't fear of black violence, but fear of black cool, and Mathers is a frozen picture of racial insecurity every time he's asked to battle. You feel the suspense *with* him, and feel the insecurities he had to confront when he was just another wannabe white rapper in Detroit.

To recap: *8 Mile* embellishes various facts from Eminem's life to create a kind of musical Western, where rhymes replace bullets in the rush towards the inevitable violent showdown. The film takes its name from the main trunk road that separates poor, black Detroit from the wealthy white suburbs to its north. Our hero Rabbit lives to the north of 8 Mile, but in a trailer, with his slutty Mom (Basinger). His attempts to make it as a rapper – and cross over that city/suburbs racial divide, from fake to real – revolve around freestyle rap battles at a local club hosted by his best friend Future (Phifer). Rabbit chokes in terror during his first battle. His girlfriend says she's pregnant, mom's a nightmare, and he's trying to make it in a world dominated by hard-looking and verbally vicious black MCs. It's a hard-knock life for our Jimmy, and he has 90-odd minutes to turn all this poverty-line stress around and send us out of the cinema with a good old-fashioned, gung-ho, can-do, all-American spring in our step. And he does. But not in the way you might imagine.

8 Mile is obsessed with the American macho tradition of rugged individualism – all kinds of help or partnership or compromise are rejected by the suspicious Rabbit, which means that the final lonely showdown takes its cue from Westerns in the *High Noon* tradition. Eminem don't need no posse. Not even no guns. Just words like fists to cut the bad guys – and rival rap crew Leaders of the Free World all dress in black – down to size.

But the final battle is one of the great set-pieces of recent cinema, and the ending – with its refusal to go along with the current obsession with instant celebrity, of fame without work – is a surprise and interestingly subversive. The film implies – no, bollocks, the film comes right out and says – that the way to salvation is through facing up to responsibility, doing a fair day's work for a fair day's pay, dealing with mundane reality no matter how gruelling and anonymous that might be. Not subversive in the context of, I dunno, a rom-com perhaps. But rock movies are all about the fantasy of transcendence through fame, of being literally above the masses when inviting adulation on a stage. *8 Mile* undercuts this completely, without making you feel that superstar Eminem is being hypocritical. The ending takes the Western convention of the hero walking off into the sunset and makes it muted and sombre. An American film that suggests that winning is no great end in itself? It's a rarity, and a welcome one.

And so is *8 Mile*'s central sex scene, between Rabbit and Alex. That is, it's a sex scene in a movie that doesn't make you want to either laugh or barf. If you were a director preparing to film some gratuitous rumpy-pumpy in the early twenty-first century, here's what you should have done, based upon this short and incendiary little scene. Choose an inappropriate setting, like a factory, in amongst heavy machinery. Tell the incidental music man to take the day off. Hire Brittany Murphy, and when you can't get away with showing penis sliding into vagina, get her to do this filthy thing where she licks her own hand and guides your leading man inside her off-screen, and then get her to do that eyes-going-out-of-focus thing that drives all men (and most women) crazy. That should do it. Don't end this 30 seconds of squelching noises with waves crashing, net curtains billowing, or tanned body doubles smooshing together in some tediously Tantric way. Remember that sex is actually quite rude and ugly, in a beautiful way.

Sadly, of course, hiring Ms Murphy is not an option since her tragic death in December 2009. Best just to hire Curtis Hanson for a day, whichever's easiest.

If Kim Basinger as a cradle-snatching trailer-trash mother is probably the most bizarre piece of casting in this book (really; no amount of smudged make-up or tousled hair can make her look like anything but Hollywood royalty), then Brittany Murphy is ideal as Rabbit's love interest. The pasty-faced dirtiness of the working-class slapper is something she doesn't seem to have to fake . . . and if you're trying to find the slimy insult in that sentence, you're barking up the wrong tree, 'cos working-class slappers rule my world. Alex is an especially great one because when she cheats on Rabbit . . . in a radio station, in full view of anyone who happens past, with a bloke Rabbit hates . . . she never says sorry. She doesn't do it for money, or to grab our hero's attention, or to punish him for anything. She just does it because she wants to get laid. She doesn't get punished for it, either. Again, unusual morals for an American film.

That just leaves time for a few details; the things that make you love a film, rather than simply admire it.

Mekhi Phifer (who plays Pratt in *ER*) gives a great performance as Future, especially as he's stuck with that most thankless of roles, the faithful black buddy-buddy of the White Star.

If you wanna know how appalling redneck rock-rapper Kid Rock got a version of 'Sweet Home Alabama' into the charts . . . it's 'inspired' by a scene from *8 Mile*.

There is an odd implication that Stephanie either wants or has had some sort of incestuous relationship with Rabbit. At one point she regales the poor boy with inappropriate details about her no-account boyfriend's reluctance to go down on her. But, before that, there's this scene where Stephanie gives Rabbit her busted car as a present. She looks lovingly and sexily into his eyes, squeezes his cheeks, calls him her 'Little Rabbit' . . . and Marshall beats a panicky retreat to bed. Hmmm.

And finally . . . even though the freestyle battles are great, the most iconic scenes are those where Rabbit writes rhymes on the bus on his way to work, on tattered bits of paper that are shoved in his back pocket. The boy stares soulfully out from between his headphones, and the streets of Detroit look as blasted and desperate and oddly beautiful as the streets of Baltimore do in *The Wire*.

And I've not even mentioned the music. Is 'Lose Yourself' the best song ever to win an Oscar? It's the only contender since the 1960s, that's for sure. Maybe Eminem hasn't made another film because *8 Mile* was just too tough an act to follow. If so . . . fair enough. He's probably right.

• •

Standing in the Shadows of Motown

2002

Starring: The Funk Brothers, Andre Braugher
Dir.: Paul Justman

★ ★ ★

Plot: Stately documentary about the most famous unknown musicians on the planet.
Key line: 'You have no idea, the *gravity*, of what went on in here, emotionally.'

If you're going to hold a viewer's interest in a low-budget documentary about a group of average-looking elderly gentlemen, you'd better make your first few minutes hit hard. Paul Justman, the director of this politely angry film about the men who played on every Tamla Motown cut until the label moved from Detroit to Los Angeles in 1973, pulls off the instant whammy with great panache.

As the film opens with staged shots of poor black children from a mythic past playing by a lake, a voiceover (by Andre Braugher, who plays Frank Pembleton in *Homicide: Life on the Street*) informs us that the elderly gentlemen we'll be watching played on 'more Number One hits than the Beach Boys, the Rolling Stones, Elvis and the Beatles combined'. The scene cuts to a pretty building in a snow-covered, present-day Detroit. Then, as a different voice reminisces, we cut to hands playing a piano. The man is wearing a classy pin-striped suit and he is playing 'The Battle Hymn of the Republic'. We see an even better-dressed black man reading a newspaper.

Jump-cut to an elderly black man sitting on his stoop in the snow. The caption informs us that he is 'Joe Hunter: Funk Brother – Keyboards'. He is talking about how the success of 'it' didn't strike him at the time, but that he eventually realized that Motown was a big deal. As his voiceover continues, 'Nobody never mentioned too much about us . . . it gets to you, you know?', we've cut back to the mysterious piano room and we see that it's Hunter playing the piano. A caption says that this is his work. The camera swings slowly around and behind the dapper entertainer and we finally see a familiar kind of reception desk sail into view. Joe Hunter, the man who played keyboards for the greatest hits of Marvin Gaye, Smokey Robinson and Diana Ross, now makes his living as a hotel pianist, playing Civil War anthems to businessmen who barely notice his presence. If this was fiction, we'd be laughing at the corniness by now. We're not laughing.

Before we get too enthusiastic, though, some context. *Standing in the Shadows* ... is based upon the book of the same name by one Allan Slutsky, a young(ish) white guitarist who cheerfully admits, on one of the accompanying DVD special features, that he's devoted a substantial chunk of his life to getting the story of Motown's unsung heroes the Funk Brothers into the public domain. At one point he compares himself to someone who devotes themselves to a great charitable cause, an unconscious revelation, one suspects, of how he feels he should be seen by his grateful grandpa protégés. He even gets to play with them these days, the proud but humble musician having made himself equal in stature to these legends of black music history by sheer obsessive patronage. This is, be warned, a man who has nicknamed himself 'Dr Licks'.

So it's inevitable that this documentary overeggs the pudding somewhat, insisting that 'anyone could have sung these songs' and made them hits, and dismissing the role of songwriters, arrangers and producers almost completely, as if Slutsky's heroes had just walked into a studio and invented the Motown sound and watched dismayed as the likes of Holland–Dozier–Holland and Smokey Robinson stole all their ideas. This is silly and dishonest and does the Funk Brothers themselves an injustice. If you want a balanced view of Motown's Hitsville USA studios, you won't find it here.

But then ... a lot of balance needed redressing. You can't argue that, say, James Jamerson's drumming and Benny Benjamin's basslines weren't so unique and innovative that they didn't amount to a form of composition, but you won't find a composing credit for any of the Funk Brothers on any Motown tune. As a simple (but staged, one suspects) little vox pop early in this film neatly contends ... everybody who loves music knows Motown's songs, singers, composers and producers, but none of us know the names of the men who actually *made* those sublime noises. After watching this movie, you will. And that makes this film a vital historical document with a serious political subtext about the exploitation of workers.

And it's only just over five minutes in before you're hit with the next surprise. When you note that the film features a reunion concert, at which the old geezers play a selection of those Motown classics with vocalists including the not especially accomplished likes of Gerald Levert, Montell Jordan and Joan Osbourne, you sigh at the inevitable *Later with Jools*-ness of it all and ready the fast-forward button. Then you hear the first eerie flute strains of the Four Tops' 'Reach Out (I'll Be There)', and Levert starts singing ... and it's great. *Really* great. I mean, keep your expectations in check if you're expecting visceral pop-soul thrills and spills, but, considering that no actual Motown artists were injured by bothering their ungracious arses with the making of this film (except the very great Martha Reeves), you've got to admit that the Funk Brothers have still got it and that the guest vocalists don't let anyone down. Performance-wise, Levert and Osbourne are revelations, and Chaka Khan's take on 'What's Going On?' is one of the most stunning and profound things I've seen and heard on a film soundtrack.

It's unsettling, too, hearing the passion of that sound, and seeing it come out of these old guys, mostly sitting down, playing as if they were making a jingle for the Milk Marketing Board. But it's also revealing that the only performance that falls flat is 'You Really Got a Hold on Me', performed with Meshell N'degeocello in a studio. Even though that studio happens to be the legendary Studio A in the original Motown HQ, something is completely missing without an audience to bounce off.

The movie's title may be unwieldy, but it is well-founded. The story is dominated and haunted by two dead men. The first of the Funk Brothers gang to die were drummer Benjamin and bassist

Jamerson, troubled geniuses killed by disappointment, drugs and booze in 1969 and 1983 respectively. The other Funk Brothers – Hunter, Richard 'Pistol' Allen, Jack 'Black Jack' Ashford, Bob Babbitt, Johnny Griffith, Uriel Jones, Joe Messina, Eddie 'Chank' Willis, and the late Eddie 'Bongo' Brown, Earl 'Chunk of Funk' Van Dyke and Robert White – seem or seemed in awe of the pair, and you feel there is an extraordinary untold story buried deep within their somewhat hagiographic treatment here. A neat little reconstruction of an incident involving Jamerson's eccentric (and stinky) travelling habits hints at a funnier, funkier movie, just waiting to be made.

There is a genuinely moving moment. One of the group's two white members, bassist Bob Babbit, is being informally interviewed by N'degeocello. She asks the question that the film has avoided for 80 minutes – did the black Funk Brother majority have any problems with Babbit or guitarist Jim Messina, especially after the hardening of Afro-American attitude in the wake of the assassination of Martin Luther King?

Babbit is obviously uncomfortable talking anyway. He tries to give his answer, which is, basically, 'No.' But he's so overwhelmed by the memory of the bond between him and the black musicians that he worked with over three decades before, and the reality that he's suddenly reunited with them after not seeing them for years . . . he just can't do it. He begins to cry, embarrassedly, apologetically.

Standing in the Shadows of Motown is not a great piece of filmmaking. Some of the reminiscences are dull. Some of the musical detail will only be interesting to nerds like me. There's no innovative approach to spark your imagination. Everybody's a little too desperate to worship at the Funk Brothers' altar. Nobody wants to point out that perhaps the reason why none of the Funk Brothers were successful after leaving Motown was because none of them could write a good song nor had a real artistic vision, unlike the Motown legends they were working for. And you long for some insight from a Robinson, Ross or Stevie Wonder.

But there is a sad yet inspiring tale here about the southern black migration to the industrial north of America, and the effect that those economic and political circumstances had upon the culture, musical pleasures and racial attitudes of the world. About how ordinary men who happened to be great artists *and* artisans built the foundations of black America's first 'cross-over' into the white world, and how a black man, Berry Gordy, paid tribute to that white power structure by replicating its cunning exploitation of skilled labour.

One day, a brave and visionary film-maker will *really* get to grips with that story. Until then, *Standing in the Shadows* ... will make you listen to the *music* of the greatest music ever made in a different way. You can't ask too much more than that.

• •

Masked and Anonymous

2003

Starring: Bob Dylan, John Goodman, Jessica Lange, Jeff Bridges, Penelope Cruz, Luke Wilson, Ed Harris, Val Kilmer, Bruce Dern, Chris Penn, Christian Slater, Mickey Rourke, Angela Bassett
Dir.: Larry Charles

★ ★ ★

**Plot: In a war-torn dystopian near-future, an old rock star called Jack Fate is released from prison to play a dodgy benefit show for a government's TV network. He encounters many stars and says many gnomic things along the way.
Key line: 'You're supposed to have all the answers, man. Come on!'**

Man ... the critics *hated* this movie. According to the generally restrained *Radio Times Guide to Films*, this strange and star-studded Bob Dylan vehicle is 'a vacuous, self-indulgent mess' and a 'pretentious ego trip', with 'a criminal waste' of talent 'spouting hideously pompous dialogue'. Roger Ebert called it 'a vanity production beyond all reason' and compared the dialogue to 'the language and philosophy of Chinese fortune cookies'. The *Village Voice* plumped for a 'self-destructive ... idiotic ... mega-dirge'. And on and on and on it goes. When we critics get permission to gang up on something, we really go to town. I feel like the lonely boy with BO and broken specs held together by Elastoplast in the corner of the playground. But *Masked and Anonymous* ... I quite like it.

The setting is some sort of parallel universe where there's some sort of global revolutionary war going on. And no, this entry isn't going to get any more sure of anything than that. A country that might be America or might be *in* Latin America is governed by the Democrat Republicans and the President is a dictator who resembles General Gaddafi. Their state-run TV network decides it needs a benefit concert to distract the peasants from revolting, but they can't get real stars like Springsteen or Billy Joel, so down-at-heel promoters Uncle Sweetheart (Goodman) and Nina Veronica (Lange) spring missing legend Jack Fate (Dylan) from a hellhole prison to do it. From then on it's bizarre cameos, obtuse *non sequiturs* and Dylan songs a-go-go. *Arriba!*

The film has some gently satirical laughs about the fact that Jack Fate is obviously just Bob Dylan. The authorities have provided a helpful list of songs they want Dylan/Fate to perform: they include key political songs by the Beatles, the Stones, The Who, Neil Young and MC5, plus Barry McGuire's 'Eve of Destruction', the 1965 hit that blatantly copied Dylan's early style and made it into a one-hit-wonder pop novelty. The always reliable Jeff Bridges plays a bitter journo who asks a reluctant Fate a bunch of questions you just *know* come from Dylan's own stock of bad memories of interviews. Questions about Frank Zappa and Hendrix and why wasn't he at Woodstock and how the guy from the Bee Gees sounds a lot like Gene Pitney, all made to imply that Fate/Dylan sold out in some treacherous way. Bridges manages to make this all seem genuinely menacing. Dylan, of course, stays silent and looks uncomfortable, which he does through most of the picture. A black girl is then brought to see Fate and sings a beautiful a cappella version of 'The Times They Are A-Changin''. Dylan is haunted by his past here,

but you can't quite tell whether he's celebrating or rejecting it ...
or maybe he's saying the two go hand in hand.

The script was co-written by Dylan and director Charles
(credited as Sergei Petrov and Rene Fontaine) and they have much
good clean fun with the whole notion of being 'Dylanesque'. The
entire script is in epithets: 'They have no ideology. They push both
Jesus and Judas aside.' 'If I know nothing else, I know at least one
thing is true: that the secret is in the ordinary; the common things
in life.' 'All of us in some way are trying to kill time. When it's all
said and done, time ends up killing us.' 'Gauguin was a stockbroker.'
'Does Jesus have to walk on water twice to make a point?' 'Have
you ever met any big stars with a set of nuts?' 'All of his songs are
recognisable. Even when they're not recognisable.' Sure, I know it
ain't Beckett or whatever. But it's more entertaining than what
passes for dialogue in the overwhelming majority of 21st-century
movies. And the soundtrack makes excellent use of unlikely Dylan
covers from around the world including 'Like a Rolling Stone', by
Articolo 31 (Italian), 'One More Cup of Coffee', by Sertab Erener
(Turkish) and 'My Back Pages', by the Magokoro Brothers
(Japanese) and the Ramones (Ramonsian). The bad guy – if he's
really a bad guy at all – gets killed by a guitar and the answer to it
all at the end of *Masked and Anonymous* is, quite literally, 'Blowing
in the Wind'. These don't strike me as the ideas of a star on an
ego-trip. Dylan seems to be taking the piss out of himself and his
reputation throughout.

There is a brilliant, haunting cameo from Giovanni Ribisi as a
piece of archetypal unknown soldier cannon fodder, gabbling at
Dylan's Fate on a bus and doomed to die violently for no good
reason. And a sequence where Uncle Sweetheart introduces Fate
to his support acts, a menagerie of circus novelty turns just like
those that supported Elvis in the early shows that Col. Tom Parker
promoted. Then Luke Wilson's Bobby Cupid arrives and gives
Fate a guitar he swears belonged to blues legend Blind Lemon
Jefferson. And *then*, Dylan/Fate performs 'Dixie' with his small
pick-up band, and it's extraordinary, and you suspect that something profound is being said about American history and which

parts of it Dylan feels made him. But, naturally, you don't know what it is, do you, Mr Jones? Sorry. Always wanted to write that line. It's a music journalist rite-of-passage.

Pretentious? Probably. Boring? Never. There's time for some kooky theories about Vietnam and AIDS, a baffling cameo from Ed Harris as a blacked-up minstrel called Oscar Vogel, who knew Fate's father, who might be the President. Maybe. Who cares? There's even some ironic Dylanology, as Cruz, Wilson and Goodman all get to interpret one of his songs. 'It's not like those other songs of his, the ones about faithless women and booze and brothels and the cruelty of society,' Goodman's Uncle Sweetheart blusters, and you realise that Dylan does read his own press after all. And always, there's Dylan's increasingly frog-like nasal rasp, and the sad, regretful songs he illuminates with it. If there's one thing Dylan's always had, it's the Blues. And *Masked and Anonymous* is as resigned to the futile search for comfort in a hostile world as everything he's sung since 1968.

Dylan's themes in his perceived peak years were: war is madness and politicians suck. Nothing original at all. What was original was the metaphor, allegory and symbolism he employed to illuminate those themes. I mean, 'A Hard Rain's A-Gonna Fall' wouldn't have been as good if it had been called 'A Big Bomb's A-Gonna Drop', would it? So Dylan does exactly the same thing here: an allegorical story about the madness of war and the shitness of politicians, where the dialogue spoken by the rabble of eccentric characters employs the same illogical fire and accusatory tone of biblical allusion and surreal humour as his songs. It works just fine, as long as you accept that things that sound profound when set to music sometimes don't when just spoken. The film walks and talks like a late-period Dylan song, in a *Time Out of Mind* style, where an apparently bemused and exhausted Bob, with his dapper pencil moustache and Hank Williams threads, stalks the old, weird America in a road movie with No Direction Home, quietly observing the rantings of ordinary freaks driven crazy by the crazies in charge. And where several favourite Dylan obsessions – huckster conmen, Al Jolson, old folk takes and jokes involving animals, the emptiness of stardom, the loneliness of living, the power of religion, the sickness of violence – collide and wrestle in the dirt and come to the conclusion that each one of us has to find our own conclusion. Annoying, when you're looking for answers from someone who was once accused of having them. But unavoidably true.

Plus, Goodman and Bridges are just plain fabulous, in an effortless way, and Val Kilmer is entertainingly preposterous, in a trying-way-too-hard way. And once you get used to the fact that Dylan is very possibly the worst actor on the planet – and if you've seen and loved Sam Peckinpah's *Pat Garrett and Billy the Kid*, then you have a head start – his 'performance' is pure charisma, a Chaplin-esque mask of blank unhappiness and shuffling vulnerability which still manages to convey a certain strength and dignity. Maybe the young and arrogant Dylan of *Don't Look Back* (see p. 61) was way cooler. But I prefer the company of this Bob, a daffy old eccentric who keeps telling everyone he's just an entertainer, and laughing darkly at the fact that no-one wants to believe him.

• •

School of Rock

2003
Starring: Jack Black, Joan Cusack, Mike White, Sarah Silverman
Dir.: Richard Linklater

★ ★ ★ ★

Plot: Chubby, manic, deluded rock star wannabe poses as substitute teacher and teaches rich kids how to rock. Valuable lessons learned.
Key lines: 'There used to be a way to stick it to The Man. It was called rock 'n' roll. But guess what? Oh no! The Man ruined that too with a little thing called ... MTV!!!'

The snatch of Jack Black dialogue above culled from this hit rock comedy contains two supersized ironies. The first is that MTV made Jack Black. The porky Jewish master of the hyperactive eyebrow and the mock portentous statement has been given heavy MTV rotation as the leader of prog-rock parody duo Tenacious D, whose promo videos for the likes of 'Wonderboy' and 'Fuck Her Gently' turned out to be much funnier than the resulting 2006 feature film, *Tenacious D in 'The Pick of Destiny'*. The *Tenacious D* movie might have been a critical and commercial disaster, but without Black's MTV exposure to children who recognise an adult kindred spirit when they see one, one suspects that the star of *King Kong* would be a perennial goofball sidekick.

The second irony is that *School of Rock* is financed by Paramount, corporate partners of . . . oh yes . . . MTV. On the DVD's commentary, Black and director Richard Linklater wonder out loud about why their paymasters let them get away with it. The answer's simple: MTV's greatest successes, from *Beavis and Butthead* and *South Park* to *Jackass* and *The Osbournes*, are entirely based around the modern, media-savvy teen's ironic take on adult stupidity. By biting the hand that feeds them, Black and *School of Rock* writer and co-star Mike White absolutely embody the postmodern ethic of behaving in a rebellious manner while merrily signing up to everything corporate America has to offer. The more MTV slags itself off, the more the viewer can convince themselves that they aren't watching MTV at all.

Well, people, The Man is sticking it to all of us all the time, and the reason he gets away with it is because he occasionally throws us a bone, in the shape of subversive entertainment like *School of Rock*. It's one of the greatest of all rock movies, of course, but its subversive nature doesn't stem from the deliberately dumb and futile cake-and-eat-it rants against The Man uttered by Black's character, Dewey Finn. It comes from its utterly inclusive vision of the lives changed and made better by rock 'n' roll. From its uplifting and completely accurate depictions of the joy of the communal creative process. And from two complimentary lines of dialogue gifted to the school band's punk rock drummer: 'One great rock show can change the world!' and 'The Sex Pistols never won anything'. Black, White (I know . . . almost too perfect) and

Linklater are well aware that the early Sex Pistols gigs were played to a few hundred British kids, and that the ripples from that tiny pool did, indeed, change the world. They also know that the Pistols, like Elvis, like Lennon, like Cobain, were geeky weirdoes from troubled and/or poor backgrounds who, without rock 'n' roll, would have just been ... geeky weirdoes. Rock is generally sold to us as a product of the starpower of men so sexy and talented that we can only shrivel and genuflect in the face of their *ubermensch* charisma. It's a marketing lie, which is why we're stuck with Bono. Rock's real mission lies in the way it transforms outcast losers into artists and image-makers who tap into our own feelings of powerlessness and inadequacy, and make us understand that that's how everyone feels, when you come right down to the gritty and the nitty. *The School of Rock* band's symbolic line-up of nerds and fatties and black and Oriental and female and gay, led by a sexless, bumptious man-child who can't really play, is rock's egalitarian impulse personified.

Being a feelgood Hollywood comedy, the movie's ending has to involve hugging, learning and a triumphant happy ever after. But White and Linklater deal with that with something close to genius. The band lose the talent contest to the band who have designed themselves along corporate rock lines. Dewey does not become a rock star. School of Rock don't *win anything*. Except the freedom to play music together. The warm improvised comedy of the band playing together as the credits roll sees all the musicians facing each other, connecting across class, gender and racial lines, for no other reason than they can. Man ... I'm almost tearing up here.

So ... why not five stars? Well, even though I appreciate the premise of the hugging and learning, there's still too much of it. Black has to do an awful lot of mugging to make up for some of the mediocre dialogue. There's not enough of the wonderful Joan Cusack as the stressed-out headmistress. And much of the film's action is based around American mistrust of book-learning, as we're encouraged to cheer on the idea that studying is essentially pointless, and boo the parents who may have understandable mis-givings about their 11-year-olds hanging around in rock clubs with a man posing as a teacher. This last point does provide one of *School of Rock*'s funniest and most telling moments, though, when Dewey finally has to confess the truth to the kids' parents, and tries, as any idealist would, to find a positive spin. 'I've been touched by your kids – and I'm pretty sure I've touched them.' As the terrifying double-meaning of Finn's sincere tribute dawns on you, the camera cuts to stunned parents, and back to a bewildered Black ... the last person, including the children, to understand the implications of what's he said. Black's Finn is an absolute innocent, so utterly removed from sex, never mind paedophilia, that you're struck hard by the facts of your own dirty mind, and how much we've all been corrupted by child abuse fear-mongering. Quite brilliant.

Nevertheless, this doesn't entirely excuse the thankless role given to Goddess of Rude Comedy Sarah Silverman as the nagging girlfriend of Dewey's pussy-whipped friend Ned, played by White. In a film where the lead character is a child in a man's body, it's no surprise that the villain is a symbolic Mom, dismissing all dreams and adventures as childish folly, obsessed with money, living only for the possibility of taking all the boys' toys away. Her disapproval of Dewey and her boyfriend's former life in a failed metal band is a key plot device ... but it leaves a sour note of sexism within the film's otherwise immaculate Rainbow Coalition ideals. She is conspicuous by her absence at the film's end, presumably either dumped by a revitalised Ned, or stuck at home, seething at her failure to castrate her own lover.

Carp and quibble over, all that's left to do is flag up great lines, great scenes. Dewey's first conversation with class bad boy and inevitable drummer, Freddy. Dewey: 'Freddy ... what do you like to do?' Freddy: 'I dunno ... burn stuff?' The scene where Dewey assigns each class member a band job, every child rendered equal by affectionately insulting nickname, the obviously gay boy who wants to be the band's stylist labelled with nothing more homophobic than 'Fancy Pants'. This is followed by a scene where the big black girl with an incredible gospel voice whom Dewey calls 'Turkey Sub' asks to leave the band because people will laugh at her size. The plump Black tones everything down to deliver an impassioned dismissal of 21st-century body fascism.

And, finally, the movie's best one-liner. Dewey tries to con Cusack's headmistress into letting him take the kids to the Battle of the Bands audition by saying he wants to take them to see the local Philharmonic. 'They do the classics,' he assures her. 'Beethoven ... Mozart ... Enya ... ' Of such petty insults priceless comedy is made.

Sadly, since *School of Rock*, Black has become tiresome. Accepting every offer that comes your way and being in stinker after stinker always lets the public know that you don't have any real confidence in your talent and figure you'd just better do everything before you lose your appeal. A self-fulfilling prophecy. Much like Will Farrell and Ben Stiller, someone has convinced Black that he is a great improv talent who just has to mug furiously in order to split our sides. But Jim Carrey he ain't. And it's a shame, because there really is something adorable, hilarious and subversive about Black's Dewey Finn. I hope I'm wrong, but suspect that *School of Rock* is the chubby gurner's peak moment.

● ●

DiG

2004

Starring: Anton Newcombe, Courtney Taylor, The Brian Jonestown Massacre, The Dandy Warhols
Dir.: Ondi Timoner

★ ★ ★ ★ ★

Plot: Inspired rockumentary skewers the myth of the insane rock 'n' roll genius.
Key line: 'They want me dead. I'm not joking around.'

THE great rock 'n' roll documentary of the 21st century thus far finds a unique story to tell. By contrasting the fates of US West

Coast friends, rivals and 1960s *pasticheurs* the Brian Jonestown Massacre and the Dandy Warhols, female director Ondi Timoner locates an essence of the ego, insanity, compromise and self-destruction that characterizes the best and worst that rock has to offer. Seven years in the making and edited to a compelling 107 minutes from thousands of hours of fly-on-the-wall footage, *DiG* found a profitable audience way beyond fans of the two bands or alternative American rock.

It begins with a man who looks like he stepped off the set of *Easy Rider* pointing at the camera and announcing, with no irony, 'I'm here to destroy this fucked-up system.' This is the star of our show, Anton Newcombe, founder of San Francisco's the Brian Jonestown Massacre, a band whose name neatly combines his twin fascinations of drug-addled 1960s rock and murderous cult leaders by sourcing Brian Jones of the Rolling Stones and Jim Jones of Jonestown massacre infamy.

Soon we are introduced to our narrator and co-star, Courtney Taylor, leader of Portland, Oregon's better-known Dandy Warhols. His voiceover tells us that he met Newcombe in 1995, that he is 'by far the craziest and most talented musician I had ever met', that Newcombe 'was my friend and my enemy, the greatest inspiration, and, ultimately, the greatest regret', and that the film we are about to watch is 'the story of us, and our bands, over seven years'. As he says this, we are watching the pair park a car in a desert. Newcombe, in full cosmic cowboy garb, gets out, and Taylor drives away and leaves him stranded while Newcombe throws stones at him – and us – in childlike frustration. A one-minute synopsis of a story of rivalry, hubris, failure and betrayal to rival any work of modern drama.

The story is told in strict chronology. It's 1995, and we see Newcombe and Taylor bigging each other up with ludicrous hyperbole and genuinely touching selflessness. Newcombe plays Timoner a Dandies demo and brags about how 'we' are going to take over the world and his pride over the two bands' plans to build a studio together. Taylor is like an awestruck child as he says, about BJM, 'I swear they're the best band in America ... They're so crazy. I've never seen them eat. All I've seen them do is drink liquor and snort drugs!' There's soon a neat contrast between the idiot lad antics of BJM's tambourine player and ironically camp Bez-style court jester Joel Gion, and the Dandies' sweet and dignified female keyboard player Zia McCabe describing BJM as her band's 'alter egos'.

The two bands' descent from mutual infatuation to all-out warfare is the meat of the matter, injecting a kind of diseased romantic drama into Timoner's original idea of a movie about how groups deal with the clash between art and commerce as they're about to join the music industry. Her instincts told her to drop her proposed film about ten West Coast unsigned bands and con-centrate on BJM, and she was rewarded with the kind of natural conflict and darkly profound subject matter reality TV humiliates people into contriving. With Newcombe on board, there's no need for a Simon Cowell character assassination nor a Bushtucker Trial. When he fixes the camera with his attempts at an intense, cha-rismatic stare and tells us of his brilliance, we are not watching Dylan or Lennon or Rotten. We're looking at David Brent with a psychedelic junkie makeover. You prepare to wince and hide behind the sofa. And you're not disappointed.

Flies in the ointment appear thick and fast. The Dandies are already signed and on their way, albeit with the usual creative control conflicts. Newcombe is constantly undermined by his little brother, BJM guitarist Matt Hollywood, a chubby dweeb whose sibling resentment comes out in sneering denunciations of all Anton's Malcolm McLarenesque plans, but who appears to be the only person able to see through his bullshit. And, just 15 minutes into the movie, we get the scene of wilful self-destruction that most BJM observers see as the moment that killed Newcombe's career.

The band set up a showcase at Los Angeles' the Viper Room (the notorious rock lig palace where River Phoenix died) to sell themselves to Elektra Records. Minutes after announcing, 'We're gonna get the biggest record deal in history', Newcombe interrupts a song to sack a member of the band, demands free drinks 'or else we're fucking leaving', threatens to have the bouncers beat up best mate Gion for stepping on a mic lead, starts throwing punches until the band end up rolling around the stage in a comic heap, and leaves the club. Bang. Best chance over.

The fascinating thing is that, at this stage, no-one's prepared to state the obvious ... that Newcombe is a damaged and obnoxious (and only moderately talented) borderline psycho who lives in a world of his own and can't deal with, and doesn't deserve, success. That key mixture of the rock/art myth about genius and madness, plus everyone's fear of missing out on the Next Big Thing leads people to keep describing his impossible behaviour as credibility, integrity, rebellion and non-conformity, rather than pathetic abuse. How much possibility is there of anyone learning how to relate to others for their own and everyone's benefit, when a guy from one of the indie labels that does sign him feeds him stuff like, 'Sometimes, people go past the boundaries of good and evil ... into another realm. And we call these people prophets. Jesus Christ was a person like this. So was Charles Manson. They transcend the normal world.' Someone off-camera shouts 'Adolf Hitler', and one Greg Shaw of Bomp! Records happily adds the exterminator of millions to his handy list of 'prophets'. Rock life has increasingly come to imitate *This Is Spinal Tap* (see p. 264), only no-one's laughing anymore.

We are, would you believe, just 18 minutes into this extraordinary movie and it already feels like you've been told a complete story. But it's the tip of the iceberg. A look at Newcombe's parents brings revelation and shocking tragedy. He verbally abuses his sobbing girlfriend on camera and she escapes to Tahiti. And the relationship between Newcombe and Taylor turns on the Dandies' break-through hit single, 'Not If You Were the Last Junkie on Earth'. Taylor plays Newcombe the single in a car, wanting his opinion. He gets blank silence. The BJM turn up at the video shoot, scarf the free food, and then take the piss out of the song and the video. Newcombe and his band have seen that their friends are going to make it, and their jealousy forces them to reveal their rank loathing for others' success, hiding behind that old self-righteous chestnut about 'selling out'. From then on, the Dandy Warhols are the Enemy.

But on the other hand, Taylor and Co. are happy to feed off their rivals' real-life heroin-fuelled dissolution, knowing it will look cool but remain a much safer pose if they don't actually have to live it. While Newcombe unsurprisingly denounced *DiG* after its release, Taylor, by his agreement to narrate, accepts the occasionally unflattering portrayal of his own ambition and somewhat vampiric attachment to his former friend.

And then . . . nope, no more plot here. Every few minutes brings a new twist to this cautionary tale about indulging junkies who need therapy rather than a round of applause for all their fuck-ups, and more description will just spoil your enjoyment. I'll just alert you to a scene involving roller-skates, a furry hat and a man making himself into a laughing stock in front of the entire music industry, and leave you to look forward to the visceral cringe.

• •

Ray

2004
Starring: Jamie Foxx, some decent actors who deserve better
Dir.: Taylor Hackford

★

Plot: Man wins 'Best Actor in Sunglasses' Oscar!
Key line: 'Mr Charles – you're not the first celebrity junkie I've treated.'

Ray was made to win Oscars. The sick, cruel, racist America stylised to fuck until it has the requisite glow of nostalgic cool around it. The leading man playing disabled and making his every word and movement as self-conscious and actorly as is humanly possible. Ludicrous story gimmicks about why Ray Charles wears sunglasses and how he just bumps into Quincy Jones busking in the street five minutes after arriving in the city and walks into his first jazz club and the other acts all conveniently fall sick. It's one of those American films that wants to fuel its audience's belief in 'manifest destiny', presenting the American Dream as a series of miracles beyond the ken of mere mortals. Even deeply ingrained redneck racism – Charles gets called a 'blind nigger' so often in the first ten minutes it starts to sound like a mantra – is easily overcome, as if it's just the curmudgeonly reaction of decent working folk before the star's starriness makes them immediately recant. The way the clichés are packed into the movie's opening scenes – right down to a dream Mommy telling Ray what to do and the hard-assed female club-owner using Charles for sex – is embarrassing. Lest we forget, Ray Charles did not look like Jamie Foxx.

The back story flashback device is especially hack(ford)neyed. The idea that the guy gets forgiven for being a total bastard by Mom and dead brother in a dream and then lives happily ever after ... fuck me, words fail me. And this whole obsession with dead brothers (see *Walk the Line*, p. 392) gives *Walk Hard: The Dewey Cox Story* (see p. 406) plenty to poke fun at. Like Hackford's earlier hit *An Officer and a Gentlemen*, this is Hollywood film-making-by-numbers, that cynical contempt for the punter's ability to react to a story without everything being underlined and thumped into our heads with a mallet.

And Foxx? Get real. This is not an acting performance. It's an impersonation. The guy was better in Michael Mann's *Collateral*, and that is a deeply stupid movie. The Oscar was a mixture of 'give it to the guy who plays disabled' and a decision that it was someone black's turn.

How bad does it get? How about this for an insulting scene in a film that pretends it's liberal? Having just made his first record, Charles is now apparently shagging every good-looking black woman who comes to see him play. The way he decides if a woman's worth fucking is by feeling her wrist. See where this is going? Cue the fat woman. He feels her fleshy wrist and recoils in horror. That's Oscar-winning stuff, all right.

There's something equally insulting about the implication that a square white guy from a major label had to tell Ray Charles how to be Ray Charles, and accomplished this feat in around 30 seconds. Ahmet Ertegun of Atlantic Records was a pioneering and brilliant A&R man. But I'm not buying, for one second, the idea that Charles was just a slick tribute act until this guy sang him an R&B ditty. Badly. The scene is in such stark contrast to the meeting between Johnny Cash and Sam Phillips in *Walk the Line*, where a real and complex and intense confrontation between the two *allows* Cash to find himself. Yet Cash was a musical ingenue at this point in his story whereas Charles was already a seasoned virtuoso. Are you really telling me it had never occurred to him to play jump-jive, or that that suggestion alone made Charles into a success? Fuck. Right. Off.

The best thing about *Ray* is that it gave some paid work to Richard Schiff from *The West Wing* and Robert Wisdom and Wendell Pierce from *The Wire*. All else is the current Hollywood vogue for showing African-Americans having natural rhythm and Olympian sexual appetites, shouting a lot very quickly, and weeping and wailing in churches. Twenty years since Spike Lee's *Do the Right Thing* and still American film can't bear to put a three-dimensional black character on screen, even when it's the man who invented soul music. Will a black president change anything in Hollyweird? It has to. It *surely* has to.

Still ... did you know that blind people, like, compensate for their blindness by developing their other senses? Who knew? Or that blind people put their sunglasses on before attempting post-coital conversation? Or that blind people are given super-hearing in seconds by their tough-loving Mommas not picking them up when they fall over? Or that every black woman Ray Charles met wanted to have sex with him but then either used him or nagged him 'cos all black women are moaning Mommas or scheming gold-digger sluts that have nothing better to do than fight over men?

And ... and ... Oh Lord Have Mercy, I've spent 146 minutes watching this dreck and this is 146 minutes of my life that I'll never get back. You know that cliché about living every moment like it's your last? Watching *Ray* makes every moment feel like your last.

This is the *Forrest Gump* of rock movies.

• •

Last Days

2005

Starring: Michael Pitt, Lukas Haas, Asia Argento, Scott Green
Dir.: Gus Van Sant

★ ★

**Plot: The final days of Kurt Cobain's life. Except that it isn't.
Key line: 'Success is subjective. Y'know?'**

As the closing credits confirm, *Last Days* is 'inspired in part by the
last days of Kurt Cobain'. But if you're wanting a film that offers
clues about what really happened at Lake Washington in the early
days of April 1994, then beware, because this definitely isn't it.
What US art-house director Gus Van Sant does offer is a curiously
disengaged study of the last days of a depressed rock star who
dresses like Kurt Cobain. Michael Pitt plays Blake, and has a way
with glassy-eyed and dysfunctional rock stars, after his Tommy
Gnosis in *Hedwig and the Angry Inch* (see p. 362). There's no
Courtney or Frances Bean or Nirvana, and although everyone in
the house in the woods where events take place behaves as if they're
on drugs, there are no actual drugs. There is a shotgun, but we
never see or hear it being fired. All similarities to persons living or
dead are purely inconsequential.

Van Sant creates an emotionless, deliberately dull but picturesque
mise en scène where the sounds of water falling, birds singing and a
fire burning overwhelm any human sounds. The director's ability
to make a bedraggled hippy walking up a country path to a house
look fascinating and feel ominous – without any incidental music –
is extraordinary.

As for Pitt – Blake is an actor's dream role. There's nothing to do but slump and mumble. You can almost hear Van Sant shouting: – 'Cut! Cut! . . . That's great Michael. But you almost got, y'know, a little animated there. Could you maybe amp up the slump, and double up on the mumble? Great, great . . . once more, with no feeling!' Having said that, the bit where he has to slowly crumple into a crouching foetal position shows great physical dexterity. Uh . . . sorry. There's something about watching *Last Days* that makes you start thinking in sentences like that. It shrinks and slows the world until you trip mentally on tiny movements or gestures onscreen. Sort of like acid, but without the fluorescent colours or the buzzing noise.

For the first ten minutes, there's nothing except Blake going for a swim, walking around, sitting around, stumbling down a grassy hillock, and mumbling incomprehensibly. When we do get something different, it's a boy and a girl (Green as Scott and Argento as Asia) in bed, asleep. Then it's back to the walking and stumbling.

Blake is filthy throughout – you can almost smell his body odour, and the dirt in the house's kitchen makes you itch.

After 15 minutes, Blake puts on a black nightie and gets a shotgun out of a closet. Not an (audible) word of dialogue so far. And then . . . a phone rings! Blake picks up the phone, and . . . *and* . . . words! Blake says nowt, but a guy on the other end of the line is trying to talk to him about an upcoming tour. Blake hangs up on him. He stares vacantly into the middle-distance.

And then other stuff does begin to happen. Confoundingly mundane stuff. And it happens very slowly and very quietly. It's quite funny, in a no-one's-laughing kind of way – Blake sitting in his negligée and biker boots in his lounge with a man from the *Yellow Pages* who is trying to sell him advertising space for Blake's locomotive shop. No, Blake doesn't really have a locomotive shop. When the *Yellow Pages* man says that he'll come back to clinch the deal on Tuesday, you know that will be far too late.

Van Sant dwells on small details. Two young male twins from the Church of Latter Day Saints come by. Van Sant puts a static camera on them, and they take on an unlikely beauty. While one starts in on the history of his religion, the other mouths the words along with him, and you get a glimpse of how the pair have practised and practised this ideantical speech, and how this routine is all their teenage lives have been.

At this point you wonder if this is a blacker-than-black comedy about the way the American mainstream constantly invades the world of the avowed outsider. When Blake passes out, the sound-track isn't 'Lithium' or 'All Apologies' – or 'The End' or 'Sister Morphine', for that matter. It's the schmaltzy video of 'On Bended Knee' by Boyz II Men. And then Blake just wakes up again, and 'life' goes on.

Van Sant makes you look at film, at the world, differently. In one scene, a private detective played by actor and magician Ricky Jay is in a car, telling a story about a magician called Billy Robinson. At first, you do the conventional thing, which is listen to the story and try to find its point. But you're very quickly distracted, and then mesmerised, by the way the trees that line the road are reflected in the windscreen, covering the actors' faces, making them – and us – seem small and ugly in comparison. But there is a point to the conversation. Robinson died on the stage of London's Wood Green Empire in 1918 trying and failing to catch a bullet in his teeth. 'To this day, there's all sorts of speculation about what really happened,' Jay informs us. 'Was it an attempt to commit suicide? He had some rocky relationship with his wife . . . '

After 46 minutes Blake finally picks up a guitar and, with the help of some multi-tracking skullduggery, plays a fabulous piece of droning and agonised post-rock psychedelia. It's much better than anything by Nirvana, except 'Smells Like Teen Spirit', 'About a Girl' and 'Sliver', which are all great. In essence, it's a man in a room picking up random instruments while the camera backs further and further away from him. But again, the whole sequence has a hyp-notic power.

Kim Gordon makes a cameo (as does Van Sant's fellow post-punk director Harmony Korine) as herself. She asks Blake if he's spoken to his daughter and calls him 'a rock 'n' roll cliché'. Probably therapy for her – her band Sonic Youth recommended Nirvana to the Geffen label and were mentors to Cobain and many others on the grunge scene. She tries to get him to leave with her, and she's motherly and real, and she fails and you feel the loss of all this, and all the friends and family who wonder if they could've saved Cobain. It's the one moment in *Last Days* where insight seems possible.

Occasionally, what you think is the next thing happening is actually something you've already seen, but started from another point in time. The device makes its point about a life that has become so aimless and repetitive that the passage of time has become irrelevant. But it's not much fun. *Last Days* is the film that fun forgot.

After all this grimly objective art, the way Van Sant chooses to show Blake's death is bizarrely corny. And you can't help wondering if the better film emerges in the final ten minutes, as the 'friends' who've shared his final days see the death on the TV news and scarper like murder suspects, without a thought for the man.

Which is why, despite being a unique and intellectually charged piece of film-making, *Last Days* gets the two-star treatment. You feel, around about the halfway mark, that Van Sant's major agenda here is not a study of the end of a life, but a challenge to the viewer to not get bored with the lack of action or emotional engagement. In both *Last Days* and 2003's *Elephant* (which is 'about' the Columbine High School shootings in much the same way that *Last Days* is 'about' Cobain's death), Van Sant's mission to look at major American news events without Hollywood sensation or sentiment is brave and valuable. Both pictures fly in the face of mainstream movie-making while remaining technically accomplished, and someone has to do that. But *Elephant* works because the victims of the shootings weren't famous. By looking at something so senseless with a coldly objective eye, Van Sant makes you understand that this could happen anywhere, at any time, because unhappy people do horrifying things, and we live and work and go to school with them, with no clue of what they're capable of.

But *Last Days* is about an iconic *individual* – an individual whom Van Sant doesn't seem interested in as anything other than a specimen in a laboratory. The sardonic humour fades through repetition and, once it does, we don't have anything here to cling on to. Sure . . . maybe severe depression does feel like this. But what you wind up concentrating upon is the film buff stuff of interesting camera angles and unusual sound design. It seems like a callous and narcissistic way to treat a suicide victim, and it makes for an impressive, but empty, cinematic experience.

Anyone with an interest in Cobain or left-field film should see it, though. Once.

● ●

Walk the Line

2005

Starring: Joaquin Phoenix, Reese Witherspoon, Ginnifer Goodwin, Robert Patrick
Dir.: James Mangold

★ ★ ★ ★

Plot: The life and times of young Johnny Cash.
Key line: 'You can't help nobody if you can't tell 'em the right story.'

By the time Johnny Cash died, he'd become a global icon of authenticity. So it's only fitting that, when you first see Joaquin Phoenix as Cash, after ten minutes or so of sad and poignant things about Cash's tough sharecropper upbringing, bad Dad and dead brother, you're almost pinned back in your seat by how real Phoenix is. He seems less to be acting Cash and more like he's channelled him from the grave. The granite demeanour. The hint of a sullen sneer just around the lips. The voice so deep it booms even when it mumbles. Yet Phoenix never settles for a mere impersonation. His richness of character is the solid foundation of a wonderful movie.

There are lots of things lots of us think we know about country's most rock 'n' roll star. But I didn't know, before seeing *Walk the Line*, that he had a wife before June Carter, or that he was selling 'home equipment' door-to-door when he first stumbled upon Sun Studios in Memphis, the tiny, incendiary building where he and Elvis and Jerry Lee Lewis would invent different kinds of white rock 'n' roll. *Walk the Line* is the opposite kind of biopic to Oliver Stone's *The Doors*: it seeks to ground the myth of the transcendent star in the realities that created him. But it also has no interest in making myth into mundanity ... when Cash stumbles upon Sun, he's also stumbling upon teenage Elvis recording 'Milk Cow Blues'. Can you imagine? You're a young musician from Nowheresville and one day you just bump into the world shifting upon its axis!

There is enormous joy here for rock buffs, but not presented in a way that will irritate the casual viewer. When Cash introduces himself to Sam Phillips – the man who did more than any other individual to usher in a new age of racial and musical miscegenation – the owner of Sun studios mentions his receptionist by name. Marion Kreisker is the woman who convinced a sceptical Phillips that he should give that funny-looking Elvis boy a second chance to record for him. Later, screenwriters Mangold and Gill Dennis use a car journey to a show to pay tribute to one of the most reported conversations in rock history, when Jerry Lee Lewis interrupted the recording of 'Great Balls of Fire' to rant bizarrely at Sam Phillips about how singing this rock 'n' roll was going to ensure that he and everyone involved was going to Hell. Best of all, in the audition scene, Phoenix and Dallas Roberts, who plays Phillips, achieve an extraordinary level of intensity when Phillips informs Cash that he simply doesn't believe him when he sings gospel. Cash is not some ready-made genius and Phillips is not a saint ... visionaries rarely are. In a small room in Memphis in the mid 1950s, you feel history being made by angry, honest conversations like this, and you realise just how much Mangold has committed to this story, and how much he wants to get away from the personality cult arse-licking of the standard biopic. He understands that he's dealing with key moments in American cultural history, and that moments like those are never about an individual's talent or destiny. They're about social change, and how groups of individuals, understanding exactly the right thing at exactly the right time, can force those changes through. In that context, the sparse and deadly version of 'Folsom Prison Blues' with which Cash/Phoenix responds to Phillips' goading is astonishing, Phoenix full of barely suppressed loathing, his voice funereal and doomed. I cry every time I watch it for what the moment must have meant to the four men in that room as they understood just what Johnny Cash could come to mean.

This is a story so solid and unsensational that Mangold can afford to make Elvis bloomin' Presley a bit-part player ('That boy Elvis sure likes to talk poon'). The recreations of Cash's music are stunning and Reese Witherspoon's bright-eyed and tough June Carter is the ideal light to Phoenix's darkness. When the pair duet on Dylan's 'It Ain't Me Babe' it transmits a joy and humour and power that stands alongside any of the 'real' musical performances in this book. Making John and June's romance more central to the tale than the music, or success, or even the Folsom Prison show that defined Cash's career, could have been a lazy move. But this is a love that lasted until both passed away, and so few of us experience that in the modern world that Mangold is absolutely right to make it the biggest thing in Cash's life. Of course, first wife Viv is therefore presented as a shrew to justify the great man's abandonment of his family. But the film is based on two Cash autobiographies, and if that's the way he presented it, then that's the way it is.

Do you ever think about that? About what it must be like to have been part of a famous person's story? When the star reveals all about their past – from their viewpoint only, mind – they're hailed as honest and wise and doing us all a great service. When the unknown strike back at being criticised in public by selling their story to a publisher or paper, they're despised as traitors and parasites. Now it's on celluloid, Vivian Cash will go down in history as a grabby domestic gold-digger who wasn't fit to be the wife of a legend. There'll never be a right of reply for her. Seems kinda wrong.

But screw that ... back to the stars, eh? Can you believe that there was ever a package tour featuring Elvis, Cash, Jerry Lee and

Roy Orbison, all playing small halls in the back of fucking beyond? What is your future like, when you've seen that show as a kid? Do you feel possessed of special knowledge about the Meaning of Life? Or does everything – sex, travel, love, kids – just seem like some cosmic anti-climax? Or was it just like most things . . . you just don't realise, at the time, that this is anything *that* special? Interestingly, the guys that play Presley and Lewis here don't even get close to sounding like them. You don't wanna start stealing the scene from the Man in Black in his own biopic, I guess.

When we get into Cash's drink and drugs demise, *Walk the Line* gets it spot-on again. Basically . . . it looks like fun, at first. And a useful way to block out pain. That's why we do it. It's difficult to tell a story about a poor southern boy who becomes a legend without some kind of all-American moralising, but Mangold does his level best to avoid it and just tell the story. After all, Cash lived until he was 71 and stayed with the love of his life. So the argument that hedonism is always a destroyer of people doesn't really hold here. Neither does Mangold try and convince us that Cash was different from the rest of us because he had a talent for singing. He got pranged. After a while he had to stop because it fucks up your head and your body, and that isn't easy, but he did it. That's the story. And many more of us have done that than been teetotal or inhaled our own vomit. The agony of being too much in love with being in love is the potential killer here.

If you're going through one of those perfectly understandable 'I despise Hollywood values' moments, then this is a film to snap you out of it. You know how hard everyone worked to get the old settings right and understand Cash and Carter's characters and make everything look and sound convincing. But it feels effortless as you watch it. It's what American film-making does best – tell a story with art and heart and lead it with beautiful people who make you feel good about – rather than threatened by – their charisma. It's slick and polished and easy on the eye and the head. But it has substance, too, and wears that substance lightly. The chemistry between Phoenix and Witherspoon is remarkable and makes you walk out of a cinema believing in the inevitable triumph of true love. Robert Patrick of *Terminator* fame is a memorable paternal monster. And the music is just plain stunning. Rock biopics are never masterpieces. But *Walk the Line* is as close as it gets.

• •

The U.S. vs. John Lennon

2006
Starring: John Lennon, Yoko Ono
Dir: David Leaf and John Scheinfeld

★ ★ ★

Plot: The price of being bigger than Jesus.
Key line: 'He would be looked upon as a tool.'

This documentary about John Lennon's running battles with the government of his adopted country in the late 1960s/early 1970s is not a spectacular piece of film-making. Contemporary footage of Lennon and Yoko Ono is spliced with footage of various anti-establishment protests, and various counter-culture talking heads comment about the times. Standard stuff. The left-wing intellectual cast-list is impressive – Noam Chomsky, Tariq Ali, Gore Vidal, Angela Davis, Walter Kronkite, the Smothers Brothers, John Sinclair and George McGovern all contribute – but none say anything especially incendiary or surprising. Lennon's music is a constant soundtrack but it's never put in a context that would explain to a casual watcher why he was perceived as such a threat by a body as powerful as the American government. Lennon's various avant-shenanigans with Yoko come off as naive at best, embarrassing at worst. In terms of either pure cinema or emotional frisson, it doesn't come close to a *Gimme Shelter* (see p. 104) or something like Michael Moore's *Bowling for Columbine*. But *The U.S. vs. John Lennon* is still a must-see film for anyone interested in both the history of rock and the revolutionary movements of the late 20th century. More specifically, it's a well-made, easily understood document of a time when rock music meant more than a branch of the entertainment business was ever meant to, and of what that means to a famous individual who decides to stand up and say rebellious stuff. If you want to know why rock lost its nerve and began to avoid political controversy, then this documentary will answer most of your questions.

Leaf and Scheinfeld choose to begin their story on 10 December 1971 at Ann Arbor, Michigan. A 15,000-strong benefit concert to rally support for John Sinclair, the Detroit-based left-wing activist and leader of the White Panther Party who had been jailed two-and-a-half years earlier for marijuana possession. Lennon and Ono top a bill that includes Stevie Wonder (and I wonder if blind, black men ended up in as many FBI files as Scouse rockers?) and radical leaders Jerry Rubin and Bobby Seale. The film fingers this as the moment when Lennon moved from hippy advocate of love and peace to potentially dangerous revolutionary. A link is then made between this key counter-cultural moment and the far bigger 1966 scandal when a facetious Lennon remark about the Beatles being 'more popular than Jesus at the moment' was twisted into blasphemy, prompting a spate of record burnings and frenzied denunciations of the Beatles across America. Lennon kept explaining what he'd meant by the comment but refused to completely back down. The other Beatles stayed solidly with him. They survived the attack and thrived and became increasingly influential upon American youth. American power decided that Lennon could be a threat. Lennon realised that he had not just survived a career-killing moment but had multiplied the Beatles' street cred and felt empowered to say what he wanted in public. The gap between the working-class rocker's ironic sense of humour and an American Christian right that was looking for excuses to attack both rock and a rising student counter-culture gave birth to a love–hate relationship between Lennon and America that was bound to end badly. There was only ever one inevitable loser in that scrap.

The movie also offers opportunities to see counter-cultural events that many under-40s have heard about but probably never seen. The 1968 Democratic Convention riots. The chaotic Grosvenor

Square anti-Vietnam war rallies in London. Martin Luther King speaking and marching. The Black Panthers. The Yippies. The murder of four student protesters at Kent State University in Ohio by the National Guard. Lennon and Ono doing press conferences in a bag. All the somewhat contrived sub-Ché Guevara trappings (rebel army shirts, black berets) of John and Yoko's radical phase. John and Yoko's infamous Amsterdam 'bed-in', which was preposterous and altogether wonderful in its mocking of the press. It's refreshing, too, to get some information about the human cost of the sick folly that was the Vietnam War without seeing gung-ho American directors and actors transforming the carnage into cool by way of method mugging and Doors songs. The non-musical material is presented simply and clearly and with such good faith you can almost forgive the inevitable montage of protest images set to 'Imagine'. Almost.

There is also a dark comedy in the film. Because, in the excellent archive footage of chat shows (it's so weird to watch famous people chain-smoking on mainstream TV!) and press conferences, Lennon is quite obviously talking almost total bollocks. Don't get me wrong – he's charismatic, charming, sincere and always witty. And he has moments, like when he tells the assembled media at the Montreal bed-in: 'We're selling it like soap. And you've got to sell and sell until the housewife thinks, "Oh – there's peace and war. That's the two products".' But the meat of statements like 'If a black man goes for a job in a bag ... there'd be no prejudice' falls from the bone under even the slightest critical scrutiny. What's funny is that, in the years after the McCarthy witch-hunts, the Kennedy assassination, Vietnam, race and youth rioting and the skullduggery of spooks like Nixon and J. Edgar Hoover, the 1970s American establishment was so insecure and paranoid that the gauche chunterings of a northern pop singer were perceived as a political threat that had to be dealt with like the proverbial butterfly being broken on a wheel. It's Lennon's limitations as a spokesman for a generation, rather than his strengths, that expose how close America was to falling apart in the early 1970s.

But you'd have to be one hard-hearted punk cynic not to get

emotional when watching the joy Lennon generates at a performance of 'Give Peace a Chance' at a bed-in. You can only
imagine the optimism in the room and wonder how the moment
affected the people lucky enough to be there. One of the things *The
U.S. vs. John Lennon* very usefully does is build up a feeling of vital
times, slowly, layer upon layer, until you get some understanding
of the emotions involved in believing that a non-violent revolution
is possible, and that your moral force is surely undeniable. I'd very
much like to feel like that, one day. That collective joy is what we
deny ourselves when we succumb to fear of struggle, separate from
one another and resign ourselves to conforming. It's a feeling we
sometimes get to replicate, at a gig, a club, even at the football. But
we pay to have those moments, and get our money's worth, and
drift apart again. All consumerist glory is fleeting.

When the film finally gets into the FBI and US Immigration's
attacks on Lennon, the optimism vanishes. The cleverness of a
strategy that embroiled Lennon in a long struggle to win his 'Green
Card' to stay in New York, therefore both distracting him from his
political interests and compelling him to keep his mouth shut and
his nose clean, was truly fiendish. And just in case anyone thinks
all this conspiracy stuff is made up, we get evidence from the likes
of former FBI agents M. Wesley Swearingen and John C. Ryan,
and erstwhile Nixon aides John Dean and the utterly unrepentant
G. Gordon Libby.

The irony, of course, is that America's gun culture killed Lennon.
If he had simply given in and come back to Britain, surely he would
have enjoyed a long and fruitful career of making awful records and
being involved in hilarious high-profile divorces. He won his battle
against The Man and it cost him his life.

But, at the same time, this was an America that had given
Lennon prime TV time to talk to Black Panther leader Bobby
Seale, perform anti-war songs, explain himself and the peacenik
cause to the masses. The split personality of the American body
politic continues to amaze – a country that can elect symbols as
powerful and diametrically opposed as George W. Bush and Barack
Obama in quick succession – and it's America's complexity and

extremes of good and evil that provide the context for a great story, which Leaf and Scheinfield present with integrity and rigour, even allowing for the tiresome hippy sentimentality of their ending.

Incidentally, if you do think – and who can blame you? – that pop stars doing politics was never anything but futile, the John Sinclair Freedom Party show might give you a wee pause for thought. The day before the show, the Michigan courts refused Sinclair's appeal to be released from prison on bond. The Monday after the Lennon performance attracted enormous publicity for Sinclair, the Michigan Supreme Court reversed its decision and released Sinclair. Sinclair is alive and well today, is still active politically and artistically, and performed in 2008 at my friend Alie Allerton's Rough Trade Vintage shop in Notting Hill, West London.

Rock is always being castigated for failing to change the world. But it changed individual lives for the better when it got its act together, braved opposition and aimed for something possible. If it doesn't do that now, it's not because it can't change anything. It's because it doesn't have the balls.

● ●

Dream Girls

2006

Starring: Beyoncé Knowles, Jamie Foxx, Eddie Murphy, Danny Glover, Jennifer Hudson, Anika Noni Rose
Dir.: Bill Condon

★ ★ ★

Plot: Half a great movie about how Motown changed the world. And half a lousy movie for dummies who like stage musicals.
Key line: 'Your voice alone is too ... *special*. We need a lighter sound to cross over to the pop charts.'

Maybe, to do this slick black Americana thing right, you just need the right director. Bill Condon made the big film version of the ubiquitous *Chicago*, and while its updated Bob Fosse-meets-MTV moves aren't my cup of tea, even I can appreciate that it is high-impact musical cinema. *Dream Girls* is another hit Broadway musical; its songs largely suck and the plot is as over-stylised and insubstantial as that of *Ray* (see p. 285). But it scores as solid, quality pop entertainment because it has one important element that its competitors lack completely ... a point. And when it doesn't have a point, it has Eddie Murphy and Jennifer Hudson.

Murphy's James Thunder Early is a fictional James Brown-alike and slimy creep, played with a light, self-mocking touch that should be taken as Acting 101 for the current generation of eye-rolling, Stepin Fetchit types that pass as black comedy actors. Murphy's gritty soul vocals are a revelation, too. Former *American Idol* contestant Hudson's Effie is the righteous, intimidating, big-boned black Princess that sorts the men from the misogynists with a grind of the hips and the sneer on her lips. Both light up this neat tale of how Tamla Motown crossed black music over to whites and ended the pre-1960s American evil that was 'race music'. It does so without preaching and with just the right amount of soap to engage those who aren't really arsed about the political subtext. And suddenly all the nostalgic sets and the million-dollar clothes budgets have a point, and look gorgeous rather than gratuitous.

At least, that's the case for the first hour of the film ... a funny and true history lesson defined by the wonderful scene where Early's bluesy 'Cadillac Car' song gets stopped in its chartbusting tracks by a squeaky clean, Brady Bunchified version on peak-time early 1960s TV, as heroines and *faux*-Supremes the Dreamettes look on, stunned, from their cramped sofa. This is almost matched by a montage of the Martin Luther King 'I Have a Dream' speech cut with the set-up of a black-owned record pressing plant, making copies of the same speech. It makes its point eloquently about the correlation between the dream of freedom and the ownership and control of the means of production ... and then fucks off quickly and cuts to an angry Ms Hudson striding into the office of Curtis Taylor Jr (Foxx) like a force of nature ... a whole other symbol of freedom. She chides Curtis for releasing the King album while she can't even get a B-side ... 'I mean, can he even sing?' ... lets the rant sink in and terrify the man ... and then reveals that she's just taking the piss, and that of course she sees the Bigger Picture. Foxx laughs uneasily, can't recover his composure, reveals, in his discomfort, that he knows that a big picture is made up of several small pictures.

By keeping the naive elements of a stage musical, clichés like montages that cover huge swathes of space and time in seconds, and onstage musical numbers that would have been far too glossy, expensive and Jazz Hands to work on a black 1960s tour, and 'Let's do the show right here!' speeches take on their own kind of hyper-real logic. But that's what happens when you're Bill Condon, and you wrote the screenplay that you're directing, and you've given yourself scenes brave enough to take on the complexities of what crossing over to the white market in the Civil Rights era really meant.

When Curtis succeeds in booking Early and the Dreamettes into a white, upmarket venue in Miami, it should be either triumph or disaster. It's neither. A godawful Rat Pack-style comic introduces Jimmy and the girls onstage with a repulsively racist joke. When they begin the song, you immediately get the new sound that Curtis has been talking about; restrained, sophisticated, pretty, romantic, unthreatening. But Early can't stick to the plan. Driven by both the lukewarm audience response and his desire for Rose's Lorrell, he lets rip, and takes the song to church. Which, in soul terms ... and this is why soul was as controversial for black elders as rock was for whites ... means taking it straight to his groin. The voice becomes ragged, bluesy and desperate. His movements are grinding and suggestive. And the response from the audience is ... exactly what it must have been at the time. A few are so disgusted that they leave. A few begin to smile and enjoy. Most are curious but non-committal. In a poor film, Jimmy would have ended generations of racism and fear of sex right there or had to beat a hasty retreat from a lynching. But things are never as good or bad as all that. Things percolate. Slowly. And cause as much confusion or disinterest as they do outrage or revolution.

Which means that the film earns the right to introduce its key plot point 43 minutes in, and trust the viewer to understand the whys and wherefores. When Curtis finally takes the Dreamettes off backing vocals and launches them as the Dreams ... he tells his girlfriend Effie that lead vocals will now be performed by Deena ... and you're right – Deena is a bit like Diana, isn't it? The truth is that the prettier, skinnier, less threatening Deena will cross over to white teens in a way that Effie's uncompromised blackness won't. Curtis is right, just as the Supremes' mentor Berry Gordy was right to make Diana Ross his first superstar. But at what cost? The subject of black musicians who compromise to cross over to white consumers is still a controversial subject among black music fans. Hip hop is celebrated for 'keeping it real' because, on the surface, it does not seek to make itself whiter or tone down its language to suit white standards. But when a well-educated, classy black man affects gangsta postures to sell his rap career, is he not just playing the same game with more modern rules? All this – plus the equally vexed question of what kind of woman is acceptable to the main-stream – is what the best of *Dream Girls* is about. And it goes about its task by asking questions rather than providing easy answers. We know all about the world-changing impact of Motown's elegant take on soul music. But did black culture win or lose from this impact?

Individuals lost, of course. They always do. The scene where Effie finds out she's being sidelined is followed by an oily ballad about how Rainbow Records is a family, and which cleverly uses all the images of the Civil Rights struggle – freedom, getting your share, community, seeing the Bigger Picture – to persuade her to submit to the will of her male owners. The song sounds like a big, bland lie, and it's meant to. This is followed by the new, improved, Deena-led Dreams' performance of the movie's theme song, which turns out to be an ironic little ditty about the production of submissive female fantasy figures for male benefit. And finally I'm starting to realise why *Dream Girls* wasn't a hit, despite winning a Best Picture Golden Globe and a Best Supporting Actress Oscar for Ms Hudson. Like *Josie and the Pussycats* (see p. 354) it has a bitter, late 1960s/1970s-derived anger at how pop is used to dupe its audience, while looking like sumptuously expensive 21st-century escapist pop product. It walks like *American Idol* but talks like *Slade in Flame*. This jaundiced view of pop's role in society didn't put bums on seats in its prime, and it sure ain't going to do it when it costs millions of dollars and showcases a pop superstar who's received little but praise for transcending her 'band' and going for solo gold. It's just too many ironies for fans of girl groups and musicals to take, being made to feel implicated for liking what they like. As dumped manager Marty (Glover) tells Early on his way out of his career, 'You can't have it all, Jimmy.' Maybe someone should have said that to Bill.

Shame it bombed, then, 'cos people missed the explosive row between the principals, all done in gospel call-and-response, which slips gracefully into Jennifer Hudson's astonishing performance of the musical's one great song, 'And I'm Telling You I'm Not Going', which ripped my heart right out of my hairy chest and stomped it into ready-made Garry escalope on my living-room floor. Poor Jamie Foxx ... the guy looks like he's been caught in the wake of a huge oestrogen tidal wave and ends up scurrying offscreen, bedraggled and bewildered and in need of sunglasses and a dead brother to remind him that he once served a practical purpose in a movie other than just trying to stay upright against the full force of Ms Hudson's atomic-powered Divatude.

But this, disappointingly, turns out to be the movie's peak moment. It all goes a bit pear-shaped when it heads out of Detroit and the light, bright 1960s and into LA and the dark old 1970s (just like Motown itself!), and starts slagging off disco, badly pastiching the Jackson 5, equating soul with maudlin self-pity, and making Curtis into a moustache-twiddling panto bad guy. And, like so many 21st-century films, it's too bloody long. It's like albums ... they should either last 40 minutes or be as good as *It Takes a*

Nation of Millions to Hold Us Back. Films should last 90 minutes or be as good as *Goodfellas.*

There are other flaws, too. Foxx often seems to be a confused bystander rather than the leading man. It's a bit odd when Murphy's Early suddenly morphs into Marvin Gaye for about 20 seconds before becoming Teddy Pendergrass. And then James Brown again. And then Brian Jones. Jimmy Early really is all things to all men.

And the music? I'm the first to admit that I don't really understand or have any feel for the stage musical. If your show is based on Motown, shouldn't you at least attempt to replicate the sound and match the power of the originals? Well, no, obviously, because then you wouldn't fulfil the first rule of the modern musical, which is that the songs should be a sugary, fussy, over-produced version of something that was good once. I don't get it.

But the biggest surprise is that the camera does not fall hopelessly in love with Beyoncé Knowles. It's an interestingly selfless choice for her first film role, a character who is seen as a symbol of compromise and who is constantly charged with being less talented than Hudson. She isn't just blown offscreen as an actress. She gets her bootylicious bits kicked all over the shop by Hudson as a singer, too. She seems like a child amongst charismatic adults here, and just disappears from her own film, in a similarly resigned way to Mariah Carey in *Glitter* (see p. 358).

The film is fascinatingly, brutally critical of Berry Gordy and Diana Ross, though. Names are never used ... but the story's just too close to the story of Motown and the Supremes to be about anyone else. What do they make of how they've been portrayed, for posterity's sake? Perhaps they can live with the film's terrible ending, the kind of ending that just has to happens in musicals ... reconciliation, hugs and kisses, the final show-stopping number. In real life, original sacked Supreme Florence Ballard died poor, depressed and alcoholic, in 1976, at the age of 32. Make a musical out of that.

• •

Walk Hard: The Dewey Cox Story

2007
Starring: John C. Reilly, Jenna Fischer, Tim Meadows
Dir.: Jake Kasdan

★ ★ ★

Plot: Rock biopics get the *Scary Movie* treatment
Key line: 'You're gonna have to give him a moment, son.
Dewey Cox needs to think about his entire life before he
plays.'

This overlooked spoof of the rock biopic should be watched after
Walk the Line (see p. 392), its chief inspiration. The first few minutes
are choice: Reilly as Cox posing pensively against a wall, the light
catching him just so's he can look suitably deep and iconic. An old
black guy says the key line above, and we're soon flashing back to
a typically mythic deep south, watching Cox and his perfect brother
defy death in increasingly daft ways before Dewey chops his older
sibling in half with a machete and is declared 'smell blind' by his
Momma. As I say, you have to watch *Walk the Line* and the insult-
ingly trite *Ray* before you know why these scenes are so funny.
Which is perhaps why *Walk Hard* . . . failed to find an audience,
despite being one of the better recent music-based comedies.

You really need to have seen a whole bunch of lame music biopics
to know why the scene where a 14-year-old Cox (still played by 42-
year-old Reilly, which is funny to anyone who has seen *Grease* [see
p. 178], come to think of it) performs a knowingly lightweight, sub-
Pat Boone ditty at his high school dance and sends the gathered
grown-ups into an anti-Devil's Music fury and the girls into a
sexual frenzy is spot-on. Or why the more repulsive Reilly looks in
his perpetual smelly-looking Y-fronts, the more pussy he seems to
get. Or why the running joke about drugs is so great, where Cox
keeps bursting into rooms where his black drummer Sam is getting
high with groups of gorgeous women and asking what's going on.

'You don't want no part of this shit,' Sam keeps saying, as the music gets all dark and ominous, before explaining what's fantastic about the drug he's inevitably going to give to his bandleader ('It turns all your bad feelings into good feelings. It's a nightmare!') Writers Judd Apatow (who had bigger 2007 comedy hits by writing and directing *Knocked Up* and co-producing *Superbad*) and Jake Kasdan are surgically accurate about the clichés of the material they've chosen to lampoon. But the movie's best scene perhaps explains why *Walk Hard* . . . isn't a full-on, *This Is Spinal Tap* (see p. 264)/*The School of Rock* (see p. 377) laff-riot.

When Cox's career hits the 1960s, the film quits lampooning rock flicks and starts lampooning rock itself. Sandwiched between a *Don't Look Back* (see p. 61)-inspired Dylan skit ('Rimjob fairy teapots . . . Stuffed cabbage is the darling of the Laundromat', Reilly sings, to a rapt theatre audience), and a pisstake of Brian Wilson's acid monstrosities that should be played to every Dadrock fan until they get over the old California loon, is a take on the Beatles' trip to India which guest-stars Jack Black as Macca and an on-fire Paul Rudd as John Lennon. Given scant screen-time, both find voices and faces for their victims that bring an immediate anarchy to the enterprise and succeed in blowing Reilly offscreen. Apart from the deep and simple joy of hearing a fictional John Lennon say, 'Paul's a big fat coont!', what the moment does is make you realise that Reilly was the wrong person for this film. A veteran comic character actor who has only recently been considered leading man material, his quietly funny qualities aren't ludicrous enough to make a convincing comedy rock star. Plus he's too ugly to look like one, but not ugly enough for that to be a joke in itself. *Walk Hard* . . . needed a Black or a Rudd (or a Christopher Guest) to make the film generally funny to people who aren't rock buffs. And rock buffs are probably too busy listening to Radiohead and practising sighing balefully to watch mainstream Hollywood comedies at all.

The film somewhat peters out after the 1960s spoofs, but rouses itself for the finale, a fine tilt at the windmill of Hall of Fame-type award ceremonies. Eddie Vedder of Pearl Jam is better than just a good sport for the deadpan way he tackles the mind-numbing sycophancy of the standard presentation speech ('If Elvis and Buddy Holly are the Cain and Abel of rock and roll, and Bruce Springsteen is Zachariah ... Iggy Pop is Methuselah ... and, of course, Neil Young is the wise prophet Ezekiel ... '). The only truly bum note is sounded by Jack White's embarrassing cameo as Elvis. There is almost a very fine film here about rock's greatest crime ... the fact that it takes itself way too seriously. It's put in its place by *The School of Rock*, which is actually laughing at the same thing, but is too busy just being funny to make a big deal out of it.

Nevertheless, if you hate *Ray* as much as I do, *Walk Hard* ... will make you laugh at what mainstream Hollywood considers intelligent film-making. Job done.

● ●

Control

2007
Starring: Sam Riley, Samantha Morton, Alexandra Maria Lara
Dir.: Anton Corbijn

★ ★

Plot: The aesthetically pleasing death of Ian Curtis.
Key line: 'Ian ... you are so depressing.'

The first seconds of *Control* tell you everything you need to know about this film. A camera tight on the profile of a pretty young man. Dapples of light play tastefully upon the monochromatic grey. And a voiceover says, 'Existence ... well, what does it matter?'

The line is from 'Isolation' by Joy Division, so writer Matt Greenhalgh can't take full responsibility for the sixth-form existentialism. The man that the pretty young boy is supposed to be wrote those words. But the choice is made by the film-makers, because Ian Curtis wrote hundreds of brilliant lines that could have opened this film. These lines are chosen because *Control* is about neither Ian Curtis nor the people who loved him nor Joy Division nor Manchester in the late 1970s nor the despair that drives one to suicide. It's about how much better beautiful young men look in a black and white photograph if they don't smile. It's about all the tragic young men whose pictures and works fill the rooms of university students who see rebellion in terms of choosing the right superficially meaningful cultural signifiers. It's about elegantly produced misery as a unit-shifting middle-class art fetish for those who'd rather gaze at their navel than risk any form of non-conformity. It's the Habitat version of the rock death cult. It's like being trapped inside a Coldplay record for two hours. After the hype and acclaim that greeted its initial release, it was one of the most disappointing films of its time. Worse ... when Morton as Curtis's wife Deborah discovers the singer's body, and 'Atmosphere' starts playing on the soundtrack at exactly the most shameless and predictable moment, I could have cheerfully tracked down Anton Corbijn and throttled him.

The first 12 minutes or so show glimpses of another, better film ... one about real, living, breathing people and the 1970s. We see teen Curtis experimenting with prescription drugs, practising being Bowie in the bedroom mirror, and meeting and courting wife Deborah, who wrote the book, *Touching from a Distance*, that the film is based upon ... a book, incidentally, that provides a far more rounded and emotionally engaging portrait of the Curtis tragedy than this film.

But Corbijn captures the essence of what we rock boys were like in the 1970s (both nerds and poseurs, basically), finds a way to make a grey Macclesfield council estate into something visually evocative, contrasts it nicely with the surrounding Cheshire countryside (although much of the film was actually shot in Nottingham). The scene where Curtis recites some Wordsworth, leaving Debbie awestruck, is both gently funny and affectionately true about the pretensions of teen romance. The pair hold hands behind her boyfriend Nick's back and the moment says more about the inevitability of their love than watching them grope would have done. So far, so good.

But as soon as the story of Joy Division is introduced, Corbijn's fetish for enigma begins to look like cowardice. The infamous 1976 Sex Pistols show that kicked off the Manchester punk scene, and which Michael Winterbottom made so funny and real in the infinitely superior *24 Hour Party People* (see p. 348), is used and wasted here. The boys who will be Joy Division stare in awe for a few seconds while a racket that barely resembles the Pistols blares for a few seconds. Scene over. Corbijn bottles out of any attempt to show why the Sex Pistols inspired the few people in this room to be Joy Division, the Factory label, the Buzzcocks, the Fall, the Smiths. He has no interest in the moment, yet without that moment it's doubtful whether Joy Division as we know them would have existed at all. From then on, we're simply expected to accept that Curtis was an inevitable rock star (it's worth pointing out that Joy Division were not stars, and that only music press junkies and committed post-punks even heard of Curtis's death at the time) and a doomed genius, and that epilepsy and being the male point in a love triangle leads to suicide. One suspects that a fair few two-timing epilepsy sufferers exist to disprove this theory. Corbijn's lack of interest in the context surrounding Curtis's life mirrors his inability to shed light on Curtis's depression. In *Control*, Ian Curtis is depressed because it looks deep and pretty, and enables the director to create lots of nicely composed shots that look like classy black and white photos. *Control* is little more than a very long montage of expertly composed stills, the kind of movie that only a photographer could get away with making. And its literal inability to *move* makes *Control* an even more narcissistic and insulting treatment of a personal tragedy than *Last Days* (see p. 388).

Control avoids the one-star treatment for four reasons. First, Sam Riley. This was his first film role, and considering that it largely consists of looking moody and being a bit of a prick, he does a great job. The second is Samantha Morton. She's the best British screen actress of her generation and if this isn't her best work, then that's because she has a thankless role. Deborah Curtis presents herself as a shy, dowdy, easily bullied girl in her book, so that's what Morton has to be. Her lines largely consist of asking Ian if he's coming to bed. Cast as the typical annoying rock wife and dowdy domestic whinger, she selflessly works to make Riley look good. But in her moments alone we again see a better film, told entirely from Deborah Curtis's perspective. A film about how it might *feel* to be a young, poor wife with a child, looking on helplessly as your husband abandons you, first for dreams of stardom, then for another woman, and then for death. In the scene where Debbie confronts Ian about his infidelity, Morton tries her damnedest with the lousy dialogue and artfully static camera to make the moment into the trauma it must have been. But Riley is just too inexperienced an actor to overcome his instructions to be broody and silent and enigmatic to meet her intensity, and the scene falls hopelessly flat.

The third is the recreation of Joy Division performances. No-one said that Corbijn can't shoot a good rock video, and he, his stars, and his cameramen move Heaven and Earth not just to impersonate old Joy Division films, but to create thrilling performances in themselves. You could seriously argue that the onstage scenes in *Control* equal or better the few filmed examples of how Joy Division performed live. And that's an achievement that has to be taken seriously.

And the fourth? It's one scene. It was the only scene, in fact, that I took out of the cinema with me when I first saw *Control*. It isn't a key scene, dramatically speaking. It doesn't have anything to do with the plot. It's just a wonderful piece of film-making.

It is some time after the Sex Pistols show. Ian Curtis walks out of his front door. We see that he's wearing a white shirt and tie, and what looks, at first, like an expensive black trenchcoat with collar turned up. 'No Love Lost' by Joy Division plays, masking all other noise. The camera stays tight on his face as he walks down the road. He looks troubled, but in an offhand way. An old man walks past him, ignored. Curtis stops, is illuminated by natural light, and lights up a fag with a match. He starts walking again. And walking. And walking. Where is this going?

Finally, he reaches a corner, and turns left. The camera lets him turn in front of us and walk away, so we see his back. The black coat has the word 'HATE' written on it, in large letters, in what looks like Tipp-Ex. The darkness of Curtis's shape is in sharp contrast to the brightness of the old terraced houses which are on a steep hill swooping down in front of him, and us. Now there are people in the street. The building in front of Curtis looks like a small school, and like something Curtis is just going to walk past. But as he gets closer, we see the sign on its wall: 'Employment Exchange' (that's what we used to call Job Centres, young person). The sign and the HATE scrawled upon Curtis's donkey jacket come into direct opposition as we realise that this building is Curtis's destination. He stops. We're still behind him, but we see his head turn to look at the sign. He punkily flicks his fag away. And then goes in the door.

At this point, we think we've just seen Corbijn's take on the hoariest of UK punk clichés ... 1970s Britain on the dole. Poor Ian is just going to sign on like thousands of other alienated yoof. But that's not it at all. Ian Curtis was a lower-middle-class boy who did OK at school and had no deprived or rebellious back-story before Joy Division. The scene switches suddenly to Curtis sitting opposite another man, in his neatly pressed shirt and tie. 'So what do you like doing, Colin?', he asks the man, smiling pleasantly. The man has Down's syndrome. Curtis *works* in the dole office.

The wit and camera movement, and use of light and rhythm, of picture to music, and sly understanding of British class politics and youth poserdom in this minute-and-a-half of pure cinema proves that Anton Corbijn is a potentially brilliant director who happened to make a dodgy first film. Or maybe an already brilliant director who just doesn't have a feel for human beings and their motivations. He's not helped by the writing. The dialogue throughout is so poor that finding any kind of 'key line' is like diving for pearls in a puddle. Characters like producer Martin Hannett, Factory head Tony Wilson, and Bernard Sumner of Joy Division and New Order all feel real and three-dimensional in *24 Hour Party People*. In *Control*, they're just props and plot-points, their personalities drawn from old copies of the *New Musical Express* and other rock films. Jokes are attempted but neither the cast nor Corbijn can time a gag. The one exception is Toby Kebbell as Joy Division manager Rob Gretton, a crude, mulleted smartarse who brings so much life to each of his scenes that you want to cheer when he appears onscreen.

The highlighting of Curtis's cruelty to Deborah has some iconoclastic courage to it. But there's no warning for it, no context. We're left guessing why this apparently decent bloke suddenly becomes a monster in the blink of an eye. The epilepsy? The cocktail of drugs to treat it? Love for Annik Honoré? Minor fame? Nothing truly connects. Instead of involving you in the story, Curtis's offhand nastiness merely irritates.

Which takes us back to Riley. Strong performance or not, Riley is simply far, far too pretty to be a totally convincing Ian Curtis. He betrays Corbijn's preoccupation with the surface of things, rather than the grubby, rich reality. Which, come to think of it, probably makes Corbijn the perfect 21st-century, post-New Labour British film director. Even though he's Dutch. Next up for Corbijn: *He Died with His Specs On* – the tragic death of Eric Morecambe, starring Jude Law as Eric and Lindsay Lohan as Ernie Wise.

● ●

I'm Not There

2007
Starring: Cate Blanchett, Christian Bale, Richard Gere, Heath Ledger, Ben Whishaw, Marcus Carl Franklin, Charlotte Gainsbourg, Julianne Moore
Dir.: Todd Haynes

★ ★

Plot: Six phases of Bob Dylan's life and myth, each played by six different actors including a woman and a small black boy, none of whom are called Bob Dylan. Wait! Come back ... Uh ... no, actually. Good call. Off you go.
Key line: 'You never know how the past will turn out.'

No film in this book disappointed me as profoundly as this one. Maybe I should have lowered my expectations, what with *I'm Not There* being an experimental superstar luvvie-fest in which six actors play seven different versions of Bob Dylan in a rambling, surreal non-narrative 'Inspired by the music and the many lives of Bob Dylan'. But the director and co-writer is Todd Haynes, maker of the brave *Velvet Goldmine* (see p. 326) and two bona fide masterpieces in *Superstar: The Karen Carpenter Story* (see p. 274) and the gorgeous and passionate Douglas Sirk tribute *Far from Heaven*. If there was one film-maker who could pull off such a preposterous art-house idea with mainstream money, it's Haynes. At least, that was the theory.

But the alarm bells begin to ring when you clock the amount of explanatory material among the DVD special features: not just a director's commentary and a long series of interviews with Haynes, but an intro to the film where experts – including that most over-quoted of Dylanologists, Greil Marcus – write helpful notes on what the entire thing actually means. Which is an intellectual's way of admitting that none of it makes any sense without someone talking you through it. Maybe Haynes should have just published the pitch and travelled round giving lectures about it to all those strange people who feel that the meaning of life is contained, somewhere, in Dylan's life and work.

I'm Not There is, on one level, a parody of everything about Bob Dylan – the facts, the mythology, the song lyrics, the iconography we've projected upon him. It's also, occasionally, a spoof of rock biopics, done with less knockabout laffs than *Walk Hard: The Dewey Cox Story*, but considerably more visual and intellectual panache.

But smarts and technique only count for so much. A point, a story and a soul count for more. And the more *I'm Not There* moves tortuously on, sniggering knowingly at its own self-regarding Dylanology, the more it feels like nothing but an in-joke between Haynes, his cast, and whichever of his friends he's had the most cerebral conversations about Dylan with. The idea of blending facts, myths and lyrics of Dylan into one study of him is great. It just isn't executed very well because, as it winks smugly at its audience of *cinéastes* with its meticulously recreated film-school impersonations of Fellini and Pennebaker (see *Don't Look Back*, p. 61) and Altman . . . it's just too damn pleased with itself to breathe. *I'm Not There* must be the first film I've ever watched where I've allowed myself to wonder about the moral implications of so much money being wasted on set design and production values and A-list actors' salaries for so little purpose. Probably because this is a movie that deconstructs film-making so successfully that you're never allowed to forget, not for a second, that you're watching film-making, rather than a film. It's so studied and enervating that it paralysed me into constructing sentences as lousy as that one.

Cate Blanchett *is* magnificent as Jude Quinn, an uncanny inter-pretation of the 'wild Mercury' Dylan . . . the electric rebel of 1965–66. But the effect is somewhat dulled by tiresomely contrived meetings with Allen Ginsberg and the Warhol set; and the conflict with British journalist Mr Jones, in honour of Dylan's 'Ballad of a Thin Man', is rendered with such hysterical literalism . . . well . . . actually it fits Dylan's most pompous and annoying song very well.

So, yes, there's a very funny Beatles parody in the Jude Quinn section. And the all-too-few sections starring Marcus Carl Franklin as an 11-year-old black Dylan doing his damnedest to be itinerant folk legend Woody Guthrie are a gently funny piss-take of both the young Robert Zimmerman's fake back-story and all the various suckers who believed it. But every time there's a witty line or image that begins to bring the film into focus, Haynes intervenes lest something real begins to happen, and escapes into carefully crafted shrugging or dreadful recreations of Dylan incidents that pull off the unlikely feat of both extracting the magic out of the myths *and* obfuscating any useful truths. From what I'd seen of Haynes' other movies, I'd convinced myself that it was impossible for him to make something that didn't engage emotionally. *I'm Not There* makes short work of that theory.

And one last specific gripe: the way Haynes decides that the Vietnam War was little more than a backdrop for the break-up of the Heath Ledger-Bob's marriage is a neat summation of the way

American film-makers have echoed the dehumanisation of everyone who died in that war, endlessly compounding the imperial felony by using dead Asians as nothing more than shorthand for the sensitive American's guilt. Vietnam mentions in films should be banned, unless they're by someone Vietnamese.

A good idea about who Dylan is occasionally flutters around the edges of the picture. That really this guy's myth is made from the fact that, when anyone, even someone he loves, asks him to commit to believing in or taking responsibility for anything, he just responds with a smartarse gnomic one-liner and runs away. Whether this is a true judgement of the man's weaknesses or not, it's at least a recognisable character trait.

But instead, Haynes concentrates on the whole endlessly repeated thing about Dylan creating a persona that has been mis-understood by lesser beings, and which he has not been able to escape.

First, I'm not convinced that Dylan has ever claimed this level of pity for himself, especially when he has successfully reinvented himself so many times, and thrived, and survived.

And, second ... who the fuck cares?

• •

Anvil: The Story of Anvil

2008
Starring: Steve 'Lips' Kudlow, Robb Reiner
Dir.: Sacha Gervasi

★ ★ ★ ★

Plot: A former drum roadie and two middle-aged Canadian Jews locate the essence of rock 'n' roll survival and platonic all-male marriage.
Key line: 'But, on the other hand, if it did get worse, at least, this time, after all is said and done, I can say that all has been said and done.'

The movie begins in 1984. A hugely successful heavy metal world package tour. We are in Japan, and seeing an enormous festival crowd going crazy for the Scorpions, Whitesnake and Bon Jovi. As the caption says, 'All of these bands went on to sell millions of records.'

But the music backdropping all this monolithic rawk power isn't 'Livin' on a Prayer'. It is a doomy, silly slice of grungey riffola called 'Metal on Metal' (no relation to the Kraftwerk masterpiece). The caption finishes its thought with the words: 'Except one . . . '

We suddenly get our first view of Anvil in their nearly pomp. A bunch of topless poodlehairs in glam-perv fetish-wear throwing every hard-rock pose in the book. You get a full-face shot of the lead singer and you immediately understand why you've never heard of Anvil until reading the gushing reviews for this documentary of their lives and work. For he is . . . a homely man. Chubby of face, snaggled of tooth and big of nose, he is Justin Hawkins of The Darkness, but without the irony. And that is and was Anvil's problem. When you look at Steve 'Lips' Kudlow, you're looking at someone who looks like a comedy actor. He sings words of doom, darkness and pubescent sex but looks like a gas fitter at a weekend swingers club.

The film will go on to include fulsome tributes to the skills and influence of Anvil from the likes of Lars Ulrich of Metallica, Lemmy of Motörhead and Slash of Guns N' Roses, who all generously ponder the cruel luck 'the demigods of Canadian metal' must have endured to have ended up in total obscurity after 12 albums and almost three decades of rocking. But all are rabidly heterosexual guys, so can't possibly point out that the man who writes the songs, sings the songs and plays lead guitar is just not someone that anyone wants to shag. And I know . . . you're thinking about Lemmy's warty visage right now and insisting that heavy rock frontmen don't have to be pretty. And you're right. But they do have to be charismatic to the point of making confused teenage boys want to look at them, even when they're ugly by conventional standards. They have to have faces that symbolise virility, or vanity, or rebellion, or violence, or an alien otherness. When we see Lips playing his guitar with a dildo, we think of the comedy turn at a hen night, rather than groupie-ravishing, parent-baiting cock-rock decadence. The guy *just hasn't got it.*

From that first close-up of Kudlow, the story is laid out before us. It's *Spinal Tap*-meets-*Almost Famous*, and yet another tale of real-life rock 'n' roll hubris to match *DiG* (see p. 381). You get ready to cringe and snigger at a deluded loser, and the idiocy of heavy metal to boot. But somewhere along the line *Anvil: The Story of Anvil* becomes an entirely different story, and eventually makes you cry, and you understand why it has been an unlikely low-budget success and inspired none other than Michael Moore to call it 'The best documentary I've seen in years.'

It's the story behind the story that guarantees that *Anvil . . .* was never meant to be a sneer-fest. Brit director Sacha Gervasi was a teenage metal fan and budding drummer. He went to a 1982 Anvil show at the Marquee and forced a meeting with his idols, declaring himself the biggest Anvil fan in the world. The band were so charmed by him that they nicknamed him . . . ahem . . . 'Teabag', and employed him as a roadie off-and-on for three years, until Gervasi's budding screenwriting career took precedence. As Anvil thudded into obscurity, Gervasi slowly but surely climbed the movie industry ladder until finally getting his big break 19 years later as co-writer of *The Terminal*, the Steven Spielberg/Tom Hanks vehicle about the refugee who spends years living in an airport.

Having become a movie player, Gervasi decides to look up his old Anvil mentors. He is amazed to learn that Lips Kudlow and drummer Robb Reiner are still treading the boards as Anvil, playing to crowds of 30 in bars and releasing albums that no-one hears. He is even more amazed to learn that 25 years of failure and frustration hasn't changed the pair of childhood friends – they are still as generous and upbeat and joined-at-the-hip as they were in the early 1980s. He decides that they are the perfect subject for a documentary (and first directing project) about the heroism of never giving up on your dreams. In short, the last thing Gervasi had come to do was bury Anvil, and you can feel, throughout the film, that Gervasi is as committed to reviving Anvil's career as he is to making a great movie. He succeeded, in both missions, but we'll come back to that later.

When we meet present-day Lips, he is driving through the Toronto snow at 7a.m., picking up and delivering school dinners. Gervasi dwells on the mundanity of Kudrow's conversation – 'One week it's pizza then shepherd's pie. The next week its shepherd's pie and then pizza, y'know?' His drummer partner Reiner is drilling rocks as part of his 'psychoactive therapy sessions'. As I mentioned before, you think you're being taken into an exercise in laugh-at-the-loser. Kudlow is all painfully inarticulate 'mustn't grumbles' and 'it can't possibly get worse'. But it can and must because, as anyone who has ever worked for 'the big break' will tell you, it's not the despair that kills you – it's the hope.

Hope for Anvil comes in the shape of a European tour, taking them temporarily from dead-end day jobs, 50th birthday gigs in front of handfuls of the kind of mates who call themselves Mad Dog and drink beer through their noses, and wives who love Lips and Robb and want them to be happy . . . but feel that their hubbies need to grow up, escape the cycle of rejection and disappointment and provide some money for their families.

But before that, Gervasi goes back into their history, and that's where the director begins to celebrate the movie's debt to the ultimate metal piss-take. Drummer Robb Reiner shares his name with the director of *This Is Spinal Tap*. Gervasi gets Reiner and Kudlow talking about their very first song – a Spanish Inquisition tribute called 'Thumb Hang' – in a diner, just as the fictional Nigel Tufnell and David St Hubbins do in the *Tap* movie. The band visit Stonehenge. We even get a shot of an amp where the switches go up to 11. And the European tour is scheduled by Tiziana, the exotic but hapless girlfriend of second guitarist Ivan Hurd, just as the exotic but hapless girlfriend of the singer takes over a disastrous US tour in *This Is Spinal Tap*.

Indeed, the fuck-ups and *Tap*-isms come so thick and fast that, according to *Village Voice* reviewer Camile Dodero, 'during the filming, one of Gervasi's cameramen locked the director in a room and demanded to know if Lips and Robb were secretly actors'.

Anvil . . . does, occasionally, seem just too packed with comic pathos to be true.

Lips running around after minor metal luminaries at the Sweden Rock Festival, none of whom remember him. Missed trains. Crowds comprising the proverbial three men and a dog. More missed trains. Promoters who want to pay the band in goulash. A festival called Monsters of Transylvania. Screaming fights, tears, smarmy Brit lawyers, and the first of many break-up-and-make-ups between Lips and Robb. It's a beautifully edited comedy of horrors that makes emotional sense to anyone who has ever tried to get something creative off the ground, regardless of what they think of metal.

But Lips is the heart and soul of this thing here. When he comes off tour he pays fulsome tribute to Tiziana and just sees the whole nightmare European experience as a blessing. He is a boundless optimist; intense, passionate, warm, slightly insane and a lovely, loveable man. You want him to win, to prove that nice plain guys don't always have to finish last. This is not the *X Factor*-style, anyone-can-live-their-dream-as-long-as-they're-pretty-and-obedi-ent schtick. This is long-term dedication to one idea, and a person who shouts and screams and cries for the love of it, and looks like a dog and refuses to compromise or give up. When Robb's sister Droid says, 'It's over. It's been over for a long time. And it's just too bad no-one's living in the real world,' you know she's right by any rational criteria that could be applied. But you still want to boo her. You still want her to be wrong. Because, by this time, Gervasi and Lips have made you feel that, if 'it' is over for Anvil, it's over for every decent one among us. And who needs to hear that?

Anvil happily play Ivan and Tiziana's wedding reception – more comic gold – and then we meet Lips and Robb's Jewish families, and see their mix of pride in and worry for their boys, and fall in love with the pair just a little harder. Robb shows us his Edward Hopper-influenced paintings, and they're great, and all evoke a wistful emptiness.

More hope arrives in the shape of Chris Tsangarides, a veteran

Brit-Cypriot rock producer who worked with Anvil in the early days. He wants to produce their latest album ... but also wants to get paid. Kudlow's very conventional big sister dips into her life savings to lend Anvil the money. It's hugely touching stuff. The quest is now to make the album, and sell it to a company. Neither goes smoothly.

Gervasi has no style as a director. He approaches the movie as a screenwriter would – a three-act story, characters and jokes, some good times and bad times, ending on a surprising and heartwarming high that has actually been slyly alluded to early in the tale. It's occasionally cheesy and sentimental, and none the worse for it.

Since this home movie deluxe became a surprise indie hit, the VH1 music TV channel has taken up Anvil's cause, putting the *This Is Thirteen* album out on their own label. Anvil tunes will soon be on the *Rock Band* video game. Music biz players who've been involved with Slayer, Oasis and Coldplay are on board. Anvil have supported AC/DC and headlined a stage at this year's Download Festival.

The movie hasn't made Anvil superstars. But it's given them something they've been failing to achieve for 25 years ... a career in music, where they make a living and have fans that number more than four figures. There are better movies in this book. But none that makes a feller feel more warm and fuzzy, or that his own problems might turn out OK too. *Anvil: The Story of Anvil* is less a rock documentary, more a quiet pep-talk from a wise and loyal friend.

● ●

Telstar

2009
Starring: Con O'Neill, Tom Burke, James Corden, Pam Ferris,
Kevin Spacey, JJ Feild, Ralf Little, Sid Mitchell
Dir.: Nick Moran

★ ★ ★ ★

Plot: How the earth inherited Joe Meek.
**Key line: 'He only started The Tornados so he could try and
lure Billy Fury into his khazi.'**

Between 1954 and 1967, Gloucestershire's Robert George Meek
invented the notion of the independent pop record producer.
Under his *nom de plume* Joe Meek, the former RAF radar
operator developed a very British answer to the sonic experiments
of Phil Spector, creating a legacy of hits recorded mainly in his
hand-built home studio above a handbag shop at 304 Holloway
Road in north London. Unable to play a musical instrument,
write sheet music or sing, he fashioned his sound out of
endless experiments with tape manipulation and home-made
echo chambers, resulting in early 1960s era-defining hits for
actor Johnny Leyton ('Johnny Remember Me') and the Honey-
combs ('Have I the Right'), and his greatest commercial triumph
'Telstar', an instrumental tribute to the new satellite technology
by his in-house band the Tornados, which became the first
British record to hit the Number One spot in America – way
back in 1962, just as an obscure beat combo called the Beatles
were signing their record deal with EMI.

Meek went on to turn down the opportunity to record the
Beatles, the Rolling Stones, David Bowie and Rod Stewart, as
the coming of the new rock music began to destroy his career at
the height of his success. Mentally disturbed, violent, struggling
to hide his homosexuality at a time when it was still illegal in
England, and reeling from a French composer's lawsuit claiming

authorship of 'Telstar', Meek sank precipitously into debt, decline and depression. On 3 February 1967 – the eighth anniversary of the death of Meek's beloved Buddy Holly – Meek turned a shotgun on his Holloway Road landlady Violet Shenton and then put the barrel in his mouth and pulled the trigger. He was 38.

You're right – that is a pretty great story, a hard one to fuck up. But that's exactly what Oliver Stone did with *The Doors* (see p. 289), lest we forget. So *Telstar*'s first-time director Nick Moran and his co-writer James Hicks deserve all the plaudits they can get for bringing edge, substance and plenty of style back to the rock biopic in one of the finest British films of recent years.

They did have one enormous thing in their favour, though. His name is Con O'Neill.

O'Neill comes from Irish stock but shared a West Country upbringing with Meek, and his camp take on the West Country burr is just one unforgettable element of one of the great powerhouse rock movie performances. His Meek is a fizzing ball of hoarse-throated fury; a stunning mixture of violence, self-loathing, sickness and lust. His breakdown, when he confronts, attacks and dismisses his lover and protégé Heinz Burt (Feild) over the hapless pop wannabe's relationship with a girl finds a terrifying, heartbreaking intensity that disturbs every bit as much as it moves.

Telstar began life as a stage-play by Hicks and the producers' decision to stick with O'Neill after his success in the theatrical role is entirely justified by the agony and menace that he conveys in every scene in the movie. It's only when you stop being engrossed in O'Neill's performance that you realize that you've not been given any reason for why Meek is such a basket-case.

Telstar's flaws lie in the lack of interest in a back-story, and a slight tendency to indulge in flashy visuals to the detriment of lending three dimensions to the tragic tale. Sure – a mixture of homosexual guilt, public humiliation (Meek was outed when arrested for cottaging in 1963), constant use of cheap speed, spiralling debts, falling sales, a lawsuit, and the failure and loss of his beloved Heinz are a pretty potent mixture for anyone to endure. But murder and suicide are extreme endgames, and Meek was already seen as a loose cannon long before his decline. It's a matter of public record that Meek and songwriting partner Geoff Goddard (brilliantly played here in post-Peter Cook style by Tom Burke) had an unhealthy fascination for the occult, and this is played with at the beginning of *Telstar*. But the whys are left frustratingly unanswered.

Nevertheless, Nick Moran proves that there's a great deal more to him than a life of playing charmingly laddish cockernee gangsters in the wake of his success starring in Guy Ritchie's *Lock, Stock and Two Smoking Barrels*. The sensitivity he displays in the poignant Meek–Heinz seduction scene, and the compositional flair apparent in the beautiful slow-motion tableau towards the end of *Telstar*, as the vampiric Meek tries to hide from the sun streaming through his windows while bowler-hatted bailiffs take his studio away, mark Moran out as a major new talent.

Telstar is a fitting place to end this book. Much of the movie takes place in Moran's reconstruction of 304 Holloway Road, and the flat's very English claustrophobia, chaos and knockabout comedy is a wonderful throwback to the classic British rock movies of the 1959–79 era. The supporting performances from Burke, Ferris, Little, Corden and a delightfully arch Spacey are superb. Even the in-jokey cameos from original Meek collaborators Jess Conrad and Chas Hodges of Chas and Dave, and current rockers Carl Barat and Justin Hawkins work. *Telstar*'s balance of the comic and the tragic, the highs of creativity and the horrors of failure, neatly sum up the impulses of the best movies in this book. The musical performances of 'Telstar' and 'Johnny Remember Me' are great too, bringing neatly to life the early 1960s tension between old-school showbiz and the sexual repressions unleashed by Elvis Presley, and turned into modern art by the Beatles and the Stones.

Telstar proves that British film isn't entirely lost in a world of smug chick flicks, soul-less shock horror movies and *Slumdog* fairytales. And that there's life in the rock movie beyond documentaries and fluffy musicals that tidy the complicated lives of stars into moral fables of sin and redemption. Film is at its best when it accepts that some things just end badly. Which is why *Telstar* ends this thing just fine.

Index